O'BRIEN'S
Collecting TOY TRAINS

Identification and Value Guide

6th EDITION

Edited by David Doyle

©2006 Krause Publications
Published by

700 East State Street • Iola, WI 54990-0001
715-445-2214 • 888-457-2873

Our toll-free number to place an order or obtain
a free catalog is (800) 258-0929.

Library of Congress Catalog Number: 2005906850

ISBN: 0-89689-304-9
ISBN 13: 978-0-89689-304-7

Designed by Donna Mummery
Edited by David Doyle and Dennis Thornton

Printed in China

CONTENTS

INTRODUCTION

No doubt the first toy train was created not long after George Stephenson's train first rode the rails in 1814. (Richard Trevithick, in 1804, built a locomotive that did not operate on rails). It is not clear which arrived in this country first, toy trains or the real thing (Peter Cooper's Tom Thumb in 1830). What is clear is that trains have held the imagination of both adults and children for 150 years. It was natural then that these toys move from wooden, cast iron or brass static or push replicas to self-propelled replicas. A few attempts were made to use actual steam power to move the miniatures around the rails, but the hazards of flame, hot water and steam, as well as the expense, prevented these toys from becoming widespread successes. Clockwork or mechanical trains were much safer, and considerably more successful, but required almost constant attention to keep running. The rewinding of the toy and lack of speed and direction control quickly shattered any illusion of realism that existed in the imagination of the operator.

Electricity, however, provided a medium through which trains could be run for extended periods of time, and by which the operator could control the speed, direction and stopping of the train. One of the first people to recognize this was Joshua Lionel Cowen, whose electric novelty company in 1901 produced an electrically powered gondola car. It was initially sold as an animated window display with which merchants could call attention to their wares, however the public saw the train as a toy for both adults and children. By the following year, Cowen changed his marketing strategy to match that of the public demand, and Lionel trains began their journey to domination of the U.S. electric train market.

Cowen, however, was by no means the only purveyor of electric trains. Harry Ives, W.O. Coleman, Louis Marx, Olympian A. C. Gilbert and a host of others climbed aboard the electric train express. The companies of these men and others created an array of products that fueled the imaginations, and filled the Christmas lists, of generations of American boys, and some girls too. By the late 1950s, electric trains had reached their zenith of popularity as toys. Jet aircraft captured the imagination of the distant-traveling public, stealing it away from the sleek streamliners like the Super Chief, California Zephyr and 20th Century Limited. Astronauts and pilots replaced engineers as favorites of youth. The newly established Interstate highway system allowed the shift of merchandise from rail travel to truck, ending the trips to the local freight house to pick up goods. And the Interstate allowed easy travel for the millions of shiny new cars being bought in America's burgeoning economy. Miniature cars, in the form of slot outfits, similarly tugged children from the rails.

Though the number of children who yearn for a train under the Christmas tree now may only be a portion of those who did 50 years ago, there are two other groups whose interest grows. One of these is the adult toy train operator. To the laymen, these enthusiasts are scarcely distinguishable from their cousins, the model railroader. The other group is the toy train collector. Typically specializing in one brand or era, these people preserve the toys, and joys, of yesterday. It is for this group that this volume has been written.

COLLECTING

Toy train collectors are their own fraternity, eagerly welcoming new buffs with a sincere interest in toy trains. Avail yourself of this knowledge base and friendship no matter if you are an experienced collector or a rookie. Something can always be learned. There is no substitute for experience in this hobby, as in any other. No book, no matter how complete, contains all the answers. Thousands of words and the best illustrations cannot equal the experience gained by holding a piece in your own hands. There is no finer place than the home of a friend and fellow collector. The piece that is not for sale can be examined, unhurried, and questions answered honestly; an excellent preparation for seeking an item in the marketplace.

The advent of Internet auctions has been a boon for collectors, particularly those in remote areas. But for those in more populous areas, there is no substitute for shopping in the company of fellow collectors at hobby shops and train shows, especially for the neophyte. Examining an item personally, with the counsel of more experienced collectors, is especially urged when purchasing expensive, repaired or forged items.

However, after gaining some experience, working with a trusted and reputable train auction company can provide access to trains that otherwise may take years, or even decades, to acquire.

Enthusiasts have been collecting toy trains perhaps as long as they have been being produced. In the United States, the largest and oldest collectors group is the Train Collector's Association, or TCA. Founded in 1954 in Yardley, Pa., the group has grown to more than 31,000 members. An annual convention is held at various locations around the country each summer. Smaller, regional groups called Divisions and Chapters dot the nation. Twice each year, one such group, the Eastern Division, hosts the largest toy train show in the world. The York Fairgrounds, in York, Pa., becomes a veritable Mecca for the toy train buff with several buildings encompassing more than 100,000 square feet of toy trains for sale, display or trade. Members of the TCA agree to abide by a code of conduct, assuring fair and honest dealings between members. The nationally recognized Grading Standards were developed by the TCA.

The TCA National Headquarters and the associated National Toy Train Museum is located in Strasburg, Pa. The Train Collectors Association can be reached at its web site, www.traincollectors.org, or by writing to:

Train Collectors Association
P.O. Box 248
300 Paradise Lane
Strasburg, PA 17579
(717) 687-8623

The second-oldest organization is the Toy Train Operating Society, formed on the West Coast in 1966. Similar in style and purpose to the TCA, traditionally the bulk of the TTOS members and events has been in the west, but it has been gradually spreading eastward. The TTOS can be contacted at:

Toy Train Operating Society
25 W. Walnut Street, Suite 308
Pasadena, CA 91103
Phone (626) 578-0673

One of the first, and certainly the largest, Lionel-specific clubs is the Lionel Collector's Club of America. Founded Aug. 1, 1970 by Jim Gates of Des Moines, Iowa, the organization has grown steadily since. The club was founded on the idea that collectors and operators of Lionel trains need an organization of their own. The club's mailing address is:

LCCA Business Office
P.O. Box 479
La Salle, IL 61301-0479

The youngster of these groups is the Lionel Operating Train Society, or LOTS. Founded in 1979 by Larry Keller of Cincinnati, this club's purpose is providing a national train club for operators of Lionel trains and accessories. Like the others, it publishes magazines, swap-lists and a membership directory. LOTS can be reached at:

LOTS Business Office
6376 West Fork Road
Cincinnati, OH 45247-5704

Condition and Rarity

To the collector, condition is everything, and train collectors have established criteria for grading trains. Two systems are currently in use, the older (good, very good, excellent, etc.) system used by the Train Collector's Association for more than years, and a newer system (C7, C8, C10 system), recently adopted by the TCA. Use of these conditions when describing the condition of collectible trains protects both the buyer and the seller.

These grading standards are as follows:

Fair: Well-scratched, chipped, dented, rusted, warped.

Good, or C2: Small dents, scratches, dirty.

Very Good, or C3: Few scratches, exceptionally clean, no major dents or rust.

Excellent, C6: Minute scratches or nicks, no dents or rust, all original, less than average wear.

Like New, C8: Only the slightest signs of handling and wheel wear, brilliant colors and crisp markings; literally like new. As a rule, Like New trains must have their original boxes in comparable condition to realize the prices listed in this guide. Trains in Like New and Mint conditions are the most desirable to collectors, and their prices are not only higher, but considerably more volatile than those of lesser condition.

Mint: Brand new, absolutely unmarred, all original and unused. Items dusty or faded from display, or with fingerprints from handling, cannot be considered mint. Although Lionel test ran its locomotives briefly at the factory, items "test run" by consumers cannot be considered mint. Most collectors expect mint items to come with all associated packaging with which they were originally supplied.

As one can imagine, Mint pieces command premium prices. The supply is extremely limited, and the demand among collectors is great, so often the billfold of the buyer, rather than a more natural supply and demand situation, limits the price of such pieces.

In addition to the categories stated above, two other classifications are important in the toy train hobby: restored and reproduction.

Restored: A number of the trains found in the marketplace have been restored. The rugged steel construction of many of the items has ensured that the item itself has survived, even if its brilliant enamel coating did not. Fortunately, many of these worn and scuffed items have been rescued from the trash bin, disassembled, stripped of their old finish, and a new finish has been applied. Coupled with mechanical repairs and polished or replaced brightwork, these trains now shine with all their previous glory. Unfortunately, some of the more larcenous types of our society chose to represent these restored items as excellent condition originals – often painting them in the more desirable color

combinations to boot. Under those circumstances, remember, it's not the train that is cheating, it's the seller.

No values are assigned in this book for restored items. The quality of restorations varies widely, ranging from spectroscopically matched paints applied to carefully stripped cars to "close enough" off the rack spray paints applied sometimes even directly over the old paint. Also, some collectors loath restored items, no matter how well done, or how honestly marked as restored. These factors combine to make assigning values to restored items virtually impossible. Use your own judgement, and remember, no matter how scarce an original is in a given color, the value of a restored item is not affected by color.

Further, collecting prewar trains is becoming an old enough hobby that some early restorations are 50 years old, and have acquired a patina of their own. For neophytes contemplating a major purchase, it is extremely important that you have absolute confidence in the seller, and hopefully the assistance of an experienced collector as well. If you are looking to add a specific item to your collection, it is extremely helpful to visit other collectors and carefully examine an original in advance. This will help you, much more than photos in this or any other book, know what an item *should* look like.

Reproduction: Reproductions allow enthusiasts to enjoy operating trains that otherwise they could not locate, could not afford, or would feel too risky to operate. A number of firms, Joe Mania Trains, Williams Reproductions, Kramer Reproductions, MTH and even Lionel itself have built excellent reproductions. Their products are clearly, but discretely, marked as reproductions. Unfortunately, other firms and individuals have reproduced items, particularly early trains, without any indication that they are not of original manufacture. These items are much more akin to being forgeries intended to deceive for great financial gain, rather than a reproduction built to permit enjoyment. None of the national train collecting organizations knowingly allows these items into their shows, or meets, but occasionally they do slip in, as they often do at independent shows. Be especially wary of 2 7/8-inch items and early Standard Gauge – both prime areas for forgeries.

Values for forgeries are not given in this book, as they are worthless on the legitimate market.

Demand is one of the key factors influencing values. The postwar Santa Fe F-3 diesel was the most produced locomotive in Lionel's history, yet clean examples still command premium prices due to demand.

Rarity, or scarcity, is also a factor influencing the value of trains. Low production quantities or extreme fragility cause some items to be substantially more difficult to find than others. When scarcity is coupled with demand the result is a premium price, while other items, extremely scarce, command only moderate prices due to lack of demand, or appreciation, on the part of collectors. In this guide we have rated each item on a scale of one to eight for rarity. One represents the most common items, such as the UTC lockon, while eight is assigned to those items hardest to find, such as the wooden 200 Electric Express gondola with Cowen's initials. It is hoped that this rarity rating will help the collector when having to choose between similar priced items to buy by answering the proverbial "how likely am I to get this chance again?" question.

Supply, as a short-term extension of rarity, whether actual or temporary, also affects price. If only one sought after item is at a given show, the seller is unlikely to negotiate or reduce his price. If, however, multiple sellers at a given event have identical items, no matter how rare, the temporary market glut can bring about temporarily reduced prices.

Lastly, the **buyer's intent** will effect what they are willing to pay. A collector who intends to add a piece to their permanent collection will obviously pay more for an item than a dealer who is purchasing for resale.

Trains in less than Very Good condition are not generally considered collectable.

As mentioned earlier, Mint condition trains are too uncommon to establish pricing on, as is the case for many prewar trains in Like New condition.

The prices listed are what a group of collectors would consider a reasonable market value when dealing at a train show, or "meet". Listed is a price they would be willing to pay to add that piece to their collection. When buying at a specialized train auction with internet access, one can expect to pay more as the pool of potential buyers is greater. The savings in fuel often offset this increased cost, by reducing lodging, and time, that would otherwise be spent tracking a given item down over time searching from show to show.

When contemplating a sale to a dealer, you should expect to receive 30 to 50% less than the value listed, with the poorer condition the trains the greater the amount of discount, due to the greater difficulty the dealer will have selling them. Remember that these prices are only a guideline. You are spending your money – what an item is worth to you is of greater importance than what it is worth to the author. Conversely, the publisher does not sell trains, this is not a mail-order catalog, and you should not expect a dealer or collector to "price match."

Boxes

Manufacturers boxed their products to ease handling and protect the trains en route and once at the market. They were strictly utilitarian, and throughout much of the postwar era, no thought was given to eye appeal. During the prewar era, it was intended that the trains be sold by attentive, trained salespeople. Self-service, and thus consumer oriented packaging, was not a factor.

Scattered throughout this book are photos of selected pieces with their original packaging. Items produced over an extended period of times sometimes used a variety of boxes during their production run, so boxes for a given piece can legitimately vary from those shown in this book. Beware, however that many unknowing (or uncaring) collectors and dealers often place items in the improper vintage box in an effort to "upgrade" the packaging.

One reason for this is that relatively speaking few boxes survive. The boxes, being pasteboard, were more fragile than the sturdy trains, and inherently would have a lower survival rate. Plus, people were buying TRAINS, not boxes – many of the boxes went out with the trash Christmas morning. Even in the early days of collecting, boxes; especially set boxes and outer master cartons, were considered bulky nuisances and were thrown away. Today, any given box is scarcer than its intended contents, and clean trains in their original boxes command a premium price in the marketplace. Even the boxes themselves have developed a collector market, but remember, to be proper the box must be not only the same stock number, but also the same vintage as the train inside.

Aids to Dating Trains

Unlike certain other collectibles, the age of a toy train is not a factor in its value. That is, an older train is not inherently more valuable than a newer train. It is rather the variations in construction throughout an item's production run that effect its scarcity, and thus value. Some toy trains are marked on the sides with "New" or "Built" dates. These dates are often totally irrelevant to when a piece was actually produced, and are decorative only. Establishing the production date of these trains is done more as a curiosity by most collectors, or when trying to properly and precisely recreate a given train set.

ACKNOWLEDGMENTS

Building on the firm foundation laid by the editors of previous editions of *O'Brien's Guide to Collecting Toy Trains*, including Elizabeth Stephan and Richard O'Brien, this volume features expanded emphasis, more detailed listings and new manufacturers, all reflecting the current trends in the collecting of vintage toy trains. When I worked on my previous books on toy trains, *The Standard Catalog of Lionel Trains* (prewar and postwar), I had the assistance of a number of friends I had made through my years of collecting trains from that maker. When I undertook this book, however, I realized that I would need to reach out for help to an even wider circle of collectors. As a result, not only has my knowledge been broadened, but so too has the circle of people that I call friends.

Many collectors and businesses shared photographs with me or allowed me to make my own images of rare and important pieces in their collections. Many knowledgeable collectors and dealers graciously reviewed the manuscript and offered corrections, criticism and commentary, and provided valuable insight on values for the items listed herein. Every effort has been made to present complete and accurate information here, and any errors herein are purely my own.

As with all my books on toy trains, collectors John and Bill Autry welcomed me with open arms, allowing me to photograph their collection not only in place, but trusting me with dozens of items to take to the Krause photo studio as well. Their generosity will not be soon forgotten.

Greg Stout, of Stout Auctions, who arguably handles the largest train collections in the country, granted us unlimited access for photography, and as a result, saved many, many hours of work and miles of driving. His phenomenal knowledge and amazing memory were tremendous assets in this project.

Train collecting is a passion for the entire Tschopp family, and they all pitched in on this project. Brothers Bob and John opened their postwar Lionel collection for photography and shared their knowledge. Their sister, Mary Burns and her husband Terry, put in a long, long day helping photograph the couple's fabulous prewar Lionel collection. Bob Sr. provided several rare Standard Gauge pieces, and teen-ager Bobby, the newest collector of the family, tireless located Lionel and Kusan trains for photography.

Photos for the Marx portion of this book would have been sparse indeed had not Ron Williams allowed me to photograph his collection. Unfortunately, space allows us to show but a small part of his vast array of trains.

Jim Nicholson is a true train collector—all sizes, all brands—and he graciously gave our photographers complete access to his amazing collection.

The Kusan and AMT chapters would not have been complete without the help of Joseph Lechner, Peter Attona and Jim Wagner. Vince Trimarco contributed photos of part of his large collection of Lionel HO gauge trains. Steve Hornick and his son Andrew, took the time to set up and photograph several pieces from their extensive Plasticville collection, adding greatly to that chapter.

The late Gary Lavinous and his team of dedicated volunteers stayed until near midnight at the National Toy Train Museum helping me photograph many of the rarest pieces shown in this volume. Though their day was nearing 18 hours long, they dismantled display cases to allow access, not only without complaining, but with genuine enthusiasm.

After long workdays, Bill Blystone then worked well into the evening photographing items from his extensive prewar collection. Clem Clement allowed us to photograph his wonderful collection of Standard gauge trains.

Barb Jones lent not only her photographic skills, but also her wonderful prewar collection and vast knowledge to this effort. Scott Douglas, another respected prewar Lionel collector, also provided photographs and information critical to this work.

The chapter on Lionel's smallest trains, and perhaps the smallest niche in prewar collecting, 00, would not have been possible without the help of Ken Shirey. Noted Standard Gauge aficionado Caryl Pettijohn provided much needed material in that area.

Dave McEntarfer contributed many photos, and much enthusiasm and experience to this project. Joe Mania, who produces exquisite reproductions of some of Lionel's earliest, rarest and most valuable trains, provided photographs of these products as an aid in differentiating authentic pieces from reproduction. His integrity is to be commended.

Parts with Character shared much knowledge and experience with me, as well as allowing needed photos to be taken.

My old friend, Jeff Kane of www.ttender.com, loaned several items from his collection for photography, as well as sharing part of his vast knowledge acquired through his years of supplying repair parts.

A handful of collectors chose to remain anonymous. Their anonymity, however, does not lessen the value of their contributions of photographs and information to this work—thank you.

HOW TO USE THIS BOOK

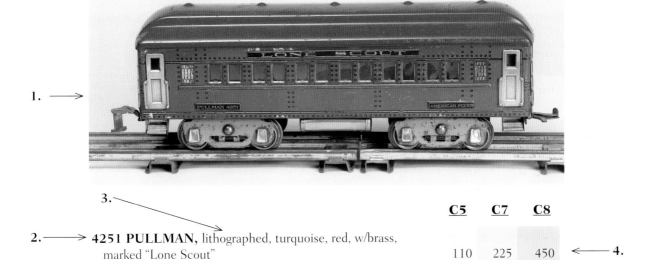

1.

3.

	C5	**C7**	**C8**
2. **4251 PULLMAN,** lithographed, turquoise, red, w/brass, marked "Lone Scout" | 110 | 225 | 450 | ← 4.

1.) Photo: In some listings, photos are supplied to better help identify and verify what Model you possess.

2.) Listing Name: Items will be listed by Model number. In most instances, if the model number does not appear on the item, the number is listed in parenthesis.

3.) Listing Description: Located directly after the Listing Name is a bried description of the listing, giving vital information to better help identification.

4.) Values: Values are listed in the columns to the right of the description. Values for each condition are in U.S. Dollars.

C5 formerly known as Good: Signs of play wear scratches, dents, minor surface rust, evidence of heavy use.

C6 formerly known as VG=Very Good: Few scratches, exceptionally clean, no major dents or rust.

C7 formerly known as EX=Excellent: Minute scratches or nicks, no dents or rust, all original, less than average wear.

C8 formerly known as LN=Like New: Only the slightest signs of handling and wheel wear, brilliant colors and crisp markings; literally like new. As a rule, Like New trains must have their original boxes in comparable condition to realize the prices listed in this guide.

Items shown in italics are the most common version. Items in bold are the most desirable. Prices are similarly coded.

Editor's note: The Train Collectors Association has changed its rating system for the condition of toy trains. Rather than Good, Excellent, Like New, etc., ratings now range from C1 through C10, with C10 being the highest, or former Mint condition. Most commonly collected are trains in C5 through C8 condition, and pricing throughout this book reflect these ratings.

AMERICAN FLYER

The company that is best remembered today as American Flyer was founded in Chicago about 1907. William Hafner, an experienced toymaker, developed a clockwork-powered train. His friend, William O. Coleman, had gained control of a struggling hardware manufacturer, the Edmonds-Metzel Manufacturing Company, and that firm's excess capacity was turned to toy production. Hafner, also a superb salesman, secured orders totaling $15,000 from Montgomery Ward and the G. Sommers & Co., and the company was firmly in the toy business. Beginning in 1908, Edmonds-Metzel trains were marketed as "American Flyer" and, in 1910, the firm's name was changed as well. Edmonds-Metzel was gone, as was hardware production, but American Flyer trains were in full swing.

By 1913, the collaboration between Hafner and Coleman, which had created the successful line, had begun to fail, resulting in Hafner leaving American Flyer. Hafner went on to form his own company, Hafner Manufacturing Company.

American Flyer introduced other types of toys to its product line, but the 1918 introduction of electric trains (the line previously had consisted of clockwork 0-gauge trains) set the company on its course for the next five decades. But the joy of a new product was dampened by the death of William Ogden Coleman. With the passing of his father, W.O. Coleman Jr. took the helm of the company.

During 1925 Flyer augmented its production of 0-gauge trains with the introduction of larger Wide Gauge trains. These trains operated on the same track as did Lionel's Standard Gauge train, but could not be marked as such because Standard Gauge was Lionel's proprietary trade name.

Three years later, one of Flyer's chief competitors, Ives, filed bankruptcy, setting the stage for the latter firm's takeover by a partnership of Lionel and American Flyer. This partnership lasted until 1930, when Lionel became sole owner of Ives. However, even with one competitor eliminated, Flyer still faced stiff competition. Toward the upper end for the Chicago firm loomed Lionel; for the economy market, American Flyer faced off against the formidable Louis Marx organization. The stiff competition forced American Flyer to withdraw from the declining Wide Gauge market after 1936.

A needed infusion of money and talent came in 1938 when Coleman sold out to famous Olympic athlete, and Erector Set proprietor, A.C. Gilbert. Gilbert moved production to Connecticut, and redesigned the line to 1/64 scale proportions the following year. At the same time, the much smaller HO gauge line was introduced. HO literally stands for Half Oh, and was considerably more realistic than even the redesigned 0 gauge line. HO remained part of the American Flyer line through 1963, even though in later years much of the line was produced by subcontractors such as Tru-Scale, Mantua or Varney.

Like other U.S. train manufacturers, Gilbert suspended production during World War II, its facilities used instead for war production. At the conclusion of hostilities, American Flyer retooled its trains for the new S gauge. Advertising of the period touted the realism of the two-rail track the new trains ran on, much to the chagrin of both Lionel and Marx, who continued to rely on three-rail track.

Despite the scale-like appearance of the new product line, and Gilbert's marketing talent, American Flyer never achieved more than the number two market position against the juggernaut of Lionel. The declining market for electric trains, and A.C. Gilbert's passing in 1961, led to the sale of the venerable firm to oil tycoon cum entertainment magnate Jack Wrather. Wrather was flush with cash from his successful "Lassie" and "Lone Ranger" television series, but sorely lacked experience in the toy market. Production of American Flyer trains ceased in 1966, and in 1967 Lionel gained ownership of the tooling and brand in exchange for liquidating the remaining inventory of American Flyer trains.

Since 1979, Lionel has offered a few American Flyer items almost every year, but this effort is a far cry from the glory days of Chicago or New Haven.

WIDE GAUGE

	C5	C7	C8
2210 LAMP, double arm	30	60	125
4000 LOCOMOTIVE, 1925-27, green, dark green, red, orange	100	200	400
4005 STOCK CAR, 1926, green	100	200	400

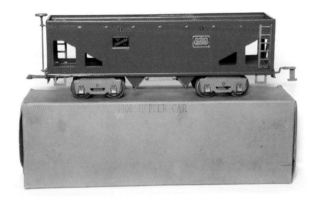

	C5	C7	C8
4006 HOPPER CAR, 1931-36, red	250	485	950
4007 SAND CAR, 1926-27, gray	300	600	1,200

	C5	C7	C8
4008 BOXCAR, 1926-27, orange	180	360	700

	C5	C7	C8
4010 TANK CAR, 1928-36, yellow	200	425	850

	C5	C7	C8
4010 TANK CAR, 1928-36, blue	420	700	1,400

	C5	C7	C8
4011 CABOOSE, 1926-32	155	310	600
4012 LUMBER CAR, 1927, blue and black, w/brass trim	65	125	250

	C5	C7	C8
4017 GONDOLA, 1928-36	105	210	400

	C5	C7	C8
4018 BOXCAR, 1928-36, beige and blue	150	300	600
4019 ENGINE, 1925-27, 0-4-0, maroon and black, w/brass trim	225	450	900

	C5	C7	C8
4020 CATTLE CAR, green and blue, 1928-36	125	250	500

	C5	C7	C8
4020 CATTLE CAR, 1928-36, two-tone blue	125	250	500

	C5	C7	C8
4021 CABOOSE, 1928-36, two-tone red w/brass trim	85	170	350
4022 MACHINERY CAR, 1928-33, orange and turquoise, w/brass trim	90	180	375
4023 LUMBER CAR, 1934-36, w/load	110	220	400

	C5	C7	C8
4039 LOCOMOTIVE, 1936, 0-4-0, brown and black, w/ brass trim	325	650	1,300
4040 BAGGAGE CAR, 1925-27, maroon	55	110	200
4040 MAIL CAR, 1925-27, lithographed, green, orange and black, marked "United States Mail Railway Post Office"	70	140	275

	C5	C7	C8
4040 MAIL CAR, 1925-27, lithographed, red	60	120	250
4041 PULLMAN, 1925-27, maroon	55	110	225
4042 CROSSING GATE, 1930-36, automatic	45	60	125
4042 OBSERVATION CAR, 1925-27, maroon	55	110	225
4080 BAGGAGE CAR, 1925-27	75	150	300
4081 WASHINGTON CAR, 1925-27	75	150	300
4082 VALLEY FORGE CAR, 1925-27	75	150	300
4090 BAGGAGE AND MAIL CAR, 1927	200	400	750
4091 PULLMAN, 1927, Annapolis	200	400	750
4092 OBSERVATION CAR, 1927, West Point	200	400	750
4122 MAIL CAR, two-tone blue	100	200	400

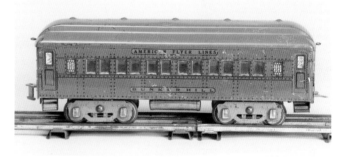

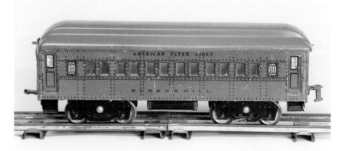

	C5	C7	C8
4141 PASSENGER CAR, Bunker Hill	300	600	1,000

	C5	**C7**	**C8**

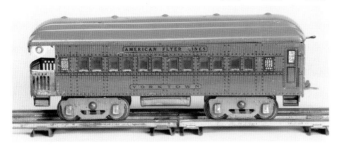

4142 OBSERVATION CAR,
Yorktown — 300, 600, 1,000

4151 PULLMAN, 1928-31,
Pleasant View — 130, 250, 500

4152 OBSERVATION CAR,
1928-31, Pleasant View — 130, 250, 500

4220 BRIDGE, 1928-33 — 450, 900, 1,750

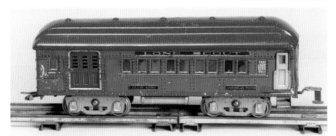

4250 CLUB CAR, 1929-31,
lithographed, turquoise and
red, w/brass trim, marked
"Lone Scout" — 110, 225, 450

4251 PULLMAN, 1929-31,
lithographed, turquoise, red,
w/brass, marked "Lone Scout" — 110, 225, 450

	C5	**C7**	**C8**

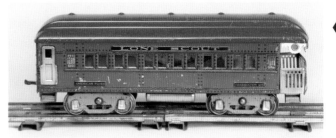

4252 OBSERVATION CAR,
1929-31, turquoise and red,
w/brass trim, marked "Lone
Scout" — 110, 225, 450

4331 PULLMAN, 1931-36,
two-tone red, w/brass inserts
and brass windows — 125, 250, 500

4332 OBSERVATION CAR,
1931-36, two-tone red, w/brass
inserts and brass windows — 225, 450, 900

4340 CLUB CAR, 1928-32,
beige, green, w/brass plates
and brass windows, marked
"Pocahontas" — 225, 450, 900

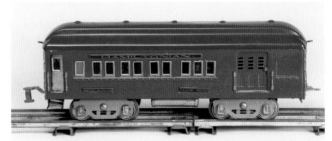

4340 CLUB CAR, 1928-32,
two-tone red w/brass trim,
marked "Hamiltonian" — 200, 400, 750

4341 PULLMAN, 1928-32,
beige, green, w/brass plates
and brass windows — 200, 400, 750

	C5	**C7**	**C8**

4341 PULLMAN, 1928-32, two-tone red, w/brass trim, marked "Hamiltonian" — 200 400 750

4341 PULLMAN, 1928-32, beige and green, w/brass trim, marked "Pocahontas" — 200 400 750

4342 OBSERVATION CAR, 1928-32, beige and green, w/brass plates and brass windows, marked "Pocahontas" — 150 300 500

4342 OBSERVATION CAR, 1928-32, two-tone red, w/brass trim, marked "Hamiltonian" — 150 300 500

4343 OBSERVATION CAR, 1928-32, beige and green, w/brass trim, marked "Pocahontas" — 175 350 600

	C5	**C7**	**C8**

4350 CLUB CAR, 1931, blue green w/red roof — 150 300 500

4351 CLUB CAR, 1931, blue green w/red roof — 150 300 500

4352 CLUB CAR, 1931, blue green w/red roof — 150 300 500

4380 BAGGAGE CAR, 1928-29, 1930-31, beige and green, w/brass trim, marked "Hancock" — 200 400 750

4380 PULLMAN, 1928-29, 1930-31, blue, w/brass trim, marked "Flying Colonel-Madison" — 200 400 750

4381 PULLMAN, 1928-29, 1930-31, blue, brass trim, marked "Flying Colonel-Adams" — 200 400 750

4381 PULLMAN, 1928-29, 1930-31, green and beige, brass trim, marked "Hancock" — 200 400 750

4382 OBSERVATION CAR, 1928-29, 1930-31, blue, w/brass trim, marked "Flying Colonel-Hancock" — 200 400 750

4382 OBSERVATION CAR, 1928-29, 1930-31, beige and green, w/brass trim, marked "Hancock" — 200 400 750

4390 CLUB CAR, 1928-34, two-tone blue, West Point — 300 600 1,000

4391 PULLMAN CAR, 1928-34, two-tone blue, Annapolis — 300 600 1,000

	C5	**C7**	**C8**

4392 OBSERVATION CAR,
1928-34, two-tone blue, Army-Navy

	300	600	1,000

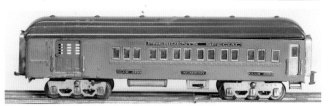

4393 DINING CAR, 1928-34, two-tone blue, marked "President's Special-Academy"

	300	600	1,000

4633 LOCOMOTIVE, 1930-31

	350	700	1,100

4635 LOCOMOTIVE, 1929-30, red w/brass trim, Shasta

	275	550	975

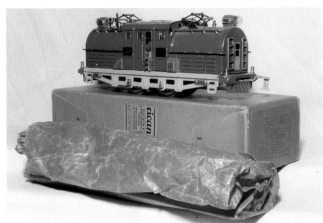

4637 LOCOMOTIVE, 1928-33, 0-4-0, Auto Bell, green and beige, w/brass trim

	600	1,200	2,000

4643 ENGINE, 1927, 0-4-0, green and black, w/brass trim

	150	300	625

	C5	**C7**	**C8**

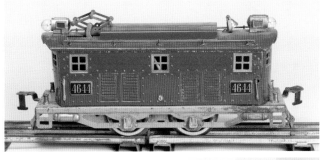

4644 ENGINE, 1928-33, 0-4-0, red and gray, w/brass trim

	125	275	550

4644RC LOCOMOTIVE, 1928-33

	225	450	900

4644 OBSERVATION CAR,
lithographed, Eagle

	110	225	450

4644 PULLMAN,
lithographed, Eagle

	110	225	450

4653 ENGINE, 1927, 0-4-0, orange and black, w/brass trim

	200	400	750

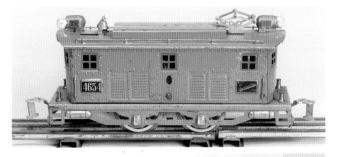

4654 LOCOMOTIVE, 1928-31

	225	450	900

	C5	C7	C8
4660 LOCOMOTIVE, 1929-30	250	500	1,000
4667 ENGINE, 1927, 0-4-0, red and black, w/brass trim	200	400	800
4670 LOCOMOTIVE, 1931, 2-4-2, black w/green stripe and brass trim, w/tender	1,000	2,000	4,000
4670 LOCOMOTIVE, 1931-32, 4-4-2, black w/green stripe and brass and nickel trim, w/tender	600	1,200	2,500
4672 LOCOMOTIVE, 1931-32, cast iron	350	700	1,500
4675 LOCOMOTIVE, 1931-32, 4-4-2	800	1,600	3,000
4677 LOCOMOTIVE, 1927	425	850	1,750

	C5	C7	C8
4678 ENGINE, 1928-29, 0-4-0, red and gray, w/brass trim	500	1,000	2,000
4680 LOCOMOTIVE, 1933, w/4671 coal tender	600	1,200	2,500
4681 LOCOMOTIVE, 1933-35, 4-4-2	750	1,500	3,000
4683 LOCOMOTIVE, 1930-31	500	1,000	2,000

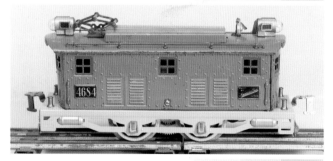

	C5	C7	C8
4684 LOCOMOTIVE, 1928-31	500	1,000	2,000

	C5	C7	C8
4685 LOCOMOTIVE, 1929-30	300	600	1,250

	C5	C7	C8
4686 ENGINE, 1928-29, 4-4-4, black red and two-tone blue, w/brass trim, marked "The Ace"	600	1,200	2,500

	C5	C7	C8
4687 ENGINE, 1927, 4-4-4, blue and black, w/brass trim	1,250	2,500	5,000
4687 LOCOMOTIVE, 1927, lithographed, blue, marked "President's Special"	1,150	2,300	4,500

	C5	C7	C8
4689 ENGINE, 1928-34, 4-4-4, peacock blue and black, w/brass and nickel trim, marked "The Commander"	2,500	5,000	9,500
4692 LOCOMOTIVE, Tri-valve steam	500	1,000	2,000
4694 LOCOMOTIVE, 4-4-2, blue w/brass and copper trim	700	1,400	2,750

	C5	C7	C8
4694 LOCOMOTIVE, 4-4-2, black w/green stripe, brass and nickel trim, w/tender	600	1,200	2,500
4693 TENDER	200	400	750
4695 LOCOMOTIVE, 1931-33	550	1,100	2,000
4696 LOCOMOTIVE, 1933-35, 2-4-2	1,400	2,800	5,500

O GAUGE

	C5	C7	C8
1 LOCOMOTIVE, 1907-16, O ga., wind-up	50	100	150
1 TRANSFORMER, 25 watt	15	20	30
1 TRANSFORMER, 35 watt	19	25	35
2 LOCOMOTIVE, 1908-16, cast iron, wind-up	70	140	200
1-1/2 TRANSFORMER, 45 watt	23	30	40
1-1/2B TRANSFORMER, 50 watt	30	40	60
2 TRANSFORMER, 75 watt	38	50	75
1-1/2 TRANSFORMER, 50 watt	30	40	60
3 LOCOMOTIVE, O ga., wind-up	45	90	125
4 LOCOMOTIVE, 0-4-0, wind-up	60	125	175
4A LOCOMOTIVE, O ga., wind-up	70	140	200
8B TRANSFORMER	42	55	75
8B TRANSFORMER, 100 watt, w/bulb covers	53	70	100
8B TRANSFORMER, 100 watt, without bulb covers	45	60	95
8B TRANSFORMER, w/ uncoupler, track, manual and buttons	53	70	100
9 LOCOMOTIVE, 1926-27, 1929-32, 0-4-0, wind-up	60	120	175
10 LOCOMOTIVE, 0-4-0, cast iron, wind-up	50	100	150
10 LOCOMOTIVE, 1925, electric	120	240	350
11 LOCOMOTIVE, 1927-32, 0-4-0, wind-up	90	180	275
12 LOCOMOTIVE, 1910-17, O ga., cast iron	50	100	150
12 SMOKE CARTRIDGES	—	4	
13 LOCOMOTIVE AND TENDER, 1917-22, 0-4-0, wind-up, black, orange and green	75	150	225
14 LOCOMOTIVE, 1925-32, 0-4-0, wind-up	45	90	150
15 LOCOMOTIVE, 1920-22, O ga., wind-up	35	70	100
16 LOCOMOTIVE, 1923-26, O ga., 0-4-0, electric	55	110	150
18B TRANSFORMER	90	120	175
19B TRANSFORMER, 300 watt w/volt and amp	75	100	150
28 LOCOMOTIVE, 0-4-0, wind-up	40	85	115
29 LOCOMOTIVE, O ga., cast iron, first electric, wind-up	75	150	225
34 LOCOMOTIVE, 1930-31, 0-4-0, wind-up	70	140	225
40 LOCOMOTIVE, 0-4-0, wind-up	70	140	225
92 SWITCH TOWER	60	80	125
96 STATION, O ga., c. 1931	30	40	60
104 KENILWORTH STATION	18	25	40
105 PULLMAN	30	60	100
119 HIAWATHA LOCOMOTIVE, O ga., tin-plate, wind-up, w/tender	60	120	175
119 HIAWATHA LOCOMOTIVE, O ga., tin-plate, electric	90	180	225
119 TENDER, 1930-32, O ga.	30	60	100
120 TENDER, O ga.	40	80	120
121 TENDER, O ga., black and white, marked "No. 121"	30	60	100
228 LOG CAR, 1939, O ga.	20	40	65
229 BOXCAR, 1939, O ga.	20	40	65
230 DUMP CAR, 1939, O ga.	20	40	65
231 TANK CAR, 1939, O ga.	20	40	65
328 TENDER, 1907-26, O ga.	30	60	100
356 TENDER, O ga., Comet	40	80	125
401 LOCOMOTIVE See 403	88	175	250
403 LOCOMOTIVE, 1939-40, O ga., 2-4-4	65	125	200
404 PULLMAN, 1939, O ga.	30	60	100
405 OBSERVATION CAR, 1939, O ga.	30	60	100

	C5	**C7**	**C8**

406 LOG CAR, 1939, green or orange — 18 / 35 / 50

	C5	**C7**	**C8**
406 LOG CAR, 1939, green or orange	18	35	50

	C5	**C7**	**C8**
407 SAND CAR, 1939, green	20	40	60

	C5	**C7**	**C8**
408 BOXCAR, 1939-40, orange	20	45	70
409 DUMP CAR, 1939, O ga.	30	65	100
410 LOCOMOTIVE, O ga.	55	110	170

	C5	**C7**	**C8**
410 TANK CAR, 1939-40, silver tank, greenframe; or green on blue frame	25	55	80

	C5	**C7**	**C8**

	C5	**C7**	**C8**
411 CABOOSE, 1939-40, similar to 3211, red	20	40	60
412 MILK CAR, 1939-40, O ga.	48	95	150

	C5	**C7**	**C8**
415 FLOODLIGHT CAR, 1939	45	90	150
416 WRECKER CAR, 1939, O ga.	100	200	300
419 LOCOMOTIVE, 1939, O ga., streamliner	135	275	400
420 LOCOMOTIVE See 422	100	200	300
421 TENDER, O ga.	35	70	100
422 LOCOMOTIVE, 1939, O ga., 2-4-2	125	250	375
423 LOCOMOTIVE, O ga.	90	175	250
424 LOCOMOTIVE, 1939, O ga., 2-4-4	60	125	185
425 LOCOMOTIVE, see 427	100	200	300

	C5	**C7**	**C8**
427 LOCOMOTIVE, 1939-40, 2-6-4	200	400	600

429 see 431

	C5	C7	C8
431 LOCOMOTIVE, 1939-40, 0-6-0	425	850	1,275
432 LOCOMOTIVE see 434	300	600	900
434 LOCOMOTIVE, 1939, O ga., 4-4-2	350	700	1,050
436 LOCOMOTIVE, 1939-40, O ga., 4-6-2	550	1,100	1,650
437 LOCOMOTIVE, 1939, O ga., 2-4-2	280	560	850
449 LOCOMOTIVE, 1939, O ga., 2-6-4	840	1,680	2,520

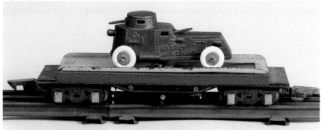

	C5	C7	C8
472 UNLOADING CAR, 1940-41, Army, w/Tootsietoy armored car	60	115	175
474 DUMP CAR, 1941, O ga., automatic	100	200	300

480 TANK CAR, 1940, yellow, Shell, or silver and blue — 25 50 75

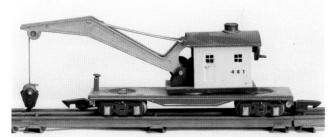

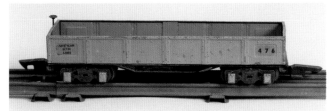

476 GONDOLA, 1940-41, green — 25 50 75

481 WRECKER CAR, 1941, black or red frame — 40 80 120

478 BOXCAR, 1940-41, 1946 white with red roof — 20 40 60

482 LUMBER CAR, 1940-41, green or black — 30 65 95

	C5	C7	C8

483 GIRDER CAR, 1941, black with orange girder — 25 | 50 | 75

484 CABOOSE, 1940-46, red — 15 | 35 | 50

486 HOPPER, 1940-41, yellow — 40 | 80 | 120

488 FLOODLIGHT CAR, 1940-41 — 50 | 100 | 150

490 WHISTLE CAR, 1940-41, gray — 40 | 75 | 115

490B WHISTLE CAR, 1940, blue — 40 | 75 | 115

	C5	C7	C8

492R MAIL PICKUP CAR, 1941, red — 30 | 60 | 90

492G MAIL PICKUP CAR, 1941, green — 30 | 60 | 90

492T MAIL PICKUP CAR, 1941, tuscan — 30 | 60 | 90

494R BAGGAGE CAR, 1940-41, red — 30 | 60 | 90

494G BAGGAGE CAR, 1940, green — 30 | 60 | 90

494B BAGGAGE CAR, 1940-41, blue — 30 | 60 | 90

494T BAGGAGE CAR, 1941, tuscan — 30 | 60 | 90

495R COACH CAR, 1940-41, red — 35 | 70 | 100

495RL COACH CAR, 1940-41, red, illuminated — 35 | 70 | 100

495G COACH CAR, 1940-41, green — 35 | 70 | 100

495GL COACH CAR, 1940-41, green, illuminated — 35 | 70 | 100

495B COACH CAR, 1940-41, blue — 35 | 70 | 100

	C5	C7	C8
495BL COACH CAR, 1940-41, blue, illuminated	35	70	100
495T COACH CAR, 1941, tuscan	35	70	100
495TL COACH CAR, 1941, tuscan, illuminated	35	70	100
496RL PULLMAN, 1941, red, illuminated	90	175	275
496GL PULLMAN, 1941, green, illuminated	90	175	275
496T PULLMAN, 1941, tuscan	90	175	275
496TL PULLMAN, 1941, tuscan, illuminated	90	175	275
497R OBSERVATION CAR, 1941, red	50	95	150
497RL OBSERVATION CAR, 1941, red, illuminated	50	95	150
497GL OBSERVATION CAR, 1941, green, illuminated	50	95	150
497T OBSERVATION CAR, 1941, tuscan	50	95	150
497TL OBSERVATION CAR, 1941, tuscan, illuminated	50	95	150

504 GONDOLA, 1939-41, diecast gray or tuscan

	C5	C7	C8
504 GONDOLA, 1939-41, diecast gray or tuscan	100	200	300

506 BOXCAR, 1939-41, Baltimore and Ohio, white

	C5	C7	C8
506 BOXCAR, 1939-41, Baltimore and Ohio, white	50	100	150

	C5	C7	C8
508 HOPPER, 1939-41, Virginian	65	130	200

	C5	C7	C8
510 CATTLE CAR, 1939-41, Missouri Pacific, brown	40	75	115

	C5	C7	C8
512 TANK CAR, 1939-41, Texaco, silver or gray	40	75	115
513 OBSERVATION CAR, 1932-35, O ga.	15	25	40
514 WRECKER CAR, 1939-41, O ga.	100	200	300
515 COACH CAR, O ga., tin-plate, lithographed, yellow, red, black and orange, early	15	25	40

	C5	C7	C8
516 CABOOSE, 1939-41, illuminated, UP or NYC	45	85	125

	C5	C7	C8
518 BAGGAGE CAR, 1931-32, O ga.	25	50	75
519 PULLMAN, 1931-32, O ga.	25	50	75

	C5	C7	C8
521 BAGGAGE-CLUB CAR, 1939-41, tuscan	100	200	300

524 PULLMAN, 1939-41, tuscan	300	600	900
531 LOCOMOTIVE, 1940-41, O ga., 4-6-4	450	900	1,350
534 LOCOMOTIVE, 1940-41, O ga., 4-8-4	1,400	2,800	4,250

545 LOCOMOTIVE, 1940, 4-4-2	50	100	150
553 LOCOMOTIVE, 1940, steam	55	110	175
555C TENDER, 1941, O ga.	30	60	90

| **556 LOCOMOTIVE,** Royal Blue, 1940-41, 4-6-2 | 55 | 115 | 175 |
| **558C TENDER,** 1941, O ga., w/chugger | 35 | 65 | 100 |

| **559 LOCOMOTIVE,** 1940-41, 4-6-2, Pennsylvania K5 | 175 | 350 | 525 |

561 STEAM LOCOMOTIVE, 1940-41, 4-6-2, Pennsylvania K5	105	210	325
564 LOCOMOTIVE, 1939, O ga., 4-6-4	1,250	2,500	2,750
564C TENDER, 1941	25	50	75
565 LOCOMOTIVE, 4-4-2, 1941, 1945-46	75	150	225
568 LOCOMOTIVE, 1939, O ga., 4-8-4	1,500	3,000	4,500

| **570 STEAM LOCOMOTIVE,** 1940-41, 4-6-4, New York Central J3, 3/16 | 150 | 300 | 450 |

571 STEAM LOCOMOTIVE, O ga., 3/16 scale, 4-8-4	200	400	600
574 LOCOMOTIVE, 1941, O ga., 0-8-0, switcher	700	1,400	2,100
574B LOCOMOTIVE, O ga., 0-8-0	1,000	2,000	3,000
597 PASSENGER AND FREIGHT STATION	35	70	100
616 LOCOMOTIVE, O ga., wind-up	75	150	225

	C5	C7	C8
617 LOCOMOTIVE, 1933-35, O ga., 2-4-2	50	100	150
622 LOCOMOTIVE, 1934, O ga.	40	80	125

	C5	C7	C8
640 STEAM LOCOMOTIVE, 1936, 0-4-2, black	100	150	225
641 LOCOMOTIVE, 1936, O ga., 2-4-2	350	700	1,050
816 LOCOMOTIVE, wind-up, three cars	300	600	900
830 LOCOMOTIVE, wind-up, two cars	140	275	425
832 LOCOMOTIVE, wind-up, three cars	140	275	425
960T LOCOMOTIVE, O ga., two cars	175	350	525
961T LOCOMOTIVE, O ga., 0-4-0, three cars	140	275	425
964T LOCOMOTIVE, O ga., three cars	200	400	600
970T HIAWATHA SET, O ga., includes locomotive tender, two coaches and observation car	335	670	1,000
1025 RAILWAY EXPRESS MAIL CAR, O ga.	30	60	90
1026 PASSENGER CAR, O ga.	15	25	40
1045 TRANSFORMER, 25 watt	15	20	35

	C5	C7	C8
1096 BOX CAB LOCOMOTIVE, 1925-27, 0-4-0, w/square headlight, rubber-stamped	75	150	225
1097 ENGINE, O ga., 0-4-0, lithographed, orange, green and red, w/nickel trim	75	150	225
1103 PASSENGER CAR	30	60	100
1104 BAGGAGE CAR, O ga.	30	60	100
1105 BAGGAGE CAR, marked "American Express"	60	120	175
1105 CANADIAN NATIONAL RAILWAYS DOMINION FLYER, O ga., lithographed, red and black, w/nickel trim	30	60	100
1106 COACH, O ga., lithographed, brown and black, marked "Dominion Flyer"	40	80	125
1106 LUMBER CAR, 1930, black	20	35	60
1106 PARLOR CAR, O ga., lithographed, yellow, black and green	30	60	100
1106 PARLOR CAR, lithographed, green w/black roof, four wheels	30	60	100

	C5	C7	C8
1093 LOCOMOTIVE, 1930-31	220	440	675
1094 LOCOMOTIVE, O ga.	350	700	1,100

	C5	C7	C8
1107 COACH CAR, O ga., lithographed	20	35	60

	C5	C7	C8
1108 BAGGAGE CAR, O ga., lithographed	25	45	75
1109 SAND CAR, O ga., lithographed, red	20	35	60
1110 BOXCAR, O ga.	25	50	75

	C5	C7	C8
1111 CABOOSE, 1919-35	25	50	75

	C5	C7	C8
1112 BOXCAR, 1919-35, NYC Reefer, lithographed 1115 on side	30	60	100
1112 BOXCAR, 1930, lithographed, yellow	35	70	110
1113 GONDOLA, 1925, lithographed, green	20	35	60
1114 CABOOSE, O ga., lithographed, red, green and white, w/brass trim	25	50	75

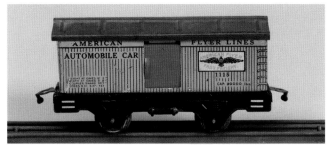

	C5	C7	C8
1115 AUTOMOBILE BOXCAR, O ga., later	40	80	125
1115 BOXCAR, see 1112			

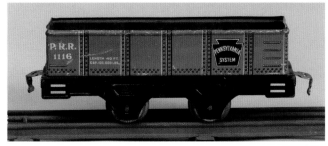

	C5	C7	C8
1116 GONDOLA	25	50	75
1116 SAND CAR, O ga.	60	120	200
1117 CABOOSE, O ga.	35	70	110
1118 TANK CAR, O ga., lithographed, gray-white and black	45	90	150
1119 STOCK CAR, O ga.	40	80	125
1120 CABOOSE, O ga.	25	50	75

	C5	C7	C8
1120 OBSERVATION CAR, 1923-29	25	50	75

	C5	**C7**	**C8**

1120 PASSENGER CAR, 1923-29 — 25 | 50 | 75

	C5	**C7**	**C8**
1121 LOCOMOTIVE, w/ whistle and tender, 2-4-0	30	60	100
1122 BLUESTREAK PASSENGER CAR, O ga.	25	50	75
1123 PASSENGER CAR, O ga., tuscan	20	40	60
1123 PASSENGER CAR, O ga.	20	40	60
1124 PULLMAN, O ga.	60	120	200
1127 CABOOSE, O ga.	15	30	50
1128 TANK CAR, O ga.	15	30	50
1141 LOG CAR, O ga.	40	80	125
1146 LOG CAR, O ga.	40	80	125
1147 OBSERVATION CAR, O ga.	50	100	150
1157 OBSERVATION CAR, O ga.	50	100	150
1200 BAGGAGE CAR, O ga., lithographed, four wheel	30	60	100
1200 BAGGAGE CAR, O ga., lithographed, eight wheel	30	60	100

	C5	**C7**	**C8**
1201 LOCOMOTIVE, 1920-24, steeple cab, black or dark green	45	90	140
1201 PASSENGER CAR, lithographed, red w/black roof	30	60	100
1202 BAGGAGE CAR, Express	35	65	100
1202 BAGGAGE CAR, O ga., Electric Service	40	80	125
1203 COACH CAR, O ga., lithographed, eight wheel, early	35	65	100
1203 PASSENGER CAR, 1933, lithographed, blue w/ black roof	35	65	100
1204 BAGGAGE CAR, 1933-34, O ga.	60	120	200

1205 BAGGAGE CAR, American Railway Express — 30 | 60 | 100

	C5	C7	C8

	C5	C7	C8

1205 MAIL CAR, 1924-26	30	60	100

1211 LOCOMOTIVE, 1920-24, steeple cab, black or dark green	45	90	150
1211 PASSENGER COACH, 1934, O ga.	30	60	100
1212 OBSERVATION CAR, 1934, O ga.	100	200	300
1213 PULLMAN, 1934, O ga.	60	120	200
1214 BAGGAGE, 1934, O ga.	60	120	200
1217 LOCOMOTIVE, 0-4-0, electric	60	120	200

1206 PASSENGER CAR, 1922-26, red or orange	40	75	125
1206 PULLMAN, O ga.	40	75	125

1207 OBSERVATION CAR, 1926	40	75	125
1208 LOCOMOTIVE, O ga.	80	160	250
1209 OBSERVATION CAR, O ga.	60	120	200

1218 LOCOMOTIVE, 1920-25, O ga., 0-4-0, black, red and yellow, electric	75	150	225

	C5	C7	C8
1219 COACH CAR, O ga.	20	40	60
1223 COACH CAR, O ga.	20	40	60
1225 LOCOMOTIVE, O ga., 1919, 0-4-0, cast iron	100	200	300
1257 OBSERVATION CAR, 1933, O ga.	120	240	375
1270 LOCOMOTIVE, O ga.	100	200	300

	C5	C7	C8
1286 PULLMAN, 1925, O ga.	45	90	150

	C5	C7	C8
1287 OBSERVATION CAR, 1925, Chicago	45	90	150
1290 TRANSFORMER	30	40	100

	C5	C7	C8
1306 PASSENGER CAR, 1922-26, four- or eight-wheel, blue, green, red or brown	25	50	75
1322RT LOCOMOTIVE, O ga., four cars	550	1,100	1,700
1621 PULLMAN, 1936-39, O ga.	65	135	200
1622 OBSERVATION CAR, 1936-39, O ga.	65	135	200

	C5	C7	C8
1641 HIAWATHA COACH, 1936-37	50	150	250

	C5	C7	C8

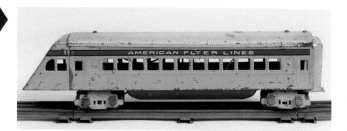

1642 HIAWATHA OBSERVATION, 1936-37 — 50 / 150 / 250

1681 LOCOMOTIVE, 1936-38, O ga., 2-6-4 — 250 / 500 / 750

1683 LOCOMOTIVE, 1936-37, O ga. — 700 / 1,400 / 2,100

1684 LOCOMOTIVE, 1936-39, O ga. — 60 / 120 / 180

1686 STEAM LOCOMOTIVE, 1937, 4-4-2, streamlined — 110 / 220 / 350

1687 LOCOMOTIVE, 1937, O ga., 2-4-2 — 350 / 700 / 1,100

1688 LOCOMOTIVE, 1937, 2-4-2 — 150 / 275 / 425

1710 LOCOMOTIVE, O ga. — 75 / 150 / 225

1730RW STREAMLINER, 1935, Union Pacific, 51 inches long — 200 / 425 / 625

1835TW TENDER — 75 / 150 / 225

2005 TRIANGLE LIGHT — 45 / 70 / 120

2010 DOUBLE ARC LAMP POST, 12 1/2 inches high — 35 / 70 / 110

2020 WATER TANK, O ga. — 50 / 100 / 150

2029 WHISTLE UNIT, remote control — 30 / 60 / 100

2043 SEMAPHORE — 175 / 225 / 400

3000 BAGGAGE, O ga., lithographed, black and two-tone green — 50 / 100 / 150

	C5	C7	C8

3001 PULLMAN, 1922-24, Illini — 50 / 100 / 150

3004 CABOOSE, O ga., illuminated — 60 / 120 / 200

3005 OBSERVATION CAR, O ga., Illini — 30 / 60 / 100

3006 FLATCAR, 1924-27 — 10 / 20 / 30

3007 SAND CAR, 1925-27 — 250 / 500 / 750

3008 BOXCAR, 1925-27, lithographed, GN, ART, B&O, or Nickel Plate — 250 / 500 / 750

3009 DUMP CAR, 1934-35, O ga., decaled — 5 / 10 / 15

3010 TANK CAR, 1925-27, O ga., gray w/black nickel trim — 50 / 100 / 150

	C5	C7	C8
3011 LOCOMOTIVE, 1926-27	100	175	275
3012 BOXCAR, 1930-35, O ga., rubber stamped	15	30	45
3012 LOCOMOTIVE, 1925-27, O ga., 0-4-0, lithographed, headlight in cab, electric	100	200	300
3013 GONDOLA, 1930-35, O ga.	25	50	75
3013 LOCOMOTIVE, O ga.	400	800	1,250
3014 CABOOSE, O ga., decaled set	25	50	75
3014 LOCOMOTIVE, O ga.	550	1,100	1,700
3015 BOXCAR, 1930-32, 1934-35, O ga.	20	40	60

	C5	C7	C8
3015 LOCOMOTIVE, 1927, green	150	275	425
3016 SAND CAR, O ga.	25	50	75
3017 CABOOSE, O ga., eight wheel	15	25	40

	C5	C7	C8
3018 TANK CAR, 1930-32, yellow and black, w/copper trim	30	65	100
3018 TANK CAR, 1934-35, eight wheel	75	175	250

	C5	C7	C8
3019 DUMP CAR, 1934, 1935, 1938, O ga., eight wheel	15	35	50
3019 ELECTRIC LOCO, 1923-24, O ga., dark green, black frame and maroon windows, rubber stamped, headlight	200	400	600

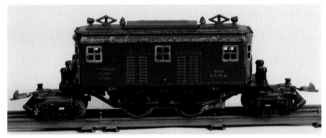

	C5	C7	C8
3020 ENGINE, 1922-25, O ga., 4-4-4, maroon and black, w/nickel trim	250	500	750

	C5	C7	C8
3020 ENGINE, 1922-25, O ga., 4-4-4, black and yellow, w/nickel trim	200	400	600

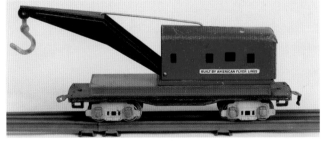

	C5	C7	C8
3025 CRANE CAR, 1936-38, O ga.	50	100	150
3045 WRECKER CAR, 1930-31, O ga.	70	140	210
3046 LUMBER CAR, 1930-32, 1934, 1935, O ga., eight wheel	20	40	60
3080 MAIL CAR, O ga.	40	80	125
3081 PULLMAN, O ga., Illini	40	80	125

	C5	C7	C8

3085 OBSERVATION CAR,
O ga., Columbia 40 80 125

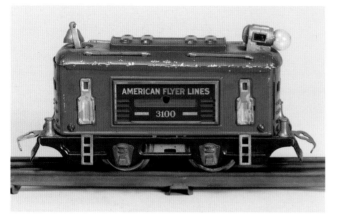

3100 LOCOMOTIVE, 1930-
33, 0-4-0 red, black, gold,
w/brass trim and plates 60 120 200

3102 LOCOMOTIVE, 1926,
lithographed 50 100 150

3103 LOCOMOTIVE, 1930 225 450 700

3105 LOCOMOTIVE, blue 140 240 400

	C5	C7	C8

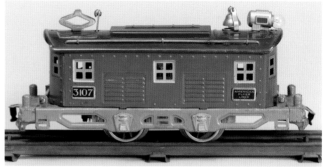

3107 LOCOMOTIVE, 1930-
32, 0-4-0 75 150 225

3107RC LOCOMOTIVE,
1930-32, O ga. 250 500 750

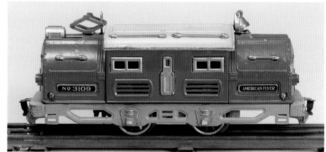

3109 ENGINE, 1930-31, 0-4-
0, green, brown, w/brass trim 100 200 300

3110 LOCOMOTIVE, 1928-
29, 0-4-0, w/headlight 125 250 375

3112 LOCOMOTIVE, 1928-
29, orange, brown or maroon
litho body 75 125 200

3113 LOCOMOTIVE, 1928-
29, O ga. 110 220 330

3113 LOCOMOTIVE, O ga.,
0-4-0, two-tone blue w/two-
tone blue coaches marked
"Nationwide Lines" made for
J.C. Penney Co., extremely rare;
set complete in original boxes 500 1,000 1,400

	C5	**C7**	**C8**

	C5	**C7**	**C8**

3113 LOCOMOTIVE, O ga., 0-4-0, two-tone blue w/two-tone blue coaches marked, American Flyer Bluebird, American Flyer Lines lettering — 150 350 600

3115 ENGINE, 1928-30, 0-4-0, peacock blue, w/brass trim — 60 120 190

3116 ENGINE, 1928-29, O ga., 0-4-0, turquoise and black, w/brass trim — 200 400 600

3117 ENGINE, 1928-29, O ga., 0-4-0, red w/brass trim — 150 300 450

3140 BAGGAGE CAR, 1932-33, O ga. — 70 140 225

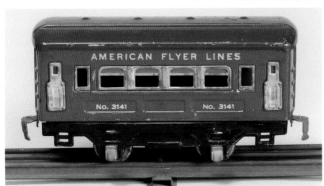

3141 PULLMAN, 1930-32, O ga., red and black, w/brass trim — 50 90 150

3142 OBSERVATION CAR, 1930-32, red, black and gold, w/brass trim — 50 90 150

3150 BAGGAGE CAR, 1930-33 — 50 90 150

3151 PASSENGER CAR, 1930-33 — 30 55 90

3152 OBSERVATION CAR, 1930-33, O ga., two-tone orange, w/brass trim — 50 100 150

	C5	C7	C8

3161 PASSENGER CAR, 1930-33 — 75 / 150 / 225

	C5	C7	C8
3161 PASSENGER CAR, 1930-33	75	150	225

	C5	C7	C8
3162 OBSERVATION CAR, 1930-33, O ga., w/brass trim	30	60	100

	C5	C7	C8
3171 PULLMAN, 1930-33, 1934, 1936-38, O ga., w/brass trim	20	40	60

	C5	C7	C8
3172 OBSERVATION CAR, 1930-33, 1934, 1936-38, O ga., w/brass trim	20	40	60

	C5	C7	C8
3176 PULLMAN, 1931, 1937, O ga.	25	50	75
3177 OBSERVATION CAR, 1931, 1937, O ga.	30	60	90
3178 COACH, 1935, O ga.	200	400	600
3179 OBSERVATION, 1935	40	75	150
3180 CLUB CAR, O ga., beige and green, w/brass trim, marked "Potomac"	40	75	120
3180 CLUB CAR, O ga., two-tone red, green, w/brass trim	25	50	75
3181 PULLMAN, 1928-30, O ga., beige and green, w/brass trim, marked "Potomac"	40	75	120
3182 LOCOMOTIVE, 1931, O ga., 0-4-0	200	400	600
3182 OBSERVATION CAR, 1928-30, O ga., beige and green, w/brass trim, marked "Potomac"	40	75	120
3184 LOCOMOTIVE, 1931, O ga., 0-4-0	250	500	750
3185 LOCOMOTIVE, 1928-30, turquoise/teal blue	225	450	700
3186 LOCOMOTIVE, 1928-29, O ga.	400	800	1,250

	C5	C7	C8
3187 LOCOMOTIVE, 1928-32, red	300	600	900
3188 LOCOMOTIVE, 1931, 0-4-0	250	500	750
3191 LOCOMOTIVE, 1931, O ga., 2-4-0, remote control reverse	160	320	500
3192 LOCOMOTIVE, 1930-31	40	80	125
3197 LOCOMOTIVE, 1930, O ga., 0-4-0	250	500	750
3198 LOCOMOTIVE, 1931, O ga., cast iron	90	180	275
3201 CABOOSE, 1932, O ga.	25	50	75

	C5	C7	C8
3206 FLATCAR, 1928-35, orange, w/lumber	45	90	150
3207 GONDOLA, 1928-38, O ga.	20	35	60
3208 BOXCAR, 1928-38, orange and blue	55	110	175
3210 TANK CAR, 1928-38	45	90	150
3211 CABOOSE, 1928-38, O ga.	40	75	120

	C5	C7	C8
3212 MILK CAR, 1938	40	80	125
3213 FLOODLIGHT CAR, 1938, O ga.	75	150	225
3216 LOG CAR, 1930-38	30	65	100
3219 DUMP CAR, 1934-38	40	80	125

	C5	C7	C8
3280 CLUB CAR, 1928-31, 1934, two-tone blue, w/brass trim, marked "Golden State" or "Jeffersonian"	180	360	550

	C5	C7	C8
3281 PULLMAN, turquoise/ teal blue, 1928-31, 1933-34	90	180	275

	C5	C7	C8

	C5	C7	C8
3281 PULLMAN, two-tone blue, w/ brass trim, marked "Golden State" or "Jeffersonian"	180	360	550

	C5	C7	C8
3282 OBSERVATION CAR, 1928-31, 1933-34, two-tone blue, w/brass trim, marked "Golden State"	180	360	550

	C5	C7	C8
3282 OBSERVATION CAR, 1928-31, 1933-34, turquoise/ teal blue	90	180	275
3302 LOCOMOTIVE, 1931, O ga., 2-4-2	250	500	750
3304 LOCOMOTIVE, 1934, O ga., 2-4-2	150	300	450
3307 LOCOMOTIVE, 1932-33, O ga., bell in cab	100	200	300
3308 LOCOMOTIVE, 1932-33, O ga., 2-4-2	150	300	450
3309 LOCOMOTIVE, 1934, O ga., 2-4-2	200	400	600

	C5	C7	C8
3310 LOCOMOTIVE, 1934, O ga., 2-4-2	100	200	300
3313 LOCOMOTIVE, 1935, O ga., 2-4-2	200	400	600
3315 LOCOMOTIVE, 1932-35, O ga.	350	700	1,100
3316 LOCOMOTIVE, 1932-35, O ga., 2-4-2	30	60	100
3322 LOCOMOTIVE, 1936	150	300	400
3323 LOCOMOTIVE, 1934, O ga., 2-4-2	250	500	750
3324 LOCOMOTIVE, 1935, O ga., 2-4-2	250	500	750
3326 LOCOMOTIVE, 1932-35, O ga., 2-4-2	65	135	200
3380 BAGGAGE CAR, O ga., red w/dark red roof and brass window inserts and decals, eight wheel, lighted	60	120	190
3381 COACH CAR, O ga., red w/dark red roof and brass window insert and decal, eight wheel, lighted	60	120	190
3382 OBSERVATION CAR, O ga., red w/dark red roof and brass window insert and decal, eight wheel, lighted	60	120	190
3541 PULLMAN, O ga.	70	140	225
3542 OBSERVATION CAR, O ga.	70	140	225

	C5	C7	C8
4603 LOCOMOTIVE, 1938, O ga., 2-4-4	150	300	450
4615 LOCOMOTIVE, 1938, O ga., 2-4-2 or 4-4-2	350	700	1,100
4629 LOCOMOTIVE, 1938, O ga.	150	300	450
4677 LOCOMOTIVE, 1938, O ga.	300	600	950
5160 CABOOSE, 1939-41, Union Pacific	25	50	75
5640 HUDSON, 1939, O ga., 4-6-4, w/tender	350	700	1,100
9217 STREET LAMP, green metal	15	30	45
9910 LOCOMOTIVE, O ga., cast aluminum, electric, Burlington Zephyr	265	525	800
9910 LOCOMOTIVE, O ga., wind-up, Burlington Zephyr	85	175	275
9910 LOCOMOTIVE, O ga., tinplate, electric, Burlington Zephyr	125	275	400
9911 BAGGAGE CAR, O ga.	150	300	450
9912 OBSERVATION CAR, O ga.	150	300	450
9913 PULLMAN, O ga.	150	300	450
9914 LOCOMOTIVE, O ga.	600	1,200	1,800
9915 LOCOMOTIVE, O ga.	400	8,00	1,200

3310 LOCOMOTIVE

S GAUGE

L/C = link-type couplers
K/C = knuckle couplers
P/M = PikeMaster couplers

	C6	C8
1 TRANSFORMER, 1949-52, 25 watt	1	3
1 TRANSFORMER, 1956, 35 watt	4	8
1A TRANSFORMER, 1957, 40 watt	3	9
1 1/2 TRANSFORMER, 1953, 45 watt	1	4
1 1/2 TRANSFORMER, 1954-55, 50 watt	1	4
2 TRANSFORMER, 1947-53, 75 watt	3	9
2B TRANSFORMER, 1947-48, 75 watt	3	10
3 TRANSFORMER, 1946, 50 watt	2	5
4B TRANSFORMER, 1949-56, 100 watt	10	22
5/5A/5B TRANSFORMER, 1946, 50 watt	2	5
6/6A TRANSFORMER, 1946, 75 watt	1	5
7B TRANSFORMER, 1946, 75 watt	2	7
8B TRANSFORMER, 1946-1952, 100 watt	11	27
9B TRANSFORMER, 1946, 150 watt	18	34
10 DC INVERTER, 1946	6	17
11 CIRCUIT BREAKER, 1946	4	10
12B TRANSFORMER, 1946-1952, 250 watt	30	110
13 CIRCUIT BREAKER, 1952-55	4	10
15B TRANSFORMER, 1953-1956, 110 watt	13	44
16 RECTIFORMER, 1950	10	36
16B TRANSFORMER, 1953, 190 watt	30	80
16B TRANSFORMER, 1954-1956, 175 watt	23	60
16C TRANSFORMER, 1958, 35 watt	6	17
17B TRANSFORMER, 190 watt	35	85

	C6	C8
18B TRANSFORMER, 1954-56, 175 watt	24	85
18B TRANSFORMER, 1953, 190 watt, dual controls	29	110
19B TRANSFORMER, 1952-1955, 300 watt, dual controls	50	145
21 IMITATION GRASS, 1949-50, grass, half-pound, full bag	15	24
21A IMITATION GRASS, 1951-56, grass, half-pound, full bag	15	26
22 SCENERY GRAVEL, 1949-56, 22 ounces, full bag	13	21
23 ARTIFICAL COAL, 1949-56, half pound, full bag	14	22
24 MULTICOLOR WIRE, 1949-56, 25 feet	3	9
25 SMOKE FLUID CARTRIDGE, 1947-1956	5	15
26 SERVICE KIT, 1952-1956	7	25
27 TRACK CLEANING FLUID, 1952-56, 8 ounces	3	8
28 TRACK BALLAST, 1950, 8 ounces	5	11
28A TRACK BALLAST, 1951-53, 8 ounces	5	12
29 IMITATION SNOW, 1950, 4 ounces	45	100
29A IMITATION SNOW, 1951-53, 4 ounces	50	110
30 HIGHWAY SIGN SET, 1949-52, three yellow, five white	42	145
30B TRANSFORMER, 1953-56, 300 watt, dual control	85	215
31 RAILROAD SIGNS, 1949-50, white, set of eight	80	270
31A RAILROAD SIGNS, 1951-52, white, set of eight	75	190
32 CITY STREET SET, 1949-1950, eight pieces	55	190
32A PARK SET, 1951, 12 pieces	55	200
33 PASSENGER AND TRAIN FIGURE SET, 1951-52, eight figures	75	215

	C6	**C8**
34 RAILWAY FIGURE SET, 1953, 25 pieces	105	770
35 BRAKEMAN W/LANTERN, three brakemen	95	160
40 SMOKE SET, 1953-55	3	4
50 DISTRICT SCHOOL, 1953-54, illuminated	55	220
160 STATION PLATFORM, 1953, non-illuminated	165	435

161 BUNGALOW, 1953, illuminated 115 270

162 FACTORY, 1953, "Mysto-Magic Company" 80 255

163 FLYERVILLE STATION, 1953 110 195

	C6	**C8**
164 BARN, 1953, illuminated	105	400
165 GRAIN ELEVATOR, 1953, illuminated	50	250
166 CHURCH, 1953, illuminated	95	290
167 TOWN HALL, 1953, illuminated	105	335
168 HOTEL, 1953, illuminated	120	375
247 TUNNEL, 1946-48, 11 inches	20	34
248 TUNNEL, 1946-48, 14 inches	20	39
249 TUNNEL, 1947-56, 11 1/2 inches	14	46
270 NEWS & FRANK STAND, 1952-53	50	140
271 WHISTLE STOP SET, 1952-53, includes Newsstand, Frank Stand, Waiting Stand	65	195
272 GLENDALE STATION, illuminated	65	215
273 SUBURBAN STATION, 1952-53, illuminated	65	215
274 HARBOR JUNCTION FREIGHT STATION, 1952-53, illuminated	55	205
275 EUREKA DINER, 1952-53, illuminated	45	200
282 STEAM 4-6-2 PACIFIC, 1952 metal tender, L/C, 1953, plastic tender, K/C, **1953, plastic tender with coal pusher, K/C**	40-**45**	85-**95**
283 STEAM 4-6-2 PACIFIC, 1954-57, C&NW, plastic tender "American Flyer" or "American Flyer Lines" lettering, K/C	30	90

	C6	C8

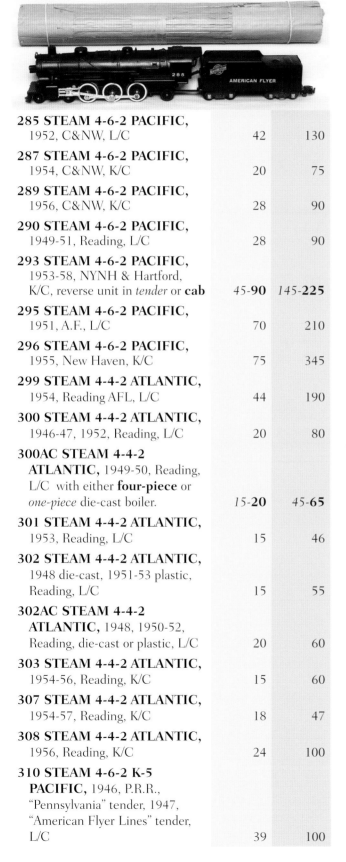

	C6	C8
285 STEAM 4-6-2 PACIFIC, 1952, C&NW, L/C	42	130
287 STEAM 4-6-2 PACIFIC, 1954, C&NW, K/C	20	75
289 STEAM 4-6-2 PACIFIC, 1956, C&NW, K/C	28	90
290 STEAM 4-6-2 PACIFIC, 1949-51, Reading, L/C	28	90
293 STEAM 4-6-2 PACIFIC, 1953-58, NYNH & Hartford, K/C, reverse unit in *tender* or **cab**	*45-90*	*145-225*
295 STEAM 4-6-2 PACIFIC, 1951, A.F., L/C	70	210
296 STEAM 4-6-2 PACIFIC, 1955, New Haven, K/C	75	345
299 STEAM 4-4-2 ATLANTIC, 1954, Reading AFL, L/C	44	190
300 STEAM 4-4-2 ATLANTIC, 1946-47, 1952, Reading, L/C	20	80
300AC STEAM 4-4-2 ATLANTIC, 1949-50, Reading, L/C with either **four-piece** or *one-piece* die-cast boiler.	*15-20*	*45-65*
301 STEAM 4-4-2 ATLANTIC, 1953, Reading, L/C	15	46
302 STEAM 4-4-2 ATLANTIC, 1948 die-cast, 1951-53 plastic, Reading, L/C	15	55
302AC STEAM 4-4-2 ATLANTIC, 1948, 1950-52, Reading, die-cast or plastic, L/C	20	60
303 STEAM 4-4-2 ATLANTIC, 1954-56, Reading, K/C	15	60
307 STEAM 4-4-2 ATLANTIC, 1954-57, Reading, K/C	18	47
308 STEAM 4-4-2 ATLANTIC, 1956, Reading, K/C	24	100
310 STEAM 4-6-2 K-5 PACIFIC, 1946, P.R.R., "Pennsylvania" tender, 1947, "American Flyer Lines" tender, L/C	39	100

	C6	C8
312 STEAM 4-6-2 K-5 PACIFIC, 1946-48, 1952, **"Pennsylvania"** tender, or "American Flyer Lines" tender, smoke in tender, or "American Flyer Lines" smoke in boiler, L/C	60	135-**175**
312AC STEAM 4-6-2 K-5 PACIFIC, 1949-51, PRR, L/C	50	135

	C6	C8
313 STEAM 4-6-2 K-5 PACIFIC, 1955-57, PRR, K/C	55	230
314AW STEAM 4-6-2 K-5 PACIFIC, 1949-50, PRR, L/C	85	315

	C6	C8
315 STEAM 4-6-2 K-5 PACIFIC, 1952, PRR, L/C	75	280

	C6	C8
316 STEAM 4-6-2 K-5 PACIFIC, 1953-54, PRR, K/C	65	240
320 STEAM 4-6-4 HUDSON, 1946, **New York Central**, or 1947 American Flyer Lines tender, L/C	45	150

	C6	C8
321 STEAM 4-6-4 HUDSON, 1946, **New York Central**, or 1947 American Flyer Lines tender, L/C	47	205
322 STEAM 4-6-4 HUDSON, 1946, **New York Central**, or 1947-48 American Flyer Lines tender, L/C	40	145-**175**
322AC STEAM 4-6-4 HUDSON, 1949-51, New York Central, L/C	40	165
324AC STEAM 4-6-4 HUDSON, 1950, New York Central, L/C	6	225
325AC STEAM 4-6-4 HUDSON, 1951, New York Central, L/C	55	175
325 STEAM 4-6-4 HUDSON, 1952, New York Central, **serif** or sans-serif "K", K/C	50-**150**	200-**325**
326 STEAM 4-6-4 HUDSON, 1953-54 small motor, 1955-57 **large motor**, New York Central, K/C	50-**100**	200-**300**

	C6	C8
332 STEAM 4-8-4 NORTHERN, 1946-49, with AC motor, L/C Tender lettered, **"Union Pacific,"** "American Flyer Lines" or "American Flyer"	150-**400**	400-**1,000**
332 STEAM 4-8-4 NORTHERN, 1947-49, with DC motor, L/C Tender lettered, **silver lettering** "American Flyer Lines" white lettering "American Flyer Lines" or "American Flyer"	150-**1,100**	400-**2,000**
332AC STEAM 4-8-4 NORTHERN, 1951, Union Pacific, L/C	150	425

	C6	C8
332DC STEAM 4-8-4 NORTHERN, 1950, Union Pacific, L/C "American Flyer Lines" or "American Flyer"	135	495
334DC STEAM 4-8-4 NORTHERN, 1950, Union Pacific, L/C	150	450

	C6	C8
K335 STEAM 4-8-4 NORTHERN, 1952, Union Pacific, K/C	130	430
336 STEAM 4-8-4 NORTHERN, 1953-57, Union Pacific, K/C	125	450

	C6	C8
342 STEAM 0-8-0 SWITCHER, 1946-48, 1952, AC or DC motor, "Nickel Plate Road," "American Flyer Lines" or "American Flyer"	100	400
342AC STEAM 0-8-0 SWITCHER, 1949-51, Nickel Plate, L/C	100	325
342DC STEAM 0-8-0 SWITCHER, 1948-50, Nickel Plate, L/C	100	325
343 STEAM 0-8-0 SWITCHER, 1953-58, Nickel Plate, K/C	10	350
346 STEAM 0-8-0 SWITCHER, 1955, Nickel Plate, K/C	200	600

	C6	C8

350 STEAM 4-6-2 PACIFIC,
1948 **wire** handrails, 1950 cast
handrail, B&O, Royal Blue, L/C — 40-**50** / 150-**200**

353 STEAM 4-6-2 PACIFIC,
1950-51, American Flyer Circus,
Pacific, 4-6-2, L/C — 125 / 450

354 STEAM 4-6-2 PACIFIC,
1954, Silver Bullet, Pacific, 4-6-2, K/C — 60 / 225

355 BALDWIN SWITCHER,
1957, C&NW, **painted** or
unpainted K/C — 65-**125** / 150-**300**

356 STEAM 4-6-2 PACIFIC,
1953, Silver Bullet, Pacific, 4-6-2, L/C, **chrome-plated** or silver-painted — 60-**65** / 75-**200**

360-361 ALCO PA&PB, 1950-51, Santa Fe, **chrome-plated** or silver-painted, L/C, priced as set — 70-**125** / 250-**600**

360-364 ALCO PA&PB, 1950-51, Santa Fe, **chrome-plated** or silver-painted, L/C, priced as set — 70-**125** / 250-**600**

370 GP-7, GENERAL MOTORS-A.F. ROAD SWITCHER, 1950-53, Coupler Bar, K/C — 50-**70** / 165-**200**

371 GP-7, GENERAL MOTORS-A.F. ROAD SWITCHER, 1954, K/C — 100 / 225

372 GP-7, 1955-1957, UNION PACIFIC, ROAD SWITCHER, K/C, marked "Built by Gilbert" or "Made by American Flyer" on side — 100-**125** / 250-**350**

374-375 GP-7, 1955, TEXAS & PACIFIC, ROAD SWITCHER, K/C, priced as set — 150 / 425

375 GP-7, 1953, GENERAL MOTORS-A.F. ROAD SWITCHER, K/C, rare — 500 / 1,100

377-78 GP-7, 1956-1957, TEXAS & PACIFIC, ROAD SWITCHER, K/C, priced as set — 175 / 500

(405) ALCO PA, 1952, Silver Streak, L/C — 75 / 300

460 A.F. BULB ASSORTMENT, 1951, 1953-54 boxed set of 54 — 35 / 125

466 ALCO PA, 1953-55, Silver Comet, chrome-plated, silver-painted with decal, or **silver-painted with heat-stamped lettering**, K/C — 75-**100** / 225-**275**

472 Alco PA, 1956, Santa Fe, K/C — 100 / 325

	C6	C8

470-471-473 ALCO PA-PB-PA, 1953-58, Santa Fe, **chrome-plated** or silver-painted, K/C, priced as set — 100-**125**   450-**525**

474-475 ALCO PA-PA, 1953-55, Silver Rocket, chrome-plated or silver-painted, K/C — 100   350

477-478 ALCO PA-PB, 1953-54, Silver Flash, **chrome-plated** or silver-painted, K/C — 150-**175**   550-**600**

	C6	C8
479 ALCO PA, 1955, Silver Flash, K/C	75	300
480 ALCO PB, 1955, Silver Flash, K/C	350	1,000

481 ALCO PA, 1956, Silver Flash, K/C — 90   150

484-485-486 ALCO PA-PB-PA, 1956-1957, Santa Fe, Blue, K/C, priced as set — 200   725

490-492 ALCO PA-PA, 1957, Northern Pacific, K/C, priced as set — 200   700

	C6	C8
490-491-493 ALCO PA-PB-PA, 1956, Northern Pacific, K/C, priced as set, rare	350	1,150

	C6	C8
494-495 ALCO PA-PA., 1956, New Haven, K/C, priced as set	200	750
497 ALCO PA, 1957, New Haven, w/Pantographs, K/C	100	350

	C6	C8
500 COMBINE CAR, 1952, AFL, **chrome-plated** or silver-painted L/C	100-**140**	350-**600**
501 COACH CAR, 1952, AFL, **chrome-plated** or silver-painted L/C	100-**140**	350-**600**

	C6	C8
502 VISTA DOME, 1952, AFL, **chrome-plated** or silver-painted L/C	100-**140**	350-**600**
503 OBSERVATION CAR, 1952, AFL, silver finish, L/C	150	650
520 KNUCKLE COUPLER KIT, 1954-56	2	5
561 DIESEL BILLBOARD, Santa Fe Alcos, 1955-56	25	65

	C6	C8
566 WHISTLING BILLBOARD, Santa Fe Alco or Steam Engine picture on billboard	15	55
568 WHISTLING BILLBOARD, 1956	20	45
571 TRUSS GIRDER BRIDGE, 1955-1956	10	45
577 WHISTLING BILLBOARD, 1946-47, "Ringling Bros. & Barnum & Bailey," **Fox Mart**	20	75-**1,750**
577NL WHISTLING BILLBOARD, 1950	25	45
578 STATION FIGURE SET, w/box 1946-52	50	175
579 SINGLE STREET LAMP, 1946-49	10	50
580 DOUBLE STREET LAMP, 1946-49	10	65
581 GIRDER BRIDGE, 1946-56, marked "Lackawanna" or "American Flyer"	10	35
582 AUTOMATIC BLINKER SIGNAL, 1946-48	55	170
583 ELECTRO MAGNETIC CRANE, 1946-49, single button control	65	200
583A ELECTRO MAGNETIC CRANE, 1950-53, double button control	65	200
584 BELL DANGER SIGNAL, 1946-47	190	850

	C6	C8
585 TOOL SHED, 1946-52	25	75

	C6	**C8**

594 ANIMATED TRACK GANG SET, 1946-47, rare — 550 — 2,250

586F WAYSIDE STATION, 1946-56 — 30 — 115

587 BLOCK SIGNAL, 1946-47 — 75 — 275

588 SEMAPHORE SIGNAL, 1946-48 — 650 — 1,900

589 PASSENGER AND FREIGHT STATION, 1946-1956, illuminated, green or **black** roof — 15 — 65-**85**

590 CONTROL TOWER, 1955-56, illuminated, manufactured by Bachman for A.C. Gilbert — 25 — 75

591 CROSSING GATE, 1946-48, single arm — 20 — 85

592 CROSSING GATE, 1946-50, double arm — 25 — 90

592a CROSSING GATE, 1951-53, double arm — 25 — 90

596 WATER TANK, 1946-56 — 40 — 80

598 TALKING STATION RECORD, 1946-1956, replacement — 10 — 20

599 TALKING STATION RECORD, 1956, replacement — 10 — 35

593 SIGNAL TOWER, 1946-54, illuminated — 35 — 85

600 CROSSING GATE, 1954-56, w/Bell — 30 — 95

	C6	C8
605 FLATCAR, 1953, AFL, w/log load, L/C	10	45
606 CRANE CAR, 1953, AFL, L/C	15	65
607 WORK CABOOSE, 1953, AFL, L/C	10	50
609 FLATCAR, 1953, AFL, w/ girder load, L/C	10	45
612 FREIGHT & PASSENGER STATION, 1946-51,1953-54, w/crane, illuminated	20	120
613 BOXCAR, 1953, Great Northern, brown, L/C, K/C	20	85
620 GONDOLA, 1953, Southern, black, L/C	25	90
622 BOXCAR, 1953, GAEX, L/C	15	80
623 REEFER, 1953, Illinois Central, orange, L/C	10	5

	C6	C8
625 TANK CAR, Shell, 1946-50, **Orange**, black or *silver*	6-**350**	30-**800**
625 TANK CAR, 1951-53, Gulf, silver, L/C	10	30
625G TANK CAR, 1951-53, Gulf, silver, L/C	10	30
627 FLATCAR, 1947-1950 C&NW, or 1950 **American Flyer Lines** w/girder load, L/C	15	25-**50**
628 FLATCAR, 1946-53, C&NW, w/log load, L/C, K/C, **wood** or metal	10-**15**	35-**55**
629 STOCK CAR, 1946-53, Missouri Pacific, red, L/C	10	40
630 CABOOSE, 1946-52, *Reading*, red, 1952 American Flyer, 1953 American Flyer Lines, L/C, K/C	5-10	20-45

	C6	C8
631 GONDOLA, 1946-53, Texas & Pacific, **unpainted** green or **gray**, or *painted* red or *green* L/C	5-**75**	20-**300**
(632) HOPPER, 1946, Virginian, L/C	30	100

	C6	C8
632 HOPPER, 1946-53, Lehigh-New England, gray, die-cast or plastic, gray, black, white, L/C	5	30
633 BOXCAR, 1946-52, B&O, L/C	10	30

	C6	C8
633 REEFER, 1946-52, B&O, L/C	40	175
634 FLOODLIGHT, 1946-49, 1953, C&NW, AFL, L/C, K/C	10	45
635 CRANE CAR, 1946-48, C&NWRY, L/C	15	60
(635) CRANE CAR, 1948-49, C&NWRY, yellow or **red** cab, L/C	10-**100**	50-**350**

	C6	C8
636 FLATCAR, 1948-53, Erie depressed center, w/spool load, **wooden** or die-cast, L/C	15-60	45-**300**
637 BOXCAR, 1949-53, MKT, yellow, L/C	10	35
638 CABOOSE, 1949-53, AFL, AF, red, L/C, K/C	5	15

	C6	C8
639 BOXCAR, 1949-52, A.F., **tuscan** or yellow, L/C	10-**15**	20-**75**
639 REEFER, 1951-52, A.F., yellow or **unpainted cream body**, L/C	5-50	20-**200**
640 HOPPER, 1949-53, A.F., gray, L/C	5	20
640 HOPPER, 1953, Wabash, black, L/C	10	35
641 GONDOLA, 1949-51, A.F., red or **gray**, L/C	10-50	25-**250**
641 GONDOLA, 1953, Frisco, brown, L/C	10	30
642 BOXCAR, 1953, A.F. or Seaboard, L/C	10	25
641 REEFER, 1952, A.F., brown or red, L/C	8	25
(643) FLATCAR, 1950-53, A.F. Circus, w/circus load, yellow or **red**, L/C	75-**125**	250-**450**
644 CRANE CAR, 1950-53, Industrial Brown hoist A.F., L/C	25	100
645 WORK CABOOSE, 1950, A.F., L/C	15	45
645A WORK CABOOSE, 1951-53, AFL, L/C	15	45
(646) FLOODLIGHT, 1950-1953, Erie, depressed center, **diecast** or plastic generator, L/C	15-45	50-**250**
647 REEFER, 1952-53, Northern Pacific, orange side, L/C	10	45

	C6	C8
648 TRACK CLEANING CAR, 1952-54, A.F., depressed center, L/C, K/C	10	35
(649) COACH CAR CIRCUS, 1950-52, yellow, L/C	45	120

	C6	C8
650 COACH CAR, 1946-53, New Haven, green or red, L/C	20	90
651 BAGGAGE, 1946-53, New Haven, green or red, L/C	10	50

	C6	C8
652 PULLMAN, 1946-53, green or red, L/C	40	200
653 COMBINE CAR, 1946-53, green or red, L/C	40	200

	C6	C8
654 OBSERVATION CAR, 1946-53, green or red, L/C	40	200
655 COACH CAR, 1953, Silver Bullet, silver or chrome, L/C	25	100
655 COACH CAR, 1953, AFL, green or red, L/C	20	75
660 COMBINE CAR, 1950-52, AFL, aluminum or chrome, L/C	20	80
661 COACH CAR, 1950-52, AFL, aluminum or chrome; L/C	40	100
662 VISTA-DOME, 1950-52, AFL, aluminum or chrome, L/C	20	100
663 OBSERVATION CAR, 1950-52, AFL, aluminum, L/C	20	80
668 MANUAL SWITCH, 1953-55, left, non-illuminated	5	10
669 MANUAL SWITCH, 1953-55, right, non-illuminated	5	10
690 TRACK TERMINAL, 1946-56	.50	1
691 TRACK PINS, 1946-48, twelve per pack	.50	1
692 FIBER TRACK PIN, 1946-48, four per pack	.25	.75
693 TRACK LOCK, 1948-56, twenty-six per pack	.05	.15
694 AUTOMATIC COUPLER TRUCK UNIT, 1946-53	3	10
700 STRAIGHT TRACK, 1946-56	.50	1.00
701 STRAIGHT TRACK, half section, 1946-56	.50	1.00
702 CURVED TRACK, 1946-56	.25	.50
703 CURVED TRACK, half section 1946-56	.25	.50
704 MANUAL UNCOUPLER, 1952-56	.25	.75
705 REMOTE UNCOUPLER, 1946-47	1	5
706 REMOTE UNCOUPLER, 1948-56	1	3
707 TRACK TERMINAL, 1946-59	.25	1
708 DIESEL WHISTLE CONTROL, 1951-56	3	10
709 LOCKOUT ELIMINATOR, 1950-55	2	10
710 STEAM WHISTLE CONTROL, 1955-56	10	45

	C6	C8
710 AUTOMATIC TRACK SECTION, 1946-47	.50	1.50
711 MAIL PICK-UPS, used w/718-719 mail cars	10	20
712 SPECIAL RAIL SECTION, 1947-56	1	2
713 MAIL HOOK, 1947-56, includes track terminal	10	25
714 LOG UNLOADING CAR, 1951-54, A.F., w/log load, L/C	15	80
715 AUTO UNLOADING CAR, 1946-54, AFL, w/load, **Armored Car**, Manoil Coupe or *Tootsietoy racer* L/C, K/C	10-25	75-**125**
716 OPERATING HOPPER, 1946-51, AFL, L/C	5	30
717 LOG UNLOADING CAR, 1946-52, AFL, w/log load, L/C	15	60

	C6	C8
718 MAIL PICKUP, 1946-54, AFL/New Haven, red or green, L/C	30	125
719 COAL DUMP CAR, 1950-54, CB&Q, painted or **unpainted** L/C	25-30	90-**120**
720/720A REMOTE CONTROL SWITCHES, left and right, w/controls, pair	20	30
722/722A MANUAL CONTROL SWITCHES, left and right, pair	10	20
725 CROSSING, 1946-56	3	7
726 RUBBER ROAD BED, black or gray, straight, 1950-56	1	2
727 RUBBER ROAD BED, black or gray, curve, 1950-56	1	2
728 RERAILER, 1956	3	15

	C6	C8

730 BUMPER, 1946-56, green or **red**

	C6	C8
730 BUMPER	10-**30**	25-**125**
731 PIKE PLANNING KIT, 1952-56	10	35

732 OPERATING BAGGAGE CAR, 1950-1954, AFL, green or red, L/C, K/C

	C6	C8
732	30	100

734 OPERATING BOXCAR, 1950-54, AF, L/C

	C6	C8
734	25	75

	C6	C8
735 ANIMATED COACH CAR, 1952-54, AFL-New Haven, red, L/C, K/C	30	100
736 OPERATING CATTLE CAR, 1950-54, Missouri Pacific, L/C	10	40

	C6	C8
(740) HAND CAR, 1952-54, AFL	20	100
741 HAND CAR AND SHED, 1953-54	75	200
(742) HAND CAR, 1955-56, AFL, reversing mechanism	40	150
747 CARDBOARD TRESTLE SET	7	25
748 OVERHEAD FOOTBRIDGE, 1951-52, gray or silver	15	40
749 STREET LAMP SET, 1950-52, plastic, set of three	7	25
750 TRESTLE BRIDGE, 1946-56, black, silver and metallic blue	15	75
751/751A LOG LOADER, 1946-50, 1952-53	40	200
752/752A SEABOARD COALER, 1946-52	100	325
753 TRESTLE BRIDGE, 1952	20	75
753 TUNNEL, 1960	20	40
754 DOUBLE TRESTLE BRIDGE, 1950-52	40	110
755 TALKING STATION, 1948-50, green or **blue** roof	50-**75**	125-**150**
755A TALKING STATION, 1951-53	50	125
758 SAM THE SEMAPHORE MAN, 1949	30	100

	C6	C8

758A SAM THE SEMAPHORE MAN, 1950-56

	C6	C8
758A SAM THE SEMAPHORE MAN, 1950-56	35	110
759 BELL DANGER SIGNAL, 1953-56	25	85
760 AUTOMATIC HIGHWAY FLASHER, 1949-56	10	40

	C6	C8
761 SEMAPHORE, 1949-56	20	75

	C6	C8
762 BILLBOARD, 1949-50, two-in-one whistle, two-button control	30	100

	C6	C8
763 MOUNTAIN SET, 1949-50, three pieces	50	175
764 EXPRESS OFFICE, 1950-51, illuminated	45	150
766 ANIMATED STATION, 1952-54, w/four plastic passengers and 735 Pullman	50	200

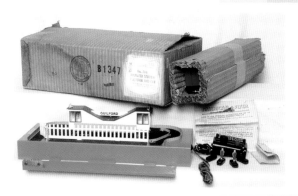

	C6	C8
K766 ANIMATED STATION, 1953-55	50	200

	C6	C8
767 ROADSIDE DINER, Branford Diner, 1950-54, illuminated	40	100

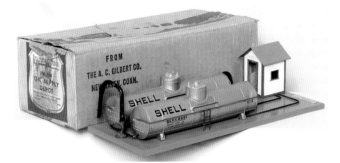

	C6	C8
768 OIL SUPPLY DEPOT, 1950-53, Shell or **Gulf**	40-**55**	125-**175**

	C6	C8

769/769A REVOLVING AIRCRAFT BEACON, 1950-56 — 15 / 60

770 BAGGAGE LOADING PLATFORM, 1950-52 — 30 / 100

771 OPERATING STOCKYARD SET, 1950-54, includes eight black and white rubber cattle w/brush bases, 736 Cattle Car — 50 / 150

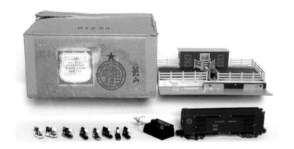

K771 OPERATING STOCKYARD SET, 1953-56, includes eight black and white rubber cattle w/brush bases, 976 Cattle Car w/knuckle couplers — 50 / 150

772 WATER TOWER, 1950-56, plain or **checkerboard** tank — 30-**40** / 100-**125**

773 OIL DERRICK, 1950-52 — 50 / 150

774 FLOODLIGHT TOWER, 1951-56, illuminated — 15 / 75

	C6	C8

775 BAGGAGE LOADING PLATFORM with L/C car, 1953-55 — 25 / 95

K775 BAGGAGE LOADING PLATFORM with K/C car, 1953-55 — 35 / 125

778 STREET LAMP SET, 1953-56, plain, mailbox and firebox, set of three — 10 / 30

779 OIL DRUM LOADER, 1955-56, w/eight oil barrels — 50 / 150

780 RAILROAD TRESTLE SET, 1953-56, plastic, twenty-four pieces — 5 / 20

781 RAILROAD ABUTMENT SET, 1953 — 20 / 65

782 RAILROAD ABUTMENT SET, 1953 — 20 / 75

783 HI-TRESTLE SECTIONS, 1953-56 — 5 / 25

784 RAILROAD HUMP SET, 1955, rare — 75 / 275

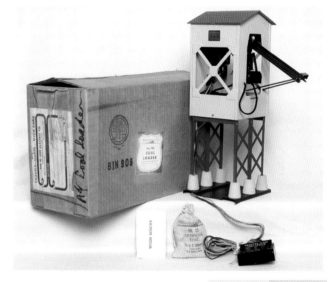

785 OPERATING COAL LOADER, 1955-56 — 125 / 325

787 LOG LOADER, 1955-56 — 75 / 275

788 SUBURBAN STATION, 1956, illuminated — 10 / 60

789 STATION AND BAGGAGE-SMASHER, 1956-57, illuminated — 60 / 275

	C6	C8
790 TRAINORAMA, 1953	50	225
792 RAILROAD TERMINAL, 1954-56	65	200
793 UNION STATION, 1955-56, illuminated	15	125

	C6	C8
794 UNION STATION, 1954, illuminated, includes firebox, mailbox and lampposts	30	125
795 UNION STATION, and Terminal, 1954	100	500
799 AUTOMATIC TALKING STATION, 1954-56	35	225
801 HOPPER, 1956-57, B&O, black, K/C	10	20
802 REEFER, 1956-57, Illinois Central, orange, K/C	10	30
803 BOXCAR, 1956-57, Santa Fe, K/C	15	30
804 GONDOLA, 1956-57, Norfolk & Western, black, K/C	5	15
805 GONDOLA, 1956-1957, Pennsylvania, K/C	5	15
806 CABOOSE, 1956, AFL, red, K/C, P/M	5	10
807 BOXCAR, 1957, Rio Grande, white, K/C	12	20
900 COMBINE CAR, 1956-57, Northern Pacific, green, K/C	100	300
901 COACH CAR, 1956-57, Northern Pacific, green, K/C	100	300

	C6	C8
902 VISTA DOME, 1956-57, Northern Pacific, green, K/C	100	300
903 OBSERVATION CAR, 1956-57, Northern Pacific, green, K/C	100	300
904 CABOOSE, 1956, AFL, red, K/C	10	25
905 FLATCAR, 1954, AFL, log load, K/C	10	40
906 CRANE CAR, 1954, AFL, K/C	15	50
907 WORK CABOOSE, 1954, AFL, K/C	15	50
909 FLATCAR, 1954, AFL, w/ girder load, K/C	10	50
910 TANK CAR, 1954, Gilbert Chemical, green, K/C	75	300
911 GONDOLA, 1955-57, C&O, black, K/C, w/silver or **brown** pipe load	10-35	40-**150**
912 TANK CAR, 1955-57, Koppers, black, K/C	20	100
913 BOXCAR, 1953-58, Great Northern, painted or decalled goat logo, K/C	13	22
914 LOG UNLOADING CAR, 1953-57, AFL, w/log load, K/C	25	43
915 AUTO UNLOADING CAR, 1953-57, AFL, w/car load, K/C	27	45
916 GONDOLA, 1955-56, D&H, K/C, w/canister load	11	18

	C6	C8
918 MAIL PICK-UP, 1953-58, American Flyer Lines or **New Haven** above doors, K/C	30-**35**	100-**125**

	C6	C8

919 COAL DUMP CAR, 1953-56, CB&Q, K/C — 25 — 115

920 GONDOLA, 1953-56, Southern, black, K/C — 10 — 30

921 HOPPER, 1953-56, CB&Q, w/coal load, K/C — 10 — 40

922 BOXCAR, 1953-57, GAEX, green, K/C — 15 — 50

923 REEFER, 1954-55, Illinois Central, orange, K/C — 15 — 25

924 HOPPER, 1953-56, Jersey Central, w/coal load, gray, K/C — 10 — 35

925 TANK CAR, 1952-57, Gulf, silver, K/C — 15 — 25

926 TANK CAR, 1955-57, Gulf, silver, K/C — 20 — 55

(928) FLATCAR, 1952-54, C&NWRY, **wooden** or die-cast, w/log load, K/C — 10-25 — 30-75

928 FLATCAR, 1956, New Haven, w/log load, K/C — 10 — 40

928 FLATCAR, 1956-57, New Haven, w/lumber load, K/C — 10 — 35

929 STOCK CAR, 1953-56, Missouri Pacific, red, K/C — 10 — 45

	C6	C8

930 CABOOSE, 1952, American Flyer, K/C — 10 — 50

930 CABOOSE, 1953-57, American Flyer Lines, K/C — 10 — 40

931 GONDOLA, 1952-55, Texas & Pacific, green, K/C — 5 — 20

933 BOXCAR, 1953-54, Baltimore & Ohio, white sides, K/C — 20 — 60

934 CABOOSE, 1954, AFL, red, K/C — 15 — 60

934 FLOODLIGHT, 1953-54, C&NWRY, K/C — 10 — 40

934 FLOODLIGHT, 1954, Southern Pacific, K/C — 15 — 60

935 CABOOSE, 1957, AFL, Bay Window, brown, K/C — 20 — 100

936 FLATCAR, 1953-54, Erie, depressed center, spool load, K/C — 15 — 45

936 FLATCAR, 1955-57, Pennsylvania, depressed center, spool load, K/C — 40 — 150

937 BOXCAR, 1953-58, MKT, yellow or yellow and brown, K/C — 10 — 40

938 CABOOSE, 1954-55, AFL, red, K/C — 5 — 15

940 HOPPER, 1953-56, Wabash, black, K/C — 10 — 30

941 GONDOLA, 1953-56, Frisco, K/C — 10 — 25

942 BOXCAR, 1954, Seaboard, K/C — 10 — 30

944 CRANE CAR, 1952-57, Industrial Brownhoist, AF, K/C — 25 — 85

945 WORK CABOOSE, 1952-57, AFL, K/C — 20 — 75

(946) FLOODLIGHT, 1953-56, Erie, depressed center, K/C — 15 — 45

947 REEFER, 1953-58, Northern Pacific, orange, K/C — 15 — 45

948 TRACK CLEANING CAR, 1953-57, American Flyer Lines, K/C — 10 — 35

C6   C8   C6   C8

951 BAGGAGE, 1953-57, AFL/ Railway Express Agency, green, tuscan or red, K/C ... 20 | 50

	C6	C8
956 FLATCAR, 1956, Monon, w/piggyback van load, K/C	25	100
957 OPERATING BOXCAR, 1957, Erie, K/C w/aluminum barrels	50	150
958 TANK CAR, 1957, Mobilgas, red, K/C	25	100
960 COMBINE CAR, 1953-56, "Columbus," chromed or silver painted with orange, green, blue, red, **chestnut** or *no* stripe	30-75	100-275

	C6	C8
952 PULLMAN, 1953-58, Pikes Peak, green or tuscan, or **tuscan with silhouttes**, K/C	35-50	175-275
953 COMBINE CAR, 1953-58, Niagara Falls, green or tuscan, or **tuscan with silhouttes**, K/C	35-50	150-250
954 OBSERVATION CAR, 1953-56, Grand Canyon, green or tuscan, or **tuscan with silhouttes**, K/C	35-50	175-275
955 COACH CAR, 1954-55, AFL, green, tuscan or silver K/C	30	100
961 COACH CAR, 1953-58, "Jefferson", chromed or silver painted with orange, green, red, **chestnut** or *no* stripe	40-100	125-300
962 VISTA-DOME, 1953-58, "Hamilton", chromed or silver painted with orange, green, blue, red, **chestnut** or *no* stripe	40-100	125-300
963 OBSERVATION CAR, 1953-58, "Washington," chromed or silver painted with orange, green, blue, red, **chestnut** or *no* stripe	40-100	125-300

	C6	C8
969 ROCKET LAUNCHER, 1957, K/C	20	90
970 WALKING BRAKEMAN CAR, 1956-57, Seaboard, K/C	30	75

	C6	C8
971 LUMBER UNLOADING CAR, 1956-57, Southern Pacific, w/lumber load, **black** or tuscan plastic painted tuscan, K/C	40-**100**	150-**300**
973 OPERATING MILK CAR, 1956, Gilbert, white, K/C, w/ plastic cans	54	88
974 OPERATING BOXCAR, 1953-54, AFL, K/C	30	90
974 OPERATING BOXCAR, 1955, Erie, K/C	50	175
975 ANIMATED COACH CAR, 1954-55, red, K/C	30	100
976 OPERATING CATTLE CAR, 1953-62, MP	25	75
977 CABOOSE, 1955-57, AFL, brown, K/C, w/moving brakeman	30	85

	C6	C8
978 OBSERVATION ACTION CAR, 1956-58, Grand Canyon, K/C	125	425
979 CABOOSE, 1957, bay window, AFL, brown, K/C, w/ moving brakeman	40	150
980 BOXCAR, 1956-57, B&O, blue, K/C	30	125

	C6	C8
981 BOXCAR, 1956, Central of Georgia, gloss or **matte** black, K/C	45-60	125-**200**
982 BOXCAR, 1956-57, BAR State of Maine, red, white and blue, K/C	50	125
983 BOXCAR, 1956-57, Missouri Pacific, blue-gray, K/C	50	150
984 BOXCAR, 1956-57, New Haven, orange, K/C	30	100
985 BOXCAR, 1957, Boston & Maine, blue, K/C	50	150

	C6	C8
988 REEFER, 1956-57, ART, orange, K/C	35	100

	C6	C8
989 REEFER, 1956-58, C&NW, K/C	50	200
994 STOCK CAR, 1957, Union Pacific, yellow, K/C	50	200
C1001 BOXCAR, 1962, WSX White's Auto Stores, yellow, P/M	300	800

	C6	C8
C2001 BOXCAR, 1962, Post, white, P/M	15	45
L2001 STEAM 4-4-0 AMERICAN, 1963, Game Train/Casey Jones	15	40

	C6	C8
L2002 STEAM 4-4-0 AMERICAN, 1963, Burlington Route	50	225
L2004 F-9, RIO GRANDE, 1962, K/C	75	250
C2009 GONDOLA, 1962-64, Texas & Pacific, light green, P/M	5	20
21004 STEAM 0-6-0 SWITCHER, 1957, P.R.R., K/C	100	375

	C6	C8
21005 STEAM 0-6-0 SWITCHER, 1957-58, P.R.R., K/C	125	500
21084 STEAM 4-6-2 PACIFIC, 1957, C&NW, K/C	40	150
21085 STEAM 4-6-2 PACIFIC, C&NW (1958-62) or CMStP&P (1963-65), K/C, P/M	30	125
(210)88 STEAM 4-4-0 AMERICAN, 1959-60, FY&P Franklin, K/C	50	150

	C6	C8
21089 STEAM 4-4-0 AMERICAN, 1960-1961, FY&PRR, Washington, K/C	75	275
21095 STEAM 4-6-2 PACIFIC, 1957, New Haven, K/C, rare	Too rarely traded to establish value	
21099 STEAM 4-6-2 PACIFIC, 1958, New Haven, K/C	100	425
21100 STEAM 4-4-2 ATLANTIC, 1957, Reading, K/C	15	40
21105 STEAM 4-4-2 ATLANTIC, 1957-58, Reading, K/C	20	50
21106 STEAM 4-4-2 ATLANTIC, 1959, Reading, K/C	60	200
21107 STEAM 4-4-2 ATLANTIC, PRR (1964, 1966) or Burlington (1965), K/C	15	40
21115 STEAM 4-6-2 K-5 PACIFIC, 1958, PRR, K/C	225	1000
21129 STEAM 4-6-4 HUDSON, 1958, New York Central, K/C	240	400

	C6	C8
21130 STEAM 4-6-4 HUDSON, 1959-60, 1962-63, New York Central, K/C	150	350
21139 STEAM 4-8-4 NORTHERN, 1958-59, Union Pacific, K/C	275	1,000

	C6	**C8**

21140 STEAM 4-8-4 NORTHERN,
1960, Union Pacific, K/C   475   1,600

**21145 STEAM 0-8-0
SWITCHER,** 1958, "Nickel
Plate Road," K/C   175   700

**21155 STEAM 0-6-0
SWITCHER,** 1958, docksider,
K/C   100   425

**21156 STEAM 0-6-0
SWITCHER,** 1959, docksider,
K/C   75   300

**21158 STEAM 0-6-0
SWITCHER,** 1960, docksider,
K/C   35   125

**21160 STEAM 4-4-2
ATLANTIC,** 1958-60, Reading,
K/C   15   40

	C6	**C8**

**21161 STEAM 4-4-2
ATLANTIC,** 1960, Reading/
American Flyer Lines or
"Prestone Car Care Express,"
K/C   10-**75**   25-**250**

**21165 STEAM 4-4-0
AMERICAN,** 1961-62, 1965-
66, Erie, K/C, P/M   10   30

**21166 STEAM 4-4-0
AMERICAN,** 1963-66,
Burlington Route, white or **black**
letters, P/M   10-**75**   25-**225**

**21168 STEAM 4-4-0
AMERICAN,** 1961-63,
Southern, P/M   25   75

21205-21205-1 EMD F-9,
Boston & Maine, 1961-62, K/C,
priced as set   115   275

21206-21206-1 EMD F-9,
Santa Fe, 1962, K/C, priced as
set   100   300

21207-21207-1 EMD F-9,
Great Northern, 1963-64, K/C,
priced as set   100   350

21210 EMD F-9, Burlington,
1961, K/C   75   250

	C6	**C8**

	C6	**C8**

21215, 21215-1 EMD F-9, Union Pacific, 1961-62, K/C, priced as set — 100 / 275

(21)234 EMD GP-7, 1961-62, Chesapeake & Ohio, long or **short** steps K/C — 150-**175** / 500-**600**

21551 ALCO PA, 1958, Northern Pacific, K/C — 125 / 375

21561 ALCO PA, 1958, New Haven, K/C — 125 / 350

21573 G.E. EP-5 ELECTRIC, 1958-59, New Haven, w/ Pantographs, K/C — 150 / 475

21720 ALCO PB, 1958, Santa Fe, K/C — 275 / 1000

21801 BALDWIN SWITCHER, 1958, C&NW, **painted** or unpainted, K/C — 45-**75** / 150-**225**

21801-1 BALDWIN SWITCHER, 1958, C&NW, **painted** or unpainted, K/C, Dummy Unit — 75-**85** / 225-**275**

21808 BALDWIN SWITCHER, 1958, C&NW, K/C — 50 / 150

(21)812 BALDWIN SWITCHER, 1959-60, Texas & Pacific — 75 / 200

21813 BALDWIN SWITCHER, 1958, 1960 M&StL, K/C — 200 / 575

	C6	C8

21831 GP-7, 1958, **Texas & Pacific** or AFL, K/C — 150-**175** / 425-**600**

21910, 21910-1, 21910-2 ALCO PA-PB-PA, 1957-58, Santa Fe, K/C, priced as set — 375 / 950

21918, 21918-1 BALDWIN SWITCHER, 1958, Seaboard, K/C, priced as set — 325 / 825

21920, 21920-1 ALCO PA-PA, 1958, Missouri Pacific, K/C, dual motors in 21920, priced as set — 350 / 1000

21920, ALCO PA, 1963-64, Missouri Pacific, K/C, single motor — 175 / 750

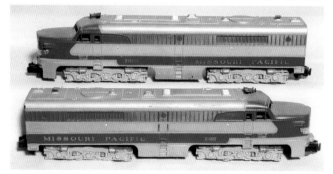

21922, 21922-1 ALCO PA-PA, 1959-60, Missouri Pacific, K/C, dual motors in 21922, priced as set — 275 / 950

	C6	C8
21925/21925-1 ALCO PA-PA, 1959-60, Union Pacific, K/C, dual motors in 21925, priced as set	250	900
21927 ALCO PA, 1960-62, Santa Fe, K/C	100	250
22004 TRANSFORMER, 1959-64, 40 watt	2	10
22006 TRANSFORMER, 1963, 25 watt	2	10
22020 TRANSFORMER, 1957-64, 50 watt	2	5
22030 TRANSFORMER, 1957-64, 100 watt	5	15
22033 TRANSFORMER, 1965, 25 watt	2	5
22034 TRANSFORMER, 1965, 110 watt	5	15
22035 TRANSFORMER, 1957-64, 175 watt	15	70
22040 TRANSFORMER, 1957-58, 110 watt	5	20
22050 TRANSFORMER, 1957-58, 175 watt	10	40
22060 TRANSFORMER, 1957-58, 175 watt, dual controls	15	45
22080 TRANSFORMER, 1957-58, 300 watt, dual controls	45	150
22090 TRANSFORMER, 1959-64, 350 watt, dual controls	50	200
23021 IMITATION GRASS, 1957-59, half pound	5	25
23022 SCENERY GRAVEL, 1957-59, 22 ounces	5	25
23023 ARTIFICIAL COAL, 1957-59, half pound	5	15
23024 MULTICOLOR WIRE, 1957-64, 25 feet	5	10

	C6	C8

	C6	C8
23600 CROSSING GATE, with Bell, 1957-58	15	75
23601 CROSSING GATE, 1959-62	15	70
23602 CROSSING GATE, 1963-64	15	70

	C6	C8
23025 SMOKE FLUID CARTRIDGES, 1957-59, box of 12	5	15
23026 SERVICE KIT, 1959-64	5	25
23027 TRACK CLEANING FLUID, 1957-59, 8 ounces	2	5
23032 RAILROAD EQUIPMENT KIT, 1960-61	35	95
23249 TUNNEL, 1957-64, 11-1/2 inches	10	40
23561 BILLBOARD HORN, 1957-59	10	45
23568 WHISTLING BILLBOARD, 1957-64	10	40
23571 TRUSS GIRDER BRIDGE, 1957-64	10	30
23581 GIRDER BRIDGE, 1957-64, marked "American Flyer"	10	35
23586 WAYSIDE STATION, 1956-59	25	100
23589 PASSENGER AND FREIGHT STATION, 1959, illuminated	15	55
23590 CONTROL TOWER, 1957-59, illuminated	20	70
23596 WATER TANK, 1957-58	25	100
23598 TALKING STATION RECORD, 1957-59	5	20
23599 TALKING STATION RECORD, 1957	10	35

	C6	C8
23743 TRACK MAINTENANCE CAR, 1960-64	90	150

	C6	C8
23750 TRESTLE BRIDGE, 1957-61	25	75
23758 SAM THE SEMAPHORE MAN, 1957	30	90
23759 BELL DANGER SIGNAL, 1956-60	10	65
23760 AUTOMATIC HIGHWAY FLASHER, 1957-60	10	40
23761 SEMAPHORE, 1957-60, two track trips	25	75
23763 BELL DANGER SIGNAL, 1961-64	10	55
23764 FLASHER SIGNAL, 1961-64	10	30

	C6	C8
23769 REVOLVING AIR-CRAFT BEACON, 1957-64	15	75
23771 OPERATING STOCKYARD SET, 1957-61	30	125

	C6	C8
23772 WATER TOWER, 1957-64	20	150
23774 FLOODLIGHT TOWER, 1957-64, illuminated	15	60
23778 STREETLAMP SET, 1957-64	10	35
23779 OIL DRUM LOADER, 1957-61, eight oil barrels	45	150
23780 GABE THE LAMPLIGHTER, 1958-59	300	1,000
23785 OPERATING COAL LOADER, 1957-60	125	350

	C6	C8
23786 TALKING STATION, 1957-59	50	150
23787 LOG LOADER, 1957-60	75	275
23788 SUBURBAN STATION, 1957-64, illuminated	10	50

	C6	C8
23789 STATION AND BAGGAGE-SMASHER, 1958-59, illuminated	50	225

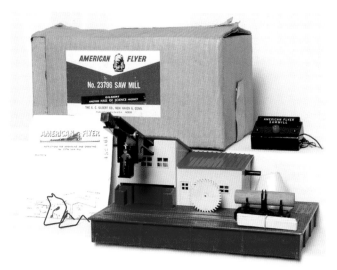

	C6	C8
23791 COW-ON-TRACK, 1957-59	25	125

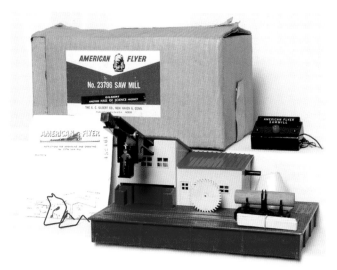

	C6	C8
23796 SAWMILL, 1957-64	100	275
23830 PIGGYBACK UNLOADER, 1959-60	40	150
24003 BOXCAR, 1958, Santa Fe, K/C	15	50
24016 BOXCAR, 1958, MKT, all yellow w/brown top, K/C	250	950
24019 BOXCAR, 1958, Seaboard, K/C	20	50

	C6	C8

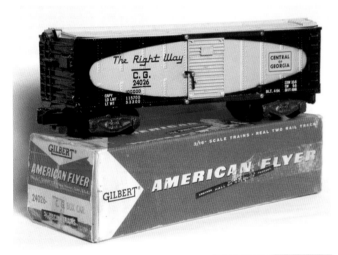

24023 BOXCAR, 1958-59, B&O, dark
blue, K/C — 35 · 150

24026 BOXCAR, 1958, Central
of Georgia, black, K/C — 35 · 175

24029 BOXCAR, 1957-60, State
of Maine, red, white and blue,
K/C — 40 · 150

	C6	C8
24030 BOXCAR, 1960, MKT, **painted** or unpainted yellow, P/M	10-40	35-**125**
24033 BOXCAR, 1958, Missouri Pacific, K/C	50	150
24036 BOXCAR, 1958-60, New Haven, orange, K/C	25	85
24039 BOXCAR, 1959, Rio Grande, white, K/C	10	50
24043 BOXCAR, 1958-60, Boston & Maine, blue, K/C	35	125
24047 BOXCAR, 1959, Great Northern, red, K/C	50	250

	C6	C8
24048 BOXCAR, 1959-62, M.St. L., red, K/C	45	150
24052 BOXCAR, 1961, UFGE Bananas, yellow, P/M	10	25
24054 BOXCAR, 1962-64 **painted**, 1966 unpainted, Santa Fe, P/M	10-20	45-**55**
(24)055 BOXCAR, 1960-61, Gold Belt Line, K/C, P/M	15	50
24056 BOXCAR, 1961, Boston & Maine, blue, **painted** or unpainted, P/M	25-75	125-**300**
24057 BOXCAR, 1962, Mounds, white or **ivory**, P/M	5-10	20-**30**
24058 BOXCAR, 1963-1964, Post, "Cereal" or **"Cereals,"** K/C, P/M	10-**15**	20-**30**

	C6	C8
24059 BOXCAR, 1963, Boston & Maine, blue, P/M	50	200
24060 BOXCAR, 1963-64, M.St. L., P/M	40	150
24065 BOXCAR, 1960-1964, New York Central, green, **K/C**, P/M	30-40	90-**125**
24066 BOXCAR, 1960, Louisville & Nashville, blue, K/C	75	200
24067 BOXCAR, 1960, Keystone Camera, orange, K/C	1,250	2,250
24068 BOXCAR, 1961, Planters Peanuts, white, P/M	1,500	3,000
24076 STOCK CAR, 1957-60, Union Pacific, yellow, K/C, P/M	25	75

	C6	C8
24077 STOCK CAR, 1959-62, Northern Pacific, red, **K/C**, P/M	60-80	200-**250**
24103 GONDOLA, 1958, 1963-64, N&W, black, K/C	5	25
24106 GONDOLA, 1960, Pennsylvania, **painted** or unpainted tuscan, K/C	5-**25**	20-**80**
24109 GONDOLA, 1957-60, C&O, black, yellow or silver lettering, K/C, w/ silver or **brown** plastic pipe load, or silver or orange cardboard pipe load	20-**35**	60-**125**

	C6	C8
24110 GONDOLA, 1959, Pennsylvania, K/C	5	15
24113 GONDOLA, 1957-59, D&H, brown, K/C, Container load	10	50
24116 GONDOLA, 1957-60, Southern, black, K/C	10	60

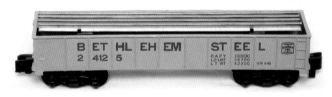

	C6	C8
24120 GONDOLA, 1960, Texas & Pacific, green, P/M	15	75
24124 GONDOLA, 1963-64, Boston & Maine, **painted** or unpainted blue, P/M	5-40	20-**175**

	C6	C8
24125 GONDOLA, 1960-64, Bethlehem Steel, **painted** or unpainted gray, K/C, P/M	10-**20**	20-**75**
24126 GONDOLA, 1961, Frisco, P/M	30	125
24127 GONDOLA, 1961-65, Monon, gray, K/C, P/M	5	15
(24130) GONDOLA, 1960, Pennsylvania, P/M	10	25
24203 HOPPER, 1958 K/C, 1963-64 **P/M**, B&O, black	10-**15**	40-**60**

	C6	C8
24206 HOPPER, 1958, CB&Q, w/coal load, brown, K/C	35	125
24209 HOPPER, 1957-60, Jersey Central{CRP}, gray, w/ hatch covers, K/C	30	100
24213 HOPPER, 1958-60, Wabash, black, K/C	15	50
24216 HOPPER, 1958-60, Union Pacific, K/C	25	90
24219 HOPPER, 1958-59, Western Maryland, K/C	35	150

	C6	C8
24309 TANK CAR, 1957-58, Gulf, silver, K/C	6	30
24310 TANK CAR, 1958-60, Gulf, silver, K/C	5	25
24313 TANK CAR, 1957-60, Gulf, silver, K/C	25	80
24316 TANK CAR, 1957-61, 1965-66, Mobilgas, red, **K/C**, P/M	5-15	25-**50**

	C6	C8
24221 HOPPER, 1959-60, C&EI, gray, K/C	40	175

	C6	C8
24319 TANK CAR, 1958, Pennsylvania Salt, K/C	150	650
24320 TANK CAR, 1960, Deep Rock, black, P/M	125	600
24321 TANK CAR, 1959, Deep Rock, black, K/C	20	100
24322 TANK CAR, 1959, Gulf, silver, K/C	20	75

	C6	C8
24222 HOPPER, 1963-64, Domino Sugar, yellow, w/hatch covers, P/M	150	500
24225 HOPPER, 1960-65, Santa Fe, red, w/gravel load, P/M	10	50
24230 HOPPER, 1961-64, Peabody, K/C, P/M	25	60

	C6	C8
24323 TANK CAR, 1959-60, Bakers, **white** with white or gray ends, K/C	100-**450**	375-**2,000**

	C6	C8			C6	C8

24324 TANK CAR, 1959-60, Hooker, orange, K/C — 35 — 150

24325 TANK CAR, 1960, Gulf, silver, K/C — 10 — 25

24328 TANK CAR, 1962-66, Shell, yellow, P/M — 10 — 25

24329 TANK CAR, 1961, 1963-66, Hooker, orange, P/M — 10 — 30

24330 TANK CAR, 1961-62, Baker's Chocolate, white, P/M — 30 — 100

24403 REEFER, 1958-59, Illinois Central, **painted** or unpainted orange, K/C — 15-**125** — 30-**275**

24409 REEFER, 1958, Northern Pacific, orange sides, K/C — 300 — 950

24419 REEFER, 1958-59, Canadian National, gray, K/C — 100 — 450

(24420) REEFER, 1958, Simmons, orange, K/C — 675 — 850

24422 BOXCAR, 1963-66, Great Northern, light green, P/M — 50 — 150

24422 REEFER, 1963-66, Great Northern, **painted** or unpainted green, fixed or opening door, P/M — 15-**65** — 25-**200**

24413 REEFER, 1957-60, ART, orange sides, K/C — 40 — 150

24416 REEFER, 1958, NW, dark green, K/C — 700 — 1700

24425 REEFER, 1960, BAR, red, K/C — 180 — 650

	C6	C8

24426 REEFER, 1960-61, Rath Packing, orange sides, K/C — 180 · 675

24516 FLATCAR, 1957-59, New Haven, w/lumber load, K/C — 15 · 45

24519 FLATCAR, 1958, Pennsylvania, depressed center, Western Electric spool load, K/C — 250 · 1,100

(24529) FLOODLIGHT, 1957-58, Erie, depressed center, K/C — 10 · 75

24533 TRACK CLEANING CAR, 1958-66, AFL, depressed center, K/C, P/M — 10 · 45

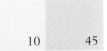

24536 FLATCAR, 1958, Monon, w/trailer load, K/C — 400 · 1,000

24537 FLATCAR, 1958, New Haven, w/pipe load, K/C — 15 · 50

	C6	C8

24539 FLATCAR, New Haven, 1958-59 silver plastic or cardboard pipe load, K/C, **1963-64** orange cardboard pipe load, P/M — 15-20 · 45-65

24540 FLATCAR, 1960, New Haven, w/pipe load, K/C — 50 · 225

24543 CRANE CAR, 1958, Industrial Brownhoist, AFL, K/C — 15 · 50

24546 WORK CABOOSE, 1958-64, AF, K/C — 15 · 45

24547 FLOODLIGHT, 1958, Erie, K/C — 250 · 750

24549 FLOODLIGHT, 1958-1966, Erie, R/C, P/M — 14 · 23

24550 FLATCAR, 1959-1964, Monon, w/trailer load, K/C — 33 · 55

24553 FLATCAR, 1958-1960, Rocket Transport, K/C — 28 · 48

24556 FLATCAR, 1959, Rock Island, wheel transport, K/C — 26 · 44

24557 FLATCAR, 1959-1960, U.S. Navy, w/Jeep load, K/C — 48 · 80

24558 FLATCAR, 1959-1960, Canadian Pacific, w/Christmas tree load, K/C — 83 · 138

	C6	C8
24559 FLATCAR, 1959, New Haven, no load, K/C	9	15
24561 CRANE CAR, 1959-1966, Industrial Brownhoist, AFL, K/C, P/M	14	23
24562 FLATCAR, 1960, N.Y. Central, no load, K/C	17	28
24564 FLATCAR, 1960, New Haven, w/pipe load, P/M	17	28
(245)65 FLATCAR, 1960-61, F.Y & P.R.R., cannon load, K/C	54	90

	C6	C8
24566 FLATCAR, 1961-1966, New Haven, auto transport, P/M	25	43
24569 CRANE CAR, 1961-1966, Industrial Brownhoist, AFL, P/M	9	15
24572 FLATCAR, 1961, U.S. Navy, w/Jeep load, P/M	60	100
24574 FLATCAR, 1960-1961, U.S. Air Force, w/fuel container load, K/C	45	75
24575 FLATCAR, 1960-1966, National, w/milk container load, P/M	21	35

	C6	C8
24577 FLATCAR, 1960-1961, 1963-1964, Illinois Central, w/jet engine container load, K/C, P/M	48	80

	C6	C8
24578 FLATCAR, 1962-1963, New Haven, w/Corvette load, P/M	54	90

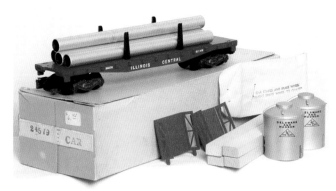

	C6	C8
24579 FLATCAR, 1960-1961, Illinois Central, w/multiload, K/C, P/M	68	113
24603 CABOOSE, 1958-1959, AFL, red, K/C	3	5
24610 CABOOSE, 1960, AFL, red, K/C	4	6

	C6	C8
24618 CABOOSE, 1958, Bay window, AFL, brown, K/C	23	38
24619 CABOOSE, 1958, Bay window, AFL, brown, K/C	23	38
24626 CABOOSE, 1958, AFL, yellow, K/C	5	8
24627 CABOOSE, 1959-1960, AFL, red, K/C	3	5
24630 CABOOSE, 1960, AFL, red, K/C	3	5
24631 CABOOSE, 1959-1961, AFL, yellow, K/C, P/M	15	25
24632 CABOOSE, 1959, AFL, yellow, K/C	24	40

	C6	C8

24633 CABOOSE, 1959-1962, bay window, AFL, silver, P/M — 27 — 45

24634 CABOOSE, 1963-1966, bay window, AFL, red, P/M — 25 — 43

24636 CABOOSE, 1960-1966, AFL, yellow, P/M, rare — 120 — 200

24636 CABOOSE, 1960-1966, AFL, red, P/M — 2 — 3

24638 CABOOSE, 1962, Bay Window, AFL, silver, P/M — 45 — 75

(247)40 COMBINE CAR, 1959-60, FY & PRR, yellow, K/C — 27 — 45

(247)50 COMBINE CAR, 1960-61, K/C — 45 — 75

24773 COMBINE CAR, 1957-1958, 1960-1962, silver, K/C, red stripe, "Columbus" — 36 — 60

24776 COMBINE CAR, 1959, silver, K/C, orange stripe, "Columbus" — 36 — 60

24793 COACH CAR, 1957-1958, 1960-1962, silver, K/C, red stripe, "Jefferson" — 36 — 60

	C6	C8

24813 VISTA-DOME, 1957-1958, 1960-1962, silver, red stripe, "Hamilton" — 45 — 75

24816 VISTA-DOME, 1959, silver, K/C, orange stripe, "Hamilton" — 45 — 75

24833 OBSERVATION CAR, 1957-1958, 1960-1962, silver, K/C, red stripe, "Washington" — 30 — 50

24836 OBSERVATION CAR, 1959, silver, K/C, orange stripe, "Washington" — 30 — 50

24837 COMBINE CAR, 1959-1960, Union Pacific, yellow and gray, K/C — 75 — 125

24838 COACH CAR, 1959-1960, Union Pacific, yellow and gray, K/C — 75 — 125

24839 VISTA-DOME, 1959-1960, Union Pacific, yellow and gray, K/C — 83 — 138

24840 OBSERVATION CAR, 1959-1960, Union Pacific, yellow and gray, K/C — 75 — 125

24843 COMBINE CAR, 1958, Northern Pacific, green, K/C — 45 — 75

24846 COACH CAR, 1958, Northern Pacific, green, K/C — 45 — 75

24849 VISTA-DOME, 1958, Northern Pacific, green, K/C — 48 — 80

24853 OBSERVATION CAR, 1958, Northern Pacific, green, K/C — 75 — 125

24856 COMBINE CAR, P/M — 90 — 150

24856 COMBINE CAR, 1958 & 1964, Missouri Pacific, silver and blue, K/C — 105 — 175

24859 COACH CAR, P/M — 90 — 150

24859 COACH CAR, 1958, 1963-1964, Missouri Pacific, silver and blue, K/C — 105 — 175

	C6	**C8**
24863 VISTA-DOME, P/M	78	130
24863 VISTA-DOME, 1958, 1963-1964, Missouri Pacific, silver and blue, K/C	90	150
24866 OBSERVATION CAR, P/M	75	125

	C6	**C8**
24866 OBSERVATION CAR, 1958, 1963-1964, Missouri Pacific, silver and blue, K/C	90	150
24867 COMBINE CAR, 1958, AFL, silver, K/C	45	75
24868 OBSERVATION CAR, 1958, AFL, silver, K/C	45	75
24869 COACH CAR, 1958, AFL, silver, K/C	45	75

	C6	**C8**
25003 LOG UNLOADING CAR, 1958-1960, AFL, log, K/C	60	100

	C6	**C8**
25016 LUMBER UNLOADING CAR, 1958-1960, Southern Pacific, w/lumber load, K/C	45	75
25019 OPERATING MILK CAR, 1957-1960, Gilbert, white, K/C, w/ plastic cans	65	108
25025 COAL DUMP CAR, 1958-1960, CB&Q, K/C	53	88

	C6	**C8**
25042 OPERATING BOXCAR, 1958, Erie, brown, K/C, w/aluminum barrels	60	100

	C6	**C8**
25044 ROCKET LAUNCHER, 1957, K/C	20	90
25045 ROCKET LAUNCHER, 1958-1960, vertical launch, K/C	25	43
25046 ROCKET LAUNCHER, 1960, 45 degrees angle launch, K/C	29	48

	C6	C8

25049 WALKING BRAKEMAN CAR, 1958-1960, Rio Grande, white, K/C — 90 | 150

25052 CABOOSE, 1960, bay window, AFL, silver, K/C, "Moving Brakeman" — 44 | 73

25056 DETONATOR CAR, 1959, USMC, yellow, K/C — 90 | 150

25056 ROCKET LAUNCHER, 1959, USMC, yellow, K/C — 90 | 150

25057 EXPLODING BOXCAR, 1960, T.N.T. — 60 | 100

	C6	C8

25058 LUMBER UNLOADING CAR, 1961-1964, Southern Pacific, w/lumber load, P/M — 36 | 60

25059 ROCKET LAUNCHER, 1961-1964, U.S.A.F., forty-five degrees angle launch, P/M — 29 | 48

25060 COAL DUMP CAR, 1961-1964, CB&Q, maroon, K/C — 45 | 75

25057 EXPLODING BOXCAR, 1961, TNT — 60 | 100

	C6	**C8**

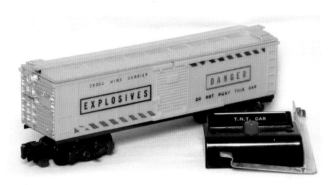

25062 EXPLODING BOXCAR,
1962-1964, mine carrier, P/M — 235 / 393

25071 TIE-JECTOR CAR, 1961-1964, AF, tie load, P/M — 11 / 18

25081 BOXCAR, 1961-1964, NYC, w/hayjector, light green, P/M — 11 / 19

25082 BOXCAR, 1961-1964, New Haven, w/hayjector, orange, P/M — 18 / 30

Item	C6	C8
25062 EXPLODING BOXCAR, 1962-1964, mine carrier, P/M	235	393
25071 TIE-JECTOR CAR, 1961-1964, AF, tie load, P/M	11	18
25081 BOXCAR, 1961-1964, NYC, w/hayjector, light green, P/M	11	19
25082 BOXCAR, 1961-1964, New Haven, w/hayjector, orange, P/M	18	30

Item	C6	C8
26015 FLATCAR, 1960-1963, USAF, w/rocket sled load, P/M	57	95
26101 SCENIC PANEL Curve, 1965	10	15
26121 SCENIC PANEL Straight, 1965	15	23
26122 SCENIC PANEL Straight, 1965	13	19
26141 SCENIC PANEL Right/Left Switch, 1965	10	15

	C6	**C8**

Item	C6	C8
26151 SCENIC PANEL Crossover, 1965	8	12
26300 STRAIGHT TRACK, P/M	15	25
26301 STRAIGHT TRACK, P/M	15	25
26302 STRAIGHT TRACK, w/ uncoupler	1	2
26310 CURVE TRACK, P/M	15	22
26320/321 REMOTE CONTROL SWITCHES, left and right w/controls P/M, Pair	13	19
26322 CROSSING, 90 degrees, P/M	2	2
26323/324 MANUAL SWITCHES, P/M, pair	5	8
26601 FIBER ROAD BG, straight	.50	1
26602 FIBER ROAD BG, curved	.50	1
26700 STRAIGHT TRACK	.50	1
26710 STRAIGHT TRACK	.50	1
26720 CURVE TRACK	.50	1
26726 RUBBER ROAD	.50	1
26726 RUBBER ROAD, half curve	.50	1
26720 CURVE TRACK, half section	.50	1
26744 MANUAL SWITCHES, pair	8	11
26745 90 DEGREES CROSSING	2	2
26746 RUBBER ROADBED, 1957-1964, black or gray, straight	.50	1
26745 RUBBER ROADBED, 1957-1964, black or gray, curved	.50	1
26749 BUMPER, 1957-1960, green	4	6
26751 PIKE PLANNING KIT, 1957-1959	8	11
26760 REMOTE CONTROL SWITCHES, left and right, w/ controls, pair	15	22
26770 MANUAL SWITCHES, pair	11	16
5300T 740 HANDCAR, w/three tipple cars: blue, green and red	130	195

HO GAUGE

	C5	C7	C8
119 FLATCAR, IC, w/three wheel sets, die-cast, gray, no number, couplers connected	25	45	75
123 REFRIGERATOR CAR, PFE, encircled SP, orange and brown	22	45	65
123 REFRIGERATOR CAR, PFE, encircled SP, all orange	100	140	180
124 REFRIGERATOR CAR, MDT, white and brown	8	15	25
125 TANK CAR, Shell, plastic w/die-cast frame, silver	10	35	45
126 TANK CAR, Sinclair, plastic w/die-cast frame, black	15	40	50

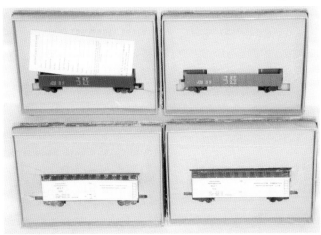

	C5	C7	C8
127 GONDOLA, T&P, embossed "A.C. Gilbert Co.," gray	12	28	40
127 GONDOLA, T&P, embossed "A.C. Gilbert Co.," green	15	25	32
128 GONDOLA, LNE, embossed "A.C. Gilbert Co.," gray	30	55	100

	C5	C7	C8
129 FLATCAR, NYNH&H, w/transformer, die-cast, black	20	35	50

	C5	C7	C8
131 CABOOSE, RDG, center cupola, illuminated, red	12	20	35
133 BAGGAGE CAR, NH, "American Flyer Style," green	40	70	110
135 COACH, NH, "American Flyer Style," green	25	65	100
155 SWITCHER, PRR, B6sb 0-6-0 slantback steam, S/CC	65	110	160
216 FLATCAR, IC, die-cast, gray, w/three wheel sets, no number, couplers connected to body, couplers connected to body, car also available in kit form	25	45	75
252 BLOCK SIGN, black	—	50	100
253 ROADSIDE DINER, yellow w/sign and antenna	—	45	95

	C5	C7	C8
257 TALKING STATION, 1950	—	150	300
258 PASSENGER STATION, metal, white/green/red	—	70	100
259 WHISTLING STATION, similar to 258, w/whistle	—	150	200
420 LOCOMOTIVE, Lack., F-3 A-unit GMD powered diesel, silver	45	75	90
421 LOCOMOTIVE, B&O, F-3 A-unit GMD powered diesel, blue and gray	50	75	100
422 LOCOMOTIVE, B&O, F-3 A-unit GMD dummy diesel, blue and ray	80	150	175
423 LOCOMOTIVE, NP, F-3 A-unit GMD powered diesel, green	85	120	140
424 LOCOMOTIVE, NP, F-3 A-unit GMD dummy diesel, green	60	100	125
425 LOCOMOTIVE, Lack., F-3 B-unit GMD dummy diesel, no number, silver	100	150	200
426 LOCOMOTIVE, B&O, F-3 B-unit GMD dummy diesel, blue and gray	100	150	200
427 LOCOMOTIVE, NP, F-3 B-unit GMD dummy diesel, green	100	150	200
430 DL-600 DEMONSTRATOR, Alco, powered, maroon and gray	50	70	100
433 SWITCHER, PRR, B6sb 0-6-0 slantback steam, S/CC	50	75	100
443 LOCOMOTIVE, NYC, J3a Hudson 4-6-4, whitewall drive wheels, S/CC	60	90	125
446 LOCOMOTIVE, NYC, J3a Hudson 4-6-4, whitewall drive wheels, w/whistle, S/CC	70	100	150
500 TANK CAR, Gulf, Varney version, silver, single dome	7	12	18
500 TANK CAR, Gulf, Gilbert version, silver, single dome	12	20	32
501 HOPPER, CB&Q, Varney version, brown, panel sides, w/Coal Load	4	8	12

	C5	C7	C8
501 HOPPER, CB&Q, Gilbert version, Brown, Smooth Sides, w/Coal Load	8	15	20
502 STOCK CAR, MKT, Varney version, yellow/brown	5	8	12
502 STOCK CAR, MKT, Gilbert version, yellow/brown	7	12	20
503 FLATCAR, NYNH&H, black, w/transformer load	22	32	45
504 REFRIGERATOR CAR, PFE, encircled SP, orange, one herald	12	24	36
504 REFRIGERATOR CAR, PFE/UP, SP/UP Heralds, orange, two herald	22	45	70
505 HOPPER, N&W, black, ink-stamped "Gilbert HO," early model	5	12	20
506 CABOOSE, RDG, red, w/center cupola,	10	18	28
506 CABOOSE, PRR, red, w/center cupola,	8	12	20
510 HOPPER, covered, Monon, Varney version, gray, w/panel side	4	8	12
510 HOPPER, covered, Monon, Gilbert version, gray, w/smooth side	10	22	30
511 TANK CAR, Gulf, silver, w/three domes	22	35	48
512 BOXCAR, NH, orange	10	15	20
513 BOXCAR, B&O, blue and orange	18	30	55
514 BOXCAR, SBD, "Silver Meteor," brown	15	30	45
516 CABOOSE, NYC, brown, lighted, w/center cupola	22	32	45
516 CABOOSE, RDG, red, lighted, center cupola	22	32	45
517 TANK CAR, Mobilgas, Varney version, red	3	10	15
517 TANK CAR, Mobilgas, Gilbert version, red	7	17	27
518 TANK CAR, Koppers, Varney version, black	10	18	30
518 TANK CAR, Koppers, Gilbert version, black	20	30	45

	C5	C7	C8
520 REFRIGERATOR CAR, CNW, "Northwestern," green and yellow	25	35	50
521 REFRIGERATOR CAR, NP, orange w/silver roof and ends	60	75	110
521 REFRIGERATOR CAR, NP, orange w/brown roof and ends	12	25	30
522 BOXCAR, B&M, blue and black	15	25	45
523 BOXCAR, D&RGW, "Cookie Box," white	18	22	30
524 REFRIGERATOR CAR, Morrell, orange and brown	15	28	40
525 HOPPER CAR, B&O, Varney version, black, panel sides, w/load	6	12	20
525 HOPPER CAR, B&O, Gilbert version, black, smooth sides, no load	10	18	28
526 REFRIGERATOR CAR, GB&W, "Green Bay Route," gray and red	22	35	55
540 COMBINE CAR, NP, green, lighted	25	35	50
541 COACH CAR, NP, green, lighted	28	38	53
542 VISTA DOME, NP, green, lighted	30	40	55
543 OBSERVATION CAR, NP, green, lighted	28	38	53
700 GIRDER BRIDGE, silver or red, "Lackawanna"	—	10	30
711 FLASHER SIGNAL	—	15	40
L1001 LOCOMOTIVE, NP, F-3 A-unit pikemaster, powered diesel, green	125	150	200
C1002 COMBINE CAR, NP, pikemaster, non-lighted, green	100	150	200
L1002 LOCOMOTIVE, C&O, F-3 A-unit pikemaster, dummy diesel, blue	110	130	170
C1003 VISTA DOME, NP, pikemaster, non-lighted, green	100	150	200

	C5	C7	C8
C1004 OBSERVATION CAR, NP, pikemaster, non-lighted, green	100	150	200
C1006 HOPPER, C&O, covered, pikemaster, yellow and white	90	150	200
C1007 HOPPER, T&P, some are covered, pikemaster, green and white	90	150	200
2764 BAGGAGE CAR, NH, AF, couplers on trucks, car also available in kit form, cataloged as item 121	28	48	85
2764 BAGGAGE CAR, NH, AF, couplers on body, car also available in kit form, cataloged as item 215	30	50	95
L3003 LOCOMOTIVE, SF, F-3 A-unit pikemaster, powered diesel, red	25	40	55
C3008 CABOOSE, SF, bay window, pikemaster, red	8	15	25

	C5	C7	C8
5318 LOCOMOTIVE, NYC, J3a Hudson 4-6-4 steam, A-C Spur Drive, headlight, remote control, Bakelite wheels w/ brass rims, cataloged as item 112, also available in kit form as HO-112	60	100	130
5318 LOCOMOTIVE, NYC, J3a Hudson 4-6-4 steam, D-C Worm Drive, smoke-in-soiler, no headlight, whitewall drive wheels, cataloged as item 151	125	170	200

	C5	C7	C8
5318 LOCOMOTIVE, NYC, J3a Hudson 4-6-4 steam, D-C worm drive, headlight, piston smoke unit in tender, whitewall drive wheels, cataloged as item 151	75	125	170
5318 LOCOMOTIVE, NYC, J3a Hudson, D-C worm drive, headlight, bellows smoke unit in tender, whitewall drive wheels, cataloged as item 151, 1947-49	75	125	170
5318 LOCOMOTIVE, NYC, J3a Hudson 4-6-4 steam, D-C worm drive, w/headlight, piston smoke unit in tender, no cab number, whitewall drive wheels, cataloged as item 151, 1947-48	80	130	175
5318 LOCOMOTIVE, NYC, J3a Hudson 4-6-4 steam, A-C Spur Drive, w/headlight, remote control, die-cast drive wheels, cataloged as item 112, also available in kit form HO-112	80	150	200
5318 LOCOMOTIVE, NYC, J3a Hudson 4-6-4 steam, A-C Spur Drive, w/headlight, remote control, Bakelite wheels w/brass rims, cataloged as item 200, also available in kit form as HO-1	60	100	130
5318 LOCOMOTIVE, NYC, J3a Hudson 4-6-4 steam, A-C spur drive, no headlight, Bakelite wheels, single red window strut, cataloged 200, also available in kit form as HO-1	75	120	150
5318 LOCOMOTIVE, NYC, J3a Hudson 4-6-4 steam, D-C Worm Drive, w/headlight, smoke unit in tender, whitewall drive wheels, cataloged as item 151	75	125	170
5802 TANK CAR, gasoline, Texaco, die-cast, silver, couplers on trucks, car also available in kit form	15	30	50

	C5	C7	C8
5802 TANK CAR, gasoline, Texaco, die-cast, silver, couplers on body, car also available in kit form	10	22	45

	C5	C7	C8
8302 COACH CAR, NH, AF, die-cast, couplers on trucks, car also available in kit form, cataloged 122, also available in kit form	25	40	80
8302 COACH CAR, NH, AF, die-cast, couplers on body, car also available in kit form, cataloged 122, also available in kit form	25	40	80
15503 GONDOLA, LNE, die-cast, black or gray, couplers on body, cataloged as item 205, car also available in kit form	10	25	45
15503 GONDOLA, LNE, die-cast, black, couplers on trucks, cataloged as item 117, car also available in kit form	10	22	45
24712 TANK CAR, gasoline, Sinclair, die-cast, black, couplers on body, cataloged as item 204, car also available in kit form	10	22	45
24712 TANK CAR, gasoline, Sinclair, die-cast, black, couplers on trucks, cataloged as item 116, car also available in kit form	15	30	50

	C5	**C7**	**C8**

	C5	**C7**	**C8**

31004 SWITCHER, PRR,
B6sb
0-6-0 slantback S/CC — 40 / 65 / 85

	C5	C7	C8
31004 SWITCHER, PRR, B6sb 0-6-0 slantback S/CC	40	65	85
31005 LOCOMOTIVE, NYC, J3a Hudson 4-6-4 steam S/CC	55	80	110
31007 LOCOMOTIVE, B&O, F-3 A-unit GMD powered diesel, blue and gray	95	140	180
31008 LOCOMOTIVE, B&O, F-3 B-unit GMD dummy diesel, blue and gray	200	300	400
31009 LOCOMOTIVE, B&O, F-3 A-unit GMD dummy diesel, blue and gray	90	140	160

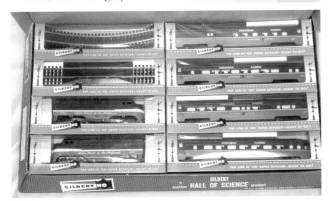

	C5	C7	C8
31010 LOCOMOTIVE, NP, F-3 A-unit GMD powered diesel, green	100	150	170
31011 LOCOMOTIVE, NP, F-3 B-unit GMD dummy diesel, green	100	125	150

	C5	C7	C8
31012 LOCOMOTIVE, NP, F-3 A-unit GMD dummy diesel, green	100	125	150
31013 LOCOMOTIVE, Industrial, transfer diesel, black, w/counterweight	80	125	160

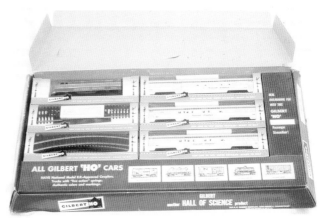

	C5	C7	C8
31014 LOCOMOTIVE, SP, F-3 A-unit GMD powered diesel, orange	110	160	200
31017 LOCOMOTIVE, C&O, Alco DL-600, 600 on number boards, blue and yellow	115	170	210
31019 SWITCHER, B&O, B6sb 0-6-0 slantback S/CC	95	155	210
31021 LOCOMOTIVE, Industrial, transfer diesel, blue, no counterweight	30	45	60
31022 LOCOMOTIVE, C&O, Alco DL-600 w/ringing bell (see 31017), blue	70	140	180
31025 LOCOMOTIVE, C&O, F-3 A-unit pikemaster powered diesel, blue plastic	25	50	75
31025 LOCOMOTIVE, C&O, F-3 A-unit pikemaster, blue	100	150	200
31031 LOCOMOTIVE, B&O, B6sb 0-6-0 slantback, no S/CC	45	70	90
31032 LOCOMOTIVE, NP, F-3 A-unit pikemaster powered diesel	50	70	95

	C5	C7	C8

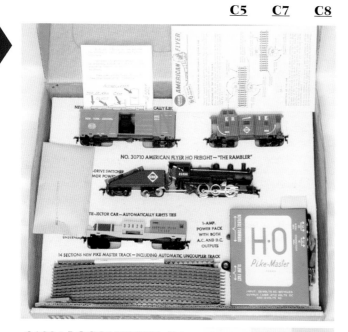

32404 CABOOSE, NYC, die-cast, red, couplers on body, cataloged as item 127, car also available in kit form, w/center cupola, 1939 — 12, 26, 55

	C5	C7	C8

31036 LOCOMOTIVE, Erie, B6sb 0-6-0 slantback switcher, no S/CC — 40, 65, 80

31037 LOCOMOTIVE, M&StL, F-3 A-unit pikemaster, w/o headlight, red/white — 95, 145, 175

31037 LOCOMOTIVE, M&StL, F-3 A-unit pikemaster powered diesel, red and white — 70, 90, 120

31038 LOCOMOTIVE, M&StL, F-3 A-unit pikemaster dummy diesel, red and white — 100, 120, 140

31039 LOCOMOTIVE, MP, F-3 A-unit GMD powered diesel, silver and blue — 150, 225, 300

31045 LOCOMOTIVE, WAB, J3a Hudson 4-6-4 steam S/CC — 70, 110, 165

31088 LOCOMOTIVE, FY&P, Franklin 4-4-0 Old Time (Tyco), green and red — 150, 250, 325

32404 CABOOSE, NYC, die-cast, red, couplers on trucks, cataloged as item 120, car also available in kit form, w/center cupola, 1939 — 12, 28, 58

32404 CABOOSE, NYC, die-cast, brown, couplers on body, cataloged as item 207, car also available in kit form, w/center cupola, 1938 — 18, 32, 65

33002 BOXCAR, NYC, w/ large NYC oval sticker, green and white — 27, 35, 45

33004 STOCK CAR, NP, "Pig Palace," red w/silver roof — 100, 150, 200

33006 STOCK CAR, GN, hay-jector eliminated, red — 80, 110, 150

33009 STOCK CAR, WAB, hay-jector eliminated, blue — 80, 110, 150

33010 STOCK CAR, UP, hay-jector eliminated, yellow — 90, 140, 190

33012 BOXCAR, SF, large Santa Fe cross, red and white — 80, 140, 180

	C5	**C7**	**C8**

33115 BALLAST CAR, MW, by TruScale, gray, Kleer-Pak or cardboard Gilbert box required — 40 / 80 / 110

33119 GONDOLA, Monon, pikemaster, white and red — 45 / 90 / 110

33120 GONDOLA, T&P, pikemaster, green and white — 60 / 100 / 130

33121 GONDOLA, NH, "Trap Rock," pikemaster, tan and yellow — 80 / 150 / 200

33122 GONDOLA, N&W, pikemaster, black — 50 / 95 / 125

33211 HOPPER, C&EI, no load, gray — 10 / 20 / 30

33212 HOPPER, SF, w/gray stone load, red — 20 / 32 / 45

33214 HOPPER, SF, covered, red and white — 10 / 22 / 35

	C5	**C7**	**C8**
33215 HOPPER, Peabody, no load, tan (tan color varies)	15	22	42
33217 HOPPER, NYC, covered, green/white	10	20	30
33219 HOPPER, B&O, no load, black	60	75	115
33220 HOPPER, CB&Q, w/ covered, red and white	160	260	375
33312 TANK CAR, Karo, "Karo Syrup," white/red	150	250	350
33313 TANK CAR, Hooker, chemical, orange/black	75	110	140
33314 TANK CAR, Cities, "Cities Service," green	350	425	500
33315 TANK CAR, SOHIO, "Sohio," black	375	450	550
33316 GONDOLA, Bethlehem Steel, w/rail load, gray and red	45	85	125
33316 GONDOLA, Bethlehem Steel, PM version, w/rail load, gray and red	80	125	155
33317 GONDOLA, NH, pikemaster, black and orange	70	130	150
33403 REFRIGERATOR CAR, BAR, large BAR sticker, red	70	100	150
33500 TANK CAR, Gulf, single dome, silver	12	25	35
33501 HOPPER CAR, CB&Q, smooth side, brown, w/coal load	18	28	40
33502 STOCK CAR, MKT, yellow and brown	55	75	95
33503 FLATCAR, NYNH&H, w/transformer Load, black	50	75	125
33505 GONDOLA, N&W, black and white	10	22	32
33506 CABOOSE, PRR, red, w/center cupola	5	12	20
33507 GONDOLA, D&H, brown, w/canister load	30	60	75

	C5	C7	C8
33507 GONDOLA, D&H, pikemaster version, brown	100	200	300
33508 GONDOLA, C&O, black and yellow, w/pipe load	20	35	55
33509 HOPPER CAR, WM, brown, w/RISS trailer load	42	55	80
33510 HOPPER CAR, Monon, covered, gray and red	80	130	170
33511 TANK CAR, Gulf, three domes, silver	12	25	35
33512 BOXCAR, NH, orange	12	24	36
33513 BOXCAR, B&O, blue and orange	30	50	75
33514 BOXCAR, SBD, "Silver Meteor," brown	20	45	65
33515 CABOOSE, C&O, lighted, yellow, w/center cupola	45	75	120
33516 CABOOSE, NYC, lighted, brown, w/center cupola	12	22	35
33517 TANK CAR, Mobil, "Mobilgas," red	12	18	25
33518 TANK CAR, Koppers, chemical, black	60	100	150
33519 CABOOSE, B&O, red, w/center cupola	10	22	35
33520 REFRIGERATOR CAR, CNW, green and yellow	75	120	150
33521 REFRIGERATOR CAR, NP, orange and brown	18	27	42
33522 BOXCAR, B&M, blue and black	25	40	60
33523 BOXCAR, D&RGW, "Cookie Box," white and red	20	30	45
33524 REFRIGERATOR CAR, Morrel Ref, Morrel, Orange and silver	25	35	65
33525 HOPPER CAR, B&O, no load, smooth side, black	45	90	120

	C5	C7	C8
33526 REFRIGERATOR CAR, GB&W, "Green Bay Route," gray and red	30	42	55
33527 FLATCAR, NH, w/ lumber load and stakes, black	20	32	45
33530 COMBINE CAR, SP, lighted, silver/orange	60	120	160
33531 COACH CAR, SP, lighted, silver and orange	60	120	160
33536 FLATCAR, PRR, w/ten stakes, brown	60	95	135
33537 TRACK CLEANING CAR, D&H, w/D&H Canister, black	22	40	65

	C5	C7	C8
33538 FLATCAR, U.S. Air Force, w/two Nike rockets, dark green	60	155	155
33539 FLATCAR, RI, w/two railcar trucks, gray and black	38	65	100
33540 COMBINE CAR, NP, lighted, green	25	35	50
33541 COACH CAR, NP, lighted, green	35	50	65
33542 VISTA DOME, NP, lighted, green	30	45	60
33543 OBSERVATION CAR, NP, lighted, green	32	45	62

	C5	**C7**	**C8**

33544 FLATCAR, CP, red, w/Christmas tree load — 100 / 175 / 225

33545 FLATCAR, National, w/Borden's Milk Tank, black and white — 20 / 40 / 80

33546 FLATCAR, IC, w/jet engine case, black — 25 / 50 / 90

33549 CRANE TENDER, MW, by TruScale, typically 642, gray, Kleer-Pak or cardboard — 40 / 70 / 100

33548 CRANE, MW, X74 Brownhoist, by TruScale, red cab, Kleer-Pak or cardboard Gilbert — 90 / 150 / 200

33555 FLATCAR, IC, w/ containers, lumber, pipes, brown — 45 / 70 / 90

33557 FLATCAR, WM, w/ Riss trailer van, brown — 42 / 55 / 80

33558 FLATCAR, IC, w/load, similar to 33555, brown — 25 / 40 / 50

33615 CABOOSE, NYC, brown, w/center cupola — 15 / 20 / 30

	C5	C7	C8
33616 CABOOSE, C&O, lighted, yellow, w/center cupola	33	55	80
33618 CABOOSE, Erie, bay window, pikemaster, red	8	15	25
33620 CABOOSE, WAB, bay window, pikemaster, blue	22	35	50
33621 CABOOSE, C&O, bay window, pikemaster, yellow	12	20	32
33623 CABOOSE, M&StL, bay window, pikemaster, red	25	42	52
33625 CABOOSE, NYC, bay window, pikemaster, red	90	125	160
33626 CABOOSE, work, Erie, no tie-jector, see 33820	85	120	150
33627 CABOOSE, PRR, bay window, pikemaster, red	32	45	65
33720 COACH, FY&P, Old Time, by Mantua-Tyco, yellow	95	150	210
33721 COMBINE CAR, MP, lighted, silver and blue	75	125	150
33722 COACH CAR, MP, lighted (sold separately only), silver and blue	120	180	200
33723 VISTA DOME, MP, lighted, silver and blue	75	125	150
33724 OBSERVATION CAR, MP, lighted, silver/blue	75	125	150

33804 BOXCAR, TNT, exploding "Boxcar," black/yellow

	40	55	90

	C5	C7	C8
33806 BOXCAR MINE, Mine Carrying/Exploding "Boxcar," yellow	30	45	70

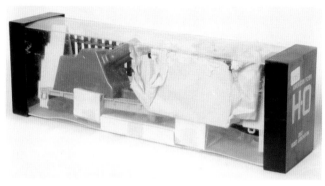

	C5	C7	C8
33812 ROCKET LAUNCHER CAR, USAF, w/Rocket, yellow/blue	25	40	80
33818 CATTLE CAR, GN, ejects hay bale, red	20	45	65
33819 CATTLE CAR, NYC, ejects hay bale, green	25	50	70
33820 CABOOSE, work, AF, Tie Car, ejects tie, orange and gray	10	20	35
33835 HOPPER CAR, C&O, dumps coal load, black	18	28	48

	C5	C7	C8
35105 MOTORIZED VEHICLE, Inspection, w/two figures, green	400	600	800
35210 RADAR TOWER, made for Ideal by Gilbert	—	15	40

	C5	C7	C8
35212 CROSSING GATE, made for Ideal by Gilbert	—	10	35
35213 OIL STORAGE DEPOT	—	40	75
35759 DRUM LOADING CONVEYOR, "Oil Depot"	—	50	100
35780 COAL LOADER, "Elm City Coal Gravel & Sand Co."	—	50	70
35785 AUTOMATIC COAL UNLOADER, w/35785 hopper car	—	50	90
35785 HOPPER CAR, C&O, dumps coal load, black	18	28	48
35790 PIGGYBACK UNLOADER, w/Riss van trailer	—	80	140

	C5	C7	C8
49611 REFRIGERATOR CAR, MDT, die-cast, white/brown, couplers on trucks, cataloged as item 114, car also available in kit form	20	40	60
49611 REFRIGERATOR CAR, MDT, die-cast, white/brown, couplers on body, cataloged as item 202, car also available in kit form	20	40	60

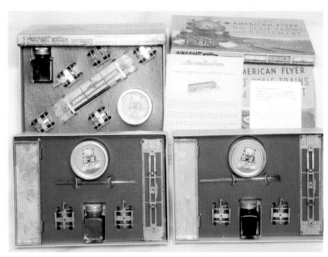

	C5	C7	C8
35901 REFRIGERATOR CAR, PFE, die-cast, orange, couplers on body, cataloged as item 201, car also available in kit form	20	40	60
35901 REFRIGERATOR CAR, PFE, die-cast, orange, couplers on trucks, cataloged as item 113, car also available kit form	20	40	60
147313 GONDOLA, PRR, die-cast, brown, couplers on body, cataloged as item 118, car also available in kit form	12	28	50
147313 GONDOLA, PRR, die-cast, brown, couplers on body, cataloged as item 206, car also available in kit form	12	28	50
352414 AUTOMATIC CROSSING WATCHMAN	—	20	45

AMT

American Model Toys (later Auburn Model Trains) was incorporated in May 1948 by John "Jack" W. Ferris in Fort Wayne, Ind. The first products of the firm were sand-cast 0 gauge aluminum passenger cars. These illuminated passenger cars included two Roomette Pullmans and an Observation. Very early in the company's history, the firm relocated from Ft. Wayne about 25 miles to Auburn, Ind.

With no other comparable 0 gauge streamlined passenger cars on the market, Ferris's fledgling firm flourished. After only a brief period producing the sand-cast cars, production switched to using extruded aluminum bodies with die-cast frames. These cars, which came in six styles – baggage, combination, Pullman, diner, Vista Dome and observation – had smooth roofs and included interior illumination. The series was offered in the markings of the Santa Fe and New York Central railroads, an obvious attempt to capitalize on the success of Lionel's streamlined F-3 diesels, introduced in 1948.

Building on the success of these 0 gauge streamliners, the firm began offering HO gauge counterparts as well as beautiful 0 gauge, scale-sized boxcars in 1951. These boxcars, much larger than the 3464-series cars Lionel was offering at the time and much more elaborately decorated, no doubt pushed Lionel into the creation of its famous 6464 boxcars. However, as had been the case with the streamliners, briefly AMT enjoyed a monopoly and good sales. This led to the offering of additional types of freight cars in 1953. These cars included stock, refrigerator, depressed center flatcars and cabooses.

Bigger news however was AMT's introduction of its own locomotive, patterned after the EMD F-7. Powered by a seven-pole Pittman motor and equipped with traction tires, these locomotives proved to have excellent performance.

Alas, despite its fine products, the firm was under assault by Lionel, which viewed it as a threat, and hampered by its own liberal credit and sales policies with distributors. Thus, when Nashville-based Kusan Corporation approached Ferris in 1953 with an offer to purchase, it was well received.

Values listed for good, excellent and like new

	C5	**C7**	**C8**

AMT SAND-CAST PASSENGER CARS

These cars, the first offered by AMT, were all illuminated, and equipped with sprung trucks.

PENNSYLVANIA

		C5	C7	C8
1001 PULLMAN, City of Altoona.		75	125	175
1002 PULLMAN, City of Fort Wayne.		75	125	175
1003 OBSERVATION, Skyline View.		75	125	175

NEW YORK CENTRAL

	C5	C7	C8
1004 PULLMAN, City of Toledo.	75	125	175
1005 PULLMAN, City of Buffalo.	75	125	175
1006 OBSERVATION, Manhattan Island.	75	125	175

EXTRUDED ALUMINUM CARS

About 1949-50, AMT began manufacturing its streamlined passenger cars with extruded aluminum bodies, rather than the sand castings used previously. Initially the bodies were extruded as a single piece (as were the similar cars introduced a few years later by Lionel), however later cars were produced with the sides and roofs formed from three separate extrusions, which then were slipped together. Even the early single piece extrusions have variations involving the thickness of the aluminum.

Other notable variations include the length of the nameplates on the cars. Except for C&NW plates, the bulk of AMT's nameplates were 4 1/4-inches long, though some occasionally turn up with 4-inch plates. Further, the Bedroom-Roomette cars could also be purchased with prototypically correct "Pullman" lettering rather than a specific road name – today this variation is difficult to locate.

The window glazing came most often in blue plastic, but some had two-piece acetate windows, the outer layer clear, the inner frosted. The vista domes also came in blue, which often warp, or white, which are frequently found cracked. Also, cars were available new with either smooth or fluted roofs. Originally, the fluted roof cars were lower cost, but today on the collector market they command a slight premium. The prices listed below are for the smooth-roof versions. Finally, the cars are listed by catalog number, rather than the number on the side of the car.

"TEXAS SPECIAL" SET: Aluminum cars with red painted trim wearing the markings of the Missouri-Kansas-Texas and Frisco jointly operated Texas Special passenger train.

	C5	C7	C8
1001 MAIL EXPRESS: Number plate reads "3407".	75	125	200

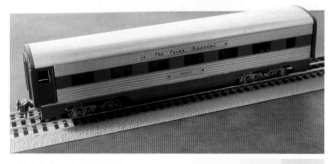

	C5	C7	C8
1002 ROOMETTE: "BOWIE".	75	125	200
1003 DINER: Number plate reads "DINER"	75	125	200

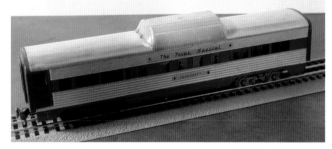

	C5	C7	C8
1004 VISTA DOME: "CROCKETT".	75	125	200

	C5	C7	C8
1005 OBSERVATION: "SAM HOUSTON".	75	125	200

	C5	C7	C8		C5	C7	C8

1006 DAY COACH: Number plate reads "3160". — 75 125 200

1007 CREW COMBINATION: Number plate reads "5260". — 75 125 200

1008 Baggage: Number plate reads "4170". — 75 125 200

SANTA FE SET: *Large letterboard reads "SANTA FE" with smaller plates carrying numbers and car names.*

2001 MAIL EXPRESS: Number plate reads "3407". — 40 75 125

2002 ROOMETTE.

The Santa Fe cars were offered with either fluted or smooth roofs. Shown here is a fluted-roof example of the Indian Scout.

(Type I) Number plate reads "INDIAN LAKE". — 40 75 125

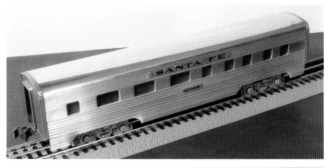

The smooth roof version of the Indian Scout is shown here.

(Type II) Number plate reads "INDIAN SCOUT". — 40 75 125

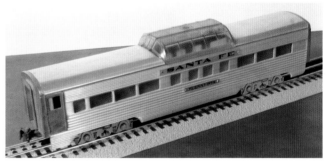

2003 DINER: "DINER". — 40 75 125

2004 VISTA DOME: "BUENA VISTA". — 40 75 125

The Santa Fe observation cars were also offered with either fluted or smooth roofs. Shown here is a fluted-roof example of the Indian Arrow.

	C5	C7	C8

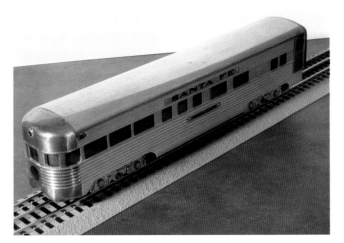

The smooth roof version of the observation car is shown here.

	C5	C7	C8
2005 OBSERVATION: "INDIAN ARROW".	40	75	125

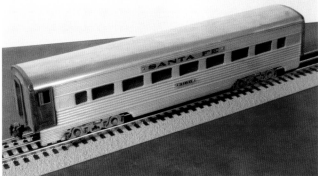

2006 DAY COACH: Number plate reads "3160".	40	75	125

2007 CREW COMBINATION: Number plate reads "5264".	40	75	125

	C5	C7	C8
2008 BAGGAGE: Number plate reads "4170".	40	75	125

NEW YORK CENTRAL SET: Large letterboard reads "NEW YORK CENTRAL" with smaller plates carrying numbers and car names.

3001 MAIL EXPRESS: Number plate reads "3407".	40	75	125
3002 ROOMETTE:			
(Type I) "CITY OF DETROIT".	40	75	125
(Type II) "CITY OF ERIE".	40	75	125
(Type III) "CITY OF UTICA".	40	75	125

3003 DINER: "DINER".	40	75	125

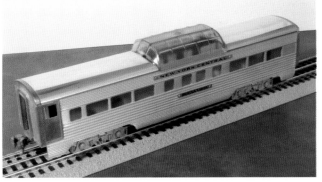

3004 VISTA DOME: "BUENA VISTA".	40	75	125

	C5	**C7**	**C8**

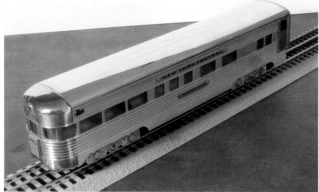

3005 OBSERVATION:
"SENECA FALLS".   40   75   125

3006 DAY COACH: Number
plate reads "3160".   40   75   125

**3007 CREW
COMBINATION:** Number
plate reads "5260".   40   75   125

3008 BAGGAGE: Number
plate reads "4170".   40   75   125

	C5	**C7**	**C8**

PENNSYLVANIA SET: Large letterboard reads "PENNSYLVANIA" with smaller plates carrying numbers and car names.

4001 MAIL EXPRESS:
Number plate reads "3407".   40   75   125

4002 ROOMETTE:

(Type I) "CITY OF
PITTSBURGH".   40   75   125

(Type II) "FORT WAYNE".   40   75   125

4003 DINER: "DINER".   40   75   125

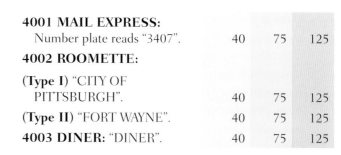

4004 VISTA DOME: "CITY
OF NEW YORK".   40   75   125

4005 OBSERVATION: "CITY
OF CHICAGO".   40   75   125

4006 DAY COACH: Number
plate reads "3160".   40   75   125

**4007 CREW
COMBINATION:** Number
plate reads "5260".   40   75   125

4008 BAGGAGE: Number
plate reads "4170".   40   75   125

	C5	C7	C8

SOUTHERN SET: All cars bear a large plate on each side reading "SOUTHERN" and small plates with additional lettering.

	C5	C7	C8
5001 MAIL EXPRESS: Number plate reads "3407".	75	125	200
5002 ROOMETTE:			
(Type I) "CATAWBA RIVER".	75	125	200
(Type II) **"POTOMAC RIVER".**	75	125	200
(Type III) **"DAN RIVER".**	75	125	200
5003 DINER: "DINER".	75	125	200
5004 VISTA DOME: "GEORGIA".	75	125	200
5005 OBSERVATION: "CRESCENT CITY".	75	125	200
5006 DAY COACH: Number plate reads "3160".	75	125	200
5007 CREW COMBINATION: Number plate reads "5260".	75	125	200
5008 BAGGAGE: Number plate reads "4170".	75	125	200

CHICAGO & NORTHWESTERN SET: These cars were attractively painted in the yellow and green scheme of the CNW. The "CHICAGO & NORTHWESTERN" nameplates on these cars are significantly larger than the nameplates on the other cars. Once again, smaller plates were used for names and numbers.

	C5	C7	C8
6001 MAIL EXPRESS: Number plate reads "3407".	80	150	250
6002 ROOMETTE: "NORTHERN PINES".	80	150	250
6003 DINER "DINER".	80	150	250
6004 VISTA DOME: "NORTHERN STREAMS".	80	150	250

	C5	C7	C8
6005 OBSERVATION: "NORTHERN STATES".	80	150	250
6006 DAY COACH: Number plate reads "3160".	Too rarely traded to establish accurate pricing.		
6007 CREW COMBINATION: Number plate reads "5260".	80	150	250
6008 BAGGAGE: Number plate reads "4170".	80	150	250

BALTIMORE & OHIO SET: Large letterboard is marked "BALTIMORE & OHIO" and small plates have additional lettering.

7001 MAIL EXPRESS: Number plate reads "3407".	Too rarely traded to establish accurate pricing.
7002 ROOMETTE: "YOUNGSTOWN".	Too rarely traded to establish accurate pricing.
7003 DINER: "DINER".	Too rarely traded to establish accurate pricing.
7004 VISTA DOME: "CAPITOL CITY".	Too rarely traded to establish accurate pricing.
7005 OBSERVATION: "WAWASEE".	Too rarely traded to establish accurate pricing.
7006 DAY COACH: Number plate reads "3160".	Too rarely traded to establish accurate pricing.
7007 CREW COMBINATION: Number plate reads "5260".	Too rarely traded to establish accurate pricing.
7008 BAGGAGE: Number plate reads "4170".	Too rarely traded to establish accurate pricing

<u>**C5**</u>   <u>**C7**</u>   <u>**C8**</u>   <u>**C5**</u>   <u>**C7**</u>   <u>**C8**</u>

AMT F-7 DIESEL LOCOMOTIVES

AMT introduced its F-7 diesel replicas in early 1953, and they remained part of the product line until AMT sold its entire toy train operation to Kusan late in 1954.

322 SANTA FE: F-7 A unit, catalog number F2, dark blue and yellow paint, yellow lettering, excess yellow; humped body, refined ventilation screen.

	C5	C7	C8
Powered	100	140	180
Dummy	50	70	110

1733 NEW YORK CENTRAL: F7 A Unit, catalog number F3; dark gray and light gray paint; white lettering

	C5	C7	C8
Powered	120	160	200
Dummy	55	80	130

2019 MISSOURI, KANSAS & TEXAS (The Texas Special): F7 A Unit, catalog number F1. Finished in the red, silver, and black paint scheme worn by the "Texas Special" passenger train. The upper portion of the nose was painted to simulate an antiglare panel.

	C5	C7	C8
Powered	120	160	225
Dummy	75	125	175

5400 CHICAGO & NORTHWESTERN: F7 A Unit, catalog number F6. Finished in yellow and green paint paint scheme. Fuel tank skirts are yellow.

	C5	C7	C8
Powered	140	190	250
Dummy	80	140	200

6755 SOUTHERN: F7 A Unit, catalog number F5; green and gray paint; with yellow lettering, gray roof, black fuel tank skirts.

	C5	C7	C8
Powered	125	160	225
Dummy	70	110	160

8644 PENNSYLVANIA: F7 A Unit, catalog number F4, bright tuscan red.

	C5	C7	C8
Powered	120	150	210
Dummy	60	100	150

BALTIMORE & OHIO: F7 A Unit, catalog number F7; painted dark blue, gray and yellow; with yellow lettering.

	C5	C7	C8
Powered	180	300	400
Dummy	100	150	200

CB&Q BURLINGTON: F7 A Unit: Silver, red and black paint; AMT production.

Too rarely traded to establish pricing.

	C5	C7	C8

BOXCARS

Introduced in March 1952, these boxcars represented a substantial improvement over competitive products. Well detailed, some of these cars were also colorfully decorated.

2227 CANADIAN PACIFIC: Cataloged as number 8007, this car was painted tuscan with white lettering. — 15 25 40

4382 MINNEAPOLIS & ST. LOUIS "MERCHANDISER": Cataloged as number 9004, this car had yellow lettering on green body paint. Its doors were green as well. — 15 30 45

13057 NICKEL PLATE: Cataloged as number 8006; this car was painted tuscan with white lettering. — 15 25 40

19509 GREAT NORTHERN: Cataloged as number 8002, these cars wore tuscan paint; with white lettering. Black doors were installed. — 15 25 40

25439 ERIE: Assigned catalog number 8003, this car was painted tuscan and decorated with black and white markings.

(Type I) Lettered "CU FT 3769", black doors. — 10 20 35

(Type II) Lettered "CU FT 3730", black doors. — 20 40 60

(Type III) Lettered "CU FT 3770", black doors. — 25 45 65

(Type IV) Reporting marks printed in two columns, fitted with tuscan doors. — 30 50 75

30565 NEW YORK, NEW HAVEN & HARTFORD: Cataloged as number 8005; black doors and white lettering highlighted this otherwise tuscan boxcar. — 15 25 40

	C5	C7	C8

34922 SANTA FE: Assigned catalog number 8004, this tuscan boxcar with black doors was lettered in white. — 10 20 30

56312 PENNSYLVANIA MERCHANDISE SERVICE: Cataloged as number 9002, the distinctive white band and red lettering of the "Merchandise Service" logo runs across the top of this brown boxcar. — 20 30 45

153902 SOUTHERN: The AMT catalog listed this tuscan with white lettering car as number 8001. — 15 25 40

174479 NEW YORK CENTRAL "PACEMAKER": Cataloged as number 9001, this car wore the distinctive red and gray "Pacemaker" paint scheme. — 15 25 40

The owner of this AMT Sentinel car replaced its original trucks and couplers with ones made by Lionel.

466096 BALTIMORE & OHIO "SENTINEL": The brilliant blue and silver "Sentinel" paint scheme adorned AMT's catalog number 9003. — 20 30 45

523977 CANADIAN NATIONAL: Cataloged as number 8008, this tuscan boxcar was decorated with green and white lettering. — 25 40 55

	C5	C7	C8

RAIL DIESEL CARS (RDCs)

The AMT Rail Diesel Cars had plastic bodies housing a seven-pole electric motor. Introduced in 1953, it continued to be offered after the Kusan takeover. All were numbered "3160" on their bodies.

	C5	C7	C8
NEW YORK CENTRAL: Catalog number 1-33.	75	110	150
PENNSYLVANIA: Catalog number 1-44.	60	90	125

	C5	C7	C8
SANTA FE: Catalog number 1-22.	80	110	140
SOUTHERN: Catalog number 1-55.	75	110	150

Following up on the success of their boxcars, in 1953 AMT launched a line of new scale-sized freight cars.

CABOOSES

	C5	C7	C8

Cabooses came with either black or yellow frames and steps, with the yellow steps warranting a premium of about 20 percent over the prices listed here.

	C5	C7	C8
104 SANTA FE: This caboose, painted in traditional red paint, was assigned catalog number C22. Its lettering was white.	30	45	65
832 PENNSYLVANIA: This caboose, painted in traditional red paint, was assigned catalog number C24. Its lettering was white.	30	45	65
1216 NEW YORK CENTRAL: This caboose too was painted in traditional red paint. Its catalog number was C23. Its lettering was white.	30	45	65

	C5	C7	C8
3162 SOUTHERN: Yet another red caboose with white lettering, this car was given catalog number C25.	40	55	85

	C5	C7	C8

90079 CHESAPEAKE & OHIO: Cataloged as number C26; this red-painted caboose had white lettering. — 45 | 65 | 100

DEPRESSED-CENTER FLATCARS

412 MONON: Cataloged as number 7351, this sand-cast aluminum car was painted gray with red lettering. — 20 | 45 | 75

GONDOLAS

51297 LOUISVILLE & NASHVILLE: This shiny black car with white lettering was given catalog number 7651. — 15 | 35 | 60

REFRIGERATOR CARS

1008 GERBER'S: Cataloged as number 7251, this multi-colored car had sides painted blue and white, its roof red, ends white, and the lettering blue. — 20 | 40 | 70

9241 SANTA FE: Cataloged with number 7252, this car had yellow sides and ends, and a red-brown roof. The lettering was black. — 20 | 35 | 65

STOCK CARS

	C5	C7	C8

32066 CHICAGO, BURLINGTON & QUINCY: This tuscan-sided car with black and white markings was given catalog number 7151. — 15 | 25 | 35

47150 MISSOURI, KANSAS & TEXAS: Assigned catalog number 7150 was this yellow-sided car with black roof and white lettering. — 20 | 30 | 45

140449 ATLANTIC COAST LINE: This tuscan car was given catalog number 7152. It had white lettering. — 15 | 25 | 35

BUDDY L

One of the most unlikely manufacturers of toy trains was Fred Lundahl. Lundahl formed the Moline Pressed Steel Company about 1910. Operating in East Moline, the company supplied heavy stamped sheet steel parts to the automotive industry, notably International Harvester for its truck production and McCormick-Deering for its agricultural products. The first steel toy that Fred built was for his son, Arthur. Arthur was known in the neighborhood as Buddy. The "L" appendage stood for Lundahl, differentiating Arthur from another child, also known as Buddy. Young Arthur had bemoaned that many of the toys his father had bought him broke prematurely through normal play.

Fred Lundahl, with a considerable amount of expertise, equipment and heavy 18 gauge steel at his disposal, fabricated for Buddy a truck robust enough to withstand youthful play in dirt and sand. By 1921, the parents of other neighborhood children were asking Fred for toys for their kids. Inspired, the next year Fred took samples of his toys to the New York Toy Fair. Despite their high cost, the rugged appeal of the big toys led to the first of what would become an avalanche of orders. In 1926, just three years after the manufacture of full-sized automotive components was abandoned in favor of toy vehicle production, an outdoor railroad was added to the product line.

In 1930, Fred Lundahl lost control of the company he founded. The company name was changed to Buddy "L" Manufacturing Company at that time, and Fred passed away later the same year. The next year was the last for the outdoor railroad as well.

	C5	**C7**	**C8**
BUDDY "L" INDUSTRIAL TRAIN HANDCAR, No. 2 ga., 1929-1931, orange, rare	1600	2500	4000

	C5	**C7**	**C8**
51 LOCOMOTIVE, No. 2 ga., 1929-1931, decals BL 12, BL 14, or BL 16, dark green	200	400	600
52 STAKE CAR, No. 2 ga., 1929-1931, flatcar, red	55	100	150
53 ROCK CAR, No. 2 ga., 1929-1931, red	55	100	150
54 GONDOLA, No. 2 ga., 1929-1931, red	55	100	150
55 BALLAST CAR, No. 2 ga., 1929-1931, side dump, red	100	175	250
56 ROCKER DUMP CAR, No. 2 ga., 1929-1931, red	100	175	250
70 STRAIGHT TRACK, No. 2 ga., 1929-1931, dark green, 24", price per section	15	20	30

	C5	**C7**	**C8**
71 CURVED TRACK, No. 2 ga., 1929-1931, dark green, per section	8	12	20
72R SWITCH, No. 2 ga., 1929-1931, dark green	35	60	90
73L SWITCH, No. 2 ga., 1929-1931, dark green	35	60	90
74 TURN-OUT CURVE, No. 2 ga., 1929-1931, dark green	7	10	15
75 NINETY DEGREES CROSSING, No. 2 ga., 1929-1931, dark green	25	35	50
76 SIXTY DEGREES CROSSING, No. 2 ga., 1929-1931, dark green	50	75	100
77 LOOSE LATCH PLATE, No. 2 ga., 1929-1931, dark green	3	5	6
78 1/4 STRAIGHT TRACK, 6", No. 2 ga., 1929-1931, dark green	15	20	30
79 1/2 STRAIGHT TRACK, 12", No. 2 ga., 1929-1931, dark green	15	20	30

	C5	C7	C8

80 THREE STALL ROUNDHOUSE AND TURNTABLE, No. 2 ga., 1929-1931, dark green

	850	1,100	2,000

81 ONE STALL ROUNDHOUSE AND TURNTABLE, No. 2 ga., 1929-1931, dark green

	600	1,000	1,500

BUDDY "L" OUTDOOR RAILROAD SUPPORTING PIERS, 3-1/4" ga., black

	110	150	200

	C5	C7	C8

TRESTLE SECTIONS, 3-1/4" ga., black

	150	250	350

1000 LOCOMOTIVE AND TENDER, 3-1/4" ga., 1921-1931, decal reads 963, black

	1,100	1,650	2,200

1001 CABOOSE, 3-1/4" ga., 1921-1931, decal 3017, red

	450	600	800

1002 BOXCAR, 3-1/4" ga., 1921-1931, red

	500	750	1,000

1003 TANK CAR, 3-1/4" ga., 1921-1931, dark red, yellow and silver

	750	1,125	1,500

1004 STOCK CAR, 3-1/4" ga., 1921-1931, red

	300	500	650

	C5	C7	C8
1005 GONDOLA, 3-1/4" ga., 1921-1931, coal car, black	400	600	750
1006 FLATCAR, 3-1/4" ga., 1926-1931, black	300	500	650

	C5	C7	C8
1007 HOPPER, 3-1/4" ga., 1928-1931, bottom dump, black	650	800	1,000
1008 BALLAST CAR, 3-1/4" ga., 1928-1931, side dump, black, 23"	650	800	1,000
1009 CONSTRUCTION CAR, 3-1/4" ga., 1930-1931, single truck, dark green, 11"	1,700	2,550	3,400

	C5	C7	C8
1020 LOCOMOTIVE WRECKING CRANE, 3-1/4" ga., 1927-1930, black, red	2,000	3,000	4,000
1021 LOCOMOTIVE DREDGE, 3-1/4" ga., 1927-1930, black and red	2,000	3,000	4,200
1022 LOCOMOTIVE PILE DRIVER, 3-1/4" ga., 1927-1930, black and red	2,600	3,900	5,500
1023 LOCOMOTIVE SHOVEL, 3-1/4" ga., 1928-1930, black and red	2,200	3,300	4,500
1200 STRAIGHT TRACK, 3-1/4" ga., 4' long	27	41	55
1201 CURVED TRACK, 3-1/4" ga., 4' long, 26' dia.	17	26	35
1202 RIGHT-HAND SWITCH, 3-1/4" ga., 7'	375	563	750

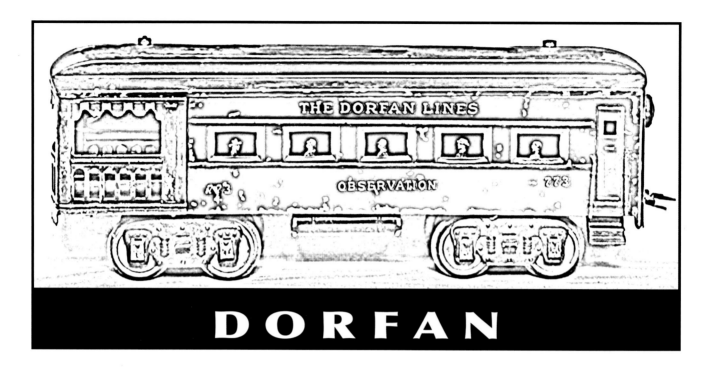

Dorfan produced trains for only 10 years, from 1924-1933, but during that time was one of the Big Four of American train making, along with Ives, Lionel and American Flyer.

Julius and Milton Forcheimer worked for their cousin's firm of Joseph Kraus & Co. in Nürnberg, Germany, until 1923. At that time, Julius left his position in production and Milton his in sales departments, and moved to the United States. They brought with them not only the German firm's chief engineer, John C. Koerber, but also the company name. Jos. Kraus & Co. marketed its trains as the "Fandor" line, named after Milton's and Julius's mothers, Fanny and Dora. Once in America, the names were reversed and Dorfan was born.

The experience afforded by this management team, coupled with the booming American toy market of the 1920s, put the new company in a prime position. Eager to set itself apart from other toy train makers, the firm introduced the die-cast zinc-alloy locomotive body. This material afforded most of the heft of cast iron toys, but was considerably more resilient. In fact, Dorfan referred to the material as "unbreakable." Dorfan's products however, did have some problems. In fact, Dorfan's claims to fame, and infamy, were one and the same.

Zinc-alloy die-casting was a relatively new science at the time, and not fully understood. Cleanliness and purity of material are very important to the quality of die-casting. Impurities in the alloy over time causes the metal to expand, become very fragile and eventually crumble. Sadly, this was the case with the bulk of Dorfan's castings. Accordingly, it is very, very difficult today to find Dorfan locomotives with intact, solid castings. Fortunately for the operator, replacement reproduction body castings have been produced by a number of small firms, allowing the well-engineered Dorfan mechanisms to continue to operate.

Dorfan produced trains in both "Wide Gauge" – running on the same size track as Lionel's Standard Gauge, and "1 3/8-inch" or narrow gauge track – equal to Lionel's 0-gauge.

However, despite the company's originality and the quality of its product, the stock market crash of 1929 and the Depression were fatal to the company. Production ceased in about 1934, and the remaining inventory relocated to the company offices, from which it was liquidated through 1936.

Dorfan's Innovations

- Die-cast locomotive bodies
- Easily assembled locomotive construction sets
- Upright lamp post
- Switchboard or "Panel Board"
- Lacquered lithographed cars
- Sets to build both locomotive and motor from same parts
- Double-track O-gauge working hopper car
- Inserted window frames in passenger cars (inserted from outside of car)
- One-unit removable drive wheels and axles
- First automatic circuit breaker

- Die-cast trucks
- Die-cast car wheels
- Ball-bearing locomotive
- O-gauge derrick car
- Die-cast steam-outline electric locomotive
- Remote-controlled train-stop signals
- Directional remote control for locomotives
- Steam-type locomotives with separate polished metal domes and stacks
- Model position-light signals
- Model signal bridge
- Remote control uncoupler

	C5	C7	C8
50 ELECTRIC LOCOMOTIVE, narrow-gauge, red.	150	200	250
51 ELECTRIC LOCOMOTIVE, 1925-33, 0-B-0, "Take-Apart" locomotive, red, brown, maroon, dark green, turquoise, orange or olive.	80	150	200
52 ELECTRIC LOCOMOTIVE, 1928-33, 0-B-0, "Take-Apart" locomotive dark green, orange, blue or olive.	75	150	225
53 ELECTRIC LOCOMOTIVE, 1927-33, 0-B-0, red, blue, black or apple green.	225	325	425
53-RC ELECTRIC LOCOMOTIVE, 1930-33, 0-B-0, red, blue, black or apple green.	225	325	425
54 LOCOMOTIVE, 0-B-0, 1930-33, silver-blue, **with** or without air tanks.	150-**175**	275-**325**	375-**425**
54-RC LOCOMOTIVE, 0-B-0, 1930-33, silver-blue, **with** or without air tanks.	150-**175**	275-**325**	375-**425**
54 LOCOMOTIVE, 0-4-0, silver and gray, w/brass trim.	180	360	
54 ELECTRIC LOCOMOTIVE, 0-B-0, 1928-33, black, blue or red.	175	250	350
70 AUTOMATIC ELECTRIC CRANE, 1929-30	1,200	1,900	2,750

	C5	C7	C8
84 see 604.			
145 ELECTRIC LOCOMOTIVE, 0-B-0, 1925-?, narrow gauge, orange or red.	150	200	275
154 STEAM LOCOMOTIVE, 0-4-0, 1929-30, narrow gauge, black.	150	200	275
155 STEAM LOCOMOTIVE, 0-4-0, 1925-30, narrow gauge, red.	125	175	250
156 STEAM LOCOMOTIVE, 0-4-0, 1928-30, narrow gauge, black.	150	200	275
157 STEAM LOCOMOTIVE, 0-4-0, 1928-30, narrow gauge, black, blue or green.	150	200	275
160 TENDER	35	70	
310 TUNNEL, 1925-30, lithographed folding tunnel, 7-3/8-inches long.	20	40	65
319 TUNNEL, 1930, 8-1/4 inches long, composition.	15	30	40
320 TUNNEL, 1925-30, 8 inches long, lithographed, folding, sign reads "Dorfan Heights".	15	30	40
321 TUNNEL, 1927-30, 11-1/4 inches long, composition.	15	30	40
322 TUNNEL, 1927-30, 12-1/4 inches long, composition.	15	30	40
323 TUNNEL, 1927-30, 14-1/4 inches long, composition.	20	35	50

	C5	C7	C8
330 SEMAPHORE, 1925-27, 7 inches tall.	10	20	30
340 DANGER SIGNAL, 1925-30, 7 inches tall, with diamond-shaped warning signs.	10	20	30
350 TELEGRAPH POLE, 1925, 7 inches tall, with two insulators on crossarm.	8	12	20
351 LAMP POST, 1925, non-operating, 7 inches long.	5	10	15
355 PULLMAN, 1925-30, narrow gauge, four wheels, 5-1/2 inches long, yellow with orange roof, red with black roof, or orange with black roof, dark red	20	45	65
356 PULLMAN, 1930, narrow gauge, four wheels, 6-3/4 inches long	30	55	85
370 TELEGRAPH POLE, 1926-30, 7 inches tall, with two insulators on crossarm.	8	12	20
375 CROSSOVER, 45-degree, two-rail, narrow gauge.	5	10	15
385 PAIR OF MANUAL TURNOUTS, two-rail, narrow gauge.	10	20	30
400 AUTOMATIC BLOCK SIGNAL, narrow gauge, 1925-30.	20	40	80
401 CONTROL BLOCK CONTROL BLOCK SIGNAL, narrow gauge, 1926-30.	20	40	80
402 SEMAPHORE, 1927-30, narrow gauge, olive green, 12 inches tall.	15	35	70
404 TRACK CONNECTOR, 1928-30, wide gauge.			
405 SWITCHBOARD, 1925-26, control stand with six knife switches.	15	25	50
406 BELL SIGNAL, 1928-30, 8 1/2-inch tall grade crossing signal with bell, narrow gauge.	15	30	60
406 POWER SWITCH HOUSE, 1926-27, structure contains a 405.	125	250	400

	C5	C7	C8
407 SWITCHBOARD, 1926-30, control stand with six knife switches.	15	25	50
410 BRIDGE, 1925-30, narrow gauge, green base with red girders and orange deck, 30 inches long.	30	70	150
411 BRIDGE, 1926-30, narrow gauge, 40 inches long due to double center span.	50	150	300
412 ELECTRA BRIDGE, 1927-30, narrow gauge, 40 inches long due to double center span, lights of four corner posts.	100	275	500
413 BRIDGE, 1927-30, Wide gauge, 42 inches long, single center span.	25	50	115
414 BRIDGE, 1928-30, Wide gauge, 56 inches long, double center span.	35	80	150
414-L BRIDGE, 1929-30, Wide gauge, 56 inches long, double center span with four lights	75	200	400
415 TELEGRAPH POLE, 1927-30, 8-1/2 inches tall, with two insulators on crossarm.	8	12	20
416 WARNING SIGNAL, 1927-30, 8-1/2 inch tall grade crossing signal, narrow gauge	20	30	40
417 POSITION-LIGHT SIGNAL, 1930.	30	50	100
417 NEWARK CENTRAL STATION, 1927-29, illuminated, three-story, lithographed.	125	200	400
418 SIGNAL BRIDGE with one Position-light Signal, 1930.	125	250	500
418 MONTCLAIR STATION, 1927-29, non-illuminated, two-story, lithographed.	75	125	200
419 SIGNAL BRIDGE with two Position-light Signal, 1930.	150	300	600

	C5	C7	C8
420 BOULEVARD LIGHT, 1925-30, 7 inches tall.	10	15	25
421 AUTOMATIC CROSSING GATE, 1929-30, narrow gauge.	20	40	75
424 STATION, 1930, non-illuminated, two-story, lithographed.	75	125	200
425 STATION, 1930, illuminated, with flag and clock, cream or blue-gray with red roof.	60	100	150
426 STATION, 1930, illuminated, three-story, lithographed.	125	200	400
427 STATION, 1930, illuminated, 18-1/2 long, 9-1/2 inches deep, cream, two clock faces fenced roof with flagpole.	400	1,000	1,500
430 LAMP POST, 1925-30, 8-1/2 inches tall, 14 volts.	10	15	25
431 LAMP POST, 1930, 13-1/2 inches tall, 110 volts.	15	25	50
432 FLAG POLE, 1930, 20-1/2 inches tall, U.S. flag can be raised and lowered.			
433 LAMP POST, 1930, 13-1/2-inches tall, 14 volts.	15	25	50
465 TRACK BINDERS (clips), 1928-30, fits both narrow and wide gauge track per dozen.			
470 PULLMAN, 1925-30, narrow gauge, four wheels, 6-3/4 inches long, dark red body and roof (1925), dark red with black roof (1926-30), green with yellow roof (1929-30), or green body and roof (1930); lettered "5402" along with one of the names Franklin, Hamilton, Washington, Jefferson.	30	50	70
475 CROSSOVER, 1925-30, narrow gauge, 45-degree, three-rail.	15	25	40
480 PULLMAN, 1925-27, narrow gauge, four wheels, 6-3/4 inches long, brown with brass plates in 1925, or orange with decal lettering in 1926-27.	40	60	85

	C5	C7	C8
485 TURNOUTS, 1925-30, narrow gauge, three-rail, pair.	15	35	75
485-L TURNOUTS, 1925-30, narrow gauge, three-rail, pair with signal lights.	25	50	90
490 PULLMAN, 1925-30, narrow gauge, 8 wheels, 7-1/4 inches long, dark green, olive green, red, blue, or **turquoise, lettering with plates** or decal.	25-**40**	40-**70**	80-**110**
491 OBSERVATION, 1926-29, narrow gauge, 8 wheels, 7-1/4 inches long, olive green, red, blue, or **turquoise, lettering with plates** or decal.	25-**40**	40-**70**	80-**110**
492 BAGGAGE CAR, 1928-30, eight wheels, 10 inches long, green, green and red or green and black.	60	120	
493 PULLMAN, 1928-30, eight wheels, 10 inches long, green, green and red or green and black.	40	65	110
494 OBSERVATION, 1928-30, eight wheels, 10 inches long, green, green and red or green and black.	50	85	125
495 PULLMAN, 1928-30, eight wheels, 7-1/4 inches long, lettered Atlanta, Boston or Seattle, maroon, orange, blue or red.	20	45	70
496 PULLMAN, 1928-30, eight wheels, 10 inches, lettered "Boston," green, green and red or green and black.	65	110	150
496 PULLMAN, 1929-30, eight wheels, 9 inches long, blue, red or silver-blue.	35	60	100
497 OBSERVATION CAR, 1929-30, eight wheels, 9 inches long, blue, red or silver-blue.	35	60	100
498 PULLMAN, 1930, eight wheels, 7-1/4 inches long, red, olive green, turquoise or brown.	40	60	85
499 OBSERVATION CAR, 1930, eight wheels, 7-1/4 inches. long, red, olive green, turquoise or brown.	40	60	85

	C5	C7	C8
600 GONDOLA, 1926-30, narrow gauge, yellow.	20	30	50
601 BOXCAR, 1926-30, narrow gauge, NYC, tan.	20	35	65
602 BOXCAR, 1926-30, narrow gauge, UP, green.	20	35	65
603 BOXCAR, 1926-30, narrow gauge, Pennsylvania, red.	20	35	65
604 TANK CAR, 1926-30 narrow gauge, red.	25	45	75

	C5	C7	C8
605 HOPPER, 1926-30, narrow gauge, gray.	20	30	45
606 CABOOSE, 1926-30, narrow gauge, red.	20	45	75
607 CABOOSE, 1928-30, narrow gauge, red.	45	65	90
609 LUMBER CAR, narrow gauge, 1929-30.	35	65	125

	C5	C7	C8
610 DERRICK, narrow gauge, 1929-30.	65	150	300
770 STEAM LOCOMOTIVE, 4-4-0.	800	1,400	2,000
770 BAGGAGE CAR, see 998.			
771 PULLMAN, see 994 or 997.			
772 PULLMAN, see 994 or 997.			
773 OBSERVATION, see 996.			

	C5	C7	C8
780 PULLMAN, 1928-30, Wide gauge, red, orange or buff.	50	80	125
781 PULLMAN, 1928, Wide gauge, red with yellow trim.	100	125	160
785 PULLMAN, 1928-29, Wide gauge, olive green.	100	125	160
786 OBSERVATION, 1928-29, Wide gauge, olive green.	100	125	160
787 PULLMAN, 1928-30, Wide gauge, red.	100	125	160
789 OBSERVATION, 1928-30, Wide gauge, red.	100	160	200

	C5	C7	C8
789 PULLMAN, Wide gauge, maroon, mustard or orange, "Mountain Brook".	100	140	175
790 PULLMAN, Wide gauge, 1927-28, maroon, red or orange, "Pleasant View".	100	140	175
790 OBSERVATION, Wide gauge, maroon, "Pleasant View".	125	180	250
791 PULLMAN, 1928, red, identical to 790 except for two red lenses in rear.	100	140	175

	C5	C7	C8
800 GONDOLA, 1928-30, orange.	75	150	300

	C5	C7	C8

801 BOXCAR, 1928-30, green, with red or green roof.

	75	150	300

804 TANK CAR, 1928-30, blue.

	100	200	325

805 HOPPER, 1928-30, red.

	100	200	325

806 CABOOSE, 1928-30, brown.

	75	150	300

809 LUMBER CAR.

	200	350	600

875 CROSSOVER, 1927-28, 45-degree, Wide Gauge.

	10	20	35

875 CROSSOVER, 1929-30, 90-degree, Wide Gauge.

	10	20	35

	C5	C7	C8

885 TURNOUTS, 1927-30, Wide gauge, manual.

	15	35	75

885-L TURNOUTS, 1927-30, Wide gauge, manual, pair with signal lights.

	25	50	90

886-L TURNOUTS, 1930, Wide gauge, remote control, pair with signal lights.

	50	100	150

890 PULLMAN, 1926-28, Wide gauge, orange, lettered "Chicago" or "Washington".

	75	125	200

891 PULLMAN, 1926-28, Wide gauge, orange, lettered "San Francisco".

	75	125	200

990 PULLMAN, 1927-28, Wide gauge, gray, olive green, crackle brown, or maroon.

	100	140	200

991 PULLMAN, 1927, Wide gauge gray body.

	125	160	225

992 OBSERVATION, 1927-28, Wide gauge, gray, olive green, crackle brown, or maroon.

	100	140	200

992 PULLMAN, 1928-29, Wide gauge, blue.

	225	350	950

993 OBSERVATION, 1928-29, Wide gauge, blue.

	225	350	950

994 PULLMAN, 1928-30, Wide gauge, green or red, lettered 771 San Francisco, or 772 Washington.

	100	150	225

995 BAGGAGE, 1928-30, Wide gauge, green or red.

	150	200	275

	C5	**C7**	**C8**
996 OBSERVATION CAR, 1928-30, Wide gauge, green, red or maroon, w/people in windows.	125	175	250
997 PULLMAN, 1928-30, Wide gauge, lettered 771 San Francisco, or 772 Washington, green, or **ivory**.	100-**225**	130-**325**	175-**875**

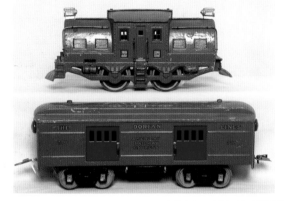

	C5	**C7**	**C8**
998 BAGGAGE, 1928-30, Wide gauge, green or **ivory**.	100-**225**	130-**325**	175-**875**
999 OBSERVATION CAR, 1928-30, Wide gauge, green or **ivory**.	100-**225**	130-**325**	175-**875**
1134 STEAM LOCOMOTIVE, 4-4-2, 1929, Wide gauge, black or green.			
1401 CONTROL BLOCK SIGNAL, 1929-30, Wide Gauge.	20	40	80
1402 SEMAPHORE, 1927-30, Wide Gauge, olive green, 12 inches tall	15	35	70
1406 BELL SIGNAL, 1928-30, 8-1/2 inch tall grade crossing signal, Wide gauge.	15	30	60
1416 WARNING SIGNAL, 1927-30, 8-1/2 inch tall grade crossing signal, Wide gauge.	20	30	40
1421 AUTOMATIC CROSSING GATE, 1929-30, Wide gauge.	20	40	75

	C5	**C7**	**C8**
3677 CABOOSE, see 606.			
3919 ELECTRIC LOCOMOTIVE, 0-B-0, 1930, orange.	275	700	1,100
3920 ELECTRIC LOCOMOTIVE, 0-B-0, 1927-30, orange, red, or green.	300	800	1,200
3930 ELECTRIC LOCOMOTIVE, 2-B-2, 1926-30, electric, orange, olive, gray, black, **blue** or green.	550-**750**	900-**1,200**	1,400-**2,200**
3931 Tank Car, see 604			

	C5	**C7**	**C8**
3931 ELECTRIC LOCOMOTIVE, 2-B-2, 1930, green, black or ivory.	1,200	1,800	3,000
5402 COACH, see 470.			
11201 see 605.			
11701 see 805.			
14048 see 600.			
29325 TANK CAR, see 804.			
121499 BOXCAR, see 801.			
126432 BOXCAR, see 602.			
253711 GONDOLA, see 800.			
486751 CABOOSE, see 606 or 806.			
517953 BOXCAR, see 603.			
S182999 BOXCAR, see 601.			

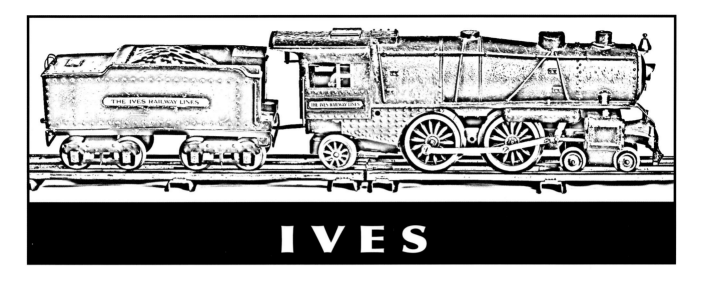

IVES

Edward Ives formed E.R. Ives and Company in 1868, when he was but 29 years old. The firm, which went through six name changes, was originally located in Plymouth, Conn., but in 1870 relocated to the more cosmopolitan Bridgeport. Ives's toys were originally made primarily of paper and were designed to be operated by air currents rising from a warm stove. Soon, however, wood, tin and even cast iron began to be used in the growing line of toys, which were now often powered by clockwork mechanisms. Despite stiff competition from foreign manufacturers, the business prospered. But just before Christmas 1900, a catastrophic fire swept through the Ives plant, reducing it to rubble. Regrouping in a new facility, the firm was back on its feet by 1901 and introduced one of its most famous lines of toys – trains. Complete railway systems were produced, with track, switches, tunnels and buildings, with the company's reliable clockwork motor powering the locomotives. These trains ran on 0 gauge track. In 1910, though, that changed as Ives began manufacturing electric trains as well.

In addition to the relatively small 0 gauge trains, Ives produced 1 gauge trains. Large trains this size, though popular in Europe, never really caught on the U.S., and in 1920, two years following Edward Ives's death, 1 gauge was replaced by Wide Gauge. Ives's wide gauge trains ran on the same size track as Lionel's Standard Gauge, but that term was trademarked, forcing Ives (and American Flyer) to term theirs Wide Gauge.

With Edward's son Harry at the helm, Ives pushed forward, fighting against a blitz of advertising – not all of it truthful – from Lionel. In 1924, the firm patented a remote control reversing switch, which was superior to any on the market. The familiar sequence of action – forward – neutral – reverse – neutral – forward is recognized as standard even today. In fact, the Ives mechanisms in general were of superb quality. Nevertheless, Lionel's ad campaign was taking its toll.

In an effort to build its market position, Ives began selling its entry-level sets at a loss. It hoped to bring consumers into the Ives camp, and then sell additional track, cars and accessories, all of which were profitable. This strategy failed, however, and in 1927, acting as chairman of the board, Harry Ives brought in Charles R. Johnson as president. But even with new blood, the company continued its downward spiral. In 1928, Ives filed for bankruptcy, with liabilities of $188,303.25. Johnson, with $245,000 worth of Christmas season stock in hand, petitioned the court to allow a private sale and quick settlement. For unknown reasons, this petition was denied, and on July 31, 1928, American Flyer and Lionel jointly purchased the Ives brand – but not the plant or tooling – for the princely sum of $73,250. Presumably this price reflected the liens of the creditors. It is believed that the Lionel-Flyer strategy was to keep the company out of the hands of other investors, who potentially could rebuild it into a formidable player in the toy train market. Harry Ives was retained as chairman through 1929, at which time he left the company. He died seven years later.

After the joint takeover, the Ives line used an amalgam of their designs, and those of the new co-owners. In 1930 Lionel took over American Flyer's stake in Ives. It is thought that the reasoning behind this was to provide Flyer with some needed tooling, which came from discontinued Lionel designs. Secondly, it gave Lionel possession of the coveted Ives reversing mechanism. The Ives operation, then existent in name only, was moved into the Lionel plant. It continued to be marketed by Lionel as a low-end product until 1933, when it was rebadged Lionel-Ives before being dropped the next year.

Lionel protected its claim to the Ives name for decades subsequent to this by manufacturing their ubiquitous track clips – used to hold pieces of sectional track together on floor setups – with the IVES name embossed in them, an ignominious end to a once proud name.

WIDE GAUGE

	C6	**C8**		**C6**	**C8**

10/10E ELECTRIC LOCOMOTIVE

10/10E ELECTRIC LOCOMOTIVE, 1931-32 peacock — 150 / 300

31 LOCOMOTIVE, 1921-1925, 0-4-0, clockwork; same general unit as No. 30, but cataloged w/brake; same body as 3250 series w/handrails; cast-iron wheels until 1924, die-cast after 1925; red or green cast-iron frame, tin body — 200 / 400

40 LOCOMOTIVE, 1904-1909, 1 ga., 4-4-0, clockwork; black cast-iron body, straight boiler w/four separate boiler bands, grab rails; nickel-plated steam dome, sand dome, bell w/front dummy headlight on top of boiler; nickel plated side rails w/separate piston rods; two rectangular cab windows on either side w/"No 40" on lithographed plate below; handbrake and reverse levers in cab; cast-iron drivers, tin pilot wheels; eight wheel tender marked "T.C.L.E. No. 40" — 1,100 / 2,200

40 TENDER, 1904-1911, eight-wheel, tin body w/rivet detail, grab rail behind body of tender; step on both sides of body; marked "T.C.L.E." inside rectangular red and gold stripes; red stripes on T-type four-wheel trucks — 250 / 500

40 LOCOMOTIVE, 1908-1909, 1 ga., 4-4-0, clockwork; Same as previous year without red and gold square outlines appear on cab roof. — 1,100 / 2,200

40 LOCOMOTIVE, 1910-1911, 1 ga., 4-4-0, clockwork; black cast-iron body w/dummy headlight on top of boiler front; three separate boiler bands, grab rails on each side of boiler; two rectangular cab windows above lithograph plate marked "IVES No. 40"; tin pony wheels, cast-iron drivers w/nickel-plated side rods w/attached piston rods; sand dome, stack and headlight part of casting, nickel bell separate; handbrake and reverse levers in cab; tender same as before — 900 / 1,800

	C6	C8

40 LOCOMOTIVE, 1912-1915, 1 ga., 4-4-0, black cast-iron body w/steam dome, sand dome, stack and dummy headlight cast together; separate brass bell; two rectangular windows on either side of cab stamped "No. 40" below; grab rails on boiler sides; cast-iron pony wheels and drive wheels w/nickel-plated drive rods w/U-shaped cross head guides; gold and red square outline on cab roof; four boiler bands painted between boiler rivets; pilot has supporting rods to boiler; reverse and handbrake levers inside cab; eight-wheel tender stamped "No. 40" 900 1,800

40 TENDER, 1912-1920, 1 ga., eight-wheel tin body and frame; rivet detail on body, tool boxes at inside front of each side w/opening lids; rivet detail on trucks, steps on both sides of frame; sides marked "No. 40" inside two white/silver rectangles; used w/late No. 40 and No. 1129 225 450

41 LOCOMOTIVE, 1908-1911, 1 ga., 0-4-0, clockwork; body casting similar to 1910 No. 40; dummy headlight, stack and steam dome part of casting w/separate brass bell; three separate boiler bands attached to body w/stanchions; cab has two windows on both sides marked "IVES No. 41" below in white on red lithographed plate; cast-iron drive wheels w/straight nickel-plated side rods; No. 40 TCLE tender w/hook coupler on front pilot 1,000 2,000

73 POLE WAGON, 1928-1930, Wide Gauge, for circus set 45 90

74 ANIMAL SET, 1928-1930, Wide Gauge, for circus set 95 190

75 CAR RUNWAYS, 1928-1930, Wide Gauge, for circus set 25 50

	C6	C8

95 BRIDGE, 1929-1930, Wide Gauge, two approach ramps w/center span w/girders 50 100

96 BRIDGE, 1929-1930, Wide Gauge, two approach ramps w/two center spans w/girders 65 130

99-1-3 BRIDGE, 1911-1920, 1 ga., two approach ramps of stone or earthen design; two viaduct center span of stonework design; flat stamped trestle sections; for mechanical 1 ga. track; 56" l. 75 150

99-1 BRIDGE, 1911-1920, 1 ga., same as contemporary No. 98, but w/two center spans. 56" l. 75 150

99-2-3 BRIDGE, 1923-1928, Wide Gauge, two approach spans, two center spans 350 700

100-1 BRIDGE, 1906-1917, 1 ga., two approach sections w/painted scenery on sides, forming a culvert between the two halves; for mechanical track; 28" l. 40 80

100-1-3 BRIDGE, 1910-1917, 1 ga., two approach sections w/painted scenery on sides, forming a culvert between the two halves; for electrical track; 28" l. 40 80

101-1 BRIDGE, 1906-1920, 1 ga., two approaches, one center span w/two viaducts, railings on both sides of track; for mechanical track; 42" l. 55 110

101-1-3 BRIDGE, 1910-1920, 1 ga., two approach ramps, center section w/two viaducts, railings on each side of track; for electrical track; 42" l. 55 110

101-2-3 BRIDGE, 1921-1922, Wide Gauge, two approach ramps, center section w/two viaducts, railing on each side of track; for electrical track 55 110

	C6	**C8**		**C6**	**C8**

170 BUFFET CAR, 1924-1925, Wide Gauge, eight-wheel; painted green w/mustard-colored window trim (1925) or tan w/red window trim (1924) body; painted roof w/clerestory strip; sliding door and four double windows; marked "The Ives Railway Lines," "170" and "Buffet" below; same lettering w/larger format and mustard colored window trim in 1925   32   65

171 BUFFET CAR, 1924, Wide Gauge, eight-wheel; green body w/red trim; sides marked "The Ives Railway Line," "171" and "Buffet"; cataloged version   32   65

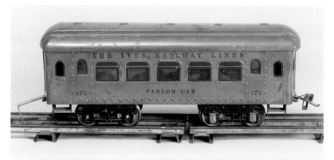

171 PARLOR CAR, 1924-1925, Wide Gauge, eight-wheel; painted green w/mustard-colored window trim (1925) or tan w/red window trim (1924); five large windows; sides marked "The Ives Railway Lines," "171" "Parlor Car"; 1925 model had larger format lettering   32   65

172 PARLOR CAR, 1924, Wide Gauge, eight wheel; green body w/red trim; marked "The Ives Railway Lines" above windows and "172," "Parlor Car" and "172" below; cataloged version   32   65

172-3 PARLOR CAR, 1924, Wide Gauge, eight-wheel; green body w/red trim; w/interior lighting; marked "The Ives Railway Lines" above windows and "172," "Parlor Car" and "172" below; cataloged version   32   65

172 OBSERVATION CAR, 1924-1925, Wide Gauge, eight-wheel; painted green w/mustard-colored trim (1925) or tan w/red window trim (1924); marked "The Ives Railway Lines" "172" above windows and "Observation" below; same lettering in 1925 w/larger format   32   65

173 OBSERVATION CAR, 1924, Wide Gauge, eight-wheel; green body w/red trim; "The Ives Railway Lines" above windows and "173," "Observation" and "173" below window; cataloged version   32   65

180 CLUB CAR, 1925-1928, Wide Gauge, 12-wheel; red, orange, or green body w/painted roof and separate clerestory strip; brass journals on trucks; passenger door at one end of side and baggage door at other; four windows; brass plate over windows marked "Pullman," brass plate below reads "Club Car"; marked "180" each door on small plate; also came rubber stamped   70   140

181 BUFFET CAR, 1912-1920, 1 ga., eight-wheel; green body w/painted roof and separate clerestory; round truss rods, steps at both ends; passenger door at left end of each side, baggage door at right; seven windows; marked "The Ives Railway Lines" above windows, and "Buffet" below; marked "No. 181" to left of baggage door   250   500

184 BUFFET CAR

181 PARLOR CAR, 1925-1928, Wide Gauge, 12-wheel; red, orange, or green body w/painted roof w/separate clerestory strip; brass journals; passenger doors at each end of side and six windows; sides marked "Made In the Ives Shops" and "181" near doors and "Pullman" above windows and "Parlor Car" below — 70 — 140

182 PARLOR CAR, 1912-1920, 1 ga., eight-wheel; green body w/painted roof w/separate clerestory strip; round truss rods; steps at each end; passenger door at each side end and 6 large windows; marked "The Ives Railway Lines" above windows and "Parlor Car" below and "No. 182" near each door — 250 — 500

182 OBSERVATION CAR, 1925-1928, Wide Gauge, 12-wheel; Red, orange, or green body w/painted roof w/separate clerestory strip; brass journals; six windows; marked "Pullman" on brass plate above windows and "Observation" below and "Made In The Ives Shops" and "182" on smaller plates — 70 — 140

183 OBSERVATION CAR, 1912-1920, 1 ga., eight-wheel; green body w/separate clerestory strip on painted roof; round truss rods; steps at each end; passenger door at front and eight various windows along side; stamped "The Ives Railway Lines" stamped above windows and "Observation" below; also stamped "No. 183" at each end — 250 — 500

184 BUFFET CAR, 1921-1925, Wide Gauge, eight-wheel; painted body generally red or green w/painted roof; passenger door w/steps at one end of side, baggage door at other and four windows; stamped lettering reads "The Ives Railway Lines" above windows and "184," "Buffet" and "184" below — 70 — 140

184 CLUB CAR, 1926-1930, Wide Gauge, eight-wheel; painted body brown, green, red, orange or cadet blue; passenger door w/steps at one end of side, baggage door at other and four windows; painted roof; brass plates over windows marked "Pullman," plates below windows read "184," "Club Car," and "Made In The Ives Shops" — 83 — 165

184-3 CLUB CAR 1926-1930, Wide Gauge, eight-wheel; painted body brown, green, red, orange or cadet blue; passenger door w/steps at one end of side, baggage door at other and four windows; interior illumination; painted roof; brass plates over windows marked "Pullman," plates below windows read "184," "Club Car," and "Made In The Ives Shops" — 83 — 165

C6   C8   **C6   C8**

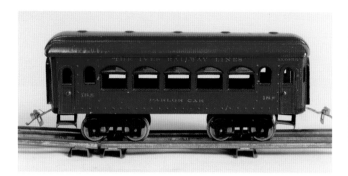

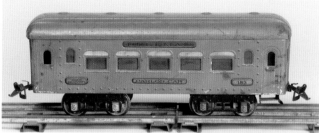

185 PARLOR CAR, 1921-1925, Wide Gauge, eight-wheel; body generally painted red or green; painted roof; passenger door w/steps at each end of side and five large windows; rubber-stamped lettering reads "The Ives Railway Lines" above windows and "185," "Parlor Car" and "185" below   118   235

185 PARLOR CAR, 1926-1930, Standard ga., eight-wheel; body painted brown, red, green, orange, or cadet blue; painted roof; passenger door w/steps at each end of side and five large windows; w/brass plates over windows read "Pullman," and "Made In The Ives Shops" and "Parlor Car" and "185" on lower plate   118   235

185-3 PARLOR CAR, 1926-1930, Wide Gauge, eight-wheel; body painted brown, red, green, orange, or cadet blue; painted roof; passenger door w/steps at each end of side and five large; interior illumination; w/brass plates over windows read "Pullman," and "Made In The Ives Shops" and "Parlor Car" and "185" on lower plate   118   235

186 OBSERVATION CAR, 1922-1925, Wide Gauge, eight-wheel; painted body painted green or red; painted roof; passenger door w/steps at front of side, steps on observation platform at sides; five large windows; "The Ives Railway Lines" rubber stamped above windows and "186," "Observation" and "186" below   118   235

186-3 OBSERVATION CAR, 1926-1930, Wide Gauge, eight-wheel; body painted brown, red, green, orange, or cadet blue; painted roof; passenger door w/steps at front of side, steps at side of observation platform; interior illumination; five large windows, brass plates above windows read "Pullman" and "186," "Observation" and "Made In The Ives Shops" below   100   200

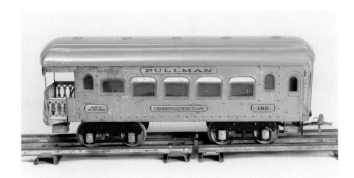

186 OBSERVATION CAR, 1926-
1930, Wide Gauge, eight-wheel; body
painted brown, red, green, orange, or
cadet blue; painted roof; passenger
door w/steps at front of side, steps
at side of observation platform; five
large windows, brass plate above
windows reads "Pullman" and "186,"
"Observation" and "Made In The Ives
Shops" below   100   200

187-3 BUFFET CAR, 1923, eight-
wheel; body painted orange, red,
green, gray, or cadet blue; painted roof
w/separate clerestory; passenger door
at end of side, w/steps, and baggage
door at other end; interior illumination
(after this year, interior lights were
standard on this series); four large
windows; stamped "The Ives Railway
Lines" above windows and "187;"
"Buffet" and "187" below; cataloged as
187-1 in 1921   118   235

187 BUFFET CAR, 1921-1928,
Wide Gauge, eight-wheel; body
painted orange, red, green, gray, or
cadet blue; painted roof w/separate
clerestory; passenger door at end
of side, w/steps, and baggage door
at other end; four large windows;
stamped "The Ives Railway Lines"
above windows and "187;" "Buffet"
and "187" below; cataloged as 187-1
in 1921   83   165

188 PARLOR CAR, 1921-1928, Wide
Gauge, eight-wheel; body painted
orange, red, green, gray, or cadet blue;
painted roof w/separate clerestory;
passenger door w/steps at each end
of side; six large windows; "The Ives
Railway Lines" above windows and
"188," "Parlor Car" and "188" below;
cataloged as 188-1 in 1921   90   180

	C6	**C8**

188-3 PARLOR CAR, 1923, Wide Gauge, eight-wheel; body painted orange, red, green, gray, or cadet blue; painted roof w/separate clerestory; passenger door w/steps at each end of side; interior illumination (after this year, interior lights were standard on this series); six large windows; "The Ives Railway Lines" above windows and "188," "Parlor Car" and "188" below; cataloged as 188-1 in 1921 — 70 — 140

189 OBSERVATION CAR, 1921-1928, Wide Gauge, eight-wheel; body painted orange, red, green, gray, or cadet blue; painted roof w/ separate clerestory; passenger door w/steps at front of side, steps at sides of observation platform six large windows; stamped "The Ives Railway Lines" above six large windows and "188," "Observation" and "188" below window; cataloged as 189-1 in 1921 — 80 — 160

189-3 OBSERVATION CAR, 1923, Wide Gauge, eight-wheel; body painted orange, red, green, gray, or cadet blue; painted roof w/separate clerestory; passenger door w/steps at front of side, steps at sides of observation platform; interior illumination (after this year, interior lights were standard on this series); six large windows; stamped "The Ives Railway Lines" above six large windows and "188," "Observation" and "188" below window; cataloged as 189-1 in 1921 — 70 — 140

	C6	**C8**

190 TANK CAR, 1921-1923, Wide Gauge, eight-wheel; same body and frame assembly as the 1 ga. tank car; gray body w/black dome w/vent pipe; frame girdles tank body w/air tank below; marked "190" and "Texas Oil" — 95 — 190

190 TANK CAR, 1923-1928, Wide Gauge, eight-wheel; orange body of tank now attached to standard car frame by saddle-type supports; w/black dome and vent pipe; grab rails and brake wheel; marked "190" and "Texas Oil" — 95 — 190

190 TANK CAR, 1929-1930, Wide Gauge, eight-wheel; collage of parts from Ives, Lionel, and Flyer — Lionel No. 215 tank car w/brass domes, American Flyer frame and Ives trucks; No. 190 car from original 1930 set which used 1921 body and frame, 1930 trucks and as a 1 ga. tank; brass plates read "Ives" and "190" — 100 — 200

| | C6 | C8 | | C6 | C8 |

191 COKE CAR, 1921-1930, Wide Gauge, eight-wheel; at first, the same as the 1 ga. Coke car, but numbered 191; brown or greenish body made up of several pieces soldered together on standard frame; stayed virtually the same throughout its history; marked "Penna R.R." and "191" on sides 70 140

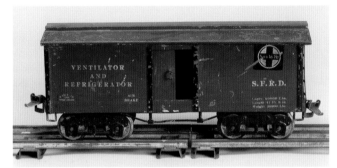

192 MERCHANDISE CAR, 1921-1928, Wide Gauge, eight-wheel; painted body and roof w/single sliding door on each side; brake wheel and ladders; marked to left of door "Ventilator and Refrigerator" and "S.F.R.D." w/the Santa Fe logo to right of door 95 190

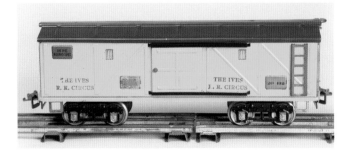

192-C CIRCUS CAR, 1928, No. 192 painted yellow w/red roof; marked for "The Ives Railway Circus" 500 1,000

20-192 MERCHANDISE CAR, 1929, Wide Gauge, green or yellow American Flyer body on Ives trucks; sliding door on each end; brass plates on Ives trucks; brass plates marked "The Ives Railway Lines" and "20-192" 300 600

192 MERCHANDISE CAR, 1930, Wide Gauge, eight-wheel; Lionel No. 214 w/Ives trucks; body painted yellow w/painted roof; double sliding doors; brass plates read "Ives" and "192" 95 190

193 LIVESTOCK CAR, 1921-1928, Wide Gauge, eight-wheel; same general car as the 1 ga. model from 1920; car made up of basic frame and ends w/separate soldered pieces constructing the body; body generally painted brown, gray or orange; painted roof; sliding door on each side; marked "The Ives Railway Lines," "193" and "Livestock" 138 275

193-C CIRCUS CAR, 1928, Wide Gauge, eight-wheel, same general car as the 1 ga. model from 1920; car made up of basic frame and ends w/ separate soldered pieces constructing the body; body painted yellow w/red roof; marked for the "The Ives Railway Circus" 500 1,000

	C6	C8		C6	C8

20-193 LIVESTOCK CAR, 1929, Wide Gauge, eight-wheel; American Flyer body and roof painted green w/ Ives trucks; single sliding door w/step on both sides at each end; brass plates read "The Ives Railway Lines" and "20-193" — 95 190

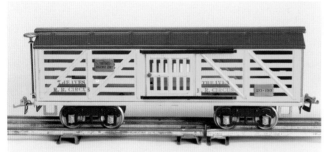

20-193-C CIRCUS CAR, 1929, Wide Gauge, eight-wheel; American Flyer body painted yellow and red roof; single sliding door w/step on both sides at each end; marked for "The Ives Railway Circus" — 500 1000

20-193 LIVESTOCK CAR, 1930, eight-wheel; Lionel No. 213 body painted orange w/red roof; Ives trucks; brass plates read "Ives" and "193" — 95 190

194 COAL CAR, 1921-1930, Wide Gauge, eight-wheel; body painted gray, black, or maroon w/black ribs; brake wheel; steps at each end; rubber stamped "Penna Coal & Coke Co." w/a P.R.R. logo in keystone — 125 250

195 CABOOSE, 1921-1927, Wide Gauge, eight-wheel; same as 1 ga. model converted to Wide Gauge trucks; red body and cupola; smoke chimney and support on roof; brake wheel on one platform; coal box beneath body; five windows; "The Ives Railway Lines" above windows and "Caboose" and "195" below window level. — 138 265

195 CABOOSE, 1928, Wide Gauge, eight-wheel; red body and cupola and black roof on both; two windows; stamped "The Ives Railway Lines" above windows and "195" and "Caboose" below — 125 250

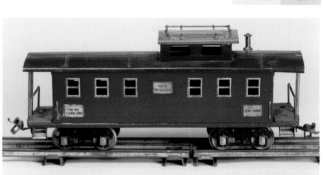

20-195 CABOOSE, 1928-1929, Wide Gauge, eight-wheel; American Flyer body on Ives trucks; red body w/red roof and red or green cupola roof; six windows w/brass window inserts and plates that read "The Ives Railway Lines" centered between windows and "Made In The Ives Shops" and "20-195" below windows — 100 200

	C6	**C8**		**C6**	**C8**

195 CABOOSE, 1930, Wide Gauge, eight-wheel; Lionel 217 caboose body on Ives trucks; short cupola w/green roof; two windows w/brass inserts, brass plates "195," "Ives," and "195" below window level; brass end railings; red body, red roof — 100 200

196 FLATCAR, 1922, Wide Gauge, eight-wheel; special version w/milk vats marked for the "Harmony Creamery" company — 400 800

196 FLATCAR, 1922-1930, Wide Gauge, eight-wheel; body painted in green, maroon, and orange; originally had a standard frame, low sides were added in 1924, sides stamped "196," "The Ives Railway Lines" and "196" — 65 130

196-C CIRCUS CAR, 1928-1929, Wide Gauge, eight-wheel; body painted in green, maroon, and orange; originally had a standard frame, low sides were added in 1924; body painted yellow and marked for "The Ives Railway Circus" — 400 800

197 LUMBER CAR, 1928-1929, Wide Gauge, eight-wheel; standard frame w/eight stakes holding wires to secure load; body painted green, orange or brown; marked "197," "The Ives Railway Lines" and "197" — 125 250

197 LUMBER CAR, 1930, Wide Gauge, eight-wheel; Lionel No. 211 car w/stakes and Ives trucks; body and stakes painted green — 125 250

20-198 GRAVEL CAR, 1929, Wide Gauge, eight-wheel; American Flyer body w/Ives trucks; black body, brass ladders; w/brake wheel; brass plates marked "The Ives Railway Lines" and "20-198" — 110 220

196-C CIRCUS CAR

	C6	C8
198 GRAVEL CAR, 1930, Wide Gauge, eight-wheel; Lionel No. 212 body w/Ives trucks; body painted black; brass brake wheels; brass plates marked "Ives" and "No. 198"	110	220
199 DERRICK CAR, 1929-1930, Wide Gauge, eight-wheel; Lionel No. 219 body on Ives trucks; body painted peacock blue w/black frame w/brass handrail on sides of cab; sides stamped "199," brass plates on rear of car read "The Ives Railway Lines" and "Ives"	370	700
200 POWER HOUSE, 1910-1914, lithographed roof and building, w/ round painted or square lithographed smokestack; houses batteries	450	900
200 FREIGHT STATION, 1923-1928, small lithographed station w/ freight punched out in open doorway; roof embossed w/shingle pattern; green or brown painted roof and base; became No. 220 in 1929	55	110
201 POWER HOUSE, 1910-1914, lithographed roof and building w/ round painted or square lithographed smokestack; made to house transformer and connections for alternating current	450	900
201 PASSENGER STATION, 1923-1928, small lithographed station w/embossed base and roof painted brown or green; goes w/No. 200 freight station	55	110
201-3 PASSENGER STATION, 1923-1928, small lithographed station w/embossed base and roof painted brown or green; goes w/No. 200 freight station; w/No. 88 lamp brackets for illumination	55	110
202 POWER HOUSE, 1910-1914, lithographed roof and building, w/ round painted or square lithographed smokestack; made to house transformer and connections for direct current	450	900

	C6	C8
203 POWER HOUSE, 1912-1914, lithographed roof and building, round painted or square lithographed smokestack; made to house two transformers and connections	850	1700
204 TRANSFORMER	10	20
205 TRANSFORMER	10	20
206 TRANSFORMER	10	20
208 TRANSFORMER	10	20
211 TRANSFORMER	10	20
212 TRANSFORMER	10	20
216 CROSSING GATE, 1923-1927, Wide Gauge, lithographed base simulating earth; two fences w/pole gate between them; manually operated	35	70
220 FREIGHT STATION, 1929-1930, lithographed building w/freight punched out in open doorway; red painted roof, green or brown painted base; formerly No. 200	55	110
221 PASSENGER STATION, 1929-1930, lithographed building w/ embossed red roof and embossed base painted brown or green; companion piece to No. 220 freight station	55	110
225 PASSENGER STATION, 1929-1930, Lionel No. 127 station; white body, red or orange roof w/ green base; brass plate above door reads "Ives R.R."	150	300

	C6	**C8**		**C6**	**C8**

226 PASSENGER STATION, 1929-1930, Lionel No. 126; crackle red finish on station w/green roof and base; brass plate over center window marked "Ives R.R. Lines" — 160 / 320

228 STATION, 1929-1930, similar to odd No. 117 w/solid base; green base and red roof w/six roof supports; four benches rest on base — 85 / 170

230 PASSENGER STATION, 1929-1930, Lionel No. 122 station w/special paint for Ives; embossed brickwork body painted yellow w/gray windows, door, and corner trim; red windows and doors open inward; brass plate over doorway reads "Waiting Room" and brass plate on roof front reads "The Ives Railway Lines" — 200 / 400

230-3XX STATION SET, 1929-1930, No. 230-X and two of No. 228 — 350 / 700

230-3 PASSENGER STATION, 1929-1930, Lionel No. 122 station w/special paint for Ives; embossed brickwork body painted yellow w/gray windows, door, and corner trim; red windows and doors open inward; interior and exterior illumination; brass plate over doorway reads "Waiting Room" and brass plate on roof front reads "The Ives Railway Lines" — 200 / 400

230-3X STATION SET, 1929-1930, No. 230-X and No. 228 — 285 / 570

241 CLUB CAR, 1928-1929, Wide Gauge, 12-wheel; American Flyer body, Ives trucks; body painted black, green, or orange; sliding baggage doors; illuminated; fourteen windows; brass plate above window reads "The Ives Railway Lines," brass plates below window read "Made In The Ives Shops," "Club Car" and "241" — 400 / 800

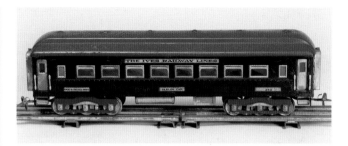

242 PARLOR CAR, 1928-1929, Wide Gauge, 12-wheel; American Flyer body on Ives trucks; black, green or orange body; passenger door at each end of side; illuminated eight windows; brass plate reads "The Ives Railway Lines" above window and "Made In The Ives Shops," "Parlor Car" and "242" — 300 / 600

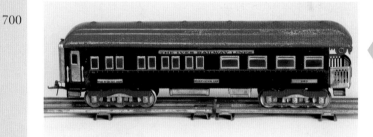

243 OBSERVATION CAR, 1928-1929, Wide Gauge, 12-wheel; American Flyer body on Ives trucks; body painted black, green, or orange painted body; illuminated; windows; w/brass platform railing; brass plates above windows read "The Ives Railway Lines"; brass plate below window reads "Made In The Ives Shops," "Observation" and "243" — 300 / 600

246 DINING CAR, 1930, Wide Gauge, 12-wheel; Lionel body on Ives trucks; body painted orange, black, blue or yellow; roof w/separate clerestory; air tanks beneath car; opening passenger door at each end of side; illuminated; five double windows; decal above windows reads "The Ives Railway Lines" and "Dining Car," "Made In the Ives Shops Dining Car" and "Ives No. 246" — 450 / 900

C6 **C8** **C6** **C8**

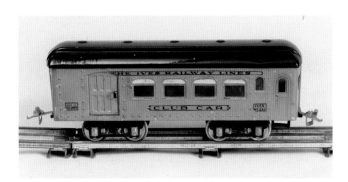

247 CLUB CAR, 1930, Wide Gauge, 12-wheel; Lionel body on Ives trucks; body painted orange, black, blue and yellow; painted roof w/separate clerestory strip; air tanks beneath car; opening passenger door at each end of side w/sliding baggage door; three double windows; illuminated; decal over door reads "The Ives Railway Lines" and "Made In The Ives Shops," "Ives No. 247" and "Club Car" 200 400

248 PULLMAN CAR, 1930, Wide Gauge, 12-wheel; Lionel body on Ives trucks; body painted orange, black, blue, or yellow; illuminated; painted roof w/separate clerestory; air tanks beneath body; opening passenger doors at each end of side; five double windows; decal above windows reads "The Ives Railway Lines," and "Made In The Ives Shops," "Ives No. 248", and "Pullman" below the windows 400 800

249 OBSERVATION CAR, 1930, Wide Gauge, 12-wheel; Lionel body on Ives trucks; body painted orange, black, blue and yellow; painted roof w/ separate clerestory; Air tanks beneath body; illuminated; passenger door at front and brass observation railing at rear; five double windows; decal above windows reads "The Ives Railway Lines," and below window level "Made In The Ives Shops," "Observation" and "Ives No. 249" below windows 400 800

250 VILLAGE HOUSE, 1929-1930, lithographed building w/painted base; Lionel No. 184 bungalow, Ives name on bottom 95 190

251 DUTCH COLONIAL HOUSE, 1929-1930, painted body and roof w/ lithographed brick chimney, Ives name on bottom. 100 200

252 VILLAGE HOUSE, 1929-1930, Lionel No. 191 Villa; crackle red finish on house w/green roof; Ives name on bottom 100 200

253 POWER HOUSE, 1929-1930, Lionel No. 435 Power station; white house, green or brown base w/red roof; Ives name on bottom 150 300

254 POWER HOUSE, 1929, Lionel No. 436 station, Ives name on bottom; larger than No. 253 160 320

255 SIGNAL TOWER, 1929-1930, Lionel No. 438 signal tower painted red-orange w/green roof; switch on back of station 150 300

	C6	C8		C6	C8

300 SEMAPHORE, 1922-1930, manual operation, single arm; track leads illuminate box behind signal arm — 40 / 80

301 SEMAPHORE, 1922-1930, Mechanical operation, double arm; track leads illuminate boxes behind signal arms — 45 / 90

302 PLATFORM SIGNAL, 1923-1928, two semaphore posts on raised platform w/ladder; manual operation, electric lights in boxes behind signal arms; same general appearance as No. 109 — 50 / 100

306 ELECTRIC STREET LAMP, 1923-1932, double gooseneck arms, cast-iron or die-cast base — 38 / 75

307 ELECTRIC STREET LAMP, 1923-1931, double gooseneck arms, cast-iron or die-cast base. — 100 / 200

308 ELECTRIC STREET LAMP, 1928-1930, single columnar lamp, die-cast — 35 / 70

310 PLATFORM SIGNAL, 1923-1926, two semaphore arms on platform w/ladder; manual operation; same as No. 302 without lights; new version of old No. 109 — 30 / 60

330 SEMAPHORE, 1924-1930, automatic, black, single arm w/ladder; electrically operated signal and lights; brass mast and Lionel signal arm in 1930 — 45 / 90

331 TARGET SIGNAL, 1924-1930, electrically operated; two colored cellophane pieces behind round target face w/white painted metal face and green base w/white post; maroon base and brass face in 1930 — 50 / 100

332 BELL SIGNAL, 1924-1930, automatic; green base, white post w/ bell in center of diamond shaped sign lettered "Railroad Crossing. Look Out For engine"; bell operated electrically; 1930 had maroon base w/brass diamond — 35 / 70

332 BAGGAGE CAR, 1931-1932, Wide Gauge, eight-wheel; Lionel car; body painted peacock blue w/orange doors w/painted roof; illuminated; four windows, two baggage doors on each side; "The Ives Railway Lines" decal below roof line marked "332," "Railway Mail" and "332" stamped below window level — 75 / 150

333 BANJO SIGNAL, 1924-1930, mechanism enclosed in white case w/front cellophane insert for light, green base, white post and body, bell on rear of signal; marked "Railroad Crossing Look Out For Engine" and "Danger Stop Look And Listen"; activated by train and operated electrically; 1930 maroon base, body, brass face — 40 / 80

334 CROSSING GATE, 1928-1930, automatic; lithographed base simulates earth and roadway; fence on one side, signal shanty on other side w/crossing gate operated by oncoming train — 95 / 190

338 BRIDGE APPROACH TELLTALE, 1924-1930, cast base, white post and arm w/hanging chains — 50 / 100

339 TRACK BUMPER, 1928-1930, Wide Gauge, Lionel bumper w/red light on top — 12 / 25

	C6	C8		C6	C8

339 PULLMAN CAR, 1931-1932, Wide Gauge, eight-wheel; Lionel car; peacock blue body w/orange trim; illuminated; six double windows w/ two passenger doors per side, steps beneath doors; "The Ives Railway Lines" on decal below roof; stamped "339," "Pullman" and "339" below window — 85 — 170

340 SPRING BUMPER, 1929-1930, Wide Gauge, sheet-steel w/spring cross bar; Lionel — 10 — 20

1129 LOCOMOTIVE, 1915-1920, 1 ga., 2-4-2; black cast-iron body, pony and drive wheels; three-piece drive rods; two separate boiler bands and nickel bell; two arched cab windows; marked "Ives No. 1129" below windows; w/No. 40 tender — 850 — 1,700

1132-R LOCOMOTIVE, Wide Gauge, same as above engines w/automatic reverse. — 950 — 1,900

1132 LOCOMOTIVE, 1921-1926, Wide Gauge, 0-4-0; black, tan, or white cast-iron body w/two boiler bands; cast-iron drive wheels w/three piece rods; nickel bell and grab rails; cast-iron or die-cast wheels; headlight in center of boiler front; two cab windows; marked "Ives 1132" below windows, w/tin No. 40 tender — 500 — 1,000

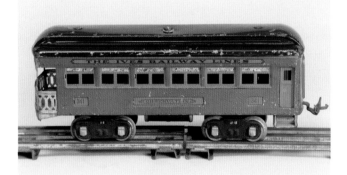

341 OBSERVATION CAR, 1931-1932, Wide Gauge, eight-wheel. Lionel car, peacock blue body w/orange w/brass platform railing; illuminated; six double windows; "The Ives Railway Lines" on decal above windows and "341," "Observation" and "341" stamped below windows — 85 — 170

1132 LOCOMOTIVE, 1928, Wide Gauge, 4-4-0; uncataloged model; cast-iron body, similar to 1927 No. 1134 but without engineer figure inside; headlight on top of boiler w/separate grab rails; die-cast wheels and four-piece drive rods; w/die-cast No. 40 tender — 950 — 1,900

1134-R LOCOMOTIVE, Wide Gauge, same as above engines w/automatic reverse — 1100 — 2200

1134 LOCOMOTIVE, 1927, Wide Gauge, 4-4-0; President Washington model; olive cast-iron body w/headlight on top of boiler; die-cast wheels w/ four-piece drive rods; engineer in cab w/tin No. 40 tender — 1050 — 2100

	C6	**C8**		**C6**	**C8**

1134 LOCOMOTIVE

1134 LOCOMOTIVE, 1928-1930, Wide Gauge, 4-4-2; die-cast body and wheels, w/die-cast No. 40 tender; headlight on boiler top or in center front; separate handrails, brass bell; brass plates marked "Made In The Ives Shops" on front of engine; also marked "The Ives Railway Lines" below cab windows and on the side of tender — 1,100 — 2,200

1760 LOCOMOTIVE, 1931, Wide Gauge, 2-4-0; black Lionel No. 384 w/Ives plate on front marked "Made In The Ives Shops"; also marked "Ives 1760" beneath cab windows; w/No. 1760 tender w/copper journals — 263 — 525

1764 LOCOMOTIVE, 1932, Wide Gauge, 4-4-4; New Haven-style electric box cab; terra-cotta and maroon; die-cast wheels w/nickel tires and nickel drive rods; brass railings and headlights at each end; brass plates read "1764" — 1,500 — 3,000

1766 PULLMAN CAR, 1932, Wide Gauge, 12-wheel; terra-cotta and maroon; illuminated; copper journals; door at each end of side w/steps and handrails; seven double windows; brass plates below windows read "1766," "Ives Lines" and "1766" — 500 — 1,000

1767 BAGGAGE CAR, 1932, Wide Gauge, 12-wheel; terra-cotta and maroon, baggage door and mail door on each side; illuminated; copper journals; brass plates read "1767," "Ives Lines" and "1767" — 500 — 1,000

1768 OBSERVATION CAR, 1932, Wide Gauge, 12-wheel; terra-cotta and maroon; door at front and seven double windows on each side; brass platform railings; copper journals; brass plates read "1768," "Observation," and "1768" — 500 — 1,000

1770 LOCOMOTIVE, 1932, Wide Gauge, 2-4-4; black Lionel No. 390 w/Ives plates marked "Made In The Ives Shops" in front and "Ives 1770" beneath car windows; No. 1770 tender w/copper journals — 350 — 700

1771 LUMBER CAR, 1931-1932, Wide Gauge, eight-wheel; black Lionel No. 511, nickel stakes, copper or nickel journals; single wood piece simulated load; stamped "Ives No. 1771" on bottom — 50 — 100

1772 GONDOLA, 1931-1932, Wide Gauge, eight-wheel; peacock Lionel No. 512, Copper or nickel journals; brass plates read "Ives" and "No. 1772" — 50 — 100

1773 CATTLE CAR, 1931-1932, Wide Gauge, eight-wheel; green Lionel No. 513, orange roof, nickel or copper journals; brass plates read "Ives" and "No. 1773" — 175 — 350

1774 BOXCAR, 1931-1932, Wide Gauge, eight-wheel; yellow No. 514 w/orange roof; nickel or copper journals; brass plates read "Ives" and "No. 1774" — 280 — 560

1775 TANK CAR, 1931-1932, Wide Gauge, eight-wheel; white Lionel No. 515 w/brass ladders and trim; nickel or copper journals; brass plates read "Ives" and "No. 1775" — 375 — 750

	C6	C8		C6	C8

1776 COAL CAR, 1931-1932, Wide Gauge, eight-wheel; red Lionel No. 516, nickel or copper journals; brass plates read "Ives" and "No. 1776" — 250 / 500

1777 CABOOSE, 1931-1932, Wide Gauge, eight-wheel; green Lionel No. 517 w/brass platforms and windows inserts; nickel or copper journals; brass plates read "Ives" and "No. 1777" — 68 / 135

1778 REEFER, 1931-1932, Wide Gauge, white Lionel No. 514R w/ peacock roof, nickel or copper journals; two doors per side, brass plates read "Ives" and "No. 1778" — 500 / 1,000

1779 DERRICK, 1931-1932, Wide Gauge, eight-wheel; green Lionel No. 219; nickel or copper journals; brass plates marked "Ives" and "No. 1779" — 325 / 650

1854 CROSSING, 1931-1932, Wide Gauge, 45 degrees — 4 / 8

1856 BUMPER, 1931-1932, Wide Gauge, sprung bar type — 10 / 20

1858 BUMPER, 1931-1932, Wide Gauge, sprung bar type w/illumination — 10 / 20

1861 TUNNEL, 1931-1932, Wide Gauge, papier-mâché, 19" l. — 15 / 30

1861 TUNNEL, 1931-1932, Wide Gauge, papier-mâché, 23" l. — 15 / 30

1864 SEMAPHORE, 1931-1932, Wide Gauge, single blade, cast base, manual operation; formerly Ives No. 300 — 45 / 90

1865 SEMAPHORE, 1931-1932, Wide Gauge, double blade, cast base, manual operation; formerly Ives No. 301 — 45 / 90

1883 BELL SIGNAL, 1931-1932, Wide Gauge, automatic; green base, brass diamond warning sign and bells on back — 60 / 120

1885 TARGET SIGNAL, 1931-1932, Wide Gauge, automatic; cast base; same as No. 331 — 65 / 130

1896 SWITCHES, 1931-1932, Wide Gauge, manual, illuminated — 15 / 30

1898 SWITCHES, 1931-1932, Wide Gauge, electrically operated, illuminated — 20 / 40

1899 CROSSING, 1931-1932, Wide Gauge, 90 degrees — 8 / 16

1901 PANEL BOARD, 1932, red; controls six separate trains or accessories by means of knife switches; Lionel No. 439 — 75 / 150

1902 FLOODLIGHT TOWER, 1932, two lights on steel tower; green and terra-cotta; Lionel No. 92 — 75 / 150

1903 SEMAPHORE, 1932, Wide Gauge, single blade, automatic; Lionel 80 — 75 / 150

1908 TRAIN CONTROL, 1932, Wide Gauge, automatic, stops and starts train; same as No. 1907 — 75 / 150

3235 LOCOMOTIVE, 1924, Wide Gauge, 0-4-0; electric box cab; green or brown tin body w/cast-iron frame and wheels; hand reverse; operating headlight, brass pantographs and brass bell; three windows per side, door on each end; marked "The Ives Railway Lines" beneath left window and "3235 N.Y.C. & H.R." beneath right window — 98 / 195

3235-R LOCOMOTIVE, 1924-1929, Wide Gauge, 0-4-0; electric box cab; green tin body w/stamped steel frame; automatic reverse; operating headlight, brass pantographs and brass bell; die-cast wheels w/nickel tires; three windows per side, door at each end; brass plates read "The Ives Railway Lines" and "Motor 3235" beneath windows — 98 / 195

	C6	C8		C6	C8

3235 LOCOMOTIVE, 1925-1927, Wide Gauge, 0-4-0; electric box cab; green or brown tin body, w/cast-iron frame; hand reverse; die-cast wheels w/nickel tires; operating headlight, brass pantographs and brass bell; three windows per side and door at each end; brass plate marked "The Ives Railway Lines" beneath left window and "Motor 3235" beneath right window — 98 — 195

3235 LOCOMOTIVE, 1928-1929, Wide Gauge, 0-4-0; electric box cab; green tin body w/stamped steel frame; operating headlight, brass pantographs and brass bell; die-cast wheels w/nickel tires; three windows per side, door at each end; brass plates read "The Ives Railway Lines" and "Motor 3235" beneath windows — 98 — 195

3236 LOCOMOTIVE, 1925-1927, Wide Gauge, 0-4-0; electric box cab; tan or red tin body w/cast-iron frame; die-cast wheels w/nickel tires; operating headlight, brass pantographs and bell; hand reverse; three windows per side, door at each end; brass plates read "The Ives Railway Lines" and "Motor 3236" — 263 — 525

3236-R LOCOMOTIVE, 1925-1930, 0-4-0; electric box cab; black, blue or red body tin body similar to Lionel No. 8; stamped steel frame w/brass journals and trim; automatic reverse; operating headlight; brass rail around roof on brass stanchions; rectangular brass plates read "Ives," "Made By The Ives Corp.," and "3236" — 263 — 525

3236 LOCOMOTIVE, 1928, Wide Gauge, 0-4-0; electric box cab; tan or red tin body w/stamped steel frame; die-cast wheels w/nickel tires; operating headlight, brass pantographs and bell; brass journals; three windows per side door at each end. Brass plates w/"The Ives Railway Lines" and "Motor 3236" — 263 — 525

3236 LOCOMOTIVE, 1929-1930, Wide Gauge, 0-4-0; electric box cab; black, blue or red, tin body similar to Lionel No. 8; stamped steel frame w/ brass journals and trim; hand reverse; operating headlight; brass rail around roof on brass stanchions; rectangular brass plates read "Ives," "Made By The Ives Corp.," and "3236" — 263 — 525

3237-R LOCOMOTIVE, 1926-1930, Wide Gauge, 0-4-0; St. Paul-type electric center cab; green or black steel body, stamped-steel frame w/separate pilots; two operating headlights, brass pantograph, bell and whistle; die-cast wheels w/nickel tires; automatic reverse; brass journals and springs on frame; brass window inserts; grab rails; brass plates read "The Ives Railway Lines" and "Motor 3237" — 325 — 650

| | **C6** | **C8** | | **C6** | **C8** |

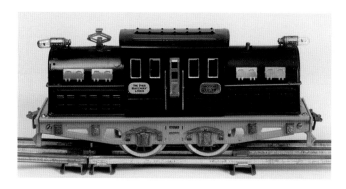

3237 LOCOMOTIVE, 1926-1930, Wide Gauge, 0-4-0; St. Paul-type electric center cab; green or black steel body, stamped-steel frame w/separate pilots; two operating headlights, brass pantograph, bell and whistle; die-cast wheels w/nickel tires; hand reverse; brass journals and springs on frame; brass window inserts; grab rails; brass plates read "The Ives Railway Lines" and "Motor 3237" — 325 — 650

3238 LOCOMOTIVE, 1913-1917, 1 ga., 2-4-2; cast-iron electric S-1 type center cab; black body some w/gray roof; two operating headlights; cast pantographs; spoked pilot and drive wheels; manual reverse; no bell or whistle; stamped "The Ives Railway Lines" to left of cab door and "Motor 3238" to right — 250 — 500

3239 LOCOMOTIVE, 1913-1916, 1 ga., 0-4-4-0; cast-iron electric S-1 type center cab; black body w/one operating headlight and one dummy; silver pantograph on each hood; axle journals on side frames do not line up w/axles; one truck has motor; manual reverse; marked "The Ives Railway Lines" beneath window to left of door and "Motor 3239" beneath right — 600 — 1,200

3239 LOCOMOTIVE, 1917-1920, 1 ga., 0-4-4-0; cast-iron electric S-3 type center cab; gray, black or olive body w/one operating and one dummy headlight; nickel pantograph, whistle and bell; axle journals now line up w/axles; one power truck; manual reverse; stamped "The Ives Railway Lines" beneath window and "Motor 3239" beneath right window — 575 — 1,150

3240 LOCOMOTIVE, 1912-1916, 1 ga.,0-4-0; cast-iron electric S-1 type center cab; black body w/two operating headlights, nickel pantographs, bell and whistle; separate grab rails; chains between trucks and between end railings; axle journals on side frames do not line up w/axles; one power truck; manual reverse; stamped "The Ives Railway Lines" beneath window and "Motor 3240" beneath right window — 900 — 1,800

3240 LOCOMOTIVE, 1917-1920, 1 ga., 0-4-4-0; cast-iron electric S-3 type center cab; black or gray body w/two operating headlights; nickel pantographs, bell and whistle; one truck has motor; axle journals line up w/axle; manual reverse; stamped "The Ives Railway Lines" stamped beneath window and "Motor 3240" beneath right window — 600 — 1,200

3240 LOCOMOTIVE, 1921, 0-4-4-0; cast-iron electric S-3 type center cab; black or gray body w/two operating headlights; nickel pantographs, bell and whistle; one truck has motor; axle journals line up w/axle; frames were altered to accommodate use on standard gauge track; manual reverse; stamped "The Ives Railway Lines" stamped beneath window and "Motor 3240" beneath right window — 1,000 — 2,000

| | C6 | C8 | | | C6 | C8 |

3241-R LOCOMOTIVE, 1921-1925, 0-4-0; red or green tin body, cast-iron frame, sometimes w/third rail pickup hoes like No. 3242; no handrails; type-S electric center cab; operating headlight, brass pantographs and brass bell; cast-iron wheels through 1924, die-cast w/nickel tires in 1925; automatic reverse; stamped "The Ives Railway Lines" beneath window and "3241 N.Y.C. & H.R." beneath right window

150   300

 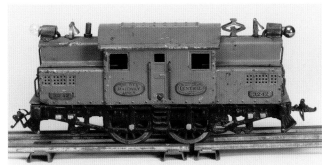 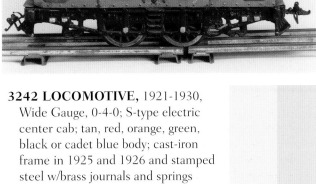

3242 LOCOMOTIVE, 1921-1930, Wide Gauge, 0-4-0; S-type electric center cab; tan, red, orange, green, black or cadet blue body; cast-iron frame in 1925 and 1926 and stamped steel w/brass journals and springs after that; die-cast wheels w/nickel tires; two operating headlights, brass pantographs; handrails; automatic reverse; brass plates read "The Ives Railway Lines," "New York Central Lines" and "3242"

225   450

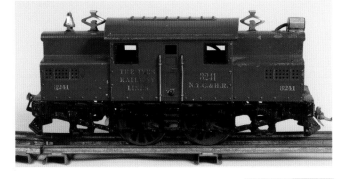

3241 LOCOMOTIVE, 1921-1925, Wide Gauge, 0-4-0; red or green tin body, cast-iron frame, sometimes w/third rail pickup hoes like No. 3242; no handrails; type-S electric center cab; operating headlight, brass pantographs and brass bell; cast-iron wheels through 1924, die-cast w/nickel tires in 1925; hand reverse; stamped "The Ives Railway Lines" beneath window and "3241 N.Y.C. & H.R." beneath right window

150   300

3242 LOCOMOTIVE, 1921-1924, Wide Gauge, 0-4-0; S-type electric center cab; red or green body; cast-iron frame w/outside rail pick-up shoes; two operating headlights and brass pantographs; cast-iron wheels; hand rails on sides and ends; stamped "The Ives Railway Lines" below window and "3242 N.Y.C. & H.R." beneath right window

225   450

3242-R LOCOMOTIVE, 1925-1930, Wide Gauge, 0-4-0; S-type electric center cab; tan, red, orange, green, black, or cadet blue body; cast-iron frame in 1925 and 1926 and stamped steel w/brass journals and springs after that; die-cast wheels w/nickel tires; two operating headlights, brass pantographs; handrails; hand reverse; brass plates read "The Ives Railway Lines," "New York Central Lines" and "3242"

225   450

	C6	C8

3243 LOCOMOTIVE, 1921-1924, Wide Gauge, 4-4-4; type-S electric center cab; green or orange tin body w/cast-iron frame; two operating headlights; handrails on sides and ends; brass pantographs, bell and whistle; cast iron wheels; stamped "The Ives Railway Lines" to left window and "3243 N.Y.C. & H.R." below right window — 450 / 900

3243-R LOCOMOTIVE, 1921-1928, Wide Gauge, 4-4-4; S-type electric center cab; black or cadet blue steel body w/stamped steel frame; grab rails on sides and ends; brass journals and trim; two operating headlights; brass pantographs, bell and whistle; die-cast wheels w/nickel tires; automatic reverse; brass plates read "The Ives Railway Lines," "New York Central Lines" and "3243" — 550 / 1,100

3243 LOCOMOTIVE, 1925-1927, Wide Gauge, 4-4-4; type-S electric center cab; red, green or orange tin body w/cast-iron frame; two operating headlights; handrails on sides and ends; brass pantographs, bell and whistle; die-cast wheels w/nickel tires; brass plates read "3243," "The Ives Railway Lines," "New York Central Lines" and "3243" — 500 / 1,000

3243 LOCOMOTIVE, 1928, Wide Gauge, 4-4-4; S-type electric center cab; black or cadet blue steel body w/ stamped steel frame; grab rails on sides and ends; brass journals and trim; two operating headlights; brass pantographs, bell and whistle; die-cast wheels w/ nickel tires; hand reverse; brass plates read "The Ives Railway Lines," "New York Central Lines" and "3243" — 500 / 1,000

3245 LOCOMOTIVE, 1928, Wide Gauge, 4-4-4; electric center cab; No. 3237 black body on black stamped-steel frame w/brass journals and springs; brass ventilator on hoods, brass window inserts and doors; two operating headlights; brass bell and pantograph; die-cast wheels w/nickel tires; brass plates read "The Ives Railway Lines" and "Motor 3245" — 1,000 / 2,000

3245-R LOCOMOTIVE, 1928-1930, Wide Gauge, 4-4-4; enter electric cab; longer steel hoods, same cab as before; black body w/orange stamped-steel frame; die-cast wheels w/nickel tires; brass ventilators, window inserts and doors; handrails on hoods, ends and by doors on sides; larger, working nickel pantographs, bell, whistle and headlight shrouds; automatic reverse; brass plates reads "Motor 3245" and "The Ives Railway Lines" — 1,000 / 2,000

3245 LOCOMOTIVE, 1929-1930, Wide Gauge, 4-4-4; enter electric cab; longer steel hoods, same cab as before; black body w/orange stamped-steel frame; die-cast wheels w/nickel tires; brass ventilators, window inserts and doors; handrails on hoods, ends and by doors on sides; larger, working nickel pantographs, bell, whistle and headlight shrouds; hand reverse; brass plates reads "Motor 3245" and "The Ives Railway Lines" — 1,000 / 2,000

	C6	C8		C6	C8

7345 MERCHANDISE CAR, 1915-1920, 1 ga., eight-wheel; yellow tin body w/blue roof w/catwalk; brake wheel; sliding door on each side; marked "Ventilator" and "Refrigerator" to left of door and "S.F.R.D. 7345" w/Santa Fe logo to right of door 150 300

7446 LIVESTOCK CAR, 1915-1920, 1 ga., eight-wheel; brown body made up of tin strips soldered together on a stock frame; brown roof w/catwalk; sliding doors also made of soldered pieces; brake wheel on one end; marked "Livestock" and "7446" below roof line and "P.R.R." and "Air Brake" on frame sides 125 250

7546 CABOOSE, 1915-1920, 1 ga., eight-wheel; red tin body and cupola w/brown roof; black smokestack, ladders and window trim; tool boxes beneath frame; five windows on each side; marked "The Ives Railway Lines" above windows and "Made In The Ives Shops," "Caboose" and "7546" windows 160 320

7648 HOPPER CAR, 1915-1920, 1 ga., eight-wheel; black or gray w/ black ribs; brake wheels and steps; marked "Penna Coal & Coke Co" w/"P.R.R." logo on sides 130 260

7849 TANK CAR, 1915-1920, 1 ga., eight-wheel; dark gray tank w/mounted trucks; catwalk frame soldered to sides of tank; Air tank below main tank; single dome w/air vent; marked "Texas Oil," w/"Air Brake" and "7849" also on sides 165 330

7950 COKE CAR, 1915-1920, 1 ga., eight-wheel; brown car made up of many soldered together; w/pieces of tin mounted to standard frame; brake wheel at one end; marked "Air Brake," "P.R.R." and "7950" on frame sides 165 330

	C6	**C8**		**C6**	**C8**

O GAUGE

	C6	C8
TRAIN SET, cast-iron, big six locomotive w/tender and two gondolas	1,875	2,500
0 LOCOMOTIVE, 1903-1905, O ga., 2-2-0; tin body, embossed boiler bands, black and red litho; four-wheel painted tender w/cast-iron wheels; arched windows on each side	225	450
0 LOCOMOTIVE, 1906, O ga., 2-2-0; tin body, embossed boiler bands; blue and white or green and white lithograph, some red and white; F.E. No. 1 tender, four-wheels, two windows per cab side w/number beneath	200	400
0 LOCOMOTIVE, 1907-1909, O ga., 2-2-0; cast-iron body, wheel arrangement reverse bicycle type, w/drivers in front; lithographed plates under cab windows "IVES No. 0," rectangular cab window; separate tin boiler bands; dummy headlight; F.E. No. 1 tender w/tin wheels	175	350
0 LOCOMOTIVE, 1910-1912, O ga., 2-2-0; cast-iron body w/lithographed number boards beneath cab windows; large drive wheels behind smaller tin wheels; dummy headlight, two separate boiler bands; F.E. No. 1 tender	150	300
0 LOCOMOTIVE, 1913-1915, O ga., 2-2-0; black cast-iron body, separate boiler bands, dummy headlight; same wheel arrangement as previous year, same general engine; number stamped beneath rectangular window; No. 1 tender	125	250
00 LOCOMOTIVE, 1930, O ga., 0-4-0; black or red cast-iron boiler, no boiler band; two rectangular windows per cab side marked "IVES No. 00" beneath; tin wheels; dummy headlight in boiler front; No. 9 tender	145	290
1 TENDER, 1903-1905, O ga., hand painted; four cast-iron wheels, tin body	100	200

	C6	C8
1 LOCOMOTIVE, 1906, O ga., 2-2-0; painted and lithographed tin in blue and white or green and white; embossed boiler bands; two rectangular windows on both sides of cab w/number beneath; F.E. No. 1 tender w/tin wheels	200	400
1 TENDER, 1906-1909, O ga., F.E. No. 1, four tin wheels, tin body, red lithograph	75	150
1 LOCOMOTIVE, 1907-1909, O ga., 2-2-0; black painted cast-iron w/two separate boiler bands, dummy headlight; drive wheels in front w/two small tin wheels trailing behind; lithographed plates below rectangular cab window read "IVES No. 1"; four-wheel F.E. No. 1 tender	175	350
1 LOCOMOTIVE, 1910-1912, O ga., 2-2-0; drive wheels behind small tin wheels, two separate boiler bands; rectangular cab window w/lithograph number board beneath; dummy headlight; four-wheel F.E. No. 1 tender	150	300
1 TENDER, 1910-1913, O ga., tin body lithographed "F.E. No. 1," four tin wheels	55	110
1 TENDER, 1914, O ga., tin body lithographed "IVES No. 1," four tin wheels	50	100
1 LOCOMOTIVE, 1926-1928, O ga., 0-4-0; cataloged in black w/one separate tin boiler band, tin wheels, no side rods; rectangular cab window stamped "IVES No. No. 11" beneath; four-wheel No. 11 tender in NYC & HR livery; dummy headlight in boiler front	125	250
1 LOCOMOTIVE, 1929, O ga., 0-4-0, same basic design as previous year, but now cataloged w/handbrake.	135	270
2 LOCOMOTIVE, 1906, O ga., 2-2-0; painted tin body, embossed boiler bands; two rectangular cab windows on either side w/number painted beneath; F.E. No. 1 tender w/tin wheels	200	400

	C6	C8

2 LOCOMOTIVE, 1907-1909, O ga., 2-2-0; black painted cast-iron w/two separate boiler bands, dummy headlight; drive wheels are in front of tin trailing wheels; rectangular cab window on both side, plates below lithographed "IVES No. 2," F.E. No. 1 tender — 175 — 350

2 LOCOMOTIVE, 1910-1912, O ga., 2-2-0, black cast-iron boiler w/two separate boiler bands, dummy headlight; drive wheels behind small tin wheels now; rectangular window on both sides of cab, plates below lithographed "IVES No. 2"; F.E. No. 1 tender — 150 — 300

2 LOCOMOTIVE, 1913-1915, O ga., 2-2-0; black cast-iron boiler, same general engine as previous year, stamped number now; Ives No. 1 tender — 135 — 270

3 LOCOMOTIVE, 1903-1905, O ga., 2-2-0; painted tin body, lithographed roof, embossed boiler bands; same as No. 0, w/stronger spring; one arched cab window per side, stack is only detail on boiler top; painted tender w/cast-iron wheels — 225 — 450

3 LOCOMOTIVE, 1906, O ga., 2-2-0; painted and lithographed tin in blue and white or green and white; embossed boiler bands; two rectangular windows per cab side w/number painted beneath; F.E. No. 1 tender w/tin wheels — 200 — 400

3 LOCOMOTIVE, 1907-1909, O ga., 2-2-0; reverse bicycle wheel pattern w/large drive wheels in front; black cast-iron body w/two separate boiler bands, dummy headlight; lithographed plate below rectangular cab window reads "Ives No. 3"; F.E. No. 1 tender — 175 — 350

3 LOCOMOTIVE, 1910-1911, O ga., 2-2-0; black cast-iron body w/dummy headlight, two separate boiler bands; drive wheels now behind small tin wheels; rectangular cab window per side, lithographed "IVES No. 3" on plate below; F.E. No. 1 tender — 150 — 300

3 LOCOMOTIVE, 1912, O ga., 0-4-0; black boiler, two separate boiler bands, dummy headlight; four cast-iron wheels w/drive rods; rectangular cab window lithographed "IVES No. 3" on plate below; F.E. No. 1 tender w/tin wheels — 125 — 250

4 LOCOMOTIVE, 1910-1912, O ga., 2-2-0; black cast-iron boiler w/two separate boiler bands, drive wheels behind small tin wheels; dummy headlight; w/rectangular cab window lithographed "IVES No. 4" on plate below; F.E. No. 1 tender — 125 — 250

4 LOCOMOTIVE, 1912, O ga., 0-4-0; black cast-iron boiler w/two separate boiler bands, dummy headlight; four cast-iron wheels w/drive rods; rectangular cab window lithographed "IVES No. 4" on plate below; F.E. No. 1 tender w/tin wheels — 115 — 230

5 LOCOMOTIVE, 1913-1916, O ga., 0-4-0; black cast-iron body, separate boiler bands; cast-iron wheels, dummy headlight on top of boiler; single rectangular cab window stamped "IVES No. 5" below; No. 1 tender — 110 — 220

5 LOCOMOTIVE, 1917-1922, O ga., 0-4-0; black cast-iron body, tin wheels, two separate boiler bands, dummy headlight in center of boiler front; two rectangular windows on both sides of cab stamped "IVES No. 5" below; No. 11 tender — 85 — 170

6 LOCOMOTIVE, 1913-1916, O ga., 0-4-0; black cast-iron body, cast-iron wheels w/straight side rods, dummy headlight on top of boiler; singular rectangular cab window stamped "IVES No. 6" below; Ives No. 1 tender — 85 — 170

6 LOCOMOTIVE, 1917-1925, O ga., 0-4-0; black cast-iron body w/cast-iron wheels w/straight drive rods; dummy headlight in center of boiler front; two rectangular windows on both sides of cab stamped "IVES No. 6" below; No. 11 tender — 85 — 170

	C6	C8

6 LOCOMOTIVE, 1926-1928, O ga., 0-4-0; black cast-iron body w/die-cast wheels w/straight drive rods; dummy headlight in boiler front center; two rectangular cab windows on both sides stamped "IVES No. 6"; NYC & HR No. 11 tender — 85 — 170

6 LOCOMOTIVE, 1929, O ga., 0-4-0; black boiler, die-cast wheels w/straight drive rods, dummy headlight in boiler front; same engine as previous year, but now a handbrake has been added; two rectangular cab windows per side stamped "IVES No. 6" below; No. 12 tender — 85 — 170

9 TENDER, 1930, O ga., same basic body and frame as No. 11 without rivet or spring detail; plain, flat surface; four tin wheels; often no stamping of legend on tender — 50 — 100

10 LOCOMOTIVE, 1930, O ga., 0-4-0; came w/Pequot set; black cast-iron body, tin wheels, without drivers; rectangular cab window marked "IVES No. 10" below; No. 11 tender — 175 — 350

10 LOCOMOTIVE, 1931-1932, 0-B-0; tin body, center cab electric style locomotive, often in peacock blue or cadet blue; St. Paul-type of engine, headlights at both ends, pantograph and bell or whistle on top of motor hoods; two windows and one door on either side and one door per end; same as 10-E w/automatic reverse — 140 — 285

11 LOCOMOTIVE, 1904-1905, 2-2-0; black cast-iron body w/tapered boiler, integral boiler bands, and dummy headlight on front top of boiler; rectangular cab window w/red area beneath; L.V.E. No. 11 tender — 175 — 350

11 TENDER, 1904-1913, O ga., LVE No. 11 tin body, four tin wheels, red lithograph — 58 — 115

11 LOCOMOTIVE, 1906-1907, O ga., 0-4-0; black cast-iron body w/four separate boiler bands, gold trim, red area below rectangular cab window; four cast-iron wheels. Dummy headlight on top of boiler. Boiler tapers towards the front like those on American Standard locomotives; LVE No. 11 tender — 165 — 330

11 LOCOMOTIVE, 1908-1909, O ga., 0-4-0, black cast-iron boiler w/three separate bands; straight boiler w/dummy headlight on top; red area below cab; L.V.E. No. 11 tender — 160 — 320

11 LOCOMOTIVE, 1910-1913, O ga., 0-4-0, black boiler and cab, lithographed plates beneath arched cab windows say "IVES No. 11"; cast-iron wheels, three separate boiler bands; L.V.E. No. 11 tender; dummy headlight on boiler top — 155 — 310

11 LOCOMOTIVE, 1914-1916, O ga., 0-4-0, black cast-iron boiler, two boiler bands, cast-iron wheels; two square windows per cab side, w/"IVES No. 11" stamped beneath them; dummy headlight on boiler top. Ives No. 11 tender. — 138 — 275

11 TENDER 1914-1930, O ga., tin body w/four tin wheels, marked "NYC & HR," Ives No. 11. — 48 — 95

12 TENDER, 1928-1930, O ga., tin body, four tin wheels; same basic tender as No. 11, but w/coal load — 45 — 90

17 LOCOMOTIVE, 1904-1905, O ga., 2-2-0, black cast-iron boiler tapers towards front; dummy headlight on boiler top, four separate boiler bands; rectangular cab window w/red area beneath; L.V.E. No. 11 tender, handbrake in cab. — 228 — 455

17 LOCOMOTIVE,, 1906-1907, O ga., 0-4-0, same body casting as No. 11, but has a handbrake located inside cab; black body, four separate boiler bands; gold trim, red area beneath cab rectangular window. cast-iron wheels, dummy headlight; boiler tapers towards front; L.V.E. No. 11 tender — 218 — 435

	C6	**C8**

17 LOCOMOTIVE,, 1908-1909, O ga., 0-4-0, black straight cast-iron body, w/three separate bands; dummy headlight on top; same as No. 11 of the period; L.V.E. No. 11 tender; handbrake — 205 410

17 LOCOMOTIVE, 1910-1913, O ga., 0-4-0, same as No. 11; black boiler cab, arched cab windows w/"IVES No. 17" beneath; cast-iron wheels, straight side rods, three separate boiler bands; dummy headlight on boiler top. L.V.E. No. 11 tender; handbrake in cab — 190 380

17 LOCOMOTIVE, 1914-1916, O ga., 0-4-0, same as No. 11 of the same period; black cast-iron body, two square windows per side, w/"IVES No. 17", stamped beneath; dummy headlight on boiler top; "IVES No. 11" tender, cast-iron wheels w/straight side rods; handbrake in cab — 180 360

17 LOCOMOTIVE, 1917-1925, O ga., 0-4-0, black boiler and cab w/dummy headlight in boiler center front, separate boiler band; handbrake in cab; NYC & HR No. 17 tender; straight side rods; single cab window w/"IVES No. 17" stamped beneath — 180 360

17 TENDER, 1917-1927, four wheels of tin, tin body, stamped lettering says "IVES No. 17" or "NYC & HR"; comes w/coal load — 45 90

17 LOCOMOTIVE, 1926-1927, O ga., 0-4-0, black cast-iron body w/one boiler band; die-cast wheels w/straight side rods, one arched cab window w/"IVES No. 17" stamped beneath; headlight back on top of boiler now; NYC & HR No. 17 tender; handbrake — 175 350

17 LOCOMOTIVE, 1928-1929, O ga., 0-4-0, black cast-iron body w/one boiler band; die-cast wheels w/straight side rods, one arched cab window w/"IVES No. 17" stamped beneath; headlight back on top of boiler now; NYC & HR No. 12 tender w/coal load; handbrake — 175 350

19 LOCOMOTIVE, 1917-1925, O ga., 0-4-0, black cast-iron boiler and cab w/handbrake, two arched windows and "IVES No. 19" beneath; cast-iron wheels w/straight drive rods, single separate boiler band; dummy headlight centered in boiler front; NYC & HR No. 17 tender — 225 450

19 LOCOMOTIVE, 1926-1927, O ga., 0-4-0, black cast-iron body w/one boiler band, dummy headlight on top of boiler; one boiler band separate; two arched cab windows marked "IVES No. 19" beneath; die-cast wheels w/straight drive rods; No. 17 NYC & HR tender — 200 400

19 LOCOMOTIVE, 1928-1929, O ga., 0-4-0, black cast-iron body w/one boiler band, dummy headlight on top of boiler; one boiler band separate; two arched cab windows marked "IVES No. 19" beneath; die-cast wheels w/straight drive rods; No. 12 tender — 200 400

20 LOCOMOTIVE, 1908-1909, O ga., 0-4-0, cast-iron body w/separate boiler bands; red area beneath two cab windows; dummy headlight on top of boiler; cast-iron wheels w/straight drive rods; reverse lever, brake speed governor; four-wheel No. 25 tender — 220 440

20 LOCOMOTIVE, 1910-1914, O ga., 0-4-0, straight boiler, cast-iron body w/grab rails on boiler sides. Dummy headlight on top of boiler, two rectangular cab windows w/lithographed plate marked beneath "IVES No. 20"; speed governor, reverse and brake; cast-iron wheels w/straight drive rods; eight wheel — 195 390

20 LOCOMOTIVE, 1915-1916, O ga., 0-4-0, straight boiler, cast-iron body w/grab rails on boiler sides. Dummy headlight on top of boiler, two rectangular cab windows w/lithographed plate stamped beneath "IVES No. 20"; speed governor, reverse and brake; cast-iron wheels w/straight drive rods; eight wheel; No. 25 tender — 195 390

	C6	C8

20 LIVESTOCK CAR, 1928-1929, Standard ga., American Flyer body on two four-wheel Ives trucks; sliding doors, brass plates; green body, red roof or orange body, red roof — 190 / 380

20 GONDOLA, 1928-1929, Standard ga., American Flyer body on two four-wheel Ives trucks — 158 / 315

20 CABOOSE, 1928-1929, Standard ga., American Flyer body on two four-wheel Ives trucks; red body, mirror roof; brass trim and plates — 140 / 280

20 GONDOLA, 1928-1929, Standard ga., black American Flyer body mounted on two four-wheel Ives trucks; brass plates and trim — 135 / 270

20 BOXCAR, 1928-1929, Standard ga., American Flyer body on two four-wheel Ives trucks; brass plates, sliding doors; yellow body w/blue roof or green body w/red roof — 190 / 380

25 LOCOMOTIVE, 1903, O ga., 4-4-0; black cast-iron body w/four cast boiler bands, dummy headlight on top of boiler, boiler tapers towards front; cast-iron wheels; three square windows on both sides of cab w/red area painted beneath; reverse and hand brake; hand-painted tin tender w/four cast-iron wheels — 325 / 650

25 LOCOMOTIVE, 1904, O ga., 4-4-0; black cast-iron body w/six separate boiler bands; dummy headlight on boiler top; three square cab windows on both sides of cab w/red area painted beneath; tin pony wheels; reverse brake; L.V.E. No. 11 tender w/tin wheels — 300 / 600

25 LOCOMOTIVE, 1905, O ga., 4-4-0; black cast-iron tapering boiler w/six separate boiler bands, dummy headlight on top of boiler; three square cab windows on both sides w/gold frame and, gold stripes beneath; tin pony wheels; handbrake and reverse; L.V.E. No. 11 tender w/red square outline on roof — 295 / 590

25 LOCOMOTIVE, 1906-1907, O ga., 4-4-2; black body, boiler tapers toward front, w/four separate boiler bands, dummy headlight on top of boiler; three square windows on both sides of cab w/gold frames and stripes, gold outline on roof; tin pony wheels; handbrake and reverse; four-wheel L.V.E. No. 25 tender, no side rods — 275 / 550

25 TENDER, 1906-1909, O ga., four tin wheels; black tin body w/red lithographed spring detail and side boards; L.V.E. No. 25 black lettering on red background — 150 / 300

25 LOCOMOTIVE, 1908-1909, O ga., 4-4-2; same general characteristics and casting as previous year; three square cab windows w/gold frames and two gold stripes beneath; gold square outline on cab roof; handbrake and reverse; L.V.E. No. 25 tender, no side rods — 263 / 525

25 LOCOMOTIVE, 1910, O ga., 4-4-2; black cast-iron body, w/ straight boiler, three separate boiler bands separate, stanchions for grab rails are cast into body; dummy headlight on top of boiler; two rectangular windows on both sides of cab, lithographed plate below reads "IVES No. 25"; handbrake and reverse; tin pony wheels; eight wheel No. 25 tender; angled side rods — 238 / 475

	C6	C8

25 TENDER, 1910-1912, O ga., eight tin wheel, black body marked "Limited Vestibule Express" in white framed in gold, blue painted interior — 150 — 300

25 LOCOMOTIVE, 1911-1914, O ga., 4-4-2; black cast-iron boiler, w/3 separate boiler bands, dummy headlight on top front of boiler, grab rails on connected by cotter pins; two rectangular windows on both sides of cab w/plate below lithographed "IVES No. 25"; red and gold trim; tin wheels on pony truck, cast-iron drivers w/angled side rods; handbrake and reverse; L.V.E. tender — 388 — 775

25 TENDER, 1913-1914, O ga., eight wheel, black tin body marked "Limited Vestibule Express" in white framed in gold — 150 — 300

25 LOCOMOTIVE, 1915-1916, O ga., 0-4-0; body casting and general detail same as previous model, some have tin pony or spoked cast-iron wheels; handbrake and reverse; latter version of tender, either marked "IVES No. 25" or "No. 25" — 225 — 450

25 TENDER, 1915-1920, O ga., eight wheel, black tin body, sides marked "IVES No. 25" in white, back marked "No. 25" in white — 145 — 295

25 TENDER, 1928-1930, O ga., die-cast body w/coal load, two four-wheel trucks w/die-cast wheels; tool boxes cast into tender sides — 150 — 300

30 LOCOMOTIVE, 1921-1927, O ga., 0-4-0 clockwork; w/electric center cab; green or red tin body on cast frame like 3250 series; cast-iron wheels until 1924, die-cast after 1925 — 200 — 400

30 LOCOMOTIVE, 1928, O ga., 0-B-0, clockwork w/electric box cab w/headlight and whistle; same body as 3258; stamped tin frame, tin lithographed body — 200 — 400

32 LOCOMOTIVE, 1921-1927, O ga., 0-4-0, clockwork; electric center cab; same body as the 3253 loco w/handrails. One door stamped "32 N.Y.C. & H.R." the other "The IVES Railway Lines"; cast-iron frame w/tin body; cast-iron wheels until 1924, die-cast from 1925-1927 — 225 — 450

50 BAGGAGE CAR, 1901-1905, O ga., four cast-iron wheels, hand-painted red, green or blue body and roof, clerestory w/white painted side — 175 — 350

50 BAGGAGE CAR, 1906-1907, O ga., red, white or yellow body lithographed to simulate wood; four tin wheels, steps, vestibules; unpunched door on each side, one marked "Limited Vestibule Express Baggage Car," the other "United States Mail Exp. Service"; black roof w/clerestory frame w/red lithographed spring detail; vestibules separate — 195 — 390

50 BAGGAGE CAR, 1908-1909, O ga., four wheel; red lithographed frame has spring detail and striped steps; white/silver body; sides marked "Limited Vestibule Express," "United States Mail Baggage Car" and "Express Service No. 50"; three doors on both sides and one on each end; black roof w/clerestory; vestibules part of body — 150 — 300

50 BAGGAGE CAR, 1910-1913, O ga., four tin wheels; lithographed yellow tin body w/open frame, black roof and clerestory; sides marked "Pennsylvania Lines"; punched center door marked "Baggage No. 50" and "Express Mail"; two doors lithographed on other side; wood sheathing on sides — 83 — 165

50 BAGGAGE CAR, 1914, four tin wheels, lithographed tin body and frame; same general car as previous year, but now marked "The Ives Railway Lines" — 75 — 150

	C6	C8

50 BAGGAGE CAR, 1915-1930, four tin wheels; red, yellow, green and tan tin body lithographed to resemble steel, tin frame; marked "The Ives Railway Lines" below roof line and "Baggage No. 50" and "U.S. Express Mail" on each side; open center doors and two lithographed doors w/open windows on side; black frame w/spring detail over wheels, black roof w/small clerestory strip. Because so many of these cars were made, the molds were rendered useless. — 25 — 50

51 PASSENGER CAR, 1901-1905, O ga., four cast-iron wheels, hand-painted tin body w/six windows on each side and vestibules at each end; roof w/clerestory strip w/white accents; red, blue or green body w/horizontal white or cream stripe beneath windows — 175 — 350

51 PASSENGER CAR, 1906-1907, O ga., four tin wheels, red lithographed spring detail on frame w/vestibule at each end; lithographed body marked "Mohawk," "Hiawatha" or "Iroquois" and "Limited Vestibule Express" below roof line; roof w/clerestory strip — 195 — 390

51 PASSENGER CAR, 1908-1909, four tin wheels, tin lithographed white body w/red detail, w/black frame w/ red lithographed detail; body marked "Limited Vestibule Express" below roof line; six windows marked "Brooklyn" below windows on lithographed plate; vestibules part of car — 170 — 260

51 PASSENGER CAR, 1910-1913, O ga., four tin wheels, tin body lithographed to resemble wood grain sheathing; black, green or gray frame w/holes over axle area; body marked "Pennsylvania Lines" below roof line; seven windows marked "Newark" below; doors replaced vestibules at end of car; roof w/clerestory strip — 95 — 190

51 PASSENGER CAR, 1914, O ga., four tin wheels, tin body, roof w/clerestory strip; same car as previous year's but w/"The Ives Railway Lines" lettered below roof line — 75 — 150

51 PASSENGER CAR, 1915-1930, O ga., four tin wheels, tin body lithographed to simulate steel; simple frame w/spring detail over axles; came in variety of colors: red, green, orange, yellow and tan; seven windows and two doors on each side; body marked "IVES Railway Lines" below roof line and "51 Chair Car 51" below windows — 25 — 50

52 PASSENGER CAR, 1908-1910, O ga., four tin wheels, tin body lithographed to simulate wood; four windows w/transoms and two doors on each side; marked "Limited Vestibule Express" below roof line and "Buffalo" below windows; roof w/clerestory strip; same body used for No. 801 trolley in 1910; cataloged as "Drawing Room Car" — 125 — 250

52 PASSENGER CAR, 1911-1913, O ga., four tin wheels, tin body lithographed to simulate wood siding; green, gray or black frame w/holes above axles; five windows and two doors on each side; body marked "Pennsylvania Lines" below roof line and "Washington" below windows; roof w/clerestory strip — 100 — 200

52 PASSENGER CAR, 1914, O ga., four tin wheels, tin body lithographed to simulate wood siding; green, gray or black frame w/holes above axles; five windows and two doors on each side; body marked "Pennsylvania Lines" below roof line and "The Ives Railway Lines" above windows; roof w/clerestory strip — 95 — 190

| | **C6** | **C8** | | **C6** | **C8** |

52 PASSENGER CAR, 1915-1930, O ga., four tin wheels, tin body lithographed to simulate steel; five windows and two doors on each side; marked "The Ives Railway Lines" below roof line and "52 Parlor Car 52" below windows; roof w/clerestory strip — **45** / **90**

53 FREIGHT CAR, 1910-1914, O ga., four tin wheels, white body, frame w/holes over axle; open doorway on both sides; marked "Pennsylvania Lines" on one side of doorway and "PA. R.R. Co." and "No. 53" on the other — **90** / **180**

53 FREIGHT CAR, 1915-1930, O ga., Same as previous frame w/spring-detail frame — **68** / **135**

54 GRAVEL CAR, 1903-1904, O ga., four cast-iron wheels, hand-painted tin body — **100** / **200**

54 GRAVEL CAR, 1905-1909, O ga., four tin wheels, tin body lithographed to simulate wood; red lithographed spring detail on frame — **95** / **190**

54 GRAVEL CAR, 1910-1914, O ga., four tin wheels, tin lithographed body on frame w/holes over axle; body marked "No. 54" — **55** / **110**

54 GRAVEL CAR, 1915-1930, O ga., four tin wheels, tin body lithographed simulated wood; later frame w/spring detail; body marked lithographed "No. 54" — **40** / **80**

55 STOCK CAR, 1910-1914, O ga., four tin wheels, yellow tin body lithographed to simulate wood; frame w/holes above axle; marked "Livestock Transportation" below roof line; no doors, just doorway on each side — **50** / **100**

55 STOCK CAR, 1915-1930, O ga., four tin wheels, tin body lithographed to simulate wood; later frame w/spring detail. Marked "Livestock Transportation" above doorway — **40** / **80**

56 CABOOSE, 1910-1914, O ga., four tin wheels, white or red tin body lithographed to simulate wood; single open door on each side, w/window on each side of door; small cupola on roof; frame w/holes over axles; marked "Pennsylvania Lines" above door — **113** / **225**

56 CABOOSE, 1915-1930, O ga., four tin wheels, tin body lithographed to simulate wood; frame w/spring detail; open door; marked "Pennsylvania Lines" over door and "Caboose No. 56" on both sides — **100** / **200**

57 LUMBER CAR, 1910-1914, O ga., four tin wheels, tin frame w/hole over axles; painted tin body, w/lumber load — **40** / **80**

57 LUMBER CAR, 1915-1930, O ga., four tin wheels, later frame w/spring detail; painted tin body w/lumber load — **30** / **60**

60 BAGGAGE CAR, 1905-1909, O ga., four tin wheels; tin body lithographed to simulate wood; tin roof w/clerestory strip; sliding lithographed door; sides marked "United States Mail Exp. Service," "Limited Vestibule Express Baggage Car" and "No. 60" — **325** / **650**

60 BAGGAGE CAR, 1910-1913, O ga., eight wheels, red, blue, white, rose or yellow tin body lithographed to simulate wood; sliding lithographed door; truss rods on frame w/single support in middle; tin roof w/separate clerestory strip; flat truss rods in 1910 and 1911, later rounded; marked "Limited Vestibule Express" below roof line, "Express Service Baggage" to left of door and "United States Mail" to right — **135** / **270**

	C6	**C8**

60 BAGGAGE CAR, 1914-1915, O ga., same as previous year, marked "The Ives Railway Lines" below roof line — 120 | 240

60 BAGGAGE CAR, 1915-1920, O ga., eight wheels, tin roof w/clerestory strip, green or red tin body lithographed to simulate steel sides w/rivet detail; lithographed in single-sliding door single in middle of side; truss rods on each side of frame; marked "The Ives Railway Lines" below roof level and "Express Service Baggage" to left of door and "U.S. Mail" to right of door — 75 | 150

60 BAGGAGE CAR, 1921-1923, O ga., eight wheels, tin roof and body. Same as previous year, without truss rods on the frame — 70 | 140

60 BAGGAGE CAR, 1924-1930, O ga., eight wheel, tin roof w/ clerestory strip; red, red-brown or blue-green lithographed without rivet detail and gold trim and brass journals; same general car as before, w/truss rods — 110 | 220

61 PASSENGER CAR, 1905-1909, O ga., four tin wheels; yellow, red, blue, buff and white bodies; tin body lithographed to simulate wood; vestibules part of body; body marked "Limited Vestibule Express" below roof line, "Express" below eight windows — 345 | 690

61 PASSENGER CAR, 1910-1913, O ga., eight wheel, white, blue, yellow, red or rose tin lithographed to simulate wood; truss rod on each side of frame and door at each end of side where vestibules were previously; tin roof w/separate clerestory strip, body marked "Limited Vestibule Express" below roof line and "Yale" below eight windows. — 155 | 310

61 CHAIR CAR, 1914-1915, O ga., green, body marked "The Ives Railway Lines" above windows and "61 Chair Car 61" below eight windows — 150 | 300

61 CHAIR CAR, 1916-1920, O ga., eight wheel; green, red or olive tin body lithographed to simulate steel w/rivet detail; truss rods on frame; door at each end of side; one-piece roof w/clerestory strip; body marked "The Ives Railway Lines" above windows and "61 Chair Car 61" below eight windows — 75 | 150

61 CHAIR CAR, 1921-1923, O ga., same car as previous year; green or red body lithographed to simulate steel; without truss rods on frame — 68 | 135

61 CHAIR CAR, 1924-1930, O ga., same car as previous year; eight wheel; red, red-brown or blue-green body lithographed to simulate steel without rivet detail; frame w/truss rods — 68 | 135

62 PARLOR CAR, 1905-1909, O ga., four-wheel, yellow, red, blue, buff and white tin body lithographed to simulate wood; tin one piece roof; three windows and two doors per side; "Limited Vestibule Express" below roof line and "Princess" below windows — 395 | 790

	C6	C8		C6	C8

62 PARLOR CAR, O ga., green, body marked "The Ives Railway Lines" above windows and "62 Parlor Car" below windows.

62 PARLOR CAR, 1910-1913, O ga., eight wheels; red, white, blue, yellow or rose tin body lithographed to simulate wood; truss rods on frame; tin roof w/ separate clerestory strip; five windows and two doors per side; marked "Limited Vestibule Express" below roof line and "Harvard" below windows — 180 — 360

62 PARLOR CAR, 1914-1915, O ga., same as previous year, w/"The Ives Railway Lines" above windows — 150 — 300

62 PARLOR CAR, 1916-1920, O ga., eight wheel; tin lithographed steel w/rivet detail; frame w/truss rods; one-piece tin roof w/clerestory strip; five windows and two doors on each side; marked "The Ives Railway Lines" below roof line and "Parlor Car" below the windows — 75 — 150

62 PARLOR CAR, 1921-1923, O ga., same car as previous year but without truss rods on frame; eight wheel; one-piece tin roof w/clerestory strip — 68 — 135

62 PARLOR CAR, 1924-1930, O ga., same car without rivet detail; eight wheel; red-brown, red, emerald green or blue-green; one-piece roof w/clerestory strip; five windows, two doors on each side; marked "The Ives Railway Lines" above windows and "62 Parlor Car 62" — 68 — 135

63 GRAVEL CAR, 1904-1907, O ga., four wheel; tin body painted w/vertical stripes w/cast-iron wheels — 70 — 140

63 GRAVEL CAR, 1908-1909, O ga., four wheel; tin lithographed body simulates wood w/tin wheels — 50 — 100

63 GRAVEL CAR, 1910-1911, O ga., eight wheel; dark green lithographed body w/incomplete lithographed on each end. Flat truss rods on frame — 48 — 95

63 GRAVEL CAR, 1912, O ga., eight wheel; dark green body w/complete lithographed at ends, flat truss rods on frame — 35 — 70

63 GRAVEL CAR, 1913-1914, O ga., eight wheel; kelly green body, same as previous year, w/half-round truss rods — 35 — 70

63 GRAVEL CAR, 1915-1916, O ga., eight wheel; gray lithographed w/pinkish tones; w/rounded truss rods; marked "63" on sides — 30 — 60

63 GRAVEL CAR, 1917-1920, O ga., eight wheel; gray lithographed tin body without pinkish coloration; rounded truss rods — 25 — 50

63 GRAVEL CAR, 1921-1923, O ga., eight wheel; gray lithographed body, no truss rods on frame — 25 — 50

63 GRAVEL CAR, 1924-1929, O ga., eight wheel; gray lithographed body, rounded truss rods on frame, journal slots on trucks — 25 — 50

63 GRAVEL CAR, 1930, O ga., eight wheel; gray lithographed body, rounded truss rods on frame, brass journals on trucks — 25 — 90

64 MERCHANDISE CAR, 1908-1909, O ga., four-wheel; painted frame and roof, single sliding door; body marked "Fast Freight Line" to left of door and "General Merchandise Car" to right — 95 — 190

64 MERCHANDISE CAR, 1910-1912, O ga., eight wheel; lithographed tin body simulates wood; tin roof, white w/lithographed blue and red stripes; T-trucks and flat truss rods on frame; single sliding door in middle of side; body marked "General Mdse. Car No. 64," "Union Line" w/star logo to left of door and "Merchandise Car No. 64 Pennsylvania Line" to right of door — 90 — 180

	C6	C8

64 MERCHANDISE CAR, 1910-1930, O ga., There are many variations of this car, and different years and different lithograph ink provided a rich palette of colors in each given herald. Because the heralds are listed at the end of the chapter, only the major changes in the car will be listed here; Union Star lines was the first, others weren't cataloged until 1913. All were produced between 1913 and 1930.

64 MERCHANDISE CAR, 1913-1917, O ga., eight wheel, tin body lithographed to simulate wood; frame w/rounded truss rods; painted tin roof; all heralds available — 100 — 200

64 MERCHANDISE CAR, 1918, O ga., eight wheel; same car, new trucks w/no detail, w/flat sides; all heralds available — 100 — 225

64 MERCHANDISE CAR, 1919-1920, O ga., eight wheel; same car, trucks w/rivet detail, no journal slots — 150 — 250

64 MERCHANDISE CAR, 1921-1923, O ga., eight wheel; same car, without truss rods on side frames — 100 — 200

64 MERCHANDISE CAR, 1924, O ga., eight wheel; same car, w/side frame truss rods — 90 — 180

64 MERCHANDISE CAR, 1925-1928, O ga., eight wheel; same general cars, trucks w/journal slots — 100 — 200

64 MERCHANDISE CAR, 1929-1930, O ga., same general car, red roof, trucks w/brass journals — 100 — 200

65 LIVESTOCK CAR, 1908-1909, O ga., four-wheel; body lithographed w/rivet detail; roof striped w/brake wheel at one end; horizontal slots punched out; striped lithographed door below "Livestock Transportation" — 63 — 125

65 LIVESTOCK CAR, 1910-1912, O ga., eight wheel; white or gray-white body lithographed to simulating wood; dark green frame w/flat truss rods; striped lithographed roof w/catwalk, punched out sides; single sliding door on each side below "Livestock Transportation" — 55 — 110

65 LIVESTOCK CAR, 1913-1917, O ga., eight wheel; painted orange body w/single sliding door on each side; painted roof w/catwalk; T-trucks; sides marked "Livestock," "Transportation" and "The Ives R.R."; c. 1916-1917 car changed to yellow lithographed body w/lithographed door; some doors have slots punched in them — 38 — 75

65 LIVESTOCK CAR, 1918, O ga., eight wheel; lithographed body in orange-yellow to simulate wood detail; trucks without detail; gray painted roof w/catwalk; sides marked "Livestock," "Transportation" and "The Ives R.R." — 25 — 50

65 LIVESTOCK CAR, 1919-1920, O ga., same as previous year, eight wheel, trucks w/detail — 25 — 50

65 LIVESTOCK CAR, 1921-1923, O ga., same as previous year, eight wheel, without truss rods on side frames — 23 — 45

65 LIVESTOCK CAR, 1924, O ga., same as previous years, w/truss rods — 23 — 45

65 LIVESTOCK CAR, 1925-1928, O ga., same as previous years, eight wheel, trucks w/journal slots. — 23 — 45

65 LIVESTOCK CAR, 1929-1930, O ga., same as previous years, w/brass journals on trucks; some lithography is now more orange than orange-yellow; roof is now painted red — 23 — 45

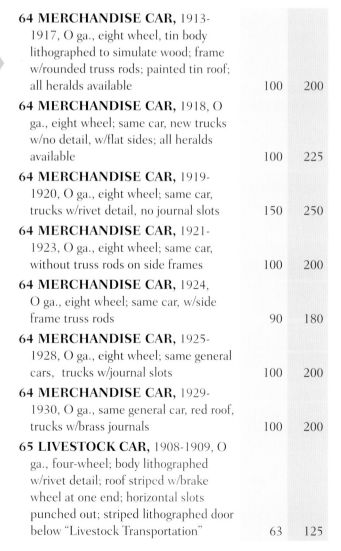

	C6	C8

66 TANK CAR, 1910-1912, O ga., eight wheel; flat truss rods on frame; painted dome and tank body mounted right onto frame, w/stripes, rivet detail and "Tank Line" painted on sides; T-trucks; red or green body — 75 150

66 TANK CAR, 1913-1915, O ga., eight wheel; frame w/round truss rods; T-trucks; black tank body on saddles w/gold band painted around each end of tank; no lettering on sides, and "TL No. 66" stamped on each end; short dome — 48 95

66 TANK CAR, 1916-1917, O ga., eight wheel; T-trucks; gray painted body on saddles mounted to frame; black dome; sides are lettered "66 Standard Oil 66," "Air Brake," "Made In The Ives Shops" and "Cap'y 100000 Gals"; ends stamped "66" — 30 60

66 TANK CAR, 1918, O ga., flat truck; same characteristics as previous year, changed "Cap'y 100000 Gals" to read "Cap'y 10,000 Gals" — 23 45

66 TANK CAR, 1919-1920, O ga., eight wheel, same as previous year, without type D-2 trucks — 23 45

66 TANK CAR, 1921-1923, O ga., eight wheel. same as before, without truss rods on frame sides — 20 60

66 TANK CAR, 1924, O ga., eight wheel, same, without truss rods on frame — 23 45

66 TANK CAR, 1925-1928, O ga., eight wheel; orange body, black dome. body mounted to frame by saddles; sides marked "66 Standard Oil 66," "Air Brake," "Made In The Ives Shops" and "Cap'y 10,000 Gals"; ends marked "66"; trucks w/journal slots — 23 45

	C6	C8

66 TANK CAR, 1929-1930, O ga., eight wheel; same car as before previous years; trucks w/brass journals. — 150 300

67 CABOOSE, 1910-1912, O ga., eight wheel; white body lithographed to simulate wood sheathing; some main roofs are lithographed w/stripes, some are painted; single lithographed sliding door on each side; sides marked "Pennsylvania Lines," "Caboose No. 67"; window to right of door marked "No. 67" below; flat truss rods on frame — 105 210

67 CABOOSE, 1913-1917, O ga., eight wheel; lithographed body w/single sliding door on each side; gray painted tin roof w/red cupola and red roof; body is red or brown-red; white lettering below roof line reads "The Ives Railway Lines"; window to left of door marked "Caboose 67" below; window to right of door marked "Caboose 67"; ends of car marked "The Ives Miniature Railway System" and "PARR/67"; rounded truss rods on frame — 43 85

67 CABOOSE, 1918, O ga., eight wheel; same as previous years w/type D-1 trucks; marked "The Ives Railway Line" below right window — 38 75

67 CABOOSE, 1919-1920, O ga., eight wheel; same as before w/type D-2 trucks — 38 75

67 CABOOSE, 1921-1923, O ga., eight wheel; same as before, no truss rods on frame sides — 38 75

67 CABOOSE, 1924, O ga., eight wheel; same as before, w/truss rods back on frame — 38 75

67 CABOOSE, 1925-1928, O ga., eight wheel; same car as previous years, w/type D-3 trucks without journals — 38 75

67 CABOOSE, 1929-1930, O ga., eight wheel; same basic car as previous years, but more of a red-orange cast to lithography and yellow lettering; green cupola roof; trucks w/brass journals — 38 75

	C6	C8

68 REEFER, 1910-1912, O ga., eight wheel; lithographed white body; lithographed roof w/catwalk; lithographed and sliding doors; T-trucks; flat truss; sides marked "Merchants Dispatch Transportation Company," "Refrigerator No. 68," "Refrigerator No. 68 Dairy Line Express" — **155 / 310**

68 REEFER, 1913-1917, O ga., eight wheel; same car as previous; white body w/painted roof; truss rods on frame are rounded; no brake wheel on roof — **143 / 285**

68 REEFER, 1918, O ga., eight wheel; same as previous year, but flat side type D-1 trucks — **138 / 275**

68 REEFER, 1919-1924, O ga., eight wheel; same as previous year, type D-2 trucks — **138 / 275**

68 REEFER, 1925-1928, O ga., eight wheel; Same as previous year; w/type D-3 trucks — **138 / 275**

68 OBSERVATION CAR, 1925-1930, O ga., eight wheel; emerald green and blue-green body tin lithographed to simulate steel; tin roof w/clerestory strip; brass observation platform; one door and five windows on both sides; brass journals; sides marked "The Ives Railway Lines" — **60 / 100**

68 REEFER, 1929-1930, O ga., eight wheel; same as previous years, w/red roof and trucks w/brass journals — **138 / 275**

69 LUMBER CAR, 1910-1912, O ga., eight wheel; black painted body w/six red stakes, lumber load held on by three chains over the top; flat truss rods on side frame; T-trucks — **65 / 130**

69 LUMBER CAR, 1913-1917, O ga., eight wheel; black painted body, six red stakes, rounded truss rods; lumber load held on by three chains; T-trucks — **50 / 100**

69 LUMBER CAR, 1918, O ga., eight wheel; black painted body, red stakes; lumber load held on by chains; flat trucks; rounded truss rods — **45 / 90**

69 LUMBER CAR, 1919-1920, O ga., eight wheel; painted body; lumber load held on by chains; rounded truss rods — **45 / 90**

69 LUMBER CAR, 1921-1923, O ga., eight wheel; red-brown painted body and stakes; lumber load held on by three chains; trucks; frame without truss rods. — **45 / 90**

69 LUMBER CAR, 1924, O ga., eight wheel; red-brown body and stakes; lumber load held on by three chains; frame has truss rods. — **45 / 90**

69 LUMBER CAR, 1925-1928, eight wheel; maroon or tan painted body and stakes; lumber load held on by three chains. — **45 / 90**

69 LUMBER CAR, 1929-1930, O ga., eight wheel; green painted body and stakes; some have short lumber load, others have regular, both held on by three chains; trucks w/brass journals — **45 / 90**

70 BAGGAGE CAR, 1904-1909, 1 ga., eight wheel; wheat and yellow tin body lithographed to simulate wood sheathing; tin wheels, black trucks w/red striping; black tin roof w/white clerestory strip; two doors and two mail windows on each side; sides marked "Twentieth Century Limited Express," "U.S. mail" and "Baggage And Express" — **325 / 650**

	C6	C8

70 BAGGAGE CAR, 1910-1915, 1 ga., eight wheel; white, yellow or brown body lithographed to simulate wood; tin wheels, tin roof w/clerestory strip; center doors on both sides and end, window next to each side door; sides marked "Twentieth Century Limited Express" or "New York Central Lines," "Baggage Express No. 70," "New York and Chicago," "United States Mail"; steps beneath each side end door; still cataloged in 1916 — 250 — 500

70 BAGGAGE CAR, 1923-1925, O ga., eight wheel; red lithographed body simulates steel; tin roof w/clerestory strip; sliding door in center and small door at each end of side; sides marked "The Ives Railway Lines," "Express Baggage Service," "60" and "U.S. Mail" — 30 — 60

70 CABOOSE, 1929-1930, O ga., eight wheel; tin roof w/red cupola roof 1929, green in 1930; catalog shows No. 67 in cut for 1929, but 1930 the car was made w/a red Lionel body — 270 — 540

71 COMBINATION CAR, 1904-1909, 1 ga., eight wheel; yellow or wheat tin lithographed to simulate wood; tin roof, black w/white painted clerestory strip; black trucks w/red striping; door at each end of side w/six windows between them; sides marked "Twentieth Century Limited Express," "Saint Louis," "Baggage," and "No. 71" — 375 — 750

71 COMBINATION CAR, 1910-1915, 1 ga., eight wheel; yellow or brown tin body lithographed to simulate wood; tin roof w/clerestory strip; two doors and three double windows on each side; white, marked "Twentieth Century Limited Express," "Baggage," "New York," "Chicago" and "Buffet Car" — 300 — 600

71 COMBINATION CAR, 1916-1920, 1 ga., eight wheel; brown tin body lithographed to simulate steel; tin roof w/clerestory strip separate; two doors per side, three double windows and one small window; marked "The Ives Railway Lines," "Baggage," "No. 71," "New York and Chicago" — 300 — 600

71 CHAIR CAR, 1923-1925, O ga., eight wheel; red lithographed body simulates steel without rivet detail; tin roof w/clerestory strip; eight windows; marked "The Ives Railway Lines," "71" "Chair Car" and "71" — 30 — 60

72 PARLOR CAR, 1904-1909, 1 ga., eight wheel; tin body lithographed to simulate wood; tin black roof w/white clerestory sides; black trucks w/red striping; door at each end of side w/four double windows between them; sides marked "Twentieth Century Limited Express," "No 72" and "San Francisco" — 488 — 975

72 PARLOR CAR, 1910-1915, 1 ga., eight wheel; white, yellow or brown tin body lithographed to simulate wood; tin roof w/clerestory strip; four double windows, three small windows, and door at each end of side, steps below door; sides marked "Twentieth Century Limited Express"; "No. 72," "Chicago," "No. 72" — 488 — 975

72 PARLOR CAR, 1916-1920, 1 ga., eight wheel; brown tin body lithographed to simulate steeple; tin roof w/clerestory strip separate; four windows, three small windows and two doors w/steps below on each side; sides marked "The Ives Railway Lines," "No. 72" and "Washington" — 425 — 850

72 DRAWING ROOM CAR, 1923-1925, O ga., eight wheel; red tin body lithographed to simulate steel without rivet detail; tin roof w/clerestory strip; five windows, two doors per side; marked "72," "Drawing room Car" and "72," "The Ives Railway Lines" — 45 — 90

72 ACCESSORY, 1928-1930, Standard ga., Pole wagon for circus set — 45 — 90

73 OBSERVATION CAR, 1916-1920, 1 ga., eight wheel; brown tin lithographed to simulate steel; tin roof w/separate clerestory strip; four double windows, three small windows, and one door on each side; sides marked "The Ives Railway Lines," "No. 73," "Observation" and "No. 73" — 300 — 600

	C6	C8
73 OBSERVATION CAR, 1923-1925, O ga., eight wheel; red tin body lithographed to simulate steel without rivet detail; tin roof w/clerestory; five windows and one door per side; brass platform at rear; sides marked "Observation" and "73," "The Ives Railway Lines"	45	90
80 TELEGRAPH POLES, 1906-1930, early examples attached right to track ties, later ones stood on their own stands	7	14
87 FLAG POLE, 1923-1930	50	100
88 LAMP BRACKET, 1923-1930, to attach to stations to illuminate them	10	20
89 WATER TOWER, 1923-1929, orange body, black frame and ladder; movable spout on counterweight; side marked "The Ives Railway Lines"	50	100
89 WATER TOWER, 1930, larger model, yellow tank w/decal mounted on Lionel base; brass plate on base marked "The Ives Railway Lines"; later reproduction has rectangular border around this lettering	175	350
90 DROP BRIDGE, 1929-1930, O ga., w/trip lever, for mechanical track	135	270
90 BRIDGE, 1912-1922, two simulated stone approaches w/culvert formed under juncture; meant for mechanical trains	45	90
90-3 BRIDGE, 1912-1922, O ga., two simulated stone approaches w/culvert formed under juncture; meant for electrical trains	45	90
91-3 BRIDGE, 1912-1922, O ga., two approach ramps w/double viaduct center; stonework design; for electrical trains	45	90
91 BRIDGE, 1912-1922, O ga., two approach ramps w/double viaduct center; stonework design; for mechanical trains	45	90
91 BRIDGE, 1923-1930, O ga., two approach ramps w/double viaduct center; earthen design; for mechanical trains; 21" long	45	90

	C6	C8
91-3 BRIDGE, 1923-1930, O ga., two approach ramps w/double viaduct center; earthen design; for electrical trains; 21" long	45	90
92 BRIDGE, 1912-1922, O ga., two approach ramps w/double viaduct center; stonework; for mechanical trains; 42" long	60	120
92-3 BRIDGE, 1912-1922, O ga., two approach ramps w/double viaduct center; stonework; for electrical trains; 42" long	60	120
92 BRIDGE, 1923-1930, O ga., w/semaphore signal; two approach ramps w/double viaduct center, and railings on sides; for mechanical trains; earthen design	50	100
92-3 BRIDGE, 1923-1930, w/semaphore signal; two approach ramps w/double viaduct center, and railings on sides; for electrical trains; earthen design	50	100
97 SWING DRAWBRIDGE, 1906-1912, O ga., two stonework approaches w/revolving center span; lattice-type griders on trestles; for mechanical track; 31" l.	175	130
97 BRIDGE, 1929-1930, Standard ga., two approach ramps w/three center spans w/girders	65	130
98 BRIDGE, 1906-1907, O ga., two approach ramps, stonework, double viaduct center; lattice-type girders on trestle; for mechanical trains; 31" l.	65	130
98 BRIDGE, 1908-1912, O ga., two approach ramps, stonework sides, double stonework viaduct; flat stamped girders on trestle; plain-sided center base, straight corner braces; for mechanical track. 31" l.	45	90
98 BRIDGE, 1911-1920, two approach ramps of stone or earthen design; one single viaduct center span of stonework design; flat stamped trestle sections; for mechanical 1 ga. track; 42" l.	50	100

	C6	C8		C6	C8

98-3 BRIDGE, 1911-1922, O ga., two approach ramps of stone or earthen design; one single viaduct center span of stonework design; flat stamped trestle sections; for electrical O ga. track; 42" l. — 45 / 90

98 BRIDGE, 1913-1922, O ga., two approach ramps of stone or earthen design; one single viaduct center span of stonework design; flat stamped trestle sections; for mechanical track — 45 / 90

98 BRIDGE, 1923-1930, O ga., two approaches of earthwork design w/ square stones along track, center span of flat steel trestles set upon stonework base; for mechanical track; 31" l. — 45 / 90

98-3 BRIDGE, 1923-1930, O ga., two approaches of earthwork design w/ square stones along track, center span of flat steel trestles set upon stonework base; for electrical track; 31" l. — 45 / 90

99 BRIDGE, 1906-1907, O ga., two approach ramps, stonework, double viaduct center; w/two center spans; lattice-type girders on trestle; for mechanical trains; 41" l. — 75 / 150

99 BRIDGE, 1908-1912, O ga., same as contemporary No. 98 but w/two center spans; 41" l. — 65 / 130

99-3 BRIDGE, 1911-1922, O ga., two approach ramps of stone or earthen design; two viaduct center span of stonework design; flat stamped trestle sections; for electrical O ga. track; 41" l. — 50 / 100

99 BRIDGE, 1913-1922, O ga., two approach ramps of stone or earthen design; two viaduct center span of stonework design; flat stamped trestle sections; for mechanical track, 41" l. — 60 / 120

99-3 BRIDGE, 1926-1928, O ga., same as No. 98 of these years; 41-1/4" l. — 50 / 100

100 BRIDGE, 1906-1917, O ga., two approach sections forming a single viaduct between the center juncture; painted groundwork; for mechanical track; 21" l. — 35 / 70

100-3 BRIDGE, 1910-1917, O ga., two approach sections forming a single viaduct between the center juncture; painted groundwork; for electrical track; 21" l. — 40 / 80

100 ACCESSORY SET, 1930-1932, includes clock, telegraph poles, crossing gate, crossing signal, single and double semaphore; 10 pieces — 55 / 110

101 BRIDGE, 1906-1922, O ga., bridge; two approaches, one center span w/two viaducts, railings on both sides of track; for mechanical trains; 31" l. — 50 / 100

100-3 BRIDGE, 1910-1922, O ga., two approach ramps, center section w/two viaducts, railings on both sides of track; for electrical track; 31" l. — 50 / 100

102 TUNNEL, 1928, papier-máché, 18" l. — 15 / 30

103 TUNNEL, 1910-1927, papier-máché, 6" l. — 12 / 25

103 TUNNEL, 1928-1930, papier-máché, 8" l. — 12 / 25

104 TUNNEL, 1906-1927, papier-máché, 8 1/2" l. — 25 / 50

104 TUNNEL, 1928-1930, papier-máché, 10" long. — 25 / 50

105 TUNNEL, 1906-1912, papier-máché, 11" long. — 12 / 25

105-E TUNNEL, 1913-1919, papier-máché, 11" long — 12 / 25

105 TUNNEL, 1913-1922, 1924-1927, papier-máché, 14" long. — 12 / 25

105 TUNNEL, 1928, papier-máché, 12" long. — 12 / 25

106 TUNNEL, 1906-1912, papier-máché, 14" long. — 15 / 30

106-E TUNNEL, 1910-1912, papier-máché, 16" long. — 15 / 30

106 TUNNEL, 1913-1928, papier-máché, 16" long. — 15 / 30

106 TUNNEL, 1929-1930, papier-máché, 19" long. — 15 / 30

107 SEMAPHORE, 1905-1917, O ga., w/check; arm on post, w/a signal and brake attachment at the base to stop mechanical train — 30 / 60

	C6	C8
107-S SEMAPHORE, 1907-1930, single arm w/wire attached to signal to operate manually	10	20
107-D SEMAPHORE, 1907-1930, double arm w/wires to operate signals manually	14	28
107 TUNNEL, 1929-1930, papier-mâché, 23" long.	18	35
108 SEMAPHORE, 1908-1917, 1 ga., w/check; arm on post w/a signal and brake attachment at the base to stop mechanical train	25	50
109 DOUBLE SEMAPHORE TOWER, 1906-1922, two signals mounted on upright base, early examples had ladder going up to platform, later ones deleted this feature	35	70
110 TRACK BUMPER, 1906-1928, for sidings, to keep trains from derailing; early examples were just a post w/two pieces of track angled up from road surface and attached to either side of the post; later ones were a more elaborate system w/a sprung bumper for the train to touch against	12	25
110-1 TRACK BUMPER, 1917, for sidings, to keep trains from derailing; early examples were just a post w/two pieces of track angled up from road surface and attached to either side of the post; later ones were a more elaborate system w/a sprung bumper for the train to touch against, for 1 ga. mechanical track	20	40
110 BRIDGE SPAN, 1931-1932, Standard ga., Lionel No. 110	30	60
111 TRACK ELEVATING POST, 1904-1907, made for O ga. mechanical track for elevated railways; see set section at end of chapter	20	40
111 CROSSING SIGN, 1912-1928	10	20
111 CROSSING SIGN, 1929, Lionel No. 0-68	10	20
112 TRACK PLATES, 1906-1932, O ga., for connecting track together at ends beneath ties	1	1
112-1 TRACK PLATES, 1912-1920, 1 ga., for connecting track together	1	1

	C6	C8
113 PASSENGER STATION, 1906-1911, red body lithographed w/cast-iron door frames and window frames; lithographed roof w/shingles and base w/tiles; sign above; marked "Ticket Office" on one side of window and "Telegraph Office" on the other	163	325
113 PASSENGER STATION, 1912-1928, painted base and roof w/red brick lithographed body; w/people in windows; front and back are identical on some models w/two doors and three windows; others have one door and two windows; tin chimney on roof	88	175
113-3 PASSENGER STATION, 1924-1928, Same as 113, w/No. 88 lamp brackets to illuminate it externally; most stations w/factory illumination have a distinctly yellow cast to the lithographed brickwork; tin chimney	88	175
114 PASSENGER STATION, 1906-1911, lithographed roof w/simulated shingles, lithographed base simulating tiles; lithographed yellow body w/red cast-iron door on window frames; some examples have lithographed plate on base w/Ives name on it, others marked "Passenger Station," "Ticket Office" and "Telegraph Office" on plates on body; cast-iron chimney on roof	95	190
114 PASSENGER STATION, 1912-1916, lithographed roof w/simulated shingles and w/lithographed base simulated tiles; body lithographed w/clerk in window on front and back, ladies in one end window and gentlemen in other; two doors on front and back of station; tin chimney on roof	73	145
114 PASSENGER STATION, 1917-1922, Same as previous year, w/painted, not lithographed, roof and base; tin chimney	65	130
114 PASSENGER STATION, 1923-1928, Same as previous years, roof has stamped shingle pattern; station body is shorter than previous years; tin chimney	65	130

	C6	C8		C6	C8

115 FREIGHT STATION, 1906-1911, lithographed block base w/ramp and platform, small yellow lithographed station set on platform; sliding door w/lithographed plate on one side and lettered "Freight," the other side lettered "Station"; body lithographed to simulate wood, roof lithographed to simulate shingles; cast-iron chimney on roof — 145   290

115 FREIGHT STATION, 1912-1916, lithographed block base w/ramp and platform; yellow lithographed body w/open door on front and back; clerk lithographed in window w/handcart carrying Ives packages; scale w/blue shadow lithographed on front and back of building; brown and green door and window trim; tin roof w/tin chimney; clerk visible in end windows — 700   1,400

115 FREIGHT STATION, 1917-1922, early examples have yellow lithographed bodies w/painted roof and flat base; painted base and roof; most are the new white lithographed body, but w/same appearance as the last version — 70   130

115 FREIGHT STATION, 1923-1928, generally the same as previous years, but w/corrugated tin roof and tin chimney; roof has vertical embossed ridges between the gutter and the roof ledge; may not have been made for all five years, but examples w/this roof seem to have an orange shadow beneath the scales, as opposed to the standard blue shadow on other models of the same station — 70   130

116 PASSENGER STATION, 1906-1911, roof w/simulated shingles, lithographed base simulates tiles; body is lithographed yellowish brick w/cast-iron doors and windows; roof has bay gable front and back marked "Grand Central Station" U-shaped bay on front and back of station w/window on each side of U; marked "Ticket Office" above one window and "Telegraph Office" above other; two cast-iron chimneys on roof — 500   1,000

116 PASSENGER STATION, 1912-1916, lithographed roof w/single pattern, bay gable front and back marked "Grand Central Station"; roof w/one, two or three cast-iron chimneys; lithographed base simulates tiles; lithographed body now w/rectangular bay in center w/windows on each side, window in center w/clerk sitting at desk; doors are now part of station body, and have lithographed stained glass pattern — 175   350

116 PASSENGER STATION, 1917-1928, lithographed body is as previous year; roof and base are now painted; bay gable at front and rear is marked "Union Station"; first examples in 1917 had a variety of combinations of old and new parts — 175   350

116-3 PASSENGER STATION, 1926-1928, same as the contemporary No. 116 station, w/two or four No. 88 lamp brackets mounted to the exterior for illumination — 160   320

117 PASSENGER STATION, 1906-1911, covered; two base pieces w/lithographed tile pattern; roof supported by eight posts; train passed through between bases; lithographed sign on roof reads "Suburban Station"; one bench between center two posts on each base — 550   1,100

117 PASSENGER STATION, 1912-1922, covered; two base pieces, each w/four posts supporting painted tin roof; train passes through between bases; one bench on each base — 450   900

	C6	C8

117 PASSENGER STATION, 1923-1928, covered; two base pieces, each w/three posts supporting painted tin roof; two benches per base; train passes between bases — 450 / 900

118 PLATFORM STATION, 1905, covered, small lithographed base w/one post supporting lithographed roof; two lithographed plates read "Suburban" and "Station" — 125 / 250

118 PLATFORM STATION, 1906-1912, covered; small lithographed base w/one post supporting lithographed roof; single lithographed plate reads "Suburban Station" on single lithographed plate — 95 / 190

119 PLATFORM STATION, 1905, covered; lithographed tile floor w/two posts supporting lithographed shingle roof; two lithographed plates read "Suburban" and "Station" — 125 / 250

119 PLATFORM STATION, 1906-1912, covered; lithographed tile floor w/two posts supporting lithographed shingle roof; one lithographed plate reads "Suburban Station" — 100 / 200

119 PLATFORM STATION, 1913-1914, covered; painted floor w/two posts supporting painted roof w/no lettering — 75 / 150

120 PLATFORM STATION, 1905, covered; lithographed tile base w/candy-stripe railing on three sides w/four wooden posts supporting lithographed shingled roof; two lithographed read "Suburban" and "Station"; came w/the plates lettered "Passenger" and "Station" — 135 / 270

120 PLATFORM STATION, 1906-1911, covered; lithographed tile base w/painted railing on one side and both ends; four posts supporting lithographed shingle roof; lithographed sign reads "Suburban Station" — 125 / 250

120 PLATFORM STATION, 1912-1916, covered; painted base w/painted railing on one side and both ends; four posts supporting painted roof w/no lettering; some of these still had lithographed roof w/lithographed sign reading "Suburban Station" — 110 / 220

121 PLATFORM STATION, 1906-1909, covered; two lithographed bases simulating tilework, one bench apiece, four posts apiece supporting roof made of metal ribs w/thirty-two pieces of stained glass among them; lattice border around bottom of roof. — 600 / 1,200

121 PLATFORM STATION, 1910-1916, covered; two lithographed covered; bases simulating tilework, two benches on each base; three posts on each base supporting roof w/metal ribs and eight separate pieces of glass; lattice border around bottom of roof — 200 / 400

121 PLATFORM STATION, 1917-1927, covered; two painted bases w/three supporting posts and two benches on each; metal ribbed roof w/eight pieces of glass; no lattice border — 160 / 320

121 CABOOSE, 1929, O ga., eight wheel; red American Flyer body No. 3211 w/Ives trucks w/brass journals; four side windows w/brass inserts and brass end railings — 100 / 200

121 CABOOSE, 1930, O ga., eight wheel; Lionel No. 817; red body w/short green cupola roof and trucks w/brass journals; brass end railings and window inserts; w/brass plates marked "121" and "Ives Lines" — 85 / 170

122 PASSENGER STATION, 1906-1916, combination of the No. 116 passenger station of these years and the No. 121 glass dome of the same period; glass dome was attached to a special shortened roof on one side of the station, and had one supporting base for the other side; see descriptions of No. 116 and No. 121 — 200 / 300

	C6	C8		C6	C8

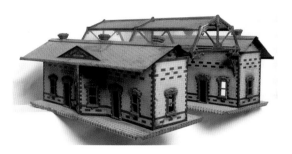

122 PASSENGER STATION, 1917-1923, combination of No. 116 and No. 121 of the same years; glass dome is supported on one side by posts coming up from a specially widened base on the No. 116 station, and by a normal No. 121 base on the other side; see contemporary No. 116 and No. 121 for further description — 200 300

122 TANK CAR, 1929-1930, O ga., eight wheel; orange Lionel No. 815 body, Ives journals w/brass trucks; brass domes, hand rail and ladders; brake wheel at both ends — 90 180

123 DOUBLE STATION, 1906-1923, combination of two No. 116 stations w/a No. 121 glass dome. For more see No. 122, No. 116 and No. 121 for description — 200 300

123 LUMBER CAR, 1910-1912, O ga., eight wheel; black flat truss rod frame w/eight red painted stakes; lumber load held on by four chains; 9" l. — 70 140

123 LUMBER CAR, 1913-1917, O ga., eight wheel; black body, red stake; lumber load held on w/four chains; round truss rods on frame; 9" l. — 55 110

123 LUMBER CAR, 1918-1924, O ga., eight wheel; tan or brown painted body and stakes, lumber load held on by four chains; round truss rods; 9" l. — 55 110

123 LUMBER CAR, 1925-1928, O ga., eight wheel; tan, brown-red or maroon body and stakes; lumber load held on by four chains; round truss rods; 9" l. — 50 100

123 LUMBER CAR, 1929-1930, O ga., eight wheel; green body and stakes; lumber load held on by four chains; rounded truss rods; trucks w/brass journals; 9" l. — 50 100

124 REEFER, 1912-1917, O ga., eight wheel; uncataloged, but first ones came w/lithographed roof w/stripes and catwalk; white body lithographed to simulate wood; sliding door in center of each side; side marked "Merchants Dispatch Transportation Company" and "Refrigerator No. 124 Dairy Express Line"; rounded truss rods w/two posts — 100 200

124 REEFER, 1918-1924, O ga., eight wheel; uncataloged, but first ones came w/lithographed roof w/stripes and catwalk; white body lithographed to simulate wood; sliding door in center of each side; door lithographed "Refrigerator No. 124" on sides; the second "e" is often misspelled as an "f" — 95 190

124 REEFER, 1925-1928, O ga., eight wheel; uncataloged, but first ones came w/lithographed roof w/stripes and catwalk; white body lithographed to simulate wood; sliding door in center of each side; door lithographed "Refrigerator No. 124" on sides; the second "e" is often misspelled as an "f" — 95 190

	C6	C8

124 REEFER, 1929-1930, O ga., eight wheel; uncataloged, but first ones came w/lithographed roof w/stripes and catwalk; white body lithographed to simulate wood; sliding door in center of each side; trucks w/brass journals; door lithographed "Refrigerator No. 124" on sides; the second "e" is often misspelled as an "f" — 95 — 190

125 MERCHANDISE CAR, 1905-1909, O ga., eight wheel; yellow body lithographed to simulate wood; red lithographed roof w/horizontal stripes; inboard trucks; single sliding lithographed door marked "Fast Freight Line" to left and "General Merchandise Car" to right — 338 — 675

125 MERCHANDISE CAR, 1910-1912, O ga., eight wheel; white body lithographed to simulate wood sheathing w/vertical stripes; w/catwalk; T-trucks, flat truss rods on sides of frame; single sliding door on each side, door marked "General Mcdse. Car No. 125"; sides marked "Union Line" and "Merchandise Car No. 125 Pennsylvania Lines" — 155 — 310

125 MERCHANDISE CAR, 1913-1917, O ga., eight wheel; same description as before but w/gray painted roof; some w/Marklin-type trucks — 138 — 275

125 MERCHANDISE CAR, 1915-1930, O ga., eight wheel; in 1915, the catalog states beneath the Union Star cut, that "No. 125 shows a Star Union Car. Under this number comes a large assortment of freights w/the heralds of different roads." — 250 — 500

125 MERCHANDISE CAR, 1918, O ga., eight wheel; same description as before but w/gray painted roof. — 138 — 275

125 MERCHANDISE CAR, 1919-1924, O ga., eight wheel; same description as before but w/gray painted roof — 125 — 250

125 MERCHANDISE CAR, 1925-1928, O ga., eight wheel; same description as before but w/gray painted roof — 125 — 250

125 MERCHANDISE CAR, 1929-1930, O ga., eight wheel; same description as before but w/red painted roof; trucks w/brass journals — 118 — 235

	C6	C8

125-81 MKT MERCHANDISE CAR, 1915-30 — 200 — 400

126 CABOOSE, 1904-1905, O ga., four-wheel; gray lithographed body, black and red roof; sliding lithographed door; sides marked "Fast Freight," "No. 126," "Caboose" — 135 — 270

126 CABOOSE, 1906-1909, four-wheel; buff-colored lithographed body, black and red lithographed roof; same general characteristics as previous years — 125 — 250

127 STOCK CAR, 1904-1909, O ga., eight wheel; gray lithographed body simulating wood, black and red horizontal striped lithographed roof; inboard trucks; sliding door on each side; marked "Livestock Transportation" — 145 — 290

127 STOCK CAR, 1910-1912, O ga., eight wheel; gray body lithographed to simulate wood; frame w/flat truss rods; lithographed cross braces on diagonal on car sides; w/catwalk and lithographed roof w/vertical stripes; sliding lithographed door, marked "Livestock Transportation" — 95 — 190

127 STOCK CAR, 1913-1917, O ga., eight wheel; yellow lithographed body w/gray painted roof; Marklin truck style; lithographed sliding door, w/"Livestock" on diagonal to left, and "Transportation" on diagonal to right; side marked "The Ives RR" — 50 — 100

127 STOCK CAR, 1918, O ga., eight wheel; yellow lithographed body w/gray painted roof; w/type D-1 trucks; lithographed sliding door, w/"Livestock" on diagonal to left, and "Transportation" on diagonal to right; side marked "The Ives RR" — 45 — 90

	C6	C8

127 STOCK CAR, 1919-1924, O ga., eight wheel; yellow lithographed body w/gray painted roof; w/type D-2 trucks; lithographed sliding door, w/"Livestock" on diagonal to left, and "Transportation" on diagonal to right; side marked "The Ives RR" — 45, 90

127 STOCK CAR, 1925-1928, O ga., eight wheel; yellow lithographed body w/gray painted roof; w/type D-3 trucks; lithographed sliding door, w/"Livestock" on diagonal to left, and "Transportation" on diagonal to right; side marked "The Ives RR" — 45, 90

127 STOCK CAR, 1929-1930, O ga., eight wheel; same lithographed pattern as previous models, but more of a yellow-orange; 1930 has some very orange examples; red roof; brass trucks have journals — 45, 90

128 GRAVEL CAR, 1905-1909, O ga., eight wheel; gray body lithographed to simulate wood; inboard trucks — 125, 250

128 GRAVEL CAR, 1910-1911, O ga., eight wheel; dark green body w/white lithographed striping, incomplete on each side; dark green frame w/flat truss rods, T-trucks; marked "New York Central" — 60, 120

128 GRAVEL CAR, 1912, eight wheel; dark green w/lithographed striping; w/frame has rounded truss rods; two support posts; marked "New York Central" — 55, 110

128 GRAVEL CAR, 1913-1915, O ga., eight wheel; lighter green lithographed body w/same general pattern as previous models; Marklin trucks; two support posts in body — 50, 100

128 GRAVEL CAR, 1916-1917, O ga., eight wheel; gray lithographed body w/reddish brown lithographed detail; two support posts across inside of body — 50, 100

128 GRAVEL CAR, 1918, O ga., eight wheel; gray lithographed body w/reddish-brown lithographed detail; rounded truss rods, type D-1 trucks; two support posts inside body — 50, 100

128 GRAVEL CAR, 1919-1924, O ga., eight wheel; gray lithographed body w/reddish-brown lithographed detail; rounded truss rods, type D-2 trucks; two support posts inside body — 50, 100

128 GRAVEL CAR, 1925-1928, O ga., eight wheel; gray lithographed body w/reddish-brown lithographed detail; rounded truss rods, type D-3 trucks; two support posts inside body — 50, 100

128 GRAVEL CAR, 1929, O ga., eight wheels; gray lithographed body w/reddish-brown lithographed detail; rounded truss rods, brass journals on the type D-4 trucks; two support posts inside body — 50, 100

128 GRAVEL CAR, 1930, O ga., eight wheel; gray lithographed body w/reddish-brown lithographed detail; frame w/rounded truss rods; brass journals on type D-4 trucks; some bodies have a lithograph that is almost white, and many examples are not punched for the two support rods across the inside of the body — 50, 100

129 PARLOR CAR, 1904-1909, O ga., eight wheel; yellow body lithograph to simulate wood (also cataloged in red); lithograph roof, some w/stripes, some have a black roof w/lithographed clerestory; inboard trucks; two doors and five windows on each side; sides marked "Limited Vestibule Express" and "Philadelphia" — 300, 600

129 DRAWING ROOM CAR, 1910-1912, O ga., eight wheel; green body lithographed to simulate wood; dark green frame w/flat truss rods, T-trucks; gray roof w/green or red clerestory strip separate; door at each end of side and four double windows; marked "Limited Vestibule Express," "Saratoga" and "129" — 70, 140

129 DRAWING ROOM CAR, 1913-1917, O ga., eight wheel; green body lithographed to simulate wood; rounded truss rods on the side frame; Marklin trucks; gray roof w/green or red clerestory strip separate; door at each end of side and four double windows; marked "Limited Vestibule Express," "Saratoga" and "129" — 70, 140

	C6	C8

129 DRAWING ROOM CAR, 1918-1924, O ga., eight wheel; green body lithographed to simulate steel; gray roof is one-piece w/clerestory strip, although some used up the existing supply of two-piece roofs; type D-2 trucks; four double windows and door at each end; marked "The Ives Railway Lines," "129" and "Saratoga" — 70 — 140

129 DRAWING ROOM CAR, 1925-1926, O ga., eight wheel; green body lithographed to simulate steel; gray roof is one-piece w/clerestory strip, although some used up the existing supply of two-piece roofs; w/type D-3 trucks; four double windows and door at each end; marked "The Ives Railway Lines," "129" and "Saratoga." Saratoga car was used in 1926 in the "Green Mountain Express" set as an observation car by bending it behind the last set of windows and adding a brass observation railing. Also cataloged in orange in 1926 — 70 — 140

129 DRAWING ROOM CAR, 1927-1929, O ga., eight wheel; orange body lithographed to simulate steel without rivet detail; orange one-piece roof w/clerestory strip; trucks; four double windows on both sides w/a door at each end of side; marked "The Ives Railway Lines," "Saratoga" and "129" — 63 — 125

129 DRAWING ROOM CAR, 1930, O ga., eight wheel; orange body lithographed to simulate steel without rivet detail; orange one-piece roof w/clerestory strip; trucks w/brass journals; four double windows on both sides w/a door at each end of side; marked "The Ives Railway Lines," "Saratoga" and "129" — 63 — 125

130 COMBINATION CAR, 1904-1909, O ga., eight wheel; yellow lithograph body; black lithographed roof w/red stripes and painted and lithographed clerestory (some roofs are just painted); inboard trucks; baggage door at one end of side, passenger door w/steps at other end of side and six windows between them; sides marked "Limited Vestibule Express," "Buffet," "Baggage" and "New York" — 150 — 300

130 COMBINATION CAR, 1910-1912, O ga., eight wheel; green body lithographed simulates wood; gray roof, gray w/red or green clerestory strip; T-truck and flat truss rods on side frames; baggage door at one end of side, passenger door w/steps at other end of side and three double windows between them; side marked "Limited Vestibule Express," "130," "Buffet" and "130" — 70 — 140

130 COMBINATION CAR, 1913-1917, O ga., eight wheel; green body lithographed simulates wood; gray roof, gray w/red or green clerestory strip; Marklin trucks and rounded truss rods on side frames; baggage door at one end of side, passenger door w/steps at other end of side and three double windows between them; side marked "Limited Vestibule Express," "130," "Buffet" and "130" — 70 — 140

130 COMBINATION CAR, 1918-1924, O ga., eight wheel; green body lithographed to simulate steel w/rivet detail; one-piece roof w/clerestory strip, all painted gray (some used up existing supply of two-piece roofs early on); baggage door at one end of windows, passenger door at other end above three double windows; type D-2 trucks; sides marked "The Ives Railway Lines," "No. 130," "Buffet," and "130" — 72 — 145

	C6	C8

130 COMBINATION CAR, 1925-1926, O ga., eight wheel; green body lithographed to simulate steel w/rivet detail; one-piece roof w/clerestory strip, all painted gray (some used up existing supply of two-piece roofs early on); baggage door at one end of windows, passenger door at other end above three double windows; type D-3 trucks; sides marked "The Ives Railway Lines," "No. 130," "Buffet," and "130"; also cataloged in orange in 1926 — 70 / 140

130 COMBINATION CAR, 1927-1929, O ga., eight wheel; orange steel lithographed body without rivet detail; brass journals on trucks; baggage door at one end of windows, passenger door at other end above three double windows; sides marked "The Ives Railway Lines," "130," "Buffet" — 60 / 120

131 BAGGAGE CAR, 1904-1909, O ga., eight wheel; yellow body lithographed to simulate wood; black and red striped roof w/painted or lithographed clerestory strip; inboard trucks; two baggage doors per side, mail window to left of first one; sides marked "U.S. Mail," "Baggage Car," "Chicago," "Limited Vestibule Express" — 250 / 500

131 BAGGAGE CAR, 1910-1912, O ga., eight wheel; green body lithographed to simulate wood; dark green frame T-trucks and flat truss rods; gray roof w/separate red or green clerestory; passenger door at each side end w/two sliding baggage doors between them; sides marked "Limited Vestibule Express," "No. 131" and "Baggage Express" — 98 / 195

131 BAGGAGE CAR, 1913-1917, O ga., eight wheel; green body lithographed to simulate wood; dark green frame Markiln trucks and rounded truss rods; gray roof w/separate red or green clerestory; passenger door at each side end w/two sliding baggage doors between them; sides marked "Limited Vestibule Express," "No. 131" and "Baggage Express" — 85 / 170

131 BAGGAGE CAR, 1924-1926, O ga., eight wheel; green body, lithographed body to simulate steel; gray one-piece roof w/clerestory strip; passenger door at end and baggage door; sides marked "The Ives Railway Lines," "No. 131," "Baggage Express" and "U.S. Mail"; also cataloged in orange in 1926 — 32 / 65

131 BAGGAGE CAR, 1927-1929, O ga., eight wheel; orange steel body lithographed without rivet detail; one passenger door at each end, two baggage doors in middle; marked "Ives Railway Lines," "No. 131," "Baggage Express" and "U.S. Mail" — 30 / 55

131 BAGGAGE CAR, 1930, O ga., eight wheel; orange steel body lithographed without rivet detail; trucks w/brass journals; one passenger door at each end, two baggage doors in middle; sides marked "Ives Railway Lines," "No. 131," "Baggage Express" and "U.S. Mail" — 30 / 55

132 OBSERVATION CAR, 1926-1929, O ga., eight wheel; one version was made from the 129 Saratoga car in 1926. Also cataloged w/orange lithographed body version; one-piece roof w/clerestory strip w/brass observation platform railing, four double windows and one door lithographed on each side; sides marked "The Ives Railway Lines," "No. 132," "Observation" — 32 / 65

	C6	**C8**

132 OBSERVATION CAR, 1930, O ga., eight wheel; orange lithographed body version; trucks w/brass journals; one-piece roof w/clerestory strip and brass observation platform railing; four double windows and one door lithographed on each side; sides marked "The Ives Railway Lines," "No. 132," "Observation" — **32** / **65**

133 PARLOR CAR, 1928-1930, O ga., eight wheel; painted body and roof w/brass window inserts, brass plates and D-3 trucks; sides marked "133 Parlor Car 133"; cataloged in various colors, but generally came in either orange or red; Same body as 135 w/less trim; not cataloged w/lights but some cars had them — **53** / **105**

134 OBSERVATION CAR, 1928-1930, O ga., eight wheel; orange or red painted body and roof w/brass window inserts, observation platform, brass plates and D-3 trucks; sides marked "134 Observation 134"; same car as 136, but less trim; not cataloged w/lights, but some cars had them — **53** / **105**

135 PARLOR CAR, 1926-1930, O ga., eight wheel; painted body and roof; interior lights; brass window inserts and brass plates; brass journals on type D-four trucks; four celluloid windows; sides marked "Pullman," "Parlor Car"; 1926 — tan body; 1927 — blue body; 1928 — orange body; 1929 — red body w/black roof and brass vestibules; 1930 — orange body w/black roof, red body w/black roof, or blue body w/red roof — **88** / **175**

136 OBSERVATION CAR, 1926-1930, O ga., eight wheel; painted body and roof; interior and platform lights; four celluloid windows w/brass window inserts and observation railing; brass journals on D-4 trucks; brass plates; sides marked "Pullman," "136 Observation 136"; 1926 — tan body; 1927 — blue body; 1928 — orange body; 1929 — red body, black roof, brass vestibules; 1930 — orange body w/black roof, or red body w/black roof, or blue body w/red roof — **88** / **175**

137 PARLOR CAR, 1928, O ga., eight wheel; black painted roof w/red body; another version of the 135 car; D-3 trucks; brass window inserts, celluloid windows; without lights or journals; brass plates read "137 Parlor Car 137" — **45** / **90**

138 OBSERVATION CAR, 1928, O ga., eight wheel; black painted roof w/red body; another version of the 136 car; brass window inserts w/celluloid windows; no lights or brass journals; D-3 trucks; brass observation platform; brass plate marked "138 Observation 138" — **45** / **90**

140 AUTOMATIC CROSSING GATES, 1906-1920, O ga., lithographed or painted base w/lithographed building and crossing gate tripped by oncoming train; for mechanical trains; 20-1/2" l. — **35** / **70**

140-3 AUTOMATIC CROSSING GATES, 1910-1920, O ga., lithographed or painted base w/lithographed building and crossing gate tripped by oncoming train; for electrical trains; 20-1/2" l. — **35** / **70**

141 PARLOR CAR, 1926-1930, O ga., eight wheel; longer than the No. 135, painted gray, orange or black body and roof; brass journals; five double windows w/brass window inserts and two doors on each side; some have vestibules, and brass plate; w/lights; "Pullman," "Parlor Car," "141" and "Made In The Ives Shops" — **80** / **160**

	C6	C8

142 OBSERVATION CAR, 1926-1930, O ga., eight wheel; body generally painted gray, orange or black, painted roof; longer than the No. 136; brass journals; five double windows w/brass window; lights; observation platform and vestibules; marked "Pullman," "Observation," "142" and "Made In The Ives Shops" — 80 — 160

145 TURNTABLE, 1910-1930, O ga., four track outside, w/inside table rotated by clockwork mechanism; brake and signal on turning table portion; painted base and table; for mechanical trains — 50 — 100

146 TURNTABLE, 1906-1919, O ga., automatic; four truck outside; inside table rotated by clockwork mechanism; brake and signal on turning table portion; painted base and table; mechanical trains — 75 — 150

176 LOCOMOTIVE, 1930, O ga., 0-4-0; black cast-iron body w/ clockwork engine and hand brake; marked "Ives No. 176" beneath cab windows; 1930 version of the No. 17 locomotive; w/No. 17 tender w/decal — 110 — 220

215 CROSSING GATE, 1923-1930, O ga., lithographed base simulating earth; two fences w/pole gate between them; manually operated — 22 — 45

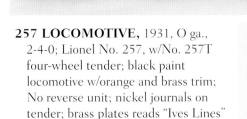

257 LOCOMOTIVE, 1931, O ga., 2-4-0; Lionel No. 257, w/No. 257T four-wheel tender; black paint locomotive w/orange and brass trim; No reverse unit; nickel journals on tender; brass plates reads "Ives Lines" and "Ives No. 257" — 200 — 400

258 LOCOMOTIVE, 1931-1932, O ga., 2-4-0 w/No. 1663 Tender; black painted locomotive w/orange and copper trim, hand reverse unit w/brass plate that reads "Ives Lines" and "Ives No. 258"; eight-wheel black tender w/brass journals — 230 — 460

339-0 TRACK BUMPER, 1928-1930, O ga., Lionel bumper w/red light on top — 12 — 25

340-0 SPRING BUMPER, 1929-1930, O ga., sheet-steel w/spring cross bar; Lionel — 10 — 20

550 BAGGAGE CAR, 1913-1915, O ga., four-wheel; painted one piece roof, lithographed body simulating wood detail Red, rose or white body; passenger door at each end of side, leaf springs on frame; marked "The Ives Railway Lines" center door and "Baggage No. 550" to left of door, and "Express Mail" to right — 58 — 115

550 BAGGAGE CAR, 1916-1926, O ga., four-wheel; green lithographed body simulates steel, painted roof; flat springs on frame; passenger door at each end of side, open doorway in center; marked "The Ives Railway Lines" above door, "Express Service Baggage 550" to left and "U.S. Mail 550" to right; sometimes 60 series cars were used for these — 58 — 115

	C6	C8

550 BAGGAGE CAR, 1927-1930, O ga., four-wheel; lithographed green steel body, flat spring frame; white body, red roof in 1927 for White Owl set, blue and buff body w/blue roof in 1930 for Blue Vagabond set, green and buff body w/blue roof in 1930 for Pequot set, also red body w/blue roof in 1930; open doorway in center of car, passenger door at each end of side; marked "The Ives Railway Lines" above doorway; "Express Service Baggage 550" to left of center door and "U.S. Mail 550" to the right. ... 58 ... 115

551 CHAIR CAR, 1913-1915, O ga., four-wheel; red, white or rose body lithographed to simulate wood sheathing; painted one-piece roof; leaf springs on frame; eight square windows and door at the end of each side "The Ives Railway Lines" lettered above eight square windows; marked "No. 61," "Yale" and "No. 61" below windows ... 55 ... 110

551 CHAIR CAR, 1916-1926, O ga., four-wheel; green body lithographed to simulate steel; painted one-piece roof; flat springs on frame; eight windows and passenger door at the end of each side; "The Ives Railway Lines" above 8 windows, "551", "Chair Car", and "551" below window level; 60 series cars were sometimes used ... 55 ... 110

551 CHAIR CAR, 1927-1930, O ga., four-wheel; green body lithographed to simulate steel; white w/red roof in 1927 for White Owl set, blue and buff w/blue roof in 1930 for Blue Vagabond, green and buff in 1930 for Pequot, also came w/red body and blue roof in 1930; painted one-piece roof; eight windows and passenger doors at the end of each side; marked "The Ives Railway Lines" above windows and "551," "Chair Car," and "551" below window ... 55 ... 110

552 PARLOR CAR, 1913-1915, O ga., four-wheel; red, white, or rose body lithographed to simulate wood; one-piece painted roof; leaf springs on frame; five wide windows and passenger door at the end of each side; marked "The Ives Railway Lines" windows, and "No. 62," "Harvard," and "No. 62" below windows ... 55 ... 110

552 PARLOR CAR, 1916-1926, O ga., four-wheel; one-piece painted roof; green body lithographed to simulate steel; flat springs on frame; five wide windows and passenger door at the end of each side; marked "The Ives Railway Lines" above windows, and "552," "Parlor Car," and "552" below ... 55 ... 110

552 PARLOR CAR, 1927-1930, O ga., four-wheel; green body lithographed to simulate steel; white w/red roof in 1927 for White Owl set, blue and buff w/blue roof in 1930 for Blue Vagabond set, green and buff in 1930 for Pequot set, also red body w/blue roof in 1930; painted one-piece roof; flat springs on frame; five wide windows and passenger door at the end of each side; marked "The Ives Railway Lines" above windows and "552," "Parlor Car" and "552" below ... 55 ... 110

558 OBSERVATION CAR, 1927-1930, O ga., four-wheel; green body lithographed to simulate steel; painted one-piece roof; white in 1927 for White Owl set, blue and buff in 1930 for Blue Vagabond set, also red w/blue roof in 1930; flat springs on frame; five wide windows and passenger door at the front of each side; brass observation railing; marked "The Ives Railway Lines" above windows and "558," "Observation" and "558" ... 55 ... 110

562 CABOOSE, 1930, O ga., four-wheel; red Lionel No. 807 body w/brass window inserts and green cupola roof; flat springs on trucks ... 68 ... 135

563 GRAVEL CAR, 1913-1930, O ga., four-wheel; gray or green body lithographed to simulate steel ... 35 ... 70

	C6	C8

564 MERCHANDISE CAR, 1913-1930, O ga., four-wheel; this series utilized the No. 64 box car series detailed in the 60 series section and in general notes — 125 / 250

565 LIVESTOCK CAR, 1913-1930, O ga., four-wheel; red orange body lithographed to simulate wood (some examples had yellow body similar to No. 65 stock car); painted one-piece roof w/catwalk; some versions had sliding door; early examples marked w/"Livestock Transportation" — 45 / 90

566 TANK CAR, 1913-1929, O ga., four-wheel; painted body frame; follows evolution of No. 66 tank car; see this car's description for more detail; ends marked "566"; sides read "Standard Oil" — 45 / 90

566 TANK CAR, 1930, O ga., Lionel No. 804 tank car w/brass domes; orange body; brass handrail and ladders; brass plates read "Ives" and "No. 566" — 60 / 120

567 CABOOSE, 1913-1930, O ga., four-wheel; lithographed body w/painted roof and cupola; see caboose No. 67 for details — 45 / 90

569 LUMBER CAR, 1913-1930, O ga., four-wheel; body and stakes painted tan, maroon, brown, green or black; two chain supports hold carries lumber load; supported load — 40 / 80

600 ELECTRIC ARC LIGHT, 1915-1922, single arm street light w/various shapes and lamp — 30 / 60

600 ELECTRIC ARC LIGHT, 1915-1922, double arm street light w/various shapes and lamps. — 40 / 80

610 PULLMAN CAR, 1931-1932, O ga., eight wheel; Lionel car; green body and roof; Air tanks beneath car; Lionel latch couplers; eight windows and passenger doors at each end of side; decal above windows reads "The Ives Lines," marked "610," "Pullman" and "610" below windows — 70 / 140

612 OBSERVATION CAR, 1931-1932, O ga., eight wheel; Lionel car; green body and roof; Lionel latch couplers; air tanks beneath car; observation platform of brass on rear; eight windows and passenger doors at the front of each side; decal above windows reads "The Ives Lines"; marked "612," "Observation" and "612" below windows — 70 / 140

800 TROLLEY, 1910-1913, O ga., four-wheel; mechanical works w/trolley pole on roof; tin wheels and hinged pilots; four windows and passenger door at each end of side; marked "Local and Suburban Service" above windows and "Trolley" below; 6-1/2" l. — 800 / 1,600

801 TROLLEY, 1910-1913, O ga., four-wheel; mechanical works w/spring pole on roof; lithographed body; tin wheels; four windows and two doors on each side; marked "Limited Vestibule Express" above windows "Buffalo" below; can also be marked "Pennsylvania Lines" "Newark" and "Washington"; 5" l. — 600 / 1,200

805 TROLLEY CAR TRAILER, 1913-1915, O ga., four-wheel; lithographed body w/cast pilot; roof w/separate clerestory; no trolley pole; cast-iron spoke wheels; five windows and one open and one blocked passenger door each on side; unpowered — 175 / 350

809 STREETCAR, 1913-1915, O ga., four-wheel; lithographed body w/cast pilot; roof w/separate clerestory; no trolley pole; cast-iron spoke wheels; five windows and one open and one blocked passenger door each on side; marked "Suburban" below windows and "Ives No. 809" on side; 7-3/4" l. — 500 / 1,000

810 TROLLEY, 1910-1912, O ga., four-wheel; same general configuration as No. 809; roof w/separate clerestory; ten caternary poles; trolley pole on roof collected current for motor; tin wheels; sides lithographed "Suburban" and "Ives No. 810" on side; 7-1/2" l. — 500 / 1,000

	C6	C8

1100 LOCOMOTIVE, 1910-1912, O ga., 2-2-0; cast black body; dummy headlight, two tin boiler bands, painted stack and bell; tin front wheels; cast drivers; no drive rods w/F.E. No. 1 tender; brass plates below rectangular window reads "Ives No. 1100" — 155 310

1100 LOCOMOTIVE, 1913-1914, O ga., 0-4-0; similar to 1912 version w/slightly different casting to accommodate front drive wheels; dummy headlight, two tin boiler bands, painted stack and bell; seven spoke wheels; w/L.V.E. No. 11 tender; lithographed plate beneath cab roof reads "Ives No. 1100" — 140 280

1100 LOCOMOTIVE, 1915-1916, O ga., 0-4-0; cast-iron black body; straight boiler w/dummy headlight on boiler top; two tin boiler bands; rectangular cab window; drive rods; seven or twelve spoke cast-iron wheels; stamped "Ives No. 1100" stamped below window; w/tender marked "Ives No. 11" — 125 250

1100 LOCOMOTIVE, 1917-1922, O ga., 0-4-0; cast-iron black body; one tin boiler band and dummy headlight in boiler front; cast-iron wheels; rectangular cab window; drive rods; w/No. 11 tender; At some point during production (probably around 1920) 1100s were made from 1116 castings w/operating headlight in boiler front, probably around — 95 190

1116 LOCOMOTIVE, 1917-1922, O ga., 0-4-0; same casting as No. 1100, but w/operating headlight in boiler front center; straight drive rods, No. 11 tender; see 1100 for more details — 150 300

1117 LOCOMOTIVE, 1910-1914, O ga., 0-4-0; black cast-iron boiler, cast-iron wheels w/angled drive rods; body extension over armature end in 1910; two tin boiler bands and dummy headlight on top of boiler; two cab windows; w/L.V.E. No. 11 tender; lithographed plates beneath windows read "Ives No. 1117" — 150 300

1117 LOCOMOTIVE, 1915-1916, O ga., 0-4-0; same boiler casting; cast-iron body and wheels w/angled drive rods; two tin boiler bands; w/Ives No. 11 tender; w/rubber stamped "Ives No. 1117" beneath windows — 140 280

1118 LOCOMOTIVE, 1910-1914, O ga., 0-4-0; same boiler No. 1117, w/operative headlight on boiler top; body covers armature in 1910 version; two tin boiler bands; cast-iron body and wheels w/angled drive rods; two cab windows; lithographed plate below windows reads "Ives No. 1118"; w/Ives No. 11 tender — 150 300

1118 LOCOMOTIVE, 1915-1916, O ga., 0-4-0; same as previous version but w/rubber stamped lettering beneath cab windows instead of lithographed plate — 140 280

1118 LOCOMOTIVE, 1917-1925, O ga., 0-4-0; larger w/higher body casting; cast-iron body, cast-iron wheels w/straight drive rods; headlight in center of boiler; one casting has extra sheeting below cab w/large rivet detail; w/Ives No. 17 tender; two rectangular windows; stamped "Ives No. 1118" below window — 110 220

1120 LOCOMOTIVE, 1916, 0-4-0; same as No. 1118; cast-iron body and wheels w/drive rods; generally stamped "Ives No. 1120" below windows, although at least one version has lithograph plates; see 1118 for more details — 388 775

1120 LOCOMOTIVE, 1928, O ga., 4-4-0; cast-iron body w/arched cab windows; die-cast wheels w/straight drive rods; separate grab rails and braces from boiler to pilot; w/No. 25 tender w/coal load; marked "Ives NYC & HR"; boiler stamped "Ives No. 1120" below windows — 475 950

1122 LOCOMOTIVE, 1929-1930, O ga., 4-4-2; die-cast body, headlight in boiler center and bell on boiler front; brass handrails, copper tubing and die-cast drive rods; die-cast wheels; drivers w/nickel tires; No. 25 die-cast tender; brass plate below cab windows reads "The Ives Railway Lines" and brass plate below boiler front reads "Made In The Ives Shops"; tender marked "The Ives Railway Lines" on brass plate — 300 600

	C6	C8

1125 LOCOMOTIVE, 1910-1913, O ga., 4-4-0; tin pony wheels; cast-iron spoked drivers w/angled rods; operating headlight on boiler top; separate handrails; two cab windows; plates below windows lithographed "Ives No. 1125"; w/eight-wheel tender w/sides lithographed "Limited Vestibule Express" — 250 — 500

1125 LOCOMOTIVE, 1914-1917, O ga., 4-4-2; cast-iron spoked pony wheels and drivers w/angled drive rods; separate grab rails, operating headlight on top of boiler; Marklin trucks; plates beneath cab windows lithographed "Ives No. 25"; w/eight-wheel No. 25 tender marked "NYC & HR" or "Ives No. 25" on sides — 250 — 500

1125 LOCOMOTIVE, 1930, O ga., 0-4-0; chunky-looking cast-iron body w/one separate boiler band; brass bell on boiler, operational headlight operates on boiler front; black or blue body; gold decal beneath cab windows read "Ives RR Lines"; "1125" cast on cab sides; w/No. 17 tender w/round Ives decal on sides and coal load — 225 — 450

1501 LOCOMOTIVE, 1931-1932, O ga., 0-4-0; mechanized red tin body, die-cast wheels without drive rod; speed governed; w/bell activated during running; hand brake; no marks on engine; sides of tender marked "1502 Ives R.R. Lines 1502" on yellow simulated letterboard — 125 — 250

1504 PULLMAN CAR, 1931-1932, O ga., four-wheel; one-piece red lithographed tin body w/blue roof and yellow trim; tin wheels; five double windows; sides marked "1504 Pullman 1504" below windows — 45 — 90

1506 LOCOMOTIVE, 1931-1932, mechanical; larger than No. 1502; tin body painted black w/die-cast wheels and straight drive rods; bell and handbrake; black No. 1507 tender w/red lithographed rectangle marked "1507 Ives R.R. Lines 1507" — 125 — 250

1512 GONDOLA, 1931-1932, O ga., four-wheel; blue tin body — 40 — 80

1513 CATTLE CAR, 1931-1932, O ga., four-wheel; green lithographed body w/sliding doors — 40 — 80

1514 BOXCAR, 1931-1932, O ga., four-wheel; yellow tin body w/blue roof and sliding doors; "Erie" logo on sides — 40 — 80

1515 TANK CAR, 1931-1932, O ga., four-wheel; silver body w/brass and copper trim; "Sunoco" logo on sides — 40 — 80

1517 CABOOSE, 1931-1932, O ga., four-wheel; red lithographed tin body w/red-brown roof; "NYC" logo on sides — 40 — 80

1550 SWITCH, 1931-1932, O ga., left and right; for clockwork trains — 8 — 16

1555 CROSSING, 1931-1932, O ga., 90 degrees for clockwork trains — 6 — 12

1558 ACCESSORY BUMPER, 1931-1932, O ga., for clockwork track — 10 — 20

1559 CROSSING GATE, 1931-1932, O ga., w/striped lithographed arm — 10 — 20

1560 STATION, 1931-1932, O ga., lithographed body and roof; housed either transformer or whistle — 40 — 80

1561 TUNNEL, 1931-1932, O ga., papier-máché; 8" l. — 10 — 20

1564 BRIDGE, 1931-1932, O ga., same as No. 91, for clockwork track — 30 — 60

1562 WATER TOWER, 1931-1932, green and maroon, w/hinged spout — 25 — 50

1563 TELEGRAPH POLE, 1931-1932 — 3 — 6

	C6	**C8**

1565 SEMAPHORE, 1931-1932, Same as No. 107-S; single arm — 10 / 20

1566 SEMAPHORE, 1931-1932, same as No. 107-D; double arm — 10 / 20

1567 CROSSING SIGN, 1931-1932, same as No. 111 — 4 / 8

1568 CLOCK, 1931-1932, tin base; lithographed face w/movable hands; diamond shaped — 4 / 8

1569 ACCESSORY SET, 1932, four telegraph poles, one clock, one crossing sign and one semaphore; w/box; seven pieces — 40 / 80

1570 GIFT SET, 1932, includes No. 1572, No. 1514, No. 1515 and No. 1517; w/box — 175 / 350

1571 TELEGRAPH POST, 1932, red and white — 3 / 6

1572 SEMAPHORE, 1932 — 6 / 12

1573 WARNING SIGNAL, 1932, square post; diamond-shaped sign — 6 / 12

1574 CLOCK, 1932, square post; diamond-shaped face w/movable hands — 4 / 8

1575 CROSSING GATE, 1932, lithographed gate, painted base; Manual. — 8 / 16

1651 LOCOMOTIVE, 1932, O ga., 0-4-0; electric-type box cab; lithographed steel in either red w/maroon roof or yellow w/blue roof; die-cast wheels; brass trim and journals; marked "Ives R.R. Lines" below roof line; also marked "1651" beneath windows — 150 / 300

1661 LOCOMOTIVE, 1932, O ga., 2-4-0; black tin body w/red trim; die-cast wheels; some versions have drive rods and a hand reverse unit; copper and brass trim; No. 1661 tender marked "Ives R.R. Lines" — 100 / 200

1663 LOCOMOTIVE, 1931-1932, O ga., 2-4-2; Lionel engine w/Ives plates; die-cast body and wheels; nickel-plated drive rods; die-cast eight-wheel tender No. 1663; both painted black cast-iron — 213 / 525

1677 GONDOLA, 1931-1932, O ga., eight wheel; blue body lithographed to simulate steel; brass journals; ovals on each side read "Ives R.R. Lines" and "1677" — 31 / 62

1678 CATTLE CAR, 1931-1932, O ga., eight wheel; green body lithographed to simulate wood w/sliding door and brass journals — 31 / 62

1679 BOXCAR, 1931-1932, O ga., eight wheel; yellow lithographed sides and blue roof; brass journals; marked "Ives R.R. Lines" and "1679" on sides — 31 / 62

1680 TANK CAR, 1931-1932, O ga., eight wheel; painted silver body w/brass and copper trim; brass journals; marked "Ives Tank Lines," "Fuel Oil" and "1680" on sides — 31 / 62

1682 CABOOSE, 1931-1932, O ga., eight wheel; red lithographed body w/red-brown roof; brass journals; sides marked "Ives R.R. Lines" in oval and "1682" in rectangle — 31 / 62

1690 PULLMAN, 1931-1932, O ga., eight wheel; red lithographed body w/maroon roof and cream trim or yellow body w/blue roof and orange trim; brass handrails and journals; six double windows and door at each end of side; "1690," "Ives R.R. Lines" and "1690" beneath windows — 35 / 70

	C6	**C8**

1691 OBSERVATION CAR,
1931-1932, O ga., eight wheel; red
lithographed body w/maroon roof and
cream trim or yellow body w/blue
roof and orange trim; brass handrails,
journals and railing; w/door at front of
each end and windows on both sides;
marked "Ives R.R. Lines" and "1691"
below windows ... 35 ... 70

1694 LOCOMOTIVE, 1932, O ga.,
4-4-4; New Haven-style electric box
cab; puff painted sides w/maroon roof
and brass trim; headlights at each end;
die-cast wheels w/nickel-plated drive
rods; punched ventilators on sides;
brass plates read "1694" "Ives Lines"
and "1694" ... 500 ... 1000

1695 PULLMAN CAR, 1932, O ga.,
12 wheel; buff painted body
w/maroon roof; copper journals;
6 double windows; decals below
windows read "1695," "The Ives Lines"
and
"1695" ... 175 ... 350

1696 BAGGAGE CAR, 1932, O ga.,
12 wheel; buff painted body w/maroon
roof; copper journals; baggage and mail
doors on each side, w/three windows
near each. "1696," "The Ives Lines"
and "1696" decals on each side ... 175 ... 350

1697 OBSERVATION CAR, 1932, O
ga., twelve wheel; buff body w/maroon
roof; brass observation platform and
copper journals; passenger door at
front and six double windows on
each side; decal below windows read
"1697," "The Ives Lines," and "1697" ... 175 ... 350

1707 GONDOLA, 1932, O ga., eight
wheel; lithographed body to simulate
wood w/cross braces; brass journals;
"Ives" logo in oval on side ... 45 ... 90

	C6	**C8**

1708 CATTLE CAR, 1932, O ga.,
eight wheel; green body lithographed
to simulate boards w/spaces between
them; ovals on sides lithographed
"1708" and "Ives" ... 135 ... 270

1709 BOXCAR, 1932, O ga., eight
wheel; lithographed blue body
w/painted roof; yellow sliding doors
and brass journals; ovals on sides read
"1709" and "Ives" ... 45 ... 90

1712 CABOOSE, 1932, O ga., eight
wheel; red lithographed body
w/maroon roof; brass journals; ovals on
sides read "1712" and "Ives" ... 45 ... 90

1810 LOCOMOTIVE, 1931-1932, O
ga., 0-4-0; electric-style box cab; green
body, red roof w/yellow trim; brass
pantograph and dummy headlight;
sides marked "Ives R.R. Lines" above
windows and ventilators and "1810"
near each end ... 95 ... 190

	C6	C8

1811 PULLMAN CAR, 1931-1932, O ga., four-wheel; green body, red roof w/yellow trim; door at each end of sides; marked "Ives R.R. Lines" above four double windows and "1811," "Pullman," "1811" below — 40 / 80

1812 OBSERVATION CAR, 1931-1932, O ga., four-wheel; green body, red roof w/yellow trim; door at front, observation platform at rear; marked "Ives R.R. Lines" above five double windows; "1812," "Observation" and "1812" below — 40 / 80

1813 BAGGAGE CAR, 1931-1932, O ga., four-wheel; green body, red roof w/yellow trim; marked "Ives R.R. Lines" between two doors and "1813," "Baggage," and "1813" at lower level of car — 40 / 80

1815 LOCOMOTIVE, 1931-1932, O ga., 0-4-0; lack tin body w/red trim; die-cast wheels and nickel drive rods; dummy headlight; no reverse; w/black No. 1815 tender marked "Ives R.R. Lines" — 95 / 190

1851 CROSSING, 1931-1932, O ga., 90 degrees — 4 / 8

1853 CROSSING, 1931-1932, O ga., 45 degrees — 4 / 8

1855 BUMPER, 1931-1932, O ga., sprung bar type — 10 / 20

1857 BUMPER, 1931-1932, O ga., sprung bar type w/illumination — 10 / 20

1851 CROSSING, 1931-1932, O ga., papier-mâché, 11" l. — 15 / 30

1860 CROSSING, 1931-1932, O ga., papier-mâché, 16" l. — 15 / 30

1863 BRIDGE APPROACH SIGNAL, 1931-1932, O ga., die-cast base; painted round post w/arm and chairs; formerly Ives No. 338 — 45 / 90

1866 FLAG POLE, 1931-1932, American flag; raised and lowered on string — 40 / 80

1867 SIGNAL TOWER, 1931-1932, Lionel No. 438 tower w/switches on back "Ives" plates — 150 / 300

	C6	C8

1868 VILLA, 1931-1932, O ga., Lionel No. 191, red and green, illuminated; "Ives" stamped on bottom — 75 / 150

1869 COLONIAL HOUSE, 1931-1932, O ga., white Lionel No. 189, illuminated; "Ives" stamped on bottom — 80 / 160

1870 COTTAGE, 1931-1932, O ga., tan and green Lionel No. 184, illuminated; w/"Ives" stamped on bottom — 75 / 150

1871 SUBURBAN STATION, 1931-1932, red and green Lionel No. 126; two windows and door; dormer on roof; marked "Ives Town" above window — 125 / 250

1872 STATION, 1931-1932, ivory and red Lionel No. 127 w/green and yellow windows, marked "Ives Town" plate above middle doors — 100 / 200

1873 CITY STATION, 1931-1932, terra-cotta Lionel No. 122 w/green roof, yellow trim and swinging doors; plate above center window reads "Ives Town" — 150 / 300

1874 CITY STATION, 1931-1932, same as 1873 but w/exterior illumination — 150 / 300

1875 FREIGHT SHED, 1931-1932, terra-cotta roof, maroon base and green piers; Lionel No. 155 w/illumination — 180 / 360

	C6	**C8**

1876 POWER HOUSE, 1931-1932, buff, terra-cotta and green Lionel No. 435 three windows on front door on each end; w/smokestack; "Ives" stamped on bottom — 145 / 290

1877 CIRCUIT BREAKER, 1931-1932, same as Lionel No. 81 but illuminated — 30 / 60

1878 CROSSING GATE, 1931-1932, O ga., automatically operated, lithographed arm, illuminated Lionel No. 077 — 30 / 60

1879 CROSSING GATE, 1931-1932, Standard ga., automatic operation, lithographed arm, illuminated; Lionel No. 77 — 30 / 60

1880 WARNING SIGNAL, 1931-1932, Standard ga., white Lionel No. 79, illuminated; brass sign face — 65 / 130

1881 SIGNAL TRAFFIC LIGHT, 1931-1932, blinking type; Lionel No. 83; yellow w/red base — 60 / 120

1882 LAMP POST, 1931-1932, electric, boulevard type; green upright die-cast base w/signal bulb — 45 / 90

1884 BELL SIGNAL, 1931-1932, O ga., automatic; green base, brass diamond warning sign and bells on back — 60 / 120

1886 TARGET SIGNAL, 1931-1932, O ga., automatic; green base, brass diamond warning sign and bells on back — 65 / 130

1887-1891 TRANSFORMERS, 1931-1932 — 10 / 20

1893 D.C. REDUCER, 1931-1932, for houses w/direct current to run transformers — 10 / 20

1894 RHEOSTAT, 1931-1932, used to control train speeds — 10 / 20

1895 SWITCHES, 1931-1932, O ga., manual, illuminated — 15 / 30

1897 SWITCHES, 1931-1932, O ga., electrically operated, illuminated — 20 / 40

1904 SEMAPHORE, 1932, O ga., single blade, automatic; Same as 1903 — 75 / 150

	C6	**C8**

1905 LAMP POST, 1932, gooseneck-style, double arm; same as No. 307 — 50 / 100

1906 FREIGHT STATION SET, boxed, 1932, includes two land trucks, a dump truck and a baggage truck; Lionel No. 163 — 75 / 150

1907 TRAIN CONTROL, 1932, O ga., automatic, stops and starts train; Lionel No. 078 — 75 / 150

1926 LIGHT BULB, 1931-1932, 6 volt, round — .50 / 1

1927 LIGHT BULB, 1931-1932, 12 volt, round — .50 / 1

1928 LIGHT BULB, 1931-1932, 18 volt, round — .50 / 1

1939 LIGHT BULB, 1931-1932, 12 volt, pear shaped — .50 / 1

1940 LIGHT BULB, 1931-1932, 18 volt, pear shaped — .50 / 1

3200 LOCOMOTIVE, 1910, O ga., 0-4-0; cast-iron S-1 type electric body; painted gold pantograph and dummy headlight on each hood; no air tanks; steps beneath door in cab center; tin wheels held on w/nuts; separate pilots; raised lettering beneath windows reads "Ives" and "3200" — 400 / 800

3200 LOCOMOTIVE, 1911, O ga., 0-4-0; cast-iron S-1 type electric center cab; green or black body; gold painted pantograph and dummy headlight on each hood; separate pilots; cast-iron six-spoke wheels; center door flanked by two windows; steps below; air tanks; raised lettering reads "Ives" and "3200" below windows — 250 / 500

3200 LOCOMOTIVE, 1912-1913, O ga., 0-4-0; cast-iron S-1 type center cab electric; maroon or black body w/separate pilots; gold painted pantograph and dummy headlight on each hood; cast-iron 10-spoke wheels; centered door on side w/steps below; air tanks; stamped "The Ives Railway Lines" below left window and "Motor 3200" beneath right window — 150 / 300

	C6	**C8**

3200 LOCOMOTIVE, 1914, O ga., 0-4-0; cast-iron S-2 type center cab electric; black painted body w/separate pilots; gold painted pantograph and dummy headlight on each hood; centered 10-spoke wheels; centered door w/steps below and air tanks; stamped "The Ives Railway Lines" beneath left window and "Motor 3200" beneath right window — 150 / 300

3200 LOCOMOTIVE, 1915-1916, O ga., 0-4-0; S-1 type cast-iron center cab electric; black body w/integral pilots; painted gold pantograph and dummy headlight on each hood; 10-Spoke wheels; center door w/steps; marked "The Ives Railway Lines" beneath left window and "Motor 3200" beneath right window — 150 / 300

3216 LOCOMOTIVE, 1917, O ga., 0-4-0; cast-iron S-1 type center cab electric, larger than 3200, shorter and smaller than 3218; squared hoods, dummy headlight on one, operating headlight on the other; cast-iron 10-spoke wheels; silver painted pantograph on each hood; center door w/steps below; stamped "The Ives Railway Lines" beneath left window and "Motor 3216" beneath right window — 175 / 350

3217 LOCOMOTIVE, 1911, O ga., 0-4-0; cast-iron S-1 type center cab electric, larger than 3216; maroon or red body; dummy headlight and pantograph on painted gold hood; separate pilots; one door and two windows on side; six-spoke wheels; raised lettering reads "Ives 3217" on sides — 275 / 550

3217 LOCOMOTIVE, 1912-1913, O ga., 0-4-0; cast-iron type S-1 center cab electric; maroon or red body; gold dummy headlight and pantograph on each hood; separate pilots; 10-spoke wheels; one door and two windows on cab side; raised lettering reads "Ives" and "3217" — 250 / 500

3217 LOCOMOTIVE, 1914, O ga., 0-4-0; cast-iron S-1 type center cab electric; black body; dummy headlight and pantograph at each end, painted silver or gold; separate pilots; cast-iron 10-spoke wheels; door and two windows on cab side, stamped lettering reads "The Ives Railway Lines" on left and "Motor 3217" to right — 150 / 300

3217 LOCOMOTIVE, 1915-1916, O ga., 0-4-0; cast-iron S-1 type center cab electric; black body; dummy headlight and pantograph on each hood; cast-iron 10-spoke wheels; pilots cast integrally to body; center door flanked by two windows on cab side center, stamped "The Ives Railway Lines" stamped beneath left window and "Motor 3217" beneath right window — 150 / 300

3218 LOCOMOTIVE, 1911, O ga., 0-4-0; cast-iron electric S-1 type center cab; maroon or red body; gold painted pantograph on each hood w/operational headlight on one and dummy on other; cast-iron six-spoke windows; separate pilots; centered door flanked by window; raised lettering reads "Ives" and "3218" — 500 / 1,000

	C6	C8		C6	C8

3218 LOCOMOTIVE, 1912-1913, O ga., 0-4-0; cast-iron electric S-type center cab; maroon or red body; gold pantograph on each hood w/operating headlight on one and dummy on other; separate pilots; cast-iron 10-spoke wheels; door and window on side; raised lettering reads "Ives" and "3218" — 450 — 900

3218 LOCOMOTIVE, 1914, O ga., 0-4-0; cast-iron electric S-1 type center cab electric; black body; silver painted pantographs; w/both dummy and operating headlight; separate pilots; 10-spoke cast-iron wheels; center door flanked by two windows; stamped "The Ives Railway Lines" to left of door and "Motor 3218" to right — 200 — 400

3218 LOCOMOTIVE, 1915-1917, O ga., 0-4-0; cast-iron electric S-1 type center cab; gray or black body; silver pantographs; dummy headlight on one hood, operating one on the other; pilots cast integrally to body; window above each door; stamped "The Ives Railway Lines" to left of door and "Motor 3218" to right — 200 — 400

3220 LOCOMOTIVE, 1916, O ga., 0-4-0; cast-iron electric S-1 type center cab; black body; silver pantographs, one dummy and one operating headlight; pilots separate from body; window above door; stamped "The Ives Railway Lines" to left of door and "Motor 3220" — 375 — 750

3238 LOCOMOTIVE, 1910-1912, O ga., 2-4-2; cast-iron electric S-1 type center cab; black body w/operating headlight on each hood; gold painted bell and whistle; manual reverse; tin pilot wheels w/10-spoke drive wheels; raised lettering reads "New York Central Lines" to left of door and "3238 NYC & HR" to right — 308 — 615

3250 LOCOMOTIVE, 1918-1924, O ga., 0-4-0; electric center cab; generally green, brown or red stamped-metal body on cast-iron frame; cast-iron spoked wheels; bell and whistle on top, operating headlight late in production; no handrails; stamped "The Ives Railway Lines" to left of cab door and "Motor 3250" or "3250 N.Y.C. & H.R." to right of cab door — 108 — 215

3250 LOCOMOTIVE, 1925, O ga., 0-4-0; electric center cab; generally green, brown or red stamped-metal body on cast-iron frame; cast-iron spoked wheels; bell and whistle on top, operating headlight; no handrails; die-cast wheels; stamped "The Ives Railway Lines" to left of cab door and "Motor 3250" or "3250 N.Y.C. & H.R." to right of cab door — 108 — 215

3251 LOCOMOTIVE, 1918-1924, O ga., 0-4-0; center electric cab; green, red or brown body and frame the same as No. 3250 w/handrails on hoods; operating headlight and bell; cast-iron wheels; stamped "The Ives Railway Lines" and "Motor 3251" or "3251 N.Y.C. & H.R." on either side of doorway — 108 — 215

3251 LOCOMOTIVE, 1925-1927, O ga., 0-4-0; center electric cab; green, red or brown tin body w/cast-iron frame; operating headlight; brass bell, brass plate to left of door; die-cast wheels w/nickel tires; marked "The Ives Railway Lines" and "Motor 3251" to right of door — 108 — 215

3252 LOCOMOTIVE, 1918-1924, O ga., 0-4-0; center electric cab; brown, red, burgundy or green body and frame the same as No. 3251; operating headlight; brass bell and handrails; cast-iron wheels; stamped "The Ives Railway Lines" to left of cab door and either "Motor 3252" or "3252 N.Y.C. & H.R." to right of cab door — 108 — 215

	C6	**C8**		**C6**	**C8**

3252 LOCOMOTIVE, 1925-1927, O ga., 0-4-0; center electric cab; red, green, orange, or brown body, same general characteristics as before except w/die-cast wheels w/or without nickel tires; brass plates to the left of cab door read "The Ives Railway Lines"; plate to the right reads "Motor 3252" · 138 275

3253 LOCOMOTIVE, 1918-1924, O ga., 0-4-0; center electric cab; red or green stamped steel body w/cast-iron frame; larger than No. 3252; one operating headlight; handrails and nickel or brass bell; cast-iron wheels; hand reverse; stamped "The Ives Railway Lines" to left of cab door and either "Motor 3253" or "3253 N.Y.C. & H.R." to right of cab door · 175 350

3253 LOCOMOTIVE, 1925-1927, O ga., 0-4-0; center electric cab; green, orange or light brown stamped-steel body w/cast-iron frame; operating headlight and brass bell; die-cast wheels w/or without nickel tires; hand reverse; brass plate to the left of cab door reads "The Ives Railway Lines" and plate to the right of door reads "Motor 3253" · 188 375

3254 LOCOMOTIVE, 1925-1927, O ga., 0-4-0; center electric cab stamped-metal body and cast-iron frame; die-cast wheels w/nickel tires; hand reverse; brass plates read "Motor 3255" to the right of cab door · 70 140

3255-R LOCOMOTIVE, 1925-1930, O ga., 0-4-0; center electric cab stamped-metal body; orange w/black frame, black w/red frame or blue w/red stamped-metal frame; brass journals; two operating headlights; grab rails and brass whistle; automatic reverse; brass plates read "Motor 3255" to the right of cab door · 110 220

3255 LOCOMOTIVE, 1928-1930, O ga., 0-4-0; center electric cab stamped-metal body; orange w/black frame, black w/red frame or blue w/red stamped-metal frame; brass journals; two operating headlights; grab rails and brass whistle; reverse lever in different position; brass plates read "Motor 3255" to the right of cab door · 125 250

3257-R LOCOMOTIVE, 1926-1930, O ga., 0-4-0; sheet metal St. Paul-type locomotive on stamped steel frame w/journals; gray, orange or black body; two operating headlights; brass bell and whistle w/hand rails; die-cast wheels w/nickel tires; cast iron or die cast pilots; automatic reverse; brass plates to the left of cab door read "The Ives Railway Lines" and brass plate to the right of cab door reads "Motor 3257" · 450 900

	C6	**C8**

3257 LOCOMOTIVE, 1926-1930, O ga., 0-4-0; sheet metal St. Paul-type locomotive on stamped steel frame w/journals; gray, orange or black body; two operating headlights; brass bell and whistle w/hand rails; die-cast wheels w/nickel tires; cast iron or die-cast pilots; hand reverse; brass plates to the left of cab door read "The Ives Railway Lines" and brass plate to the right of cab door reads "Motor 3257" — 313, 625

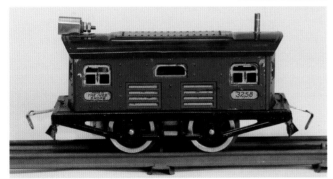

3258 LOCOMOTIVE, 1926-1930, O ga., 0-4-0; New Haven-type body; lithographed yellow body w/green roof or green body w/red roof; stamped-steel frame; operating headlight w/brass whistle; die-cast wheels w/nickel tires; two windows per side w/door on each end; lithographed plate marked "Made In The Ives Shops" and "3258" — 100, 200

3259 LOCOMOTIVE, 1927, O ga., 0-4-0; New Haven-type body; lithographed yellow body w/green roof or green body w/red roof (w/ white body and red roof for the White Owl set); stamped-steel frame; operating headlight w/brass whistle and journals; die-cast wheels w/nickel tires; two windows per side w/door on each end; lithographed plate marked "Made In The Ives Shops" and "3258" — 225, 450

3260 LOCOMOTIVE, 1928-1929, O ga., 0-4-0; stamped-steel New Haven body w/inserted ventilator and plate pieces; blue green, black or cadet blue Lionel No. 248 body; die-cast or stamped steel frame; operating headlight, brass whistle and pantograph on top; brass doors and journals; die-cast wheels w/nickel tires; two plates on side read "Made In The Ives Shops"; plate inserts stamped "Ives" and "3260" — 120, 240

3261 LOCOMOTIVE, 1929-1930, O ga., 0-4-0; stamped-steel New Haven body w/inserted ventilator and plate pieces; black Lionel No. 248 body; die-cast or stamped steel orange or red frame; operating headlight, brass whistle and pantograph on top; brass doors and journals; die-cast wheels w/ nickel tires; hand reverse; two plates on side read "Made In The Ives Shops"; plate inserts stamped "Ives" and "3261" — 120, 240

K U S A N

The history of Kusan Model Trains is indelibly linked to those trains produced by Auburn Model Toys–and unfortunately often blurred by well-meaning enthusiasts hypothesizing about the company's history. In fact, Kusan's history is pretty straightforward.

The Kusan Corporation was founded, and presided over, by Bill McLain. Kusan–the name itself taken from a Native American tribe near Coos Bay, Ore.–was a successful plastic injection molding firm based in Nashville, Tenn. In addition to producing plastic items on contract for outside firms, including the automotive industry, Kusan Corporation also made a number of plastic toys, including trucks, pistols and dolls. In 1953, there were few toy markets bigger than trains, and McLain felt that Kusan could capture part of that market. At that time, Kusan's engineers went to work creating what would become Kusan's K-series of trains.

Coincidentally, that same year, AMT had entered into its disastrous relationship with Bernie Paul. Early in 1954, Paul's General Hobbies Corporation began returning large numbers of unsold–and unpaid for–trains to the small Indiana manufacturer, which was staggered by having invested so much in the manufacture of this product, which it now appeared it would have to carry over for almost a full year.

Word of this situation reached Kusan's McLain, who saw this as an opportunity to enter the lucrative 0 gauge train market with an established product line. A purchase arrangement was made, and the inventory and tooling of AMT soon found their way to 2716 Franklin Road, Nashville, Tenn. McLain stood one large step closer to achieving his goal. Compared to the K-series cars designed by Kusan's plastics-savvy engineers, the former AMT cars were complex, labor-intensive to produce and required outside sourcing for the die-cast components. Though they provided the company with a foothold in the market, it would take inexpensively produced trains, sold in sets, to gain the market position that McClain aspired to. With Kusan's established connections in the toy industry, these sets were aimed at the mass merchandisers, to whom low retail pricing was paramount.

Producing train sets required two key elements that AMT had not had–track and transformer. Kusan purchased power packs from an outside vendor, and had them labeled as its own product. Kusan's track was designed in house, and was quite innovative. In addition to having 17 plastic crossties per section (compared to Lionel's standard of three metal ties), the center rail was removable. To utilize the track in its two-rail form, Kusan's locomotives had insulated wheels and a selector switch for two- or three-rail operation.

The company introduced easy to assemble kits, essentially K-series cars that had not gone to final assembly, in 1957. Special retail displays were offered, promoting these cars, all of which sold for less than $2 each.

Kusan successfully struggled uphill in the train market

until 1958. In that year, McLain negotiated a deal in which he would supply Sears, Roebuck and Company stores with his trains on consignment. McClain was confident with his attractively packaged, economical trains prominently displayed in the nation's largest retailer, he was poised to move his train division from the red ink to black.

Unfortunately for McClain, history tends to repeat itself. In many stores, his products were displayed poorly, in others, not at all, and after Christmas the unsold trains began to arrive at the Nashville plant en masse–a haunting reminder of AMT's fate five years previously.

Kusan's other product lines allowed the company to weather this storm, but McLain's spirit was broken. The remaining inventory of trains, with little new production, was sold through 1961. The firm continued to make other plastic toys and its custom molding operation prospered.

Kusan's train production was dead, but the tooling wasn't. In 1967, the former AMT tooling was sold by Kusan to Andrew Kriswalus, of Endicott, N.Y. Over the next several years, Kriswalus purchased the remaining dies, including those for the K-series cars, from Kusan as well. Building on the first syllable of his name, and the established KMT brand–Kris Model Trains was launched. Although he owned all the tooling, Kriswalus used only the former AMT freight car tooling.

In the early 1980s, the tooling was sold to Williams Electric Trains in Maryland, which, unlike Kriswalus, reactivated almost all of the tooling. But even this stop was not the end of the toolings' travels. In 1985, Williams sold the former Kusan tooling to Maury D. Klein of K-Line trains. Williams retained the ex-AMT tooling. The former Kusan short diesel locomotive tooling has since been sold to Ready Made Toys.

That trains are still being produced from all this tooling is proof that the lack of success by AMT and KMT was not due inferior product.

Kusan initially offered trains identical to, or at least based on, those produced by Auburn. The next year, 1956, they were joined by those of Kusan's own design, known as the K-series. Finally, the S-series, the least expensive line, was added. The S-series were relatively crude, with only four wheels and simulated truck side frames molded into the car body.

KMT F-7 DIESEL LOCOMOTIVES

	C5	C7	C8		C5	C7	C8

DIESELS

322 SANTA FE: F-7 A unit, catalog number F2, painted in Santa Fe's freight paint scheme of dark blue and yellow with yellow lettering. Typically Kusan production had better decorating than that of similar AMT items, and have improved screens on sides.

	C5	C7	C8
Powered	120	160	200
Dummy	60	80	125

1733 NEW YORK CENTRAL: F7 A Unit, catalog number F3. These locos were painted in the two-tone gray "lightning stripe" scheme of the New York Central. The lettering was white.

	C5	C7	C8
Powered	120	160	200
Dummy	55	80	130

2019 MISSOURI, KANSAS & TEXAS (The Texas Special): F7 A Unit, catalog number F1, finished in the red, silver and black paint scheme worn by the "Texas Special" passenger train. Body is straighter than that of the similar AMT unit, and has improved ventilation screens.

	C5	C7	C8
Powered	120	160	200
Dummy	75	125	175

5400 CHICAGO & NORTHWESTERN: F7 A Unit, catalog number F6, finished in yellow and green paint scheme, including "400" markings near nose. Fuel tank skirts are black.

	C5	C7	C8
Powered	140	180	225
Dummy	80	140	200

6755 SOUTHERN: F7 A Unit, catalog number F5; green and gray paint; with yellow lettering, green roof, black fuel tank skirts.

	C5	C7	C8
Powered	100	140	190
Dummy	70	110	160

8644 PENNSYLVANIA: F7 A Unit, catalog number F4, body painted dark green.

	C5	C7	C8
Powered	120	150	200
Dummy	60	100	150

BALTIMORE & OHIO: F7 A Unit, catalog number F7. The elaborately painted body of this locomotive was painted dark blue and gray. The lettering was yellow.

	C5	C7	C8
Powered	180	300	400
Dummy	100	150	200

SOUTHERN PACIFIC: F7 A Unit, loco finished in black and red Southern Pacific "Black Widow" paint scheme.

Too rarely traded to establish accurate pricing.

KMT RAIL DIESEL CARS (RDCs)

	C5	**C7**	**C8**		**C5**	**C7**	**C8**

The AMT Rail Diesel Cars had plastic bodies housing a seven-pole electric motor. Introduced in 1953, they continued to be offered after the Kusan takeover. All were numbered "3160" on their bodies.

	C5	C7	C8		C5	C7	C8
NEW YORK CENTRAL: Catalog number 1-33.	75	110	150	**SANTA FE:** Catalog number 1-22.	80	110	140
PENNSYLVANIA: Catalog number 1-44.	60	90	125	**SOUTHERN:** Catalog number 1-55.	75	110	150

EXTRUDED ALUMINUM CARS

Kusan continued to market the aluminum passenger cars originally created by AMT, at least until the existing stock–which was substantial–was exhausted.

The window glazing came most often in blue plastic, but some had two-piece acetate windows, the outer layer clear, the inner frosted. The vista domes too came in blue, which often warp, or white, which are frequently found cracked. Also, cars were available new with either smooth or fluted roofs. Originally, the fluted roof cars were lower cost, but today on the collector market they command a slight premium. The prices listed are for the smooth-roof versions. Finally, the cars are listed below by catalog number, rather than the number on the side of the car.

"TEXAS SPECIAL" SET: Aluminum cars with red painted trim wearing the markings of the Missouri-Kansas-Texas and Frisco jointly operated Texas Special passenger train.

	C5	C7	C8
1001 Mail Express: Number plate reads "3407".	75	125	200
1002 Roomette: "BOWIE".	75	125	200
1003 Diner: Number plate reads "DINER".	75	125	200
1004 Vista Dome: "CROCKETT".	75	125	200
1005 Observation: "SAM HOUSTON".	75	125	200
1006 Day Coach: Number plate reads "3160".	75	125	200
1007 Crew Combination: Number plate reads "5260"	75	125	200
1008 Baggage: Number plate reads "4170".	75	125	200

SANTA FE SET: Large letterboard reads "SANTA FE" with smaller plates carrying numbers and car names.

	C5	C7	C8
2001 Mail Express: Number plate reads "3407".	40	75	125
2002 Roomette:			
(Type I) Number plate reads "INDIAN LAKE".	40	75	125
(Type II) Number plate reads "INDIAN SCOUT".	40	75	125
2003 Diner: "DINER".	40	75	125
2004 Vista Dome: "BUENA VISTA".	40	75	125
2005 Observation: "INDIAN ARROW".	40	75	125
2006 Day Coach: Number plate reads "3160".	40	75	125
2007 Crew Combination: Number plate reads "5264".	40	75	125
2008 Baggage: Number plate reads "4170".	40	75	125

NEW YORK CENTRAL SET: Large letterboard reads "NEW YORK CENTRAL" with smaller plates carrying numbers and car names.

	C5	C7	C8
3001 Mail Express: Number plate reads "3407".	40	75	125
3002 Roomette:			
(Type I) "CITY OF DETROIT".	40	75	125
(Type II) "CITY OF ERIE".	40	75	125
(Type III) "CITY OF UTICA".	40	75	125
3003 Diner: "DINER".	40	75	125
3004 Vista Dome: "BUENA VISTA".	40	75	125
3005 Observation: "SENECA FALLS".	40	75	125
3006 Day Coach: Number plate reads "3160".	40	75	125

	C5	**C7**	**C8**
3007 Crew Combination: Number plate reads "5260".	40	75	125
3008 Baggage: Number plate reads "4170".	40	75	125

PENNSYLVANIA SET: Large letterboard reads "PENNSYLVANIA" with smaller plates carrying numbers and car names.

	C5	**C7**	**C8**
4001 Mail Express: Number plate reads "3407".	40	75	125
4002 Roomette:			
(Type I) "CITY OF PITTSBURGH".	40	75	125
(Type II) "FORT WAYNE".	40	75	125
4003 Diner: "DINER".	40	75	125
4004 Vista Dome: "CITY OF NEW YORK".	40	75	125
4005 Observation: "CITY OF CHICAGO".	40	75	125
4006 Day Coach: Number plate reads "3160".	40	75	125
4007 Crew Combination: Number plate reads "5260".	40	75	125
4008 Baggage: Number plate reads "4170".	40	75	125

SOUTHERN SET: All cars bear a large plate on each side reading "SOUTHERN" and small plates with additional lettering.

	C5	**C7**	**C8**
5001 Mail Express: Number plate reads "3407".	75	125	200
5002 Roomette:			
(Type I) "CATAWBA RIVER".	75	125	200
(Type II) "POTOMAC RIVER".	75	125	200
(Type III) "DAN RIVER".	75	125	200
5003 Diner: "DINER".	75	125	200
5004 Vista Dome: "GEORGIA".	75	125	200
5005 Observation: "CRESCENT CITY".	75	125	200
5006 Day Coach: Number plate reads "3160".	75	125	200
5007 Crew Combination: Number plate reads "5260".	75	125	200
5008 Baggage: Number plate reads "4170".	75	125	200

CHICAGO & NORTHWESTERN SET: These cars were attractively painted in the yellow and green scheme of the CNW. The "CHICAGO & NORTHWESTERN" nameplates on these cars are significantly larger than the nameplates on the other cars. Once again, smaller plates were used for names and numbers.

	C5	**C7**	**C8**
6001 Mail Express: Number plate reads "3407".	80	150	250
6002 Roomette: "NORTHERN PINES".	80	150	250
6003 Diner: "DINER".	80	150	250
6004 Vista Dome: "NORTHERN STREAMS".	80	150	250
6005 Observation: "NORTHERN STATES".	80	150	250
6006 Day Coach: Number plate reads "3160".	Too rarely traded to establish accurate pricing.		
6007 Crew Combination: Number plate reads "5260".	80	150	250
6008 Baggage: Number plate reads "4170".	80	150	250

BALTIMORE & OHIO SET: Large letterboard is marked "BALTIMORE & OHIO" and small plates have additional lettering.

	C5	**C7**	**C8**
7001 Mail Express: Number plate reads "3407".	Too rarely traded to establish accurate pricing.		
7002 Roomette: "YOUNGSTOWN".	Too rarely traded to establish accurate pricing.		

	C5	C7	C8

7003 Diner: "DINER". — Too rarely traded to establish accurate pricing.

7004 Vista Dome: "CAPITOL CITY". — Too rarely traded to establish accurate pricing.

7005 Observation: "WAWASEE". — Too rarely traded to establish accurate pricing.

7006 Day Coach: Number plate reads "3160". — Too rarely traded to establish accurate pricing.

7007 Crew Combination: Number plate reads "5260". — Too rarely traded to establish accurate pricing.

7008 Baggage: Number plate reads "4170". — Too rarely traded to establish accurate pricing.

BOXCARS

Kusan offered the series of scale-detailed boxcars Auburn had introduced in 1951, albeit with changes in some cases.

	C5	C7	C8
100 RUTLAND: Catalog number 9007, dark green and yellow.	15	30	45
2710 CHICAGO & EASTERN ILLINOIS: Tuscan, catalog number 8102.	25	45	65
4382 MINNEAPOLIS & ST. LOUIS: Cataloged as number 9004, this car had yellow lettering on green body paint. Its doors were green as well.	15	30	45
5124 MINNEAPOLIS & ST. LOUIS: Cataloged as number 9004, this car had yellow lettering on green body paint. Its doors were green as well.	15	30	45
5753 CENTRAL OF GEORGIA: Black and silver, catalog number 9009.	40	60	120
7698 CHICAGO & NORTHWESTERN: Tuscan, catalog number 8014.	40	60	120
18841 WESTERN PACIFIC: Tuscan with orange feather, catalog number 8016.	40	60	120

	C5	C7	C8
19509 GREAT NORTHERN: Cataloged as number 8002, these cars wore tuscan paint; with white lettering. Black doors were installed.	15	25	40
25439 ERIE: Assigned catalog number 8003, this car was painted tuscan and decorated with black and white markings.			
(Type I) Lettered "CU FT 3769", black doors.	10	20	35
(Type II) Lettered "CU FT 3730", black doors.	20	40	60
(Type III) Lettered "CU FT 3770", black doors.	25	45	65
(Type IV) Reporting marks printed in two columns, fitted with tuscan doors.	30	50	75
30565 NEW YORK, NEW HAVEN & HARTFORD: Cataloged as number 8005; black doors and white lettering highlighted this otherwise tuscan boxcar.	15	25	40

	C5	C7	C8
34922 SANTA FE: Assigned catalog number 8004, this tuscan boxcar with black doors was lettered in white.	10	20	30
36406 NEW HAVEN:			
(Type I) Orange, catalog number 9005.	40	60	120
(Type II) Black, catalog number 9011.	40	60	120
45396 SOO LINE: Tuscan, catalog 8015.	40	60	120
54652 MINNEAPOLIS & ST. LOUIS: Red, catalog number 9008.	40	60	120

	C5	C7	C8
77066 BOSTON AND MAINE: Blue with blue doors, catalog number 9006.	40	60	120
120119 MISSOURI PACIFIC: Blue, gray and yellow, number catalog 9010.	15	25	40
121834 SOUTHERN PACIFIC: Silver, catalog number 9012.	40	60	120
150231 UNION PACIFIC: Tuscan with yellow lettering, catalog number 8013.	40	60	120
153902 SOUTHERN: The doors of this car, like the body, were painted tuscan. It was cataloged as item 8001.	15	25	40
180190 NEW YORK CENTRAL: Tuscan with white lettering, catalog number 8011.	40	60	120
465002 BALTIMORE & OHIO: Tuscan with white lettering, catalog number 8010.	40	60	120
466096 BALTIMORE & OHIO "SENTINEL": The decal used on the Kusan-era cars was slightly smaller than that used by AMT on catalog number 9003.	20	30	45
677209 PENNSYLVANIA: Cataloged as number 8009, this tuscan boxcar was decorated with white lettering.	25	40	55

Kusan also continued to sell freight cars of other body types pioneered by Auburn.

DEPRESSED-CENTER FLATCARS

	C5	C7	C8
412 MONON: Cataloged as number 7351, this was painted gray with red lettering.	20	45	75

GONDOLAS

	C5	C7	C8
51297 LOUISVILLE & NASHVILLE: This dull black car with white lettering was given catalog number 7651.	15	35	60

REFRIGERATOR CARS

	C5	C7	C8
1008 GERBER'S: Cataloged as number 7251, this multi-colored car had sides painted blue and white, its roof and ends were tuscan, and the lettering blue.	20	40	70
9241 SANTA FE: Cataloged with number 7252, this car had dark yellow sides, and tuscan roof and ends. The lettering was black.	20	35	65

STOCK CARS

	C5	C7	C8
32066 CHICAGO, BURLINGTON & QUINCY: This tuscan-sided car with black and white markings was given catalog number 7151.	15	25	35
47150 MISSOURI, KANSAS & TEXAS: Assigned catalog number 7150 was this yellow-sided car with tuscan roof and white lettering.	20	30	45
140449 ATLANTIC COAST LINE: This tuscan car was given catalog number 7152. It had white lettering.	15	25	35

	C5	C7	C8		C5	C7	C8

BEXEL SPECIAL

THE K-SERIES LOCOMOTIVES

The locomotive for Kusan's equivalent to Lionel's 027 line was a replica of an Alco FA diesel. Originally developed as an unpowered floor toy by Kusan, it was good looking, and easily adapted for use as a powered unit. The molded-in number board of each locomotive bore the number 2716, not coincidentally the address of the company on Franklin Road in Nashville, Tenn.

BEXEL SPECIAL: Silver with black lettering, produced as a promotion of the Bexel drug company.

	C5	C7	C8
Powered	35	55	75

BEXEL SPECIAL: Blue with black lettering, produced as a promotion of the Bexel drug company.

	C5	C7	C8
Powered	60	80	100

FRISCO: Black and yellow, with yellow lettering. Cataloged with stock numbers 2 and 14.

	C5	C7	C8
Powered	10	20	30
Dummy	5	10	20

K-M-T LINES: Gray and red, catalog number 11.

Too rarely traded to establish accurate values.

BURLINGTON: Silver with black numbers, cataloged as item number 3.

	C5	C7	C8
Powered	20	30	50
Dummy	10	20	30

	C5	C7	C8

KUSAN KANNON BALL: Silver and black.

Dummy	5	10	20

MISSOURI – KANSAS – TEXAS: Red and silver, catalog number 1.

Powered	10	20	30
Dummy	5	10	20

MISSOURI PACIFIC: Blue and white, blue lettering, catalog number 4.

Powered	20	30	50
Dummy	10	20	30

MISSOURI PACIFIC: White lettering, catalog number 6.

Powered	20	30	50
Dummy	10	20	30

NACIONALES DE MEXICO: Silver with black lettering, "EL AZTECA."

Powered	20	40	60
Dummy	10	25	50

NACIONALES DE MEXICO: Yellow and gray with red lettering, "EL INTERNACIONAL."

Powered	20	40	60
Dummy	10	25	50

NEW HAVEN: Black and red "McGinnis" paint scheme, catalog number 7.

Powered	20	30	50
Dummy	10	20	30

	C5	C7	C8

SILVER STAR: Silver and red with black lettering.

Powered	30	60	90

SOUTHERN: Gray and green with yellow lettering. Catalog number 5.

Powered	10	20	30
Dummy	5	10	20

SOUTHERN PACIFIC: Black, red, orange and silver. Cataloged as item 20.

Too rarely, if ever, traded to establish accurate values.

UNION PACIFIC: Listed in catalogs with both the stock numbers 18 and 28, these yellow locomotives had gray roofs and red lettering. They wore the number 1500 on their flanks.

Powered	20	40	60
Dummy	10	25	50

U.S. 135: Yellow, gray and black with black lettering, including number 21935, catalog number 19S.

Powered	20	40	60

U.S. 135: Yellow and blue with red lettering, including number 21938, catalog number 39.

Powered	30	60	90

U.S. ARMY ATOMIC: Olive drab with white lettering, including the atomic symbol. The "fan" area of the locomotive was replaced by an aircraft-type machine gun turret. The unit was assigned catalog number 10.

Powered	10	25	50

	C5	**C7**	**C8**
U.S. ARMY ATOMIC: Black with white lettering. The "fan" area of the locomotive was replaced by an aircraft-type machine gun turret. The unit was assigned catalog number 12.			
Powered	10	25	50

	C5	**C7**	**C8**
U.S. NAVY: Two-tone gray with black lettering. Catalog number 12.			
Powered	10	25	50

THE "BEEP"

The other locomotive originating from Kusan's ownership was this grossly foreshortened GP-7. Riding on only a single truck with four wheels, the DC-powered locomotive was intended to power the Nashville firm's least expensive sets. The diminutive little locomotive soldiers on today, having survived at least two changes in tooling ownership.

As most of these units have a prominently displayed road number painted on their shell, they are listed here according to that number. The number "3206" is cast into all the numberboards, regardless of road name or painted number.

	C5	C7	C8
127 MINNEAPOLIS & ST. LOUIS: Red with white lettering, catalog number KF33, available with and without handrails.	20	40	60
248 LOUISVILLE AND NASHVILLE: Black, catalog number 23.	Too rarely traded to establish accurate value.		
501 CHESAPEAKE AND OHIO: Blue body with yellow lettering.			
(Type I) Catalog number KF25, features yellow "safety stripes" along frame edge.	20	40	60
(Type II) Catalog number KF35, no yellow "safety stripes" along frame edge.	15	35	50
612: This black locomotive, assigned catalog number B021, had no road name printed on it.	Too rarely traded to establish accurate value.		
890 GENERAL MOTORS: Silver with black lettering, this locomotive was given catalog number 37.			
(Type I) Features "safety stripes" and handrails along frame edge.	20	40	60
(Type II) No "safety stripes" or handrails.	15	35	50
3206 LOUISVILLE AND NASHVILLE: Black with white lettering.	15	35	50

	C5	C7	C8
6800 This black locomotive, had no road name printed on it, only the white "6800" number.	15	35	50
8900 USAF: Black with yellow lettering, catalog number B022.	15	25	35
9000 U.S. ARMY: Olive drab with white markings. Assigned catalog number KF24.	15	35	50
No number GRAVY TRAIN: White, unmarked, part of promotional set.	15	25	35

	C5	C7	C8
No number KUSAN: Red, catalog number B031.	15	25	35
No number KUSAN: Green with white lettering, catalog number B032.	15	25	35
No number NACIONALES DE MEXICO: Silver with black lettering.	15	35	50

	C5	C7	C8

K-SERIES FREIGHT CARS

This series of attractive but economical cars was offered in both ready-to-run, fully assembled form, as well as in kits. These kits were notably easy to assemble, and were well merchandised. Because the kit cars were fully decorated at the factory, they are difficult if not impossible to distinguish from factory-assembled cars in the absence of their boxes. Boxcars were furnished with a man who could be placed in the doorway. Cars are listed by type, and then by road number, where applicable.

BOXCARS

3206 KUSAN: Cataloged with stock number 208, this car was offered in two types:

	C5	C7	C8
(Type I) Yellow with red lettering.	5	10	15
(Type II) Red with white lettering.	5	10	15

5124 MINNEAPOLIS & ST. LOUIS: This dark green car with yellow lettering was assigned catalog number 203.

10	15	20

7989 LOUISVILLE & NASHVILLE: Given stock number 211, this blue car with yellow lettering was one of Kusan's more attractive offerings.

25	35	45

	C5	C7	C8

20065 ROCK ISLAND: Though this car was assigned only one stock number, 205, it was produced in at least five different variations.

	C5	C7	C8
(Type I) Silver with black lettering.	10	15	20
(Type II) White with black lettering.	15	20	25
(Type III) Yellow with red lettering.	Too rarely traded to establish values.		
(Type IV) Red with white lettering.	Too rarely traded to establish values.		
(Type V) Red with black lettering.	Too rarely traded to establish values.		

29048 PENNSYLVANIA: Tuscan with white lettering, this car was given catalog number 202.

	C5	C7	C8
(Type I) Includes "Don't Stand Me Still" logo.	10	15	20
(Type II) Without logo	20	25	30

	C5	**C7**	**C8**		**C5**	**C7**	**C8**

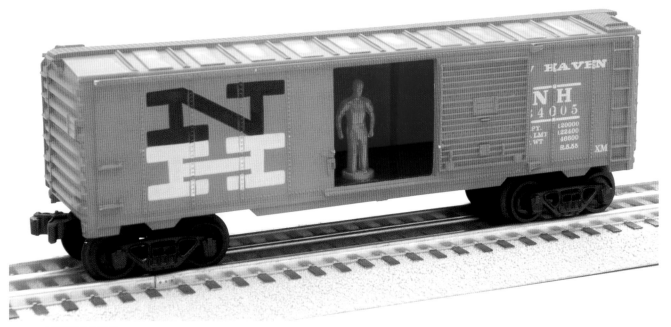

34005 NEW HAVEN

34005 NEW HAVEN: Orange with black and white lettering, this car was listed as stock number 206. 10 15 20

55001 NEW HAVEN: Black with red and white lettering, the catalog number 207 was assigned to this car. 20 30 40

62904 BURLINGTON: Catalog number 209 was given to this red car with white lettering. 15 25 35

66096 WESTERN PACIFIC: Tuscan with yellow lettering, this car was cataloged as stock number 212. 20 30 40

70203 KUSAN RAILROAD:

(Type I) Yellow with red lettering. 5 10 15

(Type II) Yellow with black lettering. 5 10 15

(Type III) Red with white lettering. 5 10 15

85023 MISSOURI– KANSAS – TEXAS: This yellow Katy boxcar had black lettering. It was given catalog number 201.

(Type I) Bright yellow. 10 15 20

(Type II) Darker yellow. 10 15 20

	C5	C7	C8

499087 UNION PACIFIC:
Yellow and black with black
lettering. — 10 · 15 · 20

	C5	C7	C8
499087 UNION PACIFIC	10	15	20
1089547 U.S. ARMY BOXCAR	15	25	45

**1089547 U.S. ARMY
BOXCAR:** Olive drab with
olive drab trucks.

**Unnumbered BEXEL
CAPSULES:** Yellow and
black.

	C5	C7	C8
Unnumbered BEXEL CAPSULES	10	15	20

FLATCARS

123 USAX: Dynamic Injection Compressortron.

(Type I) This yellow and dark
gray flatcar was given catalog
number K901. It carried a red
and gray plastic mechanism
housing decorated with red-
, white- and black-lettered
decals.

	C5	C7	C8
(Type I)	25	50	75

(Type II) Catalog number K902
was assigned to this yellow
flatcar with a red and gray
plastic mechanism housing
with black lettering.

	C5	C7	C8
(Type II)	25	50	75

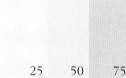

(Type III) Red cars with gray
plastic housings and black
lettering were variously
assigned catalog numbers
K903 through 906.

	C5	C7	C8
(Type III)	25	50	75

**578 NAVY RADAR
SCANNER:** Gray plastic
flat cars with gray mechanism
housings supporting red radar
antennas were given catalog
number K805.

	C5	C7	C8
578 NAVY RADAR SCANNER	25	50	75

1389 USAF MISSILE FLAT:

(Type I) Olive drab flatcar with
white lettering, with red,
white and blue rocket. Catalog
number K803.

(Type II) Black plastic flatcar
with yellow lettering with
red rocket. Catalog number
K803B.

(Type III) Unlettered black
plastic flatcar with white
rocket, assigned catalog
number K803C.

(Type IV) Olive drab flatcar
with white lettering, with
red rocket. Catalog number
K803E.

	C5	C7	C8
(Type I)	25	50	75
(Type II)	25	50	75
(Type III)	25	50	75
(Type IV)	25	50	75

	C5	C7	C8		C5	C7	C8

13445 MISSOURI– KANSAS – TEXAS: This black flatcar with white lettering was cataloged variously as stock number 401 and 407. — 5 / 10 / 15

13893 U.S. NAVY MISSILE FLAT: Gray plastic flatcar with black lettering. Assigned catalog number K803A, it hauled a white plastic rocket. — 25 / 50 / 75

24560 LOUISVILLE & NASHVILLE: This black flatcar with white lettering was cataloged as stock number 403. — 5 / 10 / 15

30100 U.S. ARMY ATOMIC REACTOR: This car was decorated with the nuclear symbol and "Danger Radiation" stamped in white.

(Type I) The olive drab version of the flatcar with red housings was assigned catalog number K801A. — 20 / 35 / 50

(Type II) Catalog number K801B was assigned to an olive drab flatcar with white plastic housings. — 25 / 40 / 55

(Type III) A black plastic flatcar with white plastic housings was given catalog number K801C. — 25 / 40 / 55

30100 U.S. ARMY SEARCHLIGHT: Olive drab flatcar with olive drab superstructure and lamp housing. Assigned catalog number K806. — 30 / 50 / 75

40916 U.S. ARMY RADAR SCANNER: Olive drab flatcar with olive drab radar assembly. White lettering decorated this car, which was given catalog number K805C. — 30 / 50 / 75

42010 U.S. ARMY CANNON:

(Type I) This olive drab flatcar, catalog number K802, mounted a large olive drab cannon. White lettering decorated the car. — 20 / 40 / 60

(Type II) A version of the car with an unpainted gray plastic body and black plastic cannon was given catalog number K802A. — Too rarely traded to establish values.

42010 U.S. ARMY Dynamic Injection Compressortron: An olive drab flatcar with white lettering formed the base for this car. Assigned catalog number K904, its gray plastic Compressortron housing lettered in black. — Too rarely traded to establish values.

	C5	**C7**	**C8**		**C5**	**C7**	**C8**

46250 FRISCO: This car was of the depressed-center design, and was given catalog number 460.

| | 25 | 40 | 60 |

83756 GULF, MOBILE AND OHIO: This black flatcar with white lettering was cataloged as stock number 402.

| | 5 | 10 | 15 |

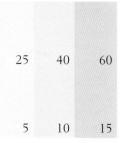

109840 U.S. ARMY RADAR SCANNER: This yellow and gray plastic flatcar with white lettering was equipped with a red and gray superstructure and a red radar array. It was given catalog number K805A.

| | 20 | 50 | 75 |

310794 BALTIMORE & OHIO: This tuscan flatcar with white lettering was cataloged as stock number 404.

| | 5 | 10 | 15 |

401098 USA SEARCHLIGHT: (Type I) Yellow flatcar with gray superstructure and red lamp housing. Decorated with black lettering and crewed by a white plastic man, this car was given catalog number K806A.

Too rarely traded to establish values.

(Type II) A second version, cataloged as stock number K806B, was based on a gray and yellow flatcar with black lettering. A gray and red plastic superstructure with white lettering with red searchlight was mounted on the car.

| | 25 | 40 | 65 |

968101 KMT SEARCHLIGHT: A black flatcar with yellow lettering was given catalog number K806C. Its superstructure was made of gray plastic parts with black lettering.

Too rarely traded to establish values.

41089547-S USAX 123: Blue and yellow with black and white lettering, this depressed center car was assigned stock number 461.

| | 25 | 35 | 55 |

Unnumbered KUSAN: Red with white lettering, catalog number 408.

| | 5 | 10 | 15 |

Unnumbered KUSAN: Yellow with red pipe load, catalog number 409.

| | 5 | 10 | 15 |

Unnumbered KUSAN: Olive drab, catalog number 411.

| | 5 | 10 | 15 |

Unnumbered KUSAN: Black with white lettering.

| | 5 | 10 | 15 |

Unnumbered: Black, unlettered.

| | 5 | 10 | 15 |

	C5	C7	C8		C5	C7	C8

GONDOLAS

1776 U.S.: This silver gondola was laden with 18 "nuclear gas bottles" – which bore a startling resemblance to milk bottles – painted in three colors. Catalog number 310 was assigned to this car.

Too rarely traded to establish value.

4190 U.S.: This dark gray gondola with light gray interior carried four red plastic air activated cement containers with the KMT logo. Assigned catalog number 308; its lettering, including the "#4190 SPACE RESEARCH" legend, was stamped in yellow.

| | 10 | 15 | 20 |

5066 READING: This black gondola with white lettering was given catalog number 305.

| | 5 | 10 | 15 |

7856 U.S. ARMY GONDOLA: This olive drab gondola with white lettering, like most of Kusan's military-themed cars, rode on olive drab trucks.

| | 20 | 40 | 60 |

54206 WESTERN MARYLAND:

(Type I) Catalog number 303 was assigned to this tuscan gondola with black lettering.

| | 5 | 10 | 15 |

(Type II) Catalog number 303B was assigned to this black gondola with white lettering.

Too rarely traded to establish value.

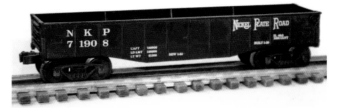

71908 NICKEL PLATE: Painted black with white lettering, this car was given catalog number 301.

| | 5 | 10 | 15 |

99032 NORFOLK & WESTERN: Painted black with white lettering, this car was given catalog number 302.

| | 5 | 10 | 15 |

569028 PITTSBURGH & LAKE ERIE: Painted black with white lettering, this car was given catalog number 304.

| | 5 | 10 | 15 |

Unnumbered GREAT NORTHERN: A tuscan gondola with white Great Northern lettering was cataloged as stock number 307.

Too rarely traded to establish value.

	C5	C7	C8

Unnumbered KUSAN: This plain-Jane car was given catalog number 309.

| (Type I) Black with white lettering. | 5 | 10 | 15 |

| (Type II) Red with white lettering. | 5 | 10 | 15 |

| **Unnumbered** All white, unlettered car was part of Gravy Train promotion. | 15 | 20 | 25 |

Unnumbered LOUISVILLE & NASHVILLE: Catalog number 306 was assigned to this black-painted, white-lettered gondola.

| | 5 | 10 | 15 |

Unnumbered: An olive drab, but undecorated car was assigned catalog number 311.

Too rarely, if ever, traded to establish value.

Unnumbered "BEXEL": This brown gondola was part of a promotional outfit.

| | 5 | 10 | 20 |

HOPPERS

316 G-E HOPPER: This black open-top hopper car was given catalog number 603. It was decorated with white lettering.

| | 25 | 40 | 60 |

800 ALUMINUM ORE HOPPER: Assigned catalog number 604, this open-topped car was painted silver and decorated with black lettering.

| | 30 | 60 | 90 |

	C5	C7	C8

18019 NEW YORK CENTRAL HOPPER: A tuscan open top hopper was decorated in New York Central markings and given catalog number 602.

| | 15 | 30 | 45 |

21640 ATLANTIC COAST LINE HOPPER: Dark gray ACL hoppers were cataloged in both open and covered versions with stock number 611.

Too rarely, if ever, traded to establish values.

36180 WABASH HOPPER: Catalog number 601; without cover; black paint, white lettering.

| | 10 | 25 | |

97786 CHICAGO & EASTERN ILLINOIS HOPPER.

(Type I) Cataloged as number 605 was this gray plastic, open-topped hopper with red lettering.

| | 15 | 25 | 35 |

(Type II) A similar car was given catalog number 610. Though gray with red lettering, this version was a replica of a covered hopper.

| | 15 | 25 | 35 |

	C5	**C7**	**C8**

TANK CARS

610 DOW TANK: Catalog number 701 was assigned to this tank car with yellow "Dow" lettering. It was produced in both gloss and matte versions.

	C5	C7	C8
610 DOW TANK	15	25	40
X723 RADIOACTIVE WASTE TANK	25	45	70
2544 CITIES SERVICE TANK	15	25	40

X723 RADIOACTIVE WASTE TANK: This silver-painted car with red lettering was given catalog number 704.

2544 CITIES SERVICE TANK: This attractive green tank car was assigned catalog number 703. The Cities Service lettering was applied in white.

2544 CITIES SERVICE TANK: Some of the Cities Service cars were further enhanced by the addition of a platform around the dome. Cars so equipped were given catalog number 710.

	C5	C7	C8
	30	40	60

	C5	**C7**	**C8**

2675 DUPONT TANK: Catalog number 702 was used by a silver-painted tank car with black and red lettering. It was offered in two versions.

	C5	C7	C8
(Type I) Without platform.	15	20	25
(Type II) With platform.	20	25	30

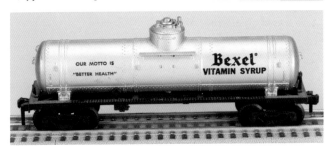

Unnumbered: Silver-painted car lettered "Bexel vitamin syrup" in black for promotional outfit.

	C5	C7	C8
	10	20	30

CABOOSES

C528 NEW HAVEN: This red caboose with white lettering was assigned catalog number 507.

763 GENERAL MOTORS: Silver lettering was applied to this red caboose, which was given catalog number 520.

	C5	C7	C8
C528 NEW HAVEN	10	15	25
763 GENERAL MOTORS	25	40	60

	C5	C7	C8

790 M-K-T (MISSOURI, KANSAS & TEXAS): The black lettering of this caboose was stamped on a yellow base color. Catalog number 501 was assigned.

| | 15 | 25 | 40 |

790 KMT: White "KMT" lettering was applied to this red-painted caboose.

Too rarely traded to establish accurate values.

900 MINNEAPOLIS & ST. LOUIS: Catalog number 518 was used for this red caboose with white lettering.

| | 20 | 40 | 60 |

901 M-K-T (MISSOURI-KANSAS - TEXAS): Catalog number 506 was assigned to this yellow and brown caboose with black lettering.

| | 10 | 15 | 20 |

901 M-K-T (MISSOURI-KANSAS - TEXAS): A similar, but red with white lettering caboose was given catalog number 519.

| | 20 | 35 | 50 |

910 MISSOURI PACIFIC: Red paint and white lettering adorned catalog number 504.

| | 10 | 20 | 30 |

2710 KUSAN LINE: This red-painted caboose, given catalog number 513, was produced in two versions.

(Type I) Yellow lettering.

| | 10 | 15 | 25 |

(Type II) White lettering.

| | 10 | 15 | 25 |

2710 KUSAN LINE: A similar, but yellow-painted caboose was given catalog number 517. It too came in two versions.

(Type I) Black lettering.

| | 10 | 15 | 25 |

	C5	C7	C8

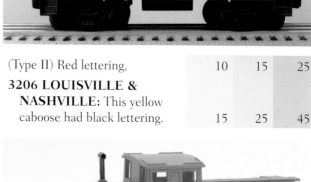

(Type II) Red lettering,

| | 10 | 15 | 25 |

3206 LOUISVILLE & NASHVILLE: This yellow caboose had black lettering.

| | 15 | 25 | 45 |

X3239 SOUTHERN: This red-painted caboose with yellow lettering was given catalog number 505.

| | 10 | 20 | 30 |

3821 UNION PACIFIC: Red paint and yellow lettering also decorated catalog number 508, a Union Pacific caboose.

| | 20 | 40 | 60 |

7989 LOUISVILLE & NASHVILLE: L&N markings were also applied to this red caboose. White lettering was used on this car, which was given catalog number 515.

| | 20 | 30 | 45 |

13518 CHICAGO, BURLINGTON & QUINCY: Assigned catalog number 503, this car was produced in two variations.

(Type I) Red paint with white lettering.

| | 20 | 40 | 60 |

(Type II) Yellow body with brown roof and black lettering.

| | 10 | 15 | 25 |

	C5	C7	C8

20200 U.S. ARMY MASTER CONTROL CENTER CABOOSE:

(Type I) Catalog number K804 was used for an olive drab with white lettering. — 25 / 35 / 45

(Type II) Catalog number K804A distinguished a gray plastic car with black lettering. — 30 / 45 / 60

35443 U.S. NAVY: A gray painted caboose with radar dish and black lettering was given catalog number 510. — 25 / 40 / 60

35443 U.S. SPACE RESEARCH: Catalog number 512 was the reference assigned this yellow and gray caboose with black lettering. — 20 / 35 / 55

35443 U.S. AIR FORCE: Catalog number 514, a gray painted caboose with yellow lettering, was produced in two variations.

(Type I) With radar dish in lieu of a smokejack. — 20 / 35 / 50

(Type II) With standard smokejack. — 15 / 30 / 45

35543 U.S. SPACE RESEARCH: This yellow and blue painted caboose with red lettering was issued with catalog number 521. — 20 / 30 / 40

	C5	C7	C8

37201 "KMT"

(Type I) Yellow with red lettering. — 5 / 10 / 15

(Type II) Red with yellow lettering. — 5 / 10 / 15

90079 CHESAPEAKE & OHIO: Though only one catalog number, 516, was used for this car, it was produced in two distinct versions.

(Type I) Red with white lettering. — 15 / 30 / 45

(Type II) Yellow with red lettering. — 20 / 40 / 60

126998 FRISCO: This red-painted car with white lettering was given catalog number 502. — 10 / 15 / 20

Unnumbered SOUTHERN PACIFIC: Yet another red-painted caboose with white lettering was given catalog number 509. — 10 / 15 / 20

Unnumbered: "Bexel Special" red caboose. — 10 / 15 / 25

Lionel-few brand names have the instantaneous recognition that Lionel enjoys early in its second century. Young or old, male or female, it seems almost everyone identifies that name with toy train. In fact, to many people the two are synonymous.

The firm bears the middle name of its founder, Joshua Lionel Cohen, the son of immigrants, who was born Aug. 25, 1877. Young Cohen, a clever inventor and shameless self-promoter with a clear head for business, formed the firm with Harry Grant on Sept. 5, 1900. Their first business was with the U.S. Navy, producing fuses for mines.

With the Navy work completed, Cohen began tinkering, trying to find a product to keep him and his partner busy and his new firm afloat. A motor he developed for a less-than-successful fan was installed under a gondola car. The car placed on a circle of steel rails connected to dry cell batteries and in 1900 the age of Lionel Electric Trains began.

As originally conceived the "train," still only a motorized gondola car, was to be an animated window display for shopkeepers to use for promoting other products. Immediately, though, it was apparent that there was more interest in the displays than the goods they held and the transition from merchandising aid to retail product was made.

In 1902, in addition to the gondola car, Lionel offered a miniature trolley, the first step towards realism. Like the gondola, the trolley ran on two-rail 2-7/8-inch gauge track. The first catalog was produced in 1900 and an American icon was born. Unfortunately, Cohen's partner Grant, though also a gifted inventor, was not a capable administrator. This led to a man joining the payroll who was arguably as influential to the company, and its trains, as Cohen himself: an Italian immigrant named Mario Caruso. Hired at age 18 as a laborer, Caruso rose to Secretary-Treasurer. He managed the company's factories, first in New York, then New Haven, followed by Newark and ultimately the massive 15-acre Irvington plant, in a no-nonsense manner. Quality, production and cost-control were always of great concern and were skillfully balanced by Caruso.

In 1906, Lionel began producing trains that rolled on "Standard Gauge" track and, in 1915, this was supplemented by the smaller "0-gauge" trains. Though Lionel made forays into other sizes, namely 00 in 1938, and, after World War II, three attempts at HO, it was to be 0-gauge where Lionel ultimately rose to notoriety. It is also the predominate size of trains produced after World War II.

During 1909, Lionel first used the slogan "Standard of the World," but it would be many years before the bold statement would become fact.

In 1910, for reasons unknown today, Cohen changed his last name to the one he is remembered by today, Cowen. A few years later, in 1918, the firm would change names as well, as the Lionel Manufacturing Company became The Lionel Corporation.

While toy train production continued in Lionel's plant during the First World War, alongside were defense products. After all, that is how the company was born. It made primarily signaling and navigational devices. This type of relationship would continue as long as The Lionel Corporation was in the manufacturing business, during both war and peacetime.

In 1923, Lionel revamped its Standard Gauge offerings, replacing the somewhat realistic, but dingy colors used previously with a veritable kaleidoscope of blues, greens, yellows and oranges…all augmented with bright brass, copper and nickel trim. These later trains constitute what is considered the classic era of Standard Gauge production.

The Depression was hard on Lionel, but harder on its competition. During the recession that preceded the Great Depression, Lionel, along with American Flyer, took over its bankrupt competitor Ives. In 1930, Lionel became the sole owner of Ives. Thirty-six years later Lionel would take over American Flyer as well.

World War II would bring a halt to Lionel's toy production, with toy train production coming to an end in June 1942. The Lionel plant, like countless others throughout the country, became totally devoted to manufacturing military products.

The complete cessation of train production for three years provided Lionel the opportunity to completely revamp its line. When production resumed in the fall of 1945, not only was Standard Gauge not mentioned, but the 0-gauge trains had totally new designed trucks and couplers, which were incompatible with the previous models, and a newly designed plastic-bodied gondola car. Over the next few years, plastics would increasingly replace the previously used metals in Lionel's products.

Joshua Cowen resigned as Chairman of the Board at the end of 1958, and less than a year later sold his stock in the firm to a syndicate headed by his eccentric and controversial great-nephew, Roy Cohn.

Ultimately, in 1969, The Lionel Toy Corporation (as it had become known in 1965) exited the toy train business by licensing the name and selling the tooling to the Fundimensions Division of General Mills. Some production was moved immediately and, by the mid-1970s, Lionel trains were no longer a presence in the huge Hillside plant.

With the exception of 1967, Lionel Trains have been, and are still, in production every year since 1945, and trains were available even in the bleak 1967. Today's Lionel trains have elaborate paint schemes and sophisticated electronics undreamed of at the dawn of the last century. Despite these advances they lack the mystique of the originals. Many of today's trains are manufactured as a collectable, to be displayed, or operated, but rarely are they played with as Josh Cowen urged his young patrons. Perhaps it is memories of a small child remembering expectations of Christmases long ago, or sneaking the new catalog to school hidden in a tablet, hoping to one day own that special item that fuels today's interest in yesterday's toys. Counter what one may think by glancing at the prices in vintage catalogs, Lionel trains were always expensive, high-quality toys. They were built to last a lifetime and many have. Now that the baby boomers have reached adulthood, many of childhood's financial constraints are lifted—the toys of youthful dreams are at last within grasp.

Lionel Prewar 2 7/8-inch and Standard Gauge

	C5	C7	C8
1 TROLLEY: 1906-14, cream body, orange band, orange roof, five windows, or white body, blue or olive band and roof, five windows, or blue body, cream band, blue roof, six windows.	1,500	2,500	4,000
1 TRAILER: Companion item to the 1 Trolley, later cataloged as 111.	1,000	1,900	2,800
2 TROLLEY: 1906-1916, "No. 2 ELECTRIC RAPID TRANSIT No. 2", yellow or red.	1,200	1,600	2,200
2 TRAILER: Companion item to the 2 Trolley, later cataloged as 200.	1,000	1,500	2,000
3 TROLLEY: 1906-13, cream or dark green body.	1,500	2,500	3,500
3 TRAILER: Non-powered trailer matching 3 trolley.	1,200	2,200	3,200
4 TROLLEY: 1906-12, cream or green body.	2,500	4,000	5,500

5 0-4-0 STEAM: 1906-1909, blued steel boiler with turned wood boiler fronts, domes and smokestacks, did not come with a tender.

	C5	C7	C8
Lettered "N.Y.C. & H.R.R.", thin-rimmed drive wheels.	800	1,000	1,200
Lettered "N.Y.C. & H.R.R.R.", thin-rimmed drive wheels.	1,000	1,200	1,500
Lettered "B. & O. R.R.", thin-rimmed drive wheels.	1,500	1,900	2,500
Lettered "PENNSYLVANIA", thin-rimmed drive wheels.	1,400	1,800	2,300
Lettered "N.Y.C. & H.R.R.R.", thick-rimmed drive wheels.	700	900	1,100

5 Special 0-4-0 STEAM: 1906-11.

	C5	C7	C8
Identical to the 5 but with the addition of a small tender. Rubber-stamped "N.Y.C. & H.R.R.R." Single truck tender.	1,100	1,300	1,600
Single-truck tender rubber-stamped "B. & O. R.R.", locomotive lettered "N.Y.C. & H.R.R.R."	1,100	1,300	1,600
Two-truck tender and loco lettered "N.Y.C. & H.R.R.R."	1,100	1,300	1,600
Two-truck tender and loco lettered "PENNSYLVANIA".	1,100	1,300	1,600

6 4-4-0 STEAM: 1906-23.

	C5	C7	C8
Steel boiler and cab, thin-rimmed drivers lettered "N.Y.C. & H.R.R.R."	600	1,000	1,600
Steel boiler and cab, thin-rimmed drivers lettered "PENNSYLVANIA".	900	1,400	1,900
Steel boiler and cab, thin-rimmed drivers lettered "B. & O. R.R."	900	1,400	1,900
Steel boiler and cab, thin-rimmed drivers lettered "B. & M. R.R."	900	1,400	1,900
Steel boiler and cab, thin-rimmed drivers, provision for train lighting, lettered "N.Y.C. & H.R.R.R."	600	1,000	1,600
Steel boiler and cab, thick-rimmed drivers, provision for train lighting, lettered "N.Y.C. & H.R.R.R."	500	800	1,200
Steel boiler and cab, thick-rimmed drivers, provision for train lighting, lettered "N.Y.C. & H.R.R.R." and "4351"	500	800	1,200

	C5	C7	C8
6 SPECIAL STEAM: 1908-09, 4-4-0, brass, with nickel trim.	2,000	2,400	3,000

	C5	C7	C8
7 STEAM: 1910-23, 4-4-0 brass and nickel, thick or **thin rims**.	1,800- **2,000**	2,000- **2,400**	2,400- **3,000**
8 TROLLEY: 1908-14, Nine or 11 windows, cream or dark green body, orange band and roof.	3,000	4,200	6,000

	C5	C7	C8
8/8E ELECTRIC: 1925-32, 0-B-0, maroon, olive, mojave, red, **peacock, pea green**.	175-**500**	215-**600**	250-**750**
9 MOTOR CAR: 1909-12, double motored, **orange, green** or dark green.	1,200-**3,000**	1,600-**4,200**	2,200-**6,000**
9E ELECTRIC: 1928-35, 0-B-0, orange, gray or two-tone green.	800	1,000	1,300
9U ELECTRIC: 1928-29, 0-B-0, orange loco kit. Assembled examples without box are worth about 50 percent less.	1,500	2,200	3,000
10 INTERURBAN: 1910-16, maroon or dark olive green.	1,000	1,600	2,200
10 ELECTRIC: 1925-29, 0-B-0, mojave, gray, peacock or **red "Macy's"**.	150-**600**	175-**750**	200-**900**
10E ELECTRIC: 1926-30, 0-B-0, *gray, peacock with a black frame,* peacock with dark green frame, State Brown, **red**.	*150-***600**	*175-***750**	*200-***900**
11 FLATCAR: 1906-26, maroon, orange, red, brown, or gray.	50	75	100
12 GONDOLA: 1906-26, red, dark olive, brown or gray.	40	65	100
13 CATTLE CAR: 1906-26, green.	50	75	100
14 BOXCAR: 1906-26, red, **yellow-orange**, or orange, also dark green "Harmony Creamery", too rarely traded to value.	50-**200**	75-**325**	100-**450**
15 OIL CAR: 1906-26 tank car, red, maroon, brown.	15	25	32
16 BALLAST CAR: 1906-26, Maroon, brown, or green.	90	125	175
17 CABOOSE: 1906-25, Red, maroon or brown.	40	60	90
18 PULLMAN: 1910-28, dark olive or yellow-orange, with or without illumination.	100	150	200

	C5	C7	C8
19 COMBINE: 1910-26, dark olive or yellow-orange, with or without illumination.	100	150	200
29 DAY COACH: 1907-14, olive or maroon.	550	750	1,000
31 COMBINE: 1921-25, dark olive, orange, brown or maroon, matches the 35 Pullman and 36 Observation.	60	70	80
32 MAIL CAR: 1921-25, dark olive, orange, brown or maroon, matches the 35 Pullman and 36 Observation.	60	70	80
33 ELECTRIC LOCOMOTIVE: 1913-24.			
0-C-0, dark olive, rubber-stamped "NEW YORK - CENTRAL – LINES".	400	600	900
0-C-0, black, rubber-stamped "NEW YORK - CENTRAL - LINES".	500	750	1,000
0-C-0, dark olive, rubber-stamped "PENN R.R."	700	1,000	1,300
0-B-0, midnight blue.	750	1,200	1,600
0-B-0, black, dark olive, dark green or gray	100	125	150
Factory repaint, colors include: red, maroon, peacock, and red with cream stripe.	300	450	600
34 ELECTRIC LOCOMOTIVE: 1912, 0-C-0 dark olive.	400	600	800
34 ELECTRIC LOCOMOTIVE: 1913, 0-B-0 dark olive.	200	285	400
35 PULLMAN: 1912-26, dark olive, orange, brown or maroon. Matches the 36 Observation.	60	70	80
Midnight-blue.	450	700	1,000
36 OBSERVATION: 1912-26, dark olive, orange, brown or maroon. Matches the 35 Pullman.	60	70	80
Midnight-blue.	450	700	1,000

	C5	**C7**	**C8**

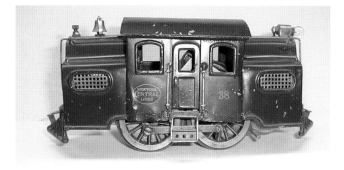

38 ELECTRIC: 1913-24, 0-B-0, Gray, green, maroon or black.

| | 100 | 120 | 150 |
| Brown. | 250 | 280 | 325 |

42 ELECTRIC: 1912; 0-B+B-0, square hoods, dark green.

| | 700 | 1,000 | 1,500 |

42 ELECTRIC: 1913, 0-B+B-0, round hoods, gray, dark gray, black, olive green, dark green, mojave.

| | 275 | 375 | 500 |
| Maroon and peacock. | 1,100 | 1,500 | 2,000 |

50 ELECTRIC: 1924, 0-B-0, dark green, **maroon**, dark gray, mojave.

| | 110- **300** | 150- **450** | 225- **600** |

	C5	**C7**	**C8**

51 STEAM: 1912-23, 4-40, black.

| | 500 | 700 | 1000 |

53 ELECTRIC: 1911, 0-C-0, 1912-21, 0-B+B-0 maroon, mojave, olive or orange.

| | 200 | 325 | 500 |

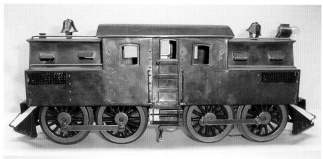

54 ELECTRIC: 1912, 0-B+B-0, 15-1/2-inch long, square-top hoods, unlettered brass body.

| | 2,500 | 3,200 | 4,000 |

54 ELECTRIC: 1913-20, 0-B+B-0, 15-1/2-inch long, round-top hoods, unlettered brass body.

| | 1,800 | 2,300 | 2,800 |

60 ELECTRIC: Mid-1910s, 0-B-0, same as 33 marked for F.A.O. Schwartz.

Too rarely, if ever, traded to establish pricing.

61 ELECTRIC: Mid-1910s, 0-B+B-0, same as 42 marked for F.A.O. Schwartz.

Too rarely, if ever, traded to establish pricing.

62: Mid-1910s, 0-B-0, same as 38 marked for F.A.O. Schwartz.

Too rarely, if ever, traded to establish pricing.

100 TROLLEY: 1910-16, assorted variations, equally valued.

| | 1,100 | 1,800 | 2,600 |

	C5	**C7**	**C8**

100 ELECTRIC LOCOMOTIVE: 1903-05, had "No. 5" stamped on its sides and ends.

	7,000	21,000	35,000

101 SUMMER TROLLEY: 1910-13.

	1,200	1,900	2,600

112 GONDOLA: 1910-26, dark olive green or gray, 6 1/2-inches long.

	200	275	375

Red, brown, dark or light gray, 9 1/2-inches long.

	50	60	75

113 CATTLE CAR: 1912-26, green.

	40	50	60

114 BOXCAR: 1912-26, red, yellow-orange or orange.

	40	50	60

	C5	**C7**	**C8**

116 BALLAST CAR: 1910-26, maroon, brown, dark green or dark gray.

	60	80	110

117 CABOOSE: 1912-26, dark red, brown, maroon or tuscan.

	30	40	60

180 PULLMAN: 1911-21, maroon or brown.

	75	100	125

181 COMBINE: 1911-21, maroon or brown.

	75	100	125

182 OBSERVATION: 1911-21, maroon or brown.

	75	100	125

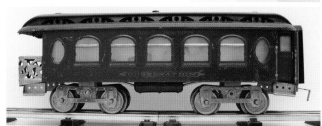

190 OBSERVATION: 1910-27, dark olive or yellow-orange, with or without illumination.

	100	150	200

| | **C5** | **C7** | **C8** | | **C5** | **C7** | **C8** |

200 MOTORIZED GONDOLA: 1901-02, wooden-bodied motorized gondola — 15,000 | 21,000 | 35,000

200 MOTORIZED GONDOLA: 1903-05, steel body. — 8,000 | 10,000 | 15,000

202 SUMMER TROLLEY: 1910-13. — 1,200 | 2,100 | 3,200

211 FLATCAR: 1926-40, black. — 100 | 150 | 225

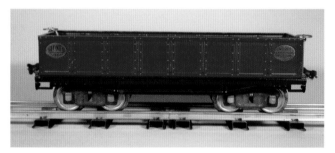

212 GONDOLA: 1926-40, gray, maroon or light green. — 75 | 115 | 150

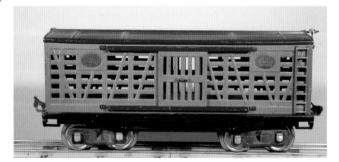

213 CATTLE CAR: 1926-40, mojave, terracotta, pea green or **cream**. — 125-**200** | 200-**350** | 275-**600**

214 BOXCAR: 1926-40, terracotta, cream or **yellow**. — 125-**300** | 175-**400** | 250-**525**

214R REFRIGERATOR CAR: 1929-40, pearl or white body. — 250 | 375 | 500

215 OIL CAR: 1926-29, pea green, ivory, buff or **aluminum-colored with Sunoco decal**. — 150-**275** | 200-**350** | 250-**450**

216 HOPPER CAR: 1926-38, dark green. — 200 | 275 | 375

	C5	C7	C8

217 CABOOSE: 1926-36, red.

| | 175 | 250 | 325 |

218 DUMP CAR: commonly with mojave-painted dump bin, rarely with pea green or gray dump bin.

| | 200 | 275 | 350 |

219 CRANE CAR: 1926-40, peacock, white or yellow cab.

| | 150 | 200 | 250 |

	C5	C7	C8

220 SEARCHLIGHT CAR: 1931-36, terracotta or green light base.

| | 225 | 300 | 375 |

300 ELECTRIC TROLLEY CAR: 1901-05.

| | 5,000 | 6,500 | 10,000 |

303 SUMMER TROLLEY: 1910-13.

| | 1,500 | 2,500 | 3,500 |

309 ELECTRIC TROLLEY TRAILER: 1904-05, non-motorized companion to the 300.

| | 8,000 | 10,000 | 15,000 |

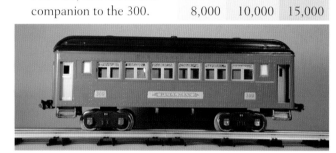

309 Pullman: 1926-39, 13-1/4-inch long illuminated passenger car painted mojave, pea green, State brown, medium or light blue. The two most valuable versions however are painted either Stephen Girard green or maroon with terracotta roof.

| | 50-150 | 75-200 | 100-275 |

220 SEARCHLIGHT CAR

	C5	**C7**	**C8**

310 BAGGAGE: 1926-39, 13-1/4-inch long companion to the 309 and 312 painted mojave, pea green, State brown, medium or light blue. The two most valuable versions however are painted either Stephen Girard green or maroon with terracotta roof.

	C5	C7	C8
310 BAGGAGE	50-150	75-200	100-275

310 TRACK: 1901-02, loose tinplated straight steel rails furnished with wooden cross ties.

Too rarely, if ever, traded to establish market pricing.

310 TRACK (Type II): 1903-05, 24 tinplated steel rails with 60 wooden cross ties.

	C5	C7	C8
310 TRACK (Type II)	75	125	200

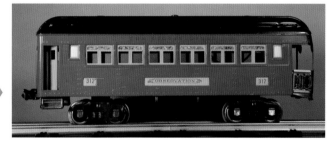

312 OBSERVATION: 1926-39, 13-1/4-inch long companion to the 309 and 310 painted mojave, pea green, State brown, medium or light blue. The two most valuable versions, however, are painted either Stephen Girard green or maroon with terracotta roof.

	C5	C7	C8
312 OBSERVATION	50-150	75-200	100-275

	C5	**C7**	**C8**

318/318E ELECTRIC: 1924-32, 0-B-0, pea green, dark gray, mojave, light gray or State Brown. A black version of the 318E was produced, and should be valued at twice the maximum listed here.

	C5	C7	C8
318/318E ELECTRIC	150-250	200-325	250-425

319 PULLMAN: 1924-30, maroon body and roof **"LIONEL LINES"** or "New York Central" markings.

	C5	C7	C8
319 PULLMAN	95-**175**	120-**250**	160-**350**

320 BAGGAGE: 1925-29, maroon body and roof **"LIONEL ELECTRIC RAILROAD"**, "New York Central" or **"Illinois Central"** markings.

	C5	C7	C8
320 BAGGAGE	95-**175**	120-**250**	160-**350**

	C5	**C7**	**C8**		**C5**	**C7**	**C8**

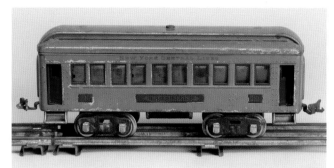

320 SWITCH AND SIGNAL: 1902-05, 17-1/2-inch long turnout with working cast iron switchstand.

Too rarely, if ever, traded to establish market pricing.

322 OBSERVATION: 1924-30, maroon body and roof **"THE LIONEL LINES"** or "New York Central" markings.

95-**175** 120-**250** 160-**350**

330 CROSSING: 1902-05, 90-degree crossover.

Too rarely, if ever, traded to establish market pricing.

337 PULLMAN: 1925-32, mojave, olive green, pea green or red with "THE LIONEL LINES", "NEW YORK CENTRAL LINES" or **"Illinois Central"** markings.

80-**175** 100-**250** 125-**350**

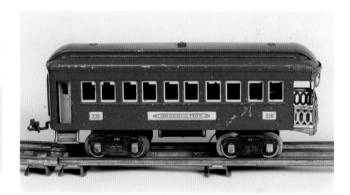

338 OBSERVATION: 1925-32, mojave, olive green, pea green or red with "THE LIONEL LINES", "NEW YORK CENTRAL LINES" or **"Illinois Central"** markings.

80-**175** 100-**250** 125-**350**

339 PULLMAN: 1925-33, gray, peacock, or **State Brown**.

40-**175** 60-**275** 90-**300**

332 BAGGAGE: 1926-33, mojave, gray, olive green, red, peacock or **State Brown**.

70-**175** 95-**275** 125-**300**

340 SUSPENSION BRIDGE: 1902-05, 24 inches-long, cast iron and wood.

Too rarely, if ever, traded to establish market pricing.

	C5	**C7**	**C8**

341 OBSERVATION: 1925-33, gray, peacock or **State Brown**.

	40-**175**	60-**275**	90-**300**

380 Electric: 1923-27, 0-B-0, 13 1/2-inch long 0-B-0, **mojave**, maroon, dark maroon.

	300-**450**	350-**525**	400-**650**

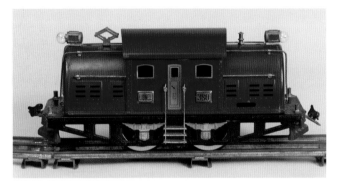

380E ELECTRIC: 1926-29, 0-B-0, maroon, dark green or **mojave**.

	450	550	650

381 ELECTRIC: 1928-29; 2-B-2, 18 inches long, State Green body.

	1,600	1,900	2,200

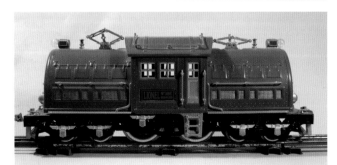

381E ELECTRIC: 1928-36, 2-B-2, 18 inches long, State Green body.

	1,500	2,100	2,700

	C5	**C7**	**C8**

381U ELECTRIC: 1928-29, 2-B-2, assembly kit in 1928-29. Much of the value of this item is predicated on the presence of the original box and tools. Inclusion of these items can increase the value up to 50 percent. Number plates marked "381U" or 381.

	1,400-**1,800**	2,400-**2,800**	3,400-**4,000**

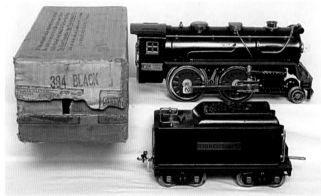

384/384E STEAM: 1930-32, 2-4-0, black with 384T or 390T tender.

	350	475	650

385E: This 23-1/2-inch long locomotive and tender was offered from 1933 through 1939. It used a sheet metal boiler and cab mounted on a die-cast frame. Its tenders had low mounted couplers for use with 500-series cars.

	400	600	800

385E STEAM: 1933-39, gunmetal, came with a 384T, 385TW or 385W tender.

	400	550	750

390 STEAM: 1929, 2-4-2, black, with 390T tender.

	500	625	850

	C5	**C7**	**C8**

390E STEAM: 1929-31, 2-4-2 black, two-tone blue or **two-tone green**, with 390T tender.

	400-**1,000**	550-**1,450**	750-**2,000**

392E STEAM: 1932-39, black or **gunmetal**, with 384T or 392T tender.

	700-**1,000**	900-**1,400**	1,200-**2,000**

400 EXPRESS TRAILER CAR: 1903-05, non-motorized version of the 200 Electric Express gondola.

	5,000	7,000	12,000

400E STEAM: 1931-39, 4-4-2, black, gunmetal or **blue**, with 400T tender.

	1,500-**2,000**	1,750-**2,500**	2,100-**3,100**

402/402E ELECTRIC: 1923-29, 0-B+B-0, mojave.

	350	425	550

	C5	**C7**	**C8**

408E ELECTRIC: 1927, 0-B+B-0, mojave, apple green or **State Brown or State Green**.

	700-**2,100**	900-**2,400**	1,200-**2,700**

412 PULLMAN, CALIFORNIA: 1929-35, 21-1/2-inch long, State Green or State Brown. Lionel's largest, most elaborate, and most expensive Standard Gauge passenger cars.

	800	1,250	1,800

400E STEAM

	C5	**C7**	**C8**

413 PULLMAN, COLORADO: 1929-35, matches the 412.

| | 800 | 1,250 | 1,800 |

414 PULLMAN, ILLINOIS: 1929-35, green or **brown**.

| | 1,000-**1,700** | 1,500-**2,300** | 2,000-**2,900** |

416 OBSERVATION, NEW YORK: 1929-35, matches the 412.

| | 800 | 1,250 | 1,800 |

418 PULLMAN: 1923-32, four or six-wheel trucks, mojave or **apple green**. Versions lettered Illinois Central bring a substantial premium.

| | 150-**300** | 225-**400** | 325-**500** |

419 COMBINATION: 1923-32, four or six-wheel trucks, mojave or **apple green**. Versions lettered Illinois Central bring a substantial premium.

| | 150-**300** | 225-**400** | 325-**500** |

	C5	**C7**	**C8**

420 PULLMAN, FAYE: 1930-40, 18-3/4-inches long, two-tone blue, six-wheel trucks and complete interiors.

| | 600 | 800 | 1,000 |

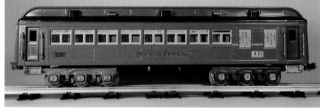

421 PULLMAN, WESTPHAL: 1930-40, 18-3/4-inches long, two-tone blue, six-wheel trucks and complete interiors.

| | 600 | 800 | 1,000 |

422 OBSERVATION, TEMPEL: 1930-40, 18-3/4-inches long, two-tone blue, six-wheel trucks and complete interiors.

| | 600 | 800 | 1,000 |

424 PULLMAN, LIBERTY BELL: 1931-40, two-tone "Stephen Girard green" and dark green.

| | 450 | 550 | 675 |

	C5	**C7**	**C8**

425 PULLMAN, STEPHEN GIRARD:
1931-40, two-tone "Stephen Girard green" and dark green.

	C5	**C7**	**C8**
	450	550	675

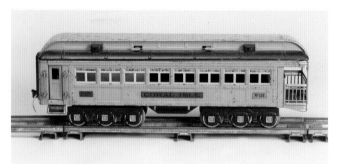

426 OBSERVATION, CORAL ISLE:
1931-40, two-tone "Stephen Girard green" and dark green.

	C5	**C7**	**C8**
	450	550	675

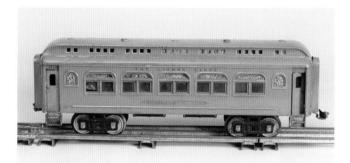

428 PULLMAN:
1926-30, dark green or **orange**, "THE LIONEL LINES" and "PARLOR CAR" markings on the upper and lower car sides respectively.

	C5	**C7**	**C8**
	225-**575**	280-**675**	350-**800**

	C5	**C7**	**C8**

429 COMBINATION:
1926-30, dark green or **orange**, "THE LIONEL LINES" and "PARLOR CAR" and "BAGGAGE" markings on the upper and lower car sides respectively.

	C5	**C7**	**C8**
	225-**575**	280-**675**	350-**800**

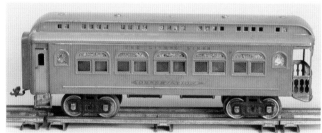

430 OBSERVATION:
1926-30, dark green or **orange**, "THE LIONEL LINES" and "OBSERVATION" markings on the upper and lower car sides respectively.

	C5	**C7**	**C8**
	225-**575**	280-**675**	350-**800**

431 DINING CAR:
1927-32, four- or six-wheel trucks, mojave, apple green, dark green or orange, matches 418, 419 and 490.

	C5	**C7**	**C8**
	400	500	600

	C5	**C7**	**C8**

	C5	**C7**	**C8**

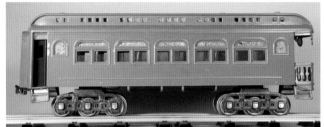

490 OBSERVATION:

1923-32, companion to the 418 Pullman and 419, four- or six-wheel trucks, mojave or **apple green**. Versions lettered Illinois Central bring a substantial premium.

	C5	C7	C8
	150-**300**	225-**400**	325-**500**

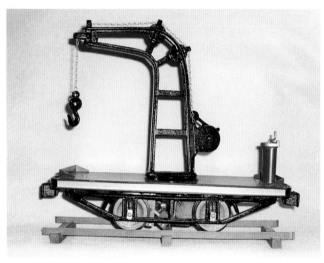

500 ELECTRIC DERRICK CAR:

motorized flatcar with manually operated derrick.

	10,000	13,000	15,000

511 FLATCAR: 1927-40,

green, with simulated lumber load.

	50	70	100

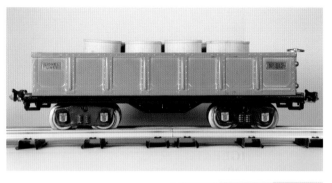

512 GONDOLA: 1927-39,

peacock, or light green.

	30	40	50

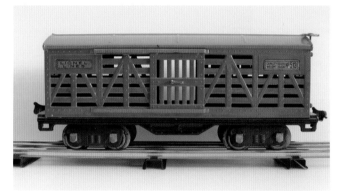

513 CATTLE CAR: 1927-

38, **olive green, cream** or orange.

	50-**75**	75-**110**	100-**150**

514 BOXCAR: 1929-40,

cream or **yellow**.

	100-**125**	125-**200**	150-**300**

514 REFRIGERATOR

CAR: 1927-28, pearl, with long plate reading "LIONEL VENTILATED REFRIGERATOR".

	200	300	400

	C5	C7	C8		C5	C7	C8

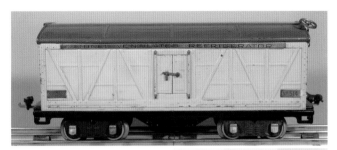

514R REFRIGERATOR CAR: 1929-40, pearl, ivory or white, peacock or **blue roof**.

100-**250**	200-**350**	300-**500**

515 TANK CAR: 1927-40, terracotta cream, silver or **orange**.

80-**350**	125-**525**	175-**725**

516 HOPPER CAR: 1928-40, painted red, **with** or without rubber-stamped lettering.

150-**200**	225-**275**	275-**375**

517 CABOOSE: 1927-40, pea green, red, or **red with black roof and orange windows or apple green**.

50-**350**	75-**500**	100-**800**

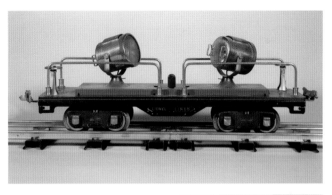

520 SEARCHLIGHT CAR: 1931, terracotta or green light platform.

100	150	200

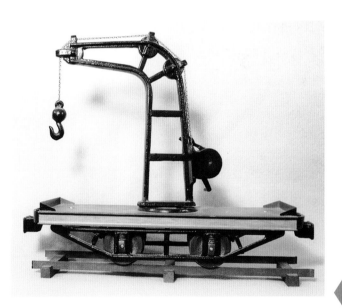

600 DERRICK TRAILER: 1903-04, 2-7/8-inch gauge, non-motorized version of the 500. Apple green or maroon and black.

7,500	10,000	15,000

C5   C7   C8   **C5   C7   C8**

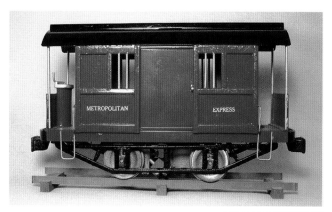

800 BOXCAR: 1904-
05, Sometimes referred
to by collectors as "jail
cars," 14-1/2-inch long
motorized boxcar lettered
"METROPOLITAN
EXPRESS."   5,000   8,000   10,000

900 BOX TRAIL CAR:
1904-05, non-powered
companion to the 800.   4,000   7,000   9,000

1000 TROLLEY: 1905, 2-
7/8-inch gauge 14-3/4-inch
long trolley maroon with a
black roof and frame.   8,000   11,000   15,000

**1050 PASSENGER
CAR TRAILER:** 1905,
non-powered matching
companion to the 1000.   9,000   12,000   16,500

1766 PULLMAN: 1934-
40, terracotta or red sides
and maroon roofs.   350   500   700

1767 PULLMAN: 1934-
40, terracotta or red
sides and maroon roofs,
matches 1766 Pullman.   350   500   700

1768 OBSERVATION:
1934-40, terracotta or red
sides and maroon roofs,
matches 1766 and 1767
Pullmans.   350   500   700

1835E STEAM: 1934-39,
black, with 384T, 1835TW
or 1835W tender.   500   650   900

	C5	**C7**	**C8**

1910 ELECTRIC: 1910-11, 0-C-0, **9-3/4-inch long**, 1912, 10-3/8-inches long, dark olive green lettered "New York - New Haven - and Hartford" or "New York Central LINES". — 500-800 — 950-1,300 — 1,400-1,900

1910 PULLMAN: Circa, 1910, uncataloged dark olive passenger car. — 900 — 1,250 — 1,700

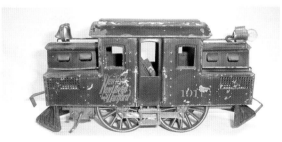

1911: 1910-12, **squared hood tops**, 1913, rounded hood tops, 0-B-0 dark olive. — 700-**900** — 950-**1,200** — 1,200-**1,800**

1911 SPECIAL: 1911-12, jumbo size version of the 1911 with 0-B+B-0 wheel arrangement, maroon "New York - New Haven - and Hartford" or "NEW YORK - CENTRAL – LINES" lettering. — 1,000 — 1,600 — 2,500

	C5	**C7**	**C8**

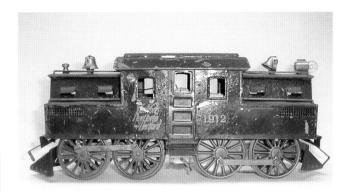

1912 (Type I): 1910-12, 15-1/2-inch long 0-B+B-0, dark green, "New York - New Haven and Hartford" or "NEW YORK - CENTRAL – LINES" lettering. — 1,200 — 1,900 — 2,600

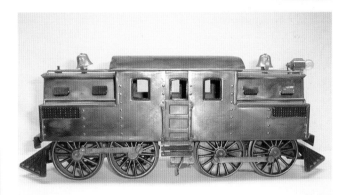

1912 SPECIAL: 1911, same as the normal 1912, but with a polished brass body. — 2,300 — 3,500 — 4,500

2200 TRAILER: A matching non-powered trailer was made to pair with the 202 trolley. — 1,100 — 2,000 — 3,000

3300 TRAILER: A matching non-powered trailer was made to pair with the 303. — 1,200 — 1,900 — 2,600

	C5	**C7**	**C8**		**C5**	**C7**	**C8**

001 STEAM LOCOMOTIVE

001 STEAM LOCOMOTIVE: 1938-42, Super-detailed OO gauge replica of a New York Central J-3a 4-6-4 Hudson. 15-1/2-inches long and numbered "5342". Chain-retained drawbar in 1938, spring-loaded pin thereafter. With or without whistle; $70 penalty for lack of whistle. — 200-250 / 400-450 / 600-700

002 STEAM LOCOMOTIVE: 1939-42, less-detailed version of the three-rail OO Hudson. With or without whistle. — 175 / 350 / 550

003 STEAM LOCOMOTIVE: 1939-42, super-detailed two-rail 00 Hudson. With or without whistle; $70 penalty for lack of whistle. — 250 / 450 / 700

004 STEAM LOCOMOTIVE: 1939-42, less-detailed two-rail 4-6-4 Hudson. — 150 / 300 / 500

4 ELECTRIC: 1928-32, 1-B-1 electric locomotive, painted orange or **gray**. — 450-600 / 650-900 / 900-1,300

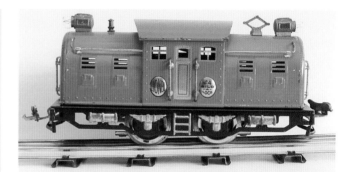

4U ELECTRIC: 1928-29, 1-B-1 electric locomotive. Kit of orange 4. To attain the values listed, the kit must be unassembled and complete with all packaging. — 1,200 / 2,000 / 4,000

0014 BOXCAR: 1938-42, super-detailed boxcar for use on three-rail track. **Yellow and maroon** "Lionel Lines" in 1938, tuscan "Pennsylvania" 1939-42. — 50-**75** / **65-125** / **80-200**

0015 TANK CAR: 1938-42, silver or black, marked **Sunoco** or Shell. — 40-**50** / 60-**75** / **80-100**

0016 HOPPER CAR: 1938-42, die-cast three-rail hopper car. **Gray** or black "SOUTHERN PACIFIC LINES". — 60-**75** / **100-125** / **150-175**

0017 CABOOSE: 1938-42, red **"Pennsylvania"** (1938) or "NYC" (1938-42) lettering. — 50-**75** / 75-**115** / **100-150**

	C5	C7	C8

0024 BOXCAR: 1939-42
semi-scale 6 7/8-inch
Pennsylvania boxcar. | 45 | 60 | 75 |

0025 TANK CAR:
1939-42, silver or black
semiscale tank car, marked
Sunoco or Shell.

0027 CABOOSE: 1939-
42, red three-rail caboose
decaled "N.Y.C. 0027".

	C5	C7	C8
0024	45	60	75
0025	40	60	80
0027	40	60	80

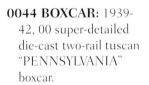

0044 BOXCAR: 1939-
42, 00 super-detailed
die-cast two-rail tuscan
"PENNSYLVANIA"
boxcar. | 45 | 70 | 100 |

0045 TANK CAR:
1939-42, 00 for two-rail
operation. Black Shell or
silver Sunoco. | 40 | 60 | 80 |

	C5	C7	C8
0045	40	60	80

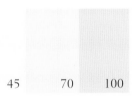

0044K BOXCAR:
1939-42, unassembled
super-detailed die-cast
boxcar finished in gray
primer. Pricing assumes
an unassembled kit, in
original packaging. | 70 | 125 | 350 |

0045K TANK CAR:
1939-42, unassembled,
and painted with gray
primer. Paint, brush and
decals were included in
the kit. Pricing assumes
an unassembled kit, in
original packaging. | 70 | 125 | 350 |

	C5	**C7**	**C8**

0046 HOPPER CAR:
1939-42, black Southern Pacific hopper for two-rail 00 operation.

	C5	C7	C8
	40	70	100

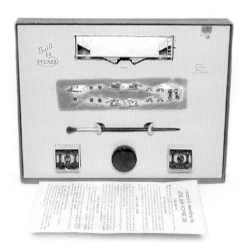

0046K HOPPER CAR:
1939-42, unassembled, and painted with gray primer. Paint, brush and decals were included in the kit. Pricing assumes an unassembled kit, in original packaging.

	C5	C7	C8
	70	125	350

0047 CABOOSE: 1939-42, red super-detailed NYC 00 caboose with smoke jack and piping, for two-rail operation.

	C5	C7	C8
	30	60	90

	C5	**C7**	**C8**

0047K CABOOSE:
1939-42, unassembled and painted with gray primer. Paint, brush and decals were included in the kit. Pricing assumes an unassembled kit, in original packaging.

	C5	C7	C8
	70	125	350

0074 BOXCAR: 1939-42, tuscan "PENNSYLVANIA" semi-scale 00 boxcar for two-rail track.

	C5	C7	C8
	45	70	100

0075 TANK CAR: 1939-42, two-rail tank car, black "SHELL" or silver "SUNOCO".

	C5	C7	C8
	20	40	60

0077 CABOOSE: 1939-42, red semi-scale NYC caboose for two-rail operation.

	C5	C7	C8
	20	40	60

150 ELECTRIC: 1917-25, 0-B-0, two different body styles. Dark green, dark olive, brown, maroon, **peacock, gray or mojave**.

	C5	C7	C8
	50-100	75-200	110-300

152 ELECTRIC: 1917-29, 0-B-0, dark green, dark olive, dark gray, light gray, pea green, mojave or **peacock**.

	C5	C7	C8
	50-400	75-550	110-700

153 ELECTRIC: 1924-25, 0-B-0, dark green, dark olive, gray, maroon, **mojave** or peacock.

	C5	C7	C8
	80-115	110-150	150-200

154 ELECTRIC: 1917-23.

	C5	C7	C8
	80	110	150

156 ELECTRIC: 1917-23, 2-B-2, dark green, olive green, **gray**, maroon or **mojave**.

	C5	C7	C8
	400-750	550-900	725-1,100

	C5	C7	C8
156X (Type I): 1923-24, less expense 0-B-0 version of the 156, olive green, gray, maroon, mojave or brown.	350	425	550
158 ELECTRIC: 1919-23, 0-B-0, dark green, gray, black.	80-100	125-140	175-200
201 STEAM: 1940-42, 0-6-0 switcher, with or without bell-ringing 2201 tender.	350-400	500-550	700-775
203 ARMORED LOCO-MOTIVE: 1917-21.	1,100	1,600	2,500
203 STEAM: 1940-41, 0-6-0 switcher, with or without bell-ringing 2203 tender.	325-400	400-475	500-575
204 STEAM: 1940-41, 2-4-2, **gunmetal** or black, with 1689T or 2689T tender.	50-**75**	70-**110**	100-**150**
224 or 224E STEAM: 1938-42, 2-6-2, black or **gunmetal** with die-cast or plastic 2224 tender, 2689W sheet metal tender.	125-**500**	165-**850**	225-**1,200**
225 or 225E STEAM: 1938-42, 2-6-2, black or **gunmetal** with die-cast or plastic bodied 2235 tender, or 2225 or 2265 sheet-metal tender.	175-**225**	250-**300**	350-**425**

	C5	C7	C8
226 or 226E STEAM: 1938-41, 2-6-4, with 2226W tender.	350	475	650

	C5	C7	C8
227 STEAM: 1939-42, 0-6-0 with 2227T or 2227B tender. Catalog number on boiler front, "8976" under cab window.	550	750	975
228 STEAM: 1939-42, 0-6-0 with 2228T or 2228B tender. Catalog number on boiler front, "8976" under cab window.	550	750	975
229 or 229E STEAM: 1939-42, 2-4-2 black or gunmetal with 2689T, 2689W, 2666T or **2666W** tender.	100-**125**	130-**175**	175-**250**
230 STEAM: 1939, 0-6-0 with 2230T or 2230B tender. Catalog number on boiler front, "8976" under cab window.	800	1300	1900
231 STEAM: 1939, 0-6-0 with 2231T or 2231B tender. Catalog number on boiler front, "8976" under cab window.	650	1200	1800

	C5	**C7**	**C8**

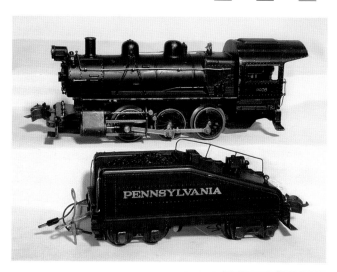

232 STEAM: 1940-41, 0-6-0 with 2232B tender. Catalog number on boiler front, "8976" under cab window.

	C5	C7	C8
232 STEAM	650	1,200	1,800

233 STEAM: 1940-42, 0-6-0 with 2233B tender. Catalog number on boiler front, "8976" under cab window.

	C5	C7	C8
233 STEAM	650	1,200	1,800

238/238E STEAM: 1936-40, 4-4-2, gunmetal or black, with 265T, 265W, 2265W or 2225W.

	C5	C7	C8
238/238E STEAM	250	300	375

	C5	**C7**	**C8**

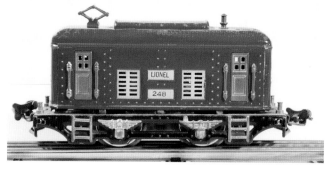

248 ELECTRIC: 1927-32, 0-B-0, dark green, peacock, **terracotta**, orange, peacock, red.

	C5	C7	C8
248 ELECTRIC	50-**150**	90-**225**	140-**325**

249/249E STEAM: 1936-39, 2-4-2, gunmetal or black, with 265T or 265W tender.

	C5	C7	C8
249/249E STEAM	75	125	200

250 ELECTRIC: 1926, 1934, 0-B-0, dark green, peacock, terracotta or orange.

	C5	C7	C8
250 ELECTRIC	150	190	250

250E STEAM: 1935-1942, 4-4-2, gloss orange, black and gray. Came with 250W, 250WX, 250T, 2250W or 2250T tender

	C5	C7	C8
250E STEAM	600	1,000	1,600

251/251E ELECTRIC: 1925-32, 0-B-0, gray, red.

	C5	C7	C8
251/251E ELECTRIC	275	325	400

	C5	**C7**	**C8**

252/252E ELECTRIC:
1926-35, 0-B-0 peacock, terracotta, yellow-orange, olive, **maroon**,

	C5	**C7**	**C8**
252/252E	75-**300**	110-**450**	150-**650**

253/253E ELECTRIC:
1924-36, 0-B-0, **maroon**, **gray**, mojave, dark green, peacock, terracotta, pea green, Stephen Girard green or **red**.

253/253E	100-**175**	150-**300**	225-**450**

254/254E ELECTRIC:
1924-34, 0-B-0, dark green, mojave, olive green, orange or **pea green**.

254/254E	150-**250**	200-**325**	250-**400**

255E STEAM: 1935-36, 2-4-2 with 263W.

255E	500	700	1000

256 ELECTRIC: 1924-30, 0-B+B-0, orange.

256	500	800	1200

257 STEAM: 1930-32, 2-4-0 with 257T or 259T tender.

257	125	200	300

258 STEAM: 1930, 2-4-0 or 2-4-2, **black** or gunmetal with 257T or 1689T tender.

258	50-**70**	80-**125**	150-**200**

259/259E STEAM:
1932-40, 2-4-2 black or gunmetal with 259T, 262T, 1588TX, 2689T or 1689W.

259/259E	50	80	125

260E STEAM: 1930, black or **gunmetal**, with 260T, **263T** or **263W**.

260E	350-**450**	450-**550**	550-**650**

261/261E STEAM: 1931, 1935, 2-4-2, black, with 257T or 261T.

261/261E	125	175	225

261/261E STEAM

	C5	**C7**	**C8**

262/262E STEAM: 1931-36, 2-4-2, black, with 262T, 265T or 265W tender. 262 more desirable than 262E.

263E STEAM: 1936-39, 2-4-2, gunmetal or **two-tone blue** with 263W or 2263W tender

	C5	**C7**	**C8**
262/262E	100-**200**	140-**250**	200-**325**
263E	300-**400**	450-**650**	625-**1,000**

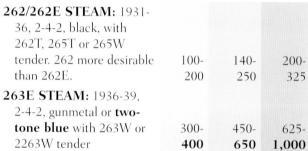

264E STEAM: 1935-40, 2-4-2, **black** or red with 261T or 265T tender.

C5	**C7**	**C8**
125-**200**	200-**275**	300-**375**

265E STEAM: 1935-40, black, gunmetal or **blue** with 261TX, 2225T, 2225W, 265TX or 265WX tender.

289E STEAM: about 1936-37, black or gunmetal with 1588, 1688T, 1688W, 1689T, or 1689W.

450 ELECTRIC: 1928-31, 0-B-0 red or apple green.

	C5	**C7**	**C8**
265E	150-**425**	225-**625**	350-**850**
289E	100	200	325
450	400	750	1125

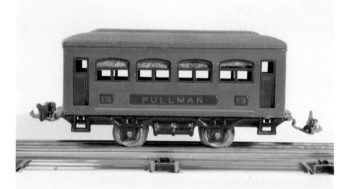

529 PULLMAN: 1926-32, olive or terracotta.

530 OBSERVATION: 1926-32, olive or terracotta.

600 PULLMAN: 1915-1925, **four wheels**, 1933-42 eight wheels, **dark green**, brown, maroon, two-tone red, light blue and aluminum.

	C5	**C7**	**C8**
529	20	30	40
530	20	30	40
600	40-**90**	55-**115**	75-**150**

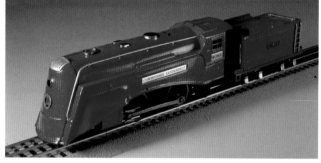

263E STEAM

	C5	C7	C8

601 PULLMAN OR OBSERVATION: 1915-1925, **four wheels**; 1933-42, eight wheels, **dark green**, brown, maroon, two-tone red, light blue and aluminum. — 40-90 | 55-115 | 75-150

602 BAGGAGE CAR: 1915-1923, **four wheels**; 1933-37, eight wheels, dark green, yellow-orange, gray, two-tone red, light blue and aluminum. — 25-80 | 40-100 | 60-135

603 PULLMAN: 1920-36, 7, 6-1/2 or **7-1/2**-inches long. Yellow-orange, red, **maroon**, green, red and black. — 25-75 | 35-100 | 50-140

604 OBSERVATION: 1920-25, 6-1/2-inches long; 1931-36, 7-1/2-inches long. Yellow-orange, green, red, **maroon**. — 25-75 | 35-100 | 50-140

605 PULLMAN: 1925-32, gray, olive green, red, **orange**, **Illinois Central**, Macy Special or Lionel Lines. — 75-300 | 110-350 | 175-400

606 OBSERVATION: 1925-32, gray, olive green, red, **orange**, **Illinois Central**, Macy Special or Lionel Lines. — 75-300 | 110-350 | 175-400

607 PULLMAN: 1926-37, peacock, red, Stephen Girard green. — 75 | 85 | 100

608 OBSERVATION: 1926-37, peacock, red, Stephen Girard green. — 75 | 85 | 100

609 PULLMAN: 1937-42, blue and silver. — 60 | 75 | 100

610 PULLMAN: 1915-42, dark green; mojave; maroon; olive green; terracotta body, maroon roof, and cream trim; light red or blue with aluminum roof; pea green; red-lettered **Macy Special**. — 45-200 | 55-300 | 70-400

611 OBSERVATION: 1937-42, blue and silver. — 60 | 75 | 100

612 OBSERVATION: 1915-42, dark green; mojave; maroon; olive green; terracotta body, maroon roof, and cream trim; light red or blue with aluminum roof; pea green; red-lettered **Macy Special**. — 45-200 | 55-300 | 70-400

613 PULLMAN: 1931-40, terracotta, two-tone blue, **light red and aluminum**. — 100-200 | 140-300 | 200-400

614 OBSERVATION: 1931-40, terracotta, two-tone blue, **light red and aluminum**. — 100-200 | 140-300 | 200-400

615 BAGGAGE: 1931-40, terracotta, two-tone blue, **light red and aluminum**. — 100-200 | 140-300 | 200-400

	C5	**C7**	**C8**

616 FLYING YANKEE:
1935-41, the 616E or the
similar whistle-equipped
616W headed replicas of
the streamlined, articulated
Boston and Maine "Flying
Yankee." Chrome or painted
aluminum, with gunmetal,
black, red or olive green trim.
Complete train. — 300 / 400 / 550

617 COACH: Matches 616,
or blue. — 50 / 60 / 75

618 OBSERVATION:
Matches 617. — 50 / 60 / 75

619 COMBINATION:
Matches 617. — 100 / 140 / 200

620 SEARCHLIGHT CAR:
1937-38, red. — 50 / 65 / 85

629 PULLMAN: 1924-32,
dark green, peacock, orange
or red. — 25 / 32 / 40

630 OBSERVATION: 1924-
32, dark green, peacock,
orange or red. — 25 / 32 / 40

**636W UP CITY OF
DENVER POWER UNIT:**
1936-39, streamlined
diesel painted yellow with a
brown roof. Came with two
637 coaches and one 638
observation car from 1936
through 1939. Price for set. — 500 / 650 / 1100

	C5	**C7**	**C8**

651 FLATCAR: 1935-38,
green. — 20 / 30 / 45

652 GONDOLA: 1935-42,
yellow or orange. — 25 / 35 / 50

653 HOPPER: 1933-42,
Stephen Girard Green. — 30 / 50 / 75

654 TANK CAR: 1933-42,
aluminum, orange, gray,
Sunoco or Shell. — 25 / 35 / 50

655 BOXCAR: 1933-41,
cream or **tuscan** body. — 30-**45** / 40-**60** / 55-**80**

656 STOCK CAR: 1935-42,
light gray or **burnt orange**. — 60-**75** / 75-**100** / 100-**140**

657 CABOOSE: 1933-42,
red. — 15 / 25 / 35

659 ORE DUMP: 1935-42,
dark green. — 50 / 60 / 75

700 ELECTRIC: 1915-16,
0-B-0. — 500 / 625 / 775

	C5	**C7**	**C8**		**C5**	**C7**	**C8**

700E STEAM

700K STEAM

700K STEAM: 1938-42, 4-6-4 Scale-detailed Hudson in kit form.

	C5	C7	C8
Assembled:	2,500	1,000	4,000
Unassembled:	5,000	8,000	12,000

701 ELECTRIC: 1915-1916, 0-B-0.

	400	500	625

700E STEAM: 1937-42, 4-6-4 Hudson, scale-detailed.

	1,300	2,000	2,800

700EWX STEAM: 4-6-4 Hudson. A number of customers liked the scale detailed appearance of Lionel's Hudson, but had extensive model railroad systems made of conventional tubular track. The 700EWX, available by special order, had blind (lacking flanges) center drivers, while the profile of the flanges of the other drivers was also slightly different.

	1,500	2,250	3,000

701 STEAM: 1939-42, 0-6-0 switcher with 701T tender, cab lettered "8976".

	350	500	700

	C5	**C7**	**C8**

702 BAGGAGE CAR:
1917-21, unlettered gray, for
armored train. — 125 · 200 · 300

703 ELECTRIC: 1915-16,
2-B-2, dark green. — 1,100 · 1,700 · 2,500

706 ELECTRIC: 1915-1916,
0-B-0, dark green. — 325 · 475 · 650

714 BOXCAR: 1940-42, scale
replica Pennsylvania boxcar. — 425 · 575 · 750

714K BOXCAR: 1940-42,
unpainted and unassembled
scale boxcar. — 600 · 1,000 · 1,500

Assembled: — 300 · 400 · 550

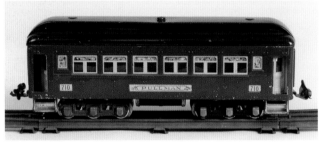

710 PULLMAN: 1924-34,
olive green, "NEW YORK
CENTRAL LINES", or
orange "NEW YORK
CENTRAL LINES",
"ILLINOIS CENTRAL
LINES" or "THE LIONEL
LINES, **red or blue "THE
LIONEL LINES"**, four or
six-wheeled trucks. — 125-**300** · 175-**375** · 225-**475**

712 OBSERVATION:
1924-34, olive green,
"NEW YORK CENTRAL
LINES", or orange "NEW
YORK CENTRAL LINES",
"ILLINOIS CENTRAL
LINES" or "THE LIONEL
LINES, **red or blue "THE
LIONEL LINES"**, four or
six-wheeled trucks. — 125-**300** · 175-**375** · 225-**475**

715 TANK CAR: 1940 Shell,
1941-42 **Sunoco** scale
model tank car. — 300-**400** · 500-**600** · 725-**850**

715K TANK CAR: 1940-42,
unpainted and unassembled
scale tank car. — 500 · 850 · 1300

Assembled: — 350 · 550 · 800

716 HOPPER: 1940-42,
black die-cast scale hopper. — 300 · 450 · 625

716K HOPPER: 1940-42,
primered only, unassembled
scale hopper car. — 600 · 900 · 1,500

Assembled: — 275 · 425 · 575

717 CABOOSE: 1940-42,
Scale caboose. — 350 · 475 · 650

	C5	C7	C8

717K CABOOSE: 1940-42, unpainted and unassembled scale tank car.

| | 600 | 1,000 | 1,500 |
| Assembled: | 300 | 400 | 550 |

728 ELECTRIC: 1916, 0-B-0, "Quaker".

Too infrequently traded to establish accurate values.

732 ELECTRIC: 1916, 0-B-0, "Quaker".

Too infrequently traded to establish accurate values.

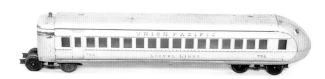

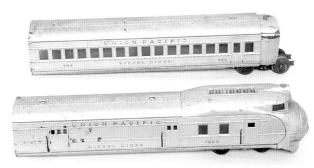

752 UNION PACIFIC M10000: 1935-41, yellow and brown or painted aluminum finish; three- or four-car sets. Price listed for three-car sets, additional cars add $100-$200, yellow and brown adds a similar premium.

| | 600 | 1000 | 1400 |

763 STEAM: 1937-40, semi-scale Hudson. Black or gunmetal, with 263W, 2263W, 2226W or 2226WX tender.

| | 1,100 | 1,800 | 2,750 |

782/783/784 HIAWATHA CARS: 1935-41, orange sides, gray roof, maroon frame. Part of streamlined articulated Hiawatha passenger set pulled by 250E locomotive.

| | 600 | 1,200 | 1,800 |

	C5	C7	C8

792/793/794 RAIL CHIEF CARS: 1937-41, red sides, maroon roof, maroon frame. Part of streamlined articulated Rail Chief passenger set pulled by 700E locomotive. Matches 793, 794, does not include vestibule.

| | 800 | 2,500 | 3,800 |

800 BOXCAR: 1915-27, orange, Wabash or Pennsylvania markings.

| | 25 | 40 | 50 |

801 CABOOSE: 1915-26.

| | 30 | 40 | 65 |

802 STOCK CAR: 1915-27, green.

| | 25 | 40 | 55 |

803 HOPPER: 1923-34, dark green or peacock.

| | 25 | 35 | 50 |

804 TANK CAR: 1923-41, gray, terracotta, aluminum-painted or **yellow-orange**.

| | 15-35 | 25-45 | 35-60 |

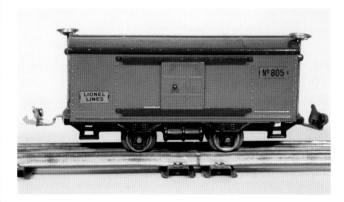

805 BOXCAR: 1927-34, pea green, cream or orange.

| | 20 | 35 | 50 |

	C5	C7	C8

806 CATTLE CAR: 1927-34, **pea green**, orange or maroon.

	C5	C7	C8
	30-60	45-90	65-125

807 CABOOSE: 1927-42, peacock, red.

	C5	C7	C8
807 CABOOSE	20	30	40
809 DUMP CAR	60	70	85

809 DUMP CAR: 1930-32, orange or green dump bin.

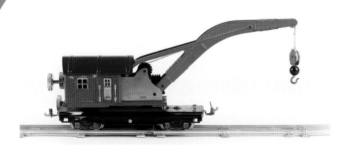

810 DERRICK: 1930-42, terracotta, cream cab or **yellow**.

	C5	C7	C8
810 DERRICK	125-175	150-210	225-250
811 FLATCAR	35-60	45-75	60-100

811 FLATCAR: 1926-42, maroon or **aluminum**-colored body.

	C5	C7	C8

812 GONDOLA: 1926-42, mojave, dark green, 45N green, **Stephen Girard green** or orange.

	C5	C7	C8
	25-60	35-75	45-100

813 STOCK CAR: 1926-42, orange, cream or **rubber-stamped tuscan**.

814 BOXCAR: 1926-42, cream, yellow or orange.

814R: 1929-42. Ivory or white with black frame, white with aluminum frame, all with blue roofs, or **white with brown roof**.

	C5	C7	C8
813 STOCK CAR	75-1,500	110-2,250	150-3,250
814 BOXCAR	60	90	125
814R	100-1,500	150-2,000	225-2,750

815 TANK CAR: 1926-27, pea green, aluminum or **orange**.

	C5	C7	C8
	50-200	75-300	110-550

	C5	**C7**	**C8**

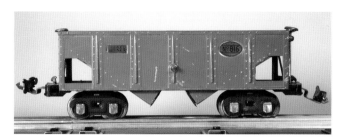

816 HOPPER: 1927-42, olive green, red or **black with plates,** or rubber-stamped black.

	C5	C7	C8
	60-**1,400**	100-**2,500**	150-**3,500**

817 CABOOSE: 1926-, peacock or red, or red with brown roof. — 35-200 | 55-300 | 75-400

820 SEARCHLIGHT CAR: 1931-42, terracotta or green light base. — 100 | 125 | 160

820 BOXCAR: 1915-26, **dark olive A.T. & S.F,** yellow-orange "ILLINOIS CENTRAL RAILROAD" or orange "UNION PACIFIC". — 40-**175** | 55-**225** | 80-**300**

821 STOCK CAR: 1925-26, green. — 50 | 65 | 90

831 FLATCAR: 1927-42, black or dark, pale, or 45N green. — 20 | 30 | 40

900 AMMUNITION BOXCAR: 1917-21, unlettered gray, included with 203 armored motor car. — 125 | 225 | 350

901 GONDOLA: 1917-27, brown, maroon, gray or green. — 35 | 45 | 60

902 GONDOLA: 1927-31, dark green, peacock or Stephen Girard green. — 20 | 30 | 40

	C5	**C7**	**C8**

1010 ELECTRIC: 1931-32, 0-B-0, orange. — 75 | 110 | 150

1011 PULLMAN: 1931-32, light orange body with green or olive roof. — 50 | 60 | 75

1015 STEAM: 1931-32, 0-4-0 with 1016 tender. — 100 | 150 | 200

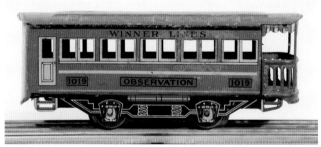

1019 OBSERVATION: 1931-32, orange body, with green or olive roof. — 50 | 60 | 75

1020 BAGGAGE: 1931-32, light orange body, with green or olive roof. — 60 | 75 | 100

	C5	C7	C8
1035 STEAM: 1931-32, 0-4-0, black with copper trim.	75	100	125
1506 STEAM: 1935, 0-4-0, clockwork, with Mickey Mouse riding in its 1509 tender.	225	325	450
1506L STEAM: 1933-34, 0-4-0, clockwork. No Mickey Mouse rode on this version.	80	100	125
1508 STEAM: 1935, 0-4-0, clockwork, streamlined, painted red, with Mickey Mouse riding in its 1509 tender.	325	450	600
1511 STEAM: 1936-37, 0-4-0, clockwork, black or red, with 1516T oil-style tender.	100	125	150

	C5	C7	C8
1512 GONDOLA: 1931-37, blue or blue-green.	5	10	20

	C5	C7	C8
1514 BOXCAR: 1931-37, light yellow, with or without Baby Ruth logo.	15	20	30

	C5	C7	C8
1515 TANK CAR: 1931-37, aluminum-colored, lithographed **Union Tank Lines, Fuel Oil** or Sunoco.	15-25	25-45	35-70

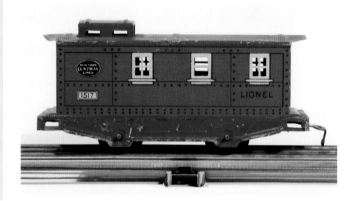

	C5	C7	C8
1517 CABOOSE: 1931-37, no Lionel markings. Red, orange "NEW YORK – CENTRAL – LINES" legend.	20	30	40
1518 CIRCUS DINING CAR: 1935, part of an uncataloged Mickey Mouse-themed circus outfit.	100	150	225
1519 MICKEY MOUSE BAND: 1935, part of an uncataloged Mickey Mouse-themed circus outfit.	100	150	225
1520 MICKEY MOUSE CIRCUS: 1935, part of an uncataloged Mickey Mouse-themed circus outfit.	100	150	225
1588 STEAM: 1936-37, clockwork, black, with 1588T tender.	125	175	225

1588 STEAM

	C5	C7	C8

1630 PULLMAN: 1938-41, blue with gray or aluminum-colored windows, roof, and underframe. 30 45 65

1631 OBSERVATION: 1938-41, blue with gray or aluminum-colored windows, roof, and underframe. 30 45 65

1651E ELECTRIC: 1933, 0-B-0, red. 100 140 200

1661E STEAM: 1933, 2-4-0, with 1661T tender. 70 100 150

1662 STEAM: 1940-42, 0-4-0, with 2201T or 2203B tender. 225 300 400

	C5	C7	C8

1663 STEAM: 1940-42, 0-4-0, with 2201T. 200 300 400

1664/1664E STEAM: 1938-42, 2-4-2 black or gunmetal, with 1689T, 1689W or 2666W. 50 75 100

1666/1666E STEAM: 1938-42, 2-6-2 black or gunmetal with 1689W, 2689T, 2689W, 2666T or 2666W tender. 75 100 125

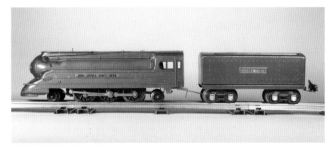

1668/1668E STEAM: 1937-41, 2-4-2, Pennsylvania, streamlined, gunmetal or black, with 1689W tender. 75 100 125

	C5	**C7**	**C8**

1677 GONDOLA: 1933-38, blue, peacock or red. 20 30 40

1679 BOXCAR: 1933-39, yellow "Baby Ruth" or "CURTISS BABY RUTH" on sides. 12 18 25

1679X BOXCAR: 1936-42, the 1679X differed from the normal production by lacking journal boxes. 20 25 30

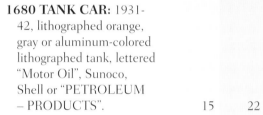

1680 TANK CAR: 1931-42, lithographed orange, gray or aluminum-colored lithographed tank, lettered "Motor Oil", Sunoco, Shell or "PETROLEUM – PRODUCTS". 15 22 30

	C5	**C7**	**C8**

1680X TANK CAR: 1936-42, orange, **gray** or aluminum-colored with Sunoco, Shell or "Gas-Sunoco-Oils" markings. 15-30 22-40 30-55

1681/1681E: 1934, 2-4-0, black or **red**, with 1661T tender. 50-75 80-100 110-150

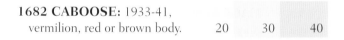

1682 CABOOSE: 1933-41, vermilion, red or brown body. 20 30 40

1684 STEAM: 1941-42, 2-4-2 die-cast, black or gunmetal. 40 55 75

1681/1681E

	C5	C7	C8

1685 PASSENGER CAR:
1933-37, gray, blue or red, four- or **six-wheel trucks**.
175-250 | 275-350 | 350-500

1686 BAGGAGE CAR:
1933-37, gray, blue or red, four- or **six-wheel trucks**.
175-250 | 275-350 | 350-500

1687 OBSERVATION CAR:
1933-37, gray, blue or red, four- or **six-wheel trucks**.
175-250 | 275-350 | 350-500

1688/1688E STEAM: 1936-40, 2-4-2, Pennsylvania streamlined boiler and cab, gunmetal or black, with 1689T or 1689W tender.
40 | 55 | 75

1689E STEAM: 1936-37, 2-4-2, black or gunmetal *Commodore Vanderbilt*-style streamlined locomotive with 1689T, 1689W, 1688T or 1688W tender.
75 | 100 | 125

1690 PULLMAN: 1933-1940, dark red with yellow windows, medium red and cream windows or orange-red.
30 | 40 | 55

	C5	C7	C8

1691 OBSERVATION: 1933-1940, dark red with yellow windows, medium red and cream windows or orange-red.
30 | 40 | 55

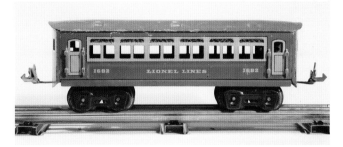

1692 PULLMAN: 1939, lithographed blue.
40 | 50 | 65

1693 OBSERVATION: 1939, lithographed blue.
40 | 50 | 65

1700E DIESEL: 1935-37, chrome-finished, or painted yellow, orange or aluminum. Yellow too scarce to value.
150 | 200 | 250

1701 COACH: 1935-37, chrome-finished, or painted red, yellow, orange or aluminum. Yellow too scarce to value.
25 | 35 | 50

1702 OBSERVATION: 1935-37, chrome finished, or painted red, yellow, orange or aluminum. Yellow too scarce to value.
25 | 35 | 50

1703 FRONT END CAR: 1935-37, chrome finished, or painted red, yellow, orange or aluminum. Yellow too scarce to value.
50 | 75 | 100

	C5	**C7**	**C8**

1717 GONDOLA: 1933-40, yellow. | 15 | 25 | 35

1717X GONDOLA: 1940, yellow, equipped with latch couplers. | 30 | 45 | 60

1719 BOXCAR: 1933-42, lithographed Stephen Girard or light green. | 20 | 30 | 40

1719X BOXCAR: 1942, lithographed light Stephen Girard green. | 25 | 35 | 45

1722 CABOOSE: 1933-42, orange, light red or orange red. | 20 | 30 | 40

1722X CABOOSE: 1939-1940, orange-red. | 20 | 30 | 40

	C5	**C7**	**C8**

1811 PULLMAN: 1934-37, peacock, gray or red. | 30 | 45 | 65

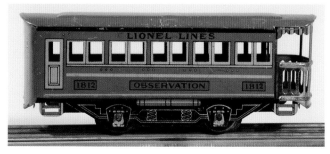

1812 OBSERVATION: 1934-37, peacock, gray or red. | 30 | 45 | 65

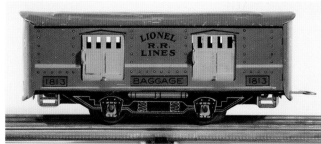

1813 BAGGAGE: 1934-37, peacock, gray or red. | 30 | 45 | 65

1816 DIESEL: 1935, clockwork-powered, chrome-finished, came with a matching 1817 coach and 1818 observation with orange vestibules and frames. | 100 | 150 | 200

1816W DIESEL: 1936-37, clockwork-powered, chrome-finished, came with a matching 1817 coach and 1818 observation with orange vestibules and frames. | 110 | 160 | 225

	C5	C7	C8			C5	C7	C8

1817 COACH: 1935-37, chrome-finished, fluted body. Sold in sets with matching 1816 or 1816W locomotive and 1818 observation. — 20 / 35 / 50

1818 OBSERVATION: 1935-37, chrome-finished, fluted body. Sold in sets with matching 1816 or 1816W locomotive and 1818 observation. — 20 / 35 / 50

2623 PULLMAN: 1941-42, "2623 MANHATTAN 2623". — 125 / 200 / 300

2624 PULLMAN: "2624 MANHATTAN 2624". — 800 / 1,500 / 3,000

2600 PULLMAN: 1938-40. — 80 / 125 / 175

2601 OBSERVATION: 1938-40. — 80 / 125 / 175

2602 BAGGAGE: 1938-40. — 80 / 125 / 175

2613 PULLMAN: 1938-42, blue body with two-tone blue roofs or **State green with a two-tone State green and dark green roof.** — 90-200 / 165-300 / 250-400

2614 OBSERVATION: 1938-42, blue body with two-tone blue roofs or **State green with a two-tone State green and dark green roof.** — 90-200 / 165-300 / 250-400

2615 BAGGAGE: 1938-42, blue body with two-tone blue roofs or **State green with a two-tone State green and dark green roof.** — 90-200 / 165-300 / 250-400

2620 SEARCHLIGHT CAR: 1938-40, red. — 50 / 80 / 120

2623 PULLMAN: 1941-42, "2623 IRVINGTON 2623". — 200 / 300 / 425

2630 PULLMAN: 1938-42, blue with aluminum or **gray roof.** — 25-**35** / 50-**60** / 75-**90**

2631 OBSERVATION: 1938-42, blue with aluminum or **gray roof.** — 25-**35** / 50-**60** / 75-**90**

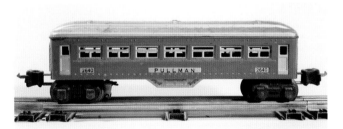

2640 PULLMAN: 1938-42, illuminated, blue or State green. — 25 / 50 / 75

	C5	**C7**	**C8**

2641 OBSERVATION:
1938-42, illuminated, blue or
State green. | 25 | 50 | 75

2642 PULLMAN: 1941-42,
tuscan with gray windows. | 40 | 60 | 85

2643 OBSERVATION:
1941-42, tuscan with gray
windows. | 40 | 60 | 85

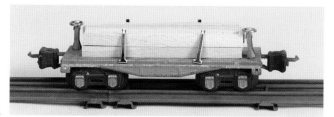

2651 FLATCAR: 1938-40,
green or **black**. | 25-**50** | 35-**75** | 50-**115**

2652 GONDOLA: 1939-42,
yellow or orange. | 25 | 35 | 50

2653 HOPPER: 1938-39,
Stephen Girard Green or
black. | 30-**75** | 50-**200** | 75-**350**

	C5	**C7**	**C8**

2654 TANK CAR: 1938-42,
aluminum-colored, orange or
gray, Sunoco or Shell. | 30 | 40 | 55

2655 BOXCAR: 1938-41,
yellow with maroon or tuscan
roof. | 40 | 55 | 75

2656 STOCK CAR: 1938-
40, light gray or burnt
orange. | 60-**100** | 75-**125** | 100-**165**

2657 CABOOSE: 1938-42,
light red. | 15 | 22 | 30

2657X: 1938-42, light
red, equipped with
electrocouplers for use with
switcher sets. | 20 | 30 | 40

2659 DUMP CAR: 1938-42,
with dark green dump bin. | 75 | 100 | 125

2660 CRANE: 1938-42. | 60 | 75 | 100

	C5	**C7**	**C8**

	C5	**C7**	**C8**

2672 CABOOSE: 1942, Pennsylvania, painted tuscan. No window frames, smokejack or steps.

	20	30	40

2682 CABOOSE: 1938-41, red Lionel Lines or tuscan New York Central.

	15	22	30

2682X CABOOSE: 1940-41, caboose with two automatic couplers.

	20	30	40

2717 GONDOLA: 1938-42, lithographed, yellow.

	20	30	40

2677 GONDOLA: 1940-42, dark red lithographed gondola.

	35	50	70

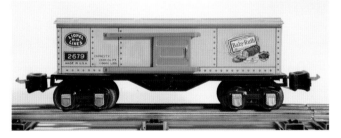

2719 BOXCAR: 1938-42, lithographed light peacock.

	15	25	40

2722 CABOOSE: 1938-42, orange-red body.

	20	30	45

2679 BOXCAR: 1938-42, yellow lithographed, "Baby Ruth" or a "Curtiss Baby Ruth Candy."

	15	25	40

2680 TANK CAR: 1938-42, gray or aluminum-painted, Sunoco, or orange with Shell markings.

	15	25	35

2755 TANK CAR: 1941-42, aluminum or gray.

	50-**100**	80-**150**	125-**225**

	C5	**C7**	**C8**		**C5**	**C7**	**C8**

2810 CRANE

2757 CABOOSE: 1941-1942, tuscan with Pennsylvania markings, separately installed steps, smokejack and red window frames.

	20	30	45

2757X: 1941-42, same as 2757, but with automatic box couplers on both ends. Requires box for full value.

	30	45	60

2758 AUTOMOBILE BOXCAR: 1941-42, tuscan double door.

40	50	65

2810 CRANE: 1938-42, cream or yellow cab.

175	210	250

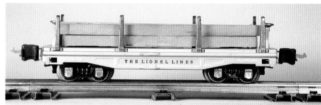

2811 FLATCAR: 1938-42, aluminum-colored.

65	95	135

2812 GONDOLA: 1938-42, 45N orange or green gateman.

30	40	50

2812X GONDOLA: 1940-42, dark orange car.

40	50	70

	C5	C7	C8		C5	C7	C8

2815 TANK CAR: 1938-42, aluminum-colored Sunoco, or orange Shell.

	C5	C7	C8
2815 Tank Car	100	150	225

2813 STOCK CAR: 1938-39, cream or tuscan.

	C5	C7	C8
2813 Stock Car	150	225	350

2814 BOXCAR: 1938-42, cream or **orange**.

	C5	C7	C8
2814 Boxcar	75-750	150-1,500	250-2,500

2816 HOPPER: 1938-42, red or **black**.

	C5	C7	C8
2816 Hopper	125-150	175-250	250-425

2814R REFRIGERATOR CAR: 1938-40, white, blue or brown roof.

	C5	C7	C8
2814R Refrigerator Car	250-750	325-1,500	450-2,500

2817 CABOOSE: 1938-42, red body, red or **brown** **roof**.

	C5	C7	C8
2817 Caboose	75-100	100-200	125-300

| | **C5** | **C7** | **C8** | | **C5** | **C7** | **C8** |

2957 CABOOSE: 1940-42, semi scale. 125 250 400

3651 LOG DUMP: 1939-40, black. 20 35 60

2820 SEARCHLIGHT CAR: 1938-42, light green light base. 125 175 225

3652 OPERATING GONDOLA: 1939-41, yellow. 30 50 75

2954 BOXCAR: 1940-42, semiscale tuscan Pennsylvania boxcar. 150 250 400

3659 OPERATING DUMP CAR: 1938-42, red dump bin. 30 50 75

3811 LOG DUMP CAR: 1939-42, black. 35 50 80

2955 TANK CAR: 1940, black with Shell markings, 1941-42 Sunoco markings. 200 350 525

2956 HOPPER: 1940-42, semi scale hopper. 200 400 625

3814 MERCHANDISE CAR: 1939-40, tuscan boxcar with operating mechanism, includes cube-like plastic "boxes." 125 175 225

	C5	C7	C8

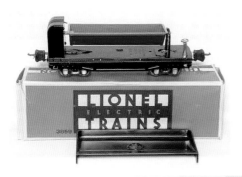

3859 OPERATING DUMP CAR: 1938-42, light red.

	C5	C7	C8
3859 OPERATING DUMP CAR	60	85	115

ACCESSORIES

1 BILD-A-MOTOR: 1928-31, mounted on a red or black base.

	C5	C7	C8
1 BILD-A-MOTOR	60	90	150

	C5	C7	C8
2 BILD-A-MOTOR: 1928-31.	100	125	225
011 PAIR OF REMOTE CONTROL SWITCHES: 1933-37.	20	30	40
011L LEFT HAND REMOTE CONTROL SWITCH: 1933-37.	10	15	20
011R RIGHT HAND REMOTE CONTROL SWITCH: 1933-37.	10	15	20

	C5	C7	C8
012 PAIR OF REMOTE CONTROL SWITCHES: 1927-33.	25	30	40
012L LEFT HAND REMOTE CONTROL SWITCH: 1927-33.	12	15	20
012R RIGHT HAND REMOTE CONTROL SWITCH: 1927-33.	12	15	20
013 REMOTE CONTROL SWITCH SET: 1929-31.	100	140	200

	C5	C7	C8
20 90-DEGREE CROSSING: 1909-42, black or pea green.	3	7	10
20X 45-DEGREE CROSSING: 1928-32, Standard gauge.	5	10	15
020 90-DEGREE CROSSING: 1915-61.	4	6	8
020X 45-DEGREE CROSSING: 1915-59. 4	7	10	
21 MANUAL SWITCH: 1915-25.	12	20	35
021 PAIR OF MANUAL SWITCHES: 1915-27.	15	25	40
021L LEFT HAND MANUAL SWITCH: 1915-37.	7	12	20
021R RIGHT HAND MANUAL SWITCH: 1915-37.	7	12	20
22 MANUAL SWITCH: 1906-25.	17	25	35
022 PAIR OF MANUAL SWITCHES: 1915-26. Priced per pair.	25	40	65

	C5	C7	C8
022 REMOTE CONTROL SWITCHES: 1938-42, 1945-66.	60	75	90
022L LEFT HAND REMOTE CONTROL SWITCH: 1938-42, 1950-61.	35	45	55
022R RIGHT HAND REMOTE CONTROL SWITCH: 1938-42, 1950-61.	35	45	55

	C5	C7	C8
23 BUMPER: 1906-33, red, black, green or yellow-orange.	20	30	40
023 BUMPER: 1915-33, red or black.	15	25	35

	C5	C7	C8
25 ILLUMINATED BUMPER: 1927-42, cream or black.	20	25	35
025 ILLUMINATED BUMPER: 1928-42, cream or black.	15	20	25

	C5	C7	C8
27 LIGHTING SET: 1911-23.	15	30	45

	C5	C7	C8
0031 CURVED TRACK: 1939-42.	8	14	20
32 MINIATURE FIGURES: 1909-18.	70	100	150
0032 STRAIGHT TRACK: 1939-42.	12	18	30

	C5	C7	C8
0034 CURVED TRACK: 1939-42.	12	18	25

	C5	**C7**	**C8**

35 BOULEVARD LAMP:
1940-42, 1945-49. Painted
aluminum color or gray.

	C5	C7	C8
	20	35	55

41 CONTACTOR: 1936-42.

	C5	C7	C8
	1	5	8

**042 PAIR OF MANUAL
SWITCHES:** 1938-1942,
1946-59.

	C5	C7	C8
	40	50	60

**042L LEFT HAND
MANUAL SWITCH:**
1938-1942, 1946-59.

	C5	C7	C8
	20	25	30

	C5	**C7**	**C8**

**042R RIGHT HAND
MANUAL SWITCH:**
1938-1942, 1946-59.

	C5	C7	C8
	20	25	30

**43/043 BILD-A-MOTOR
GEAR SET:** 1929.

	C5	C7	C8
	40	60	90

**43 LIONEL CRAFT
PLEASURE BOAT:** 1933-
36.

	C5	C7	C8
	325	550	750

**44 LIONEL CRAFT
RACING BOAT:** 1935-36.

	C5	C7	C8
	500	800	1,250

	C5	**C7**	**C8**

	C5	**C7**	**C8**

47 DOUBLE CROSSING
GATE: 1933-42, roadway area painted ivory, the remainder of the accessory base was painted 45N green.

	C5	**C7**	**C8**
47 Double Crossing Gate	60	100	150

45 AUTOMATIC GATEMAN, 045 AUTOMATIC GATEMAN, 45N AUTOMATIC GATEMAN: 1935-42, 1945.

	C5	**C7**	**C8**
45 Automatic Gateman	30	45	60

46 SINGLE CROSSING
GATE: 1939-42, roadway area painted ivory, the remainder of the accessory base was painted 45N green.

	C5	**C7**	**C8**
46 Single Crossing Gate	75	100	125

48W WHISTLE STATION: 1937-42.

49 AIRPORT: 1937-39.

	C5	**C7**	**C8**
48W Whistle Station	30	45	60
49 Airport	400	700	1,100

	C5	**C7**	**C8**

	C5	**C7**	**C8**

50 REMOTE CONTROL AIRPLANE: 1936.

	C5	C7	C8
50 REMOTE CONTROL AIRPLANE: 1936.	425	650	850

50 WARTIME FREIGHT TRAIN: 1943.

	C5	C7	C8
50 WARTIME FREIGHT TRAIN: 1943.	200	300	500

	C5	C7	C8
51 AIRPORT: 1936, 1938.	200	300	500
0051 CURVED TRACK: 1939-42.	6	12	18

	C5	C7	C8
0052 STRAIGHT TRACK: 1939-42.	12	18	30
52 LAMP POST: 1933-41.	35	55	75
53 LAMP POST: 1931-42, ivory, aluminum, light mojave, gray, or white.	25	35	45
0054 CURVED TERMINAL TRACK: 1939-42.	12	18	25
54 LAMP POST: 1929-35, maroon, pea green or State brown.	40	60	80
55 REMOTE CONTROL AIRPLANE: 1937-39.	325	550	750
56 LAMP POST: 1924-42, 1946-49, **copper**, green, pea green, dark green, gray, dark gray or aluminum.	30-**40**	45-**55**	60-**90**

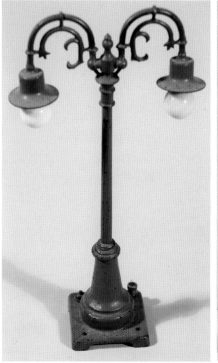

54 LAMP POST   *56 LAMP POST*

57 *LAMP POST*

58 *LAMP POST*

59 *LAMP POST*

060 *TELEGRAPH POST*

	C5	C7	C8
57 LAMP POST 1922-42, orange.	30-60	45-**85**	60-**115**
58 LAMP POST: 1922-42, dark green, pea green, orange, cream, peacock or maroon.	30	40	60
59 LAMP POST: 1920-36, dark green, olive green, light green, maroon, State brown or red.	35	55	75
60 TELEGRAPH POST: 1920-35, peacock, Stephen Girard green, dark gray, apple-green or aluminum color.	20	25	30
060 TELEGRAPH POST: 1929-42, orange, gray, green, aluminum or gray.	20	25	30

	C5	C7	C8
61 LAMP POST: 1914-32, 1934-36, olive green, mojave, dark green, pea green, maroon, State brown, and black.	40	50	60
0061 CURVED TRACK: 1938-42, 00.	5	10	15
62 SEMAPHORE: 1920-32, bases painted dark green, olive green, apple green, pea green or **yellow**.	30-**40**	40-**50**-	50-**60**
0062 STRAIGHT TRACK: 1938-42, 00.	6	12	18
63 SEMAPHORE: 1915-21: red and black.	25	40	55

	C5	C7	C8
0063 CURVED TRACK: 1938-42.	12	18	24
0064 CURVED TERMINAL TRACK: 1938.	10	15	20

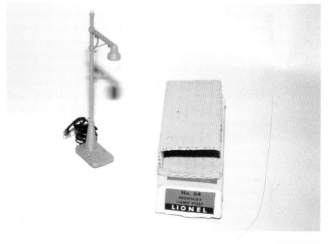

	C5	C7	C8
64 HIGHWAY LAMP POST: 1940-49, green.	45	60	75
64 SEMAPHORE: 1915-21.	30	45	65
65 SEMAPHORE: 1915-26.	30	45	65
0065 STRAIGHT TRACK: 1938.	12	18	24

	C5	C7	C8
63 LAMP POST: 1933-42.	150	200	250

	C5	**C7**	**C8**

65 WHISTLE CONTROLLER: 1935.

	C5	**C7**	**C8**
65 WHISTLE CONTROLLER: 1935.	3	5	7
0066 STRAIGHT TRACK: 1938-42.	12	18	24

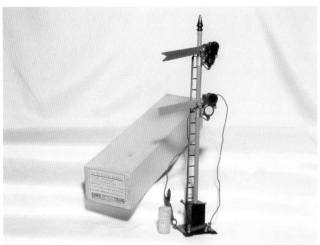

66 SEMAPHORE: 1915-26 upper arm red and black, lower arm green and black.

	C5	**C7**	**C8**
66 SEMAPHORE: 1915-26 upper arm red and black, lower arm green and black.	30	45	65

66 WHISTLE CONTROLLER: 1936-38.

	C5	**C7**	**C8**
66 WHISTLE CONTROLLER: 1936-38.	3	5	7

	C5	**C7**	**C8**
67 LAMP POST: 1915-32, dark or state green, rarely in peacock.	75	115	150

67 WHISTLE CONTROLLER: 1936-38.

	C5	**C7**	**C8**
67 WHISTLE CONTROLLER: 1936-38.	3	5	7

	C5	**C7**	**C8**
68 WARNING SIGNAL: 1920-39, dark olive, orange, maroon, pea green, peacock or white.	5	10	15
068 WARNING SIGNAL: 1925-42, orange or pea green.	5	10	15

	C5	**C7**	**C8**

	C5	**C7**	**C8**

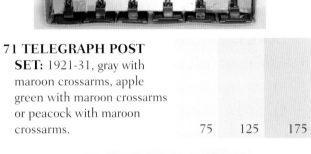

71 TELEGRAPH POST
  SET: 1921-31, gray with
  maroon crossarms, apple
  green with maroon crossarms
  or peacock with maroon
  crossarms.   75   125   175

**69 ELECTRIC WARNING
  BELL SIGNAL, 069
  ELECTRIC WARNING
  BELL SIGNAL, 69N
  ELECTRIC WARNING
  BELL SIGNAL:** 1921-35,
olive, maroon, dark green,
white, red, aluminum or
9E orange paint and black
lettering   30   45   60

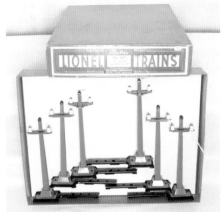

071 TELEGRAPH POST
  SET: 1929-42, gray with
  light red crossarms, green
  with red crossarms or orange
  with maroon crossarms.   75   125   175

**0070 90-DEGREE
  CROSSING:** 1938-42.   4   8   12
70 ACCESSORY OUTFIT:
  1921-32.   75   125   175

	C5	C7	C8

	C5	C7	C8
0072 PAIR OF REMOTE CONTROL SWITCHES 0066 STRAIGHT TRACK: 1938-42.	125	200	300
0072L REMOTE CONTROL SWITCH: 1939-42.	60	90	140

	C5	C7	C8
0072R REMOTE CONTROL SWITCH: 1939-42.	60	90	140
76 BLOCK SIGNAL, 076 BLOCK SIGNAL: 1923-28.	30	50	80

	C5	C7	C8
76 WARNING BELL AND SHACK: 1939-42, brass or die-cast sign.	85	150	250

	C5	C7	C8
77 AUTOMATIC CROSSING GATE, 077 AUTOMATIC CROSSING GATE, 77N AUTOMATIC CROSSING GATE: 1923-39.	30	40	50
78 TRAIN CONTROL BLOCK SIGNAL, 078 TRAIN CONTROL BLOCK SIGNAL: 1924-32, various colors.	40	70	100

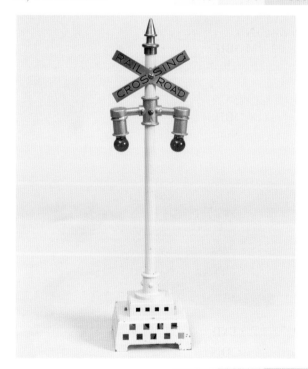

	C5	C7	C8
79 FLASHING HIGHWAY SIGNAL: 1928-40, cream base, and a pole painted either cream or mojave.	100	125	150

	C5	**C7**	**C8**

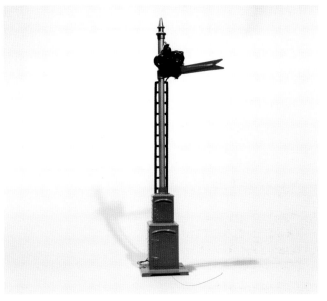

80 SEMAPHORE, 080 SEMAPHORE: 1926-35, various colors.

	C5	C7	C8
80 SEMAPHORE	50	75	110

80N SEMAPHORE: 1936-42, light red base, aluminum-painted pole and black ladder.

	C5	C7	C8
80N SEMAPHORE	50	75	110

80 RACING AUTOMOBILE SET: 1912-16 36-inch diameter track.

	C5	C7	C8
80 RACING	1,500	2,200	3,500

81 RACING AUTOMOBILE SET: 1912-16, 30-inch diameter track.

	C5	C7	C8
81 RACING	1,500	2,200	3,500

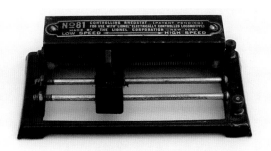

81 RHEOSTAT: 1927-33.

	C5	C7	C8
81 RHEOSTAT	5	10	15

82 TRAIN CONTROL SEMAPHORE, 082 TRAIN CONTROL SEMAPHORE: 1927-35, peacock or 45N-green base.

	C5	C7	C8
82 TRAIN CONTROL	50	80	110

82N SEMAPHORE: 1936-42, green base, aluminum-painted pole, black ladder and nickel finial.

	C5	C7	C8
82N SEMAPHORE	50	80	110

83 TRAFFIC AND CROSSING SIGNAL: 1927-42, **mojave** or red base.

	C5	C7	C8
83 TRAFFIC AND CROSSING SIGNAL	50-75	100-150	175-250

84 SEMAPHORE, 084 SEMAPHORE: 1927-32, dark green or maroon base, orange or cream pole.

	C5	C7	C8
84 SEMAPHORE	40	80	130

	C5	**C7**	**C8**

84 DOUBLE RACING AUTOMOBILE SET: 1912-16, combination of 80 and 81 sets.

2,500	3,300	4,500

85 DOUBLE RACING AUTOMOBILE SET: 1912-16, included straight track.

3,000	4,000	5,700

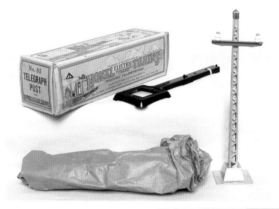

85 TELEGRAPH POST: 1929-42, orange or **aluminum**-colored post.

12-**20**	25-**40**	45-**65**

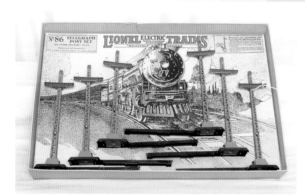

86 TELEGRAPH POST SET: 1929-42, six orange or **aluminum**-colored posts, original box critical to value.

100-**125**	200-**250**	400-**500**

	C5	**C7**	**C8**

87 RAILROAD CROSSING SIGNAL: 1927-42, orange, tan, mojave or **dark green** base.

75-**125**	125-**225**	200-**350**

88 BATTERY RHEOSTAT: 1915-27.

5	10	15

88 DIRECTION CONTROLLER: 1933-42.

5	10	15

89 FLAG POLE: 1923-34.

50	75	110

90 FLAG POLE: 1927-42, brass, nickel or black pedestal.

75	110	150

91 CIRCUIT BREAKER: 1930-42, mojave or State brown, two or three terminals.

25	35	45

	C5	C7	C8

	C5	C7	C8

092 ILLUMINATED
SIGNAL TOWER: 1923-
27, terracotta or white walls.

	C5	C7	C8
	50-**90**	90-**150**	150-**225**

93 WATER TOWER: 1931-
42, 1946-49, pea green,
aluminum or gray tank.

	C5	C7	C8
	25	35	60

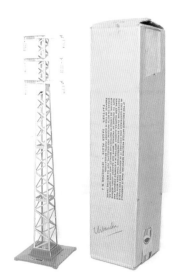

92 FLOODLIGHT
TOWER: 1931-42, pea
green, **gray** or aluminum-
painted supporting structure.

	C5	C7	C8
	75-**125**	125-**175**	175-**225**

94 HIGH TENSION
TOWER: 1932-42,
gunmetal, **mojave**,
aluminum or **gray** tower.

	C5	C7	C8
	100-**150**	175-**300**	275-**500**

	C5	**C7**	**C8**

95 RHEOSTAT: 1934-42, brass or nickel instruction plate.

	10	15	20

096 TELEGRAPH POST: 1934-35.

	15	20	25

96 COAL ELEVATOR: 1938-40.

	100	175	275

097 TELEGRAPH POST AND SIGNAL SET: 1934-35.

	200	275	375

	C5	**C7**	**C8**

97 MOTORIZED COAL ELEVATOR: 1938-42, aluminum-painted supporting structure, except 1942 when **gray**.

	100-**125**	175-**200**	225-**275**

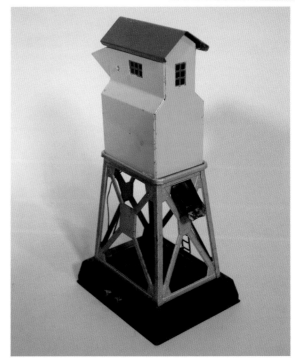

98 COAL BUNKER: 1938-40, cream-colored house on aluminum structure.

	200	325	500

	C5	C7	C8

99/099 TRAIN CONTROL BLOCK SIGNAL: 1932-35, black or red base with cream, or mojave poles.

	C5	C7	C8
	40	75	125

99N TRAIN CONTROL BLOCK SIGNAL: 1936-42, red base and ladder with aluminum-painted pole.

	C5	C7	C8
	40	75	125

	C5	C7	C8

100 BRIDGE APPROACHES: 1920-31, Standard gauge.

	C5	C7	C8
	10	20	40

101 BRIDGE: 1920-31, Standard gauge.

	C5	C7	C8
	100	150	225

102 BRIDGE: 1920-31, Standard gauge. — 125 | 175 | 250

103 BRIDGE: 1920-31, Standard gauge. The original box is a significant portion of the value listed. — 150 | 200 | 275

104 BRIDGE CENTER SPAN: 1920-31, pea green. — 20 | 30 | 40

104 TUNNEL: 1909-14. — 50 | 80 | 125

105 BRIDGE APPROACHES: 1920-31, 0-gauge. — 10 | 20 | 30

106 BRIDGE: 1920-31, 0 gauge, cream, light mustard, or pea green sides. — 50 | 75 | 110

106 AC REDUCER: 1909-14. Too infrequently traded to establish accurate value.

	C5	**C7**	**C8**
106 RHEOSTAT: 1911-14	Too infrequently traded to establish accurate value		
107 DC REDUCER: 1911-38	Too infrequently traded to establish accurate value		
108 BATTERY RHEOSTAT: 1912-14	Too infrequently traded to establish accurate value		
108 BRIDGE: 1920-31, 0 gauge, cream or light mustard sides.	75	100	150
109 BRIDGE: 1920-31, 0 gauge, cream or light mustard sides.	100	150	200
109 TUNNEL: 1913, Standard gauge, papier-mâché.	75	125	200
110 BRIDGE CENTER SPAN: 1920-31, pea green.	20	30	40
111 BULB ASSORTMENT: 1920-31, set of **wooden** or cardboard individual bulb containers with bulbs.	250-**500**	500-**1,000**	1,000-**2,000**

112 STATION: 1931-34, cream, beige or ivory walls.   150   250   375

113 STATION: 1931-34.   200   400   600

	C5	**C7**	**C8**
114 STATION: 1931-34, cream, beige or ivory walls.	500	1000	1600
115 STATION: 1935-42, 1946-49, includes train-stop circuit.	250	350	500

	C5	**C7**	**C8**
116 STATION: 1935-42, mojave or red base.	700	1,200	1,800
117 STATION: 1935-42.	100	200	300
118 TUNNEL: 1915-32.	20	35	50
118L TUNNEL: 1927, illuminated version of the 118.	40	75	150
119 TUNNEL: 1915-42.	20	35	50

119L TUNNEL: 1927-33, illuminated version of the 119.   40   75   150

	C5	C7	C8
120 TUNNEL: 1915-27, papier-mâché or steel.	35	75	125
120L TUNNEL: 1927-42, illuminated version of 120.	50	100	200
121 STATION: 1908-26, wooden or steel construction.	150	200	250
122 STATION: 1920-31, gray or gray-speckled base.	75	150	225
123 STATION: 1920-23.	150	225	350

	C5	C7	C8
123 TUNNEL: 1933-42.	75	150	225

	C5	C7	C8
126 STATION: 1923-36, lithographed walls, or red or **mustard-painted** walls.	75-**200**	125-**275**	200-**375**

	C5	C7	C8
127 STATION: 1923-36, white, cream, **mustard** or ivory-colored walls.	75-**100**	110-**150**	150-**225**

	C5	C7	C8
124 STATION: 1920-30, 1933-36, terracotta walls, tan, dark gray or **pea green** base.	100-**200**	200-**300**	300-**400**
125 STATION: 1923-25, red brick and a dark mojave base with a pea green roof, and white windows.	100	150	225
125 TRACK TEMPLATE: 1938.	2	5	10
128 STATION AND TERRACE: 1928-42, came with 124, 113 or **115** station.	1,000-**1,200**	1,500-**1,800**	2,100-**2,500**

	C5	**C7**	**C8**
128 TUNNEL: 1920.	Too rarely, if ever, traded to establish market pricing.		
129 TERRACE: 1928-42, light mojave with pea green decoration or **cream with red trim**.	600-**800**	900-**900**	1200-**1,700**
129 TUNNEL: 1920.	Too rarely, if ever, traded to establish market pricing.		
130 TUNNEL: 1920.	Too rarely, if ever, traded to establish market pricing.		
130 TUNNEL: 1926.	200	400	1,000
130L TUNNEL: 1927-33, **1927** edition was 1926, 130 with the addition of lighting, 1928 and up was smaller (18 1/2 x 14 1/2-inch base).	100-**200**	200-**400**	500-**1,000**
131 CORNER ELEVATION: 1924-28.	125	250	500
132 CORNER GRASS PLOT: 1924-28.	125	250	500
133 HEARTSHAPE GRASS PLOT: 1924-28.	125	250	500
134 OVAL GRASS PLOT: 1924-28.	125	250	500

	C5	**C7**	**C8**
134 STATION: 1937-42.	175	275	450
135 SMALL CIRCULAR GRASS PLOT: 1924-28.	100	200	400
136 LARGE ELEVATION: 1924-28.	125	250	500

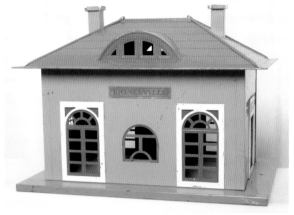

	C5	**C7**	**C8**
136 STATION: 1937-42, cream or **mustard** walls.	75-**125**	125-**250**	175-**400**
137 STATION: 1937-42, ivory or walls, vermilion roof, green or yellow door and window frames.	100	150	225

140L TUNNEL: 1927-32.	600	1,200	2,000

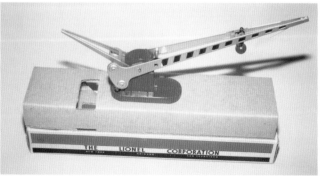

152 AUTOMATIC CROSSING GATE: 1940-42, aluminum or gray gate.	20	40	55

	C5	C7	C8

	C5	C7	C8

155 FREIGHT SHED:

	C5	C7	C8
1930-42, yellow base with maroon roof or **white base and gray roof**.	175-**225**	250-**325**	350-**450**

153 AUTOMATIC BLOCK SIGNAL AND CONTROL:

	C5	C7	C8
1940-42, 1945-59, gray or silver-colored post on a green die-cast base.	30-40	40-55	50-70
153C CONTACTOR: 1940-42.	1	2	10

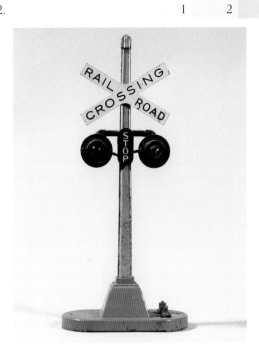

156 ILLUMINATED STATION PLATFORM:

	C5	C7	C8
1939-42, 1946-51, green base and red roof, silver or **gray posts**.	60-**90**	100-**150**	150-**225**

154 AUTOMATIC HIGHWAY SIGNAL:

	C5	C7	C8
1940-69, black or **Hiawatha orange** base	30-**50**	40-**75**	50-**100**

C5 **C7** **C8**   **C5** **C7** **C8**

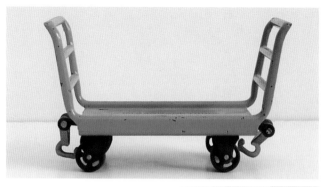

161 BAGGAGE TRUCK:
1930-32, 1942.

	C5	C7	C8
161 BAGGAGE TRUCK	30	40	55

	C5	C7	C8
157 HAND TRUCK: 1930-32, 1942 red.	20	30	40
158 STATION SET: 1940-42.	400	700	1,000
159C BLOCK CONTROL CONTACTOR SET: 1940-42.	10	15	25
160 UNLOADING BIN: 1938-42.	1	1	2

	C5	C7	C8
162 DUMP TRUCK: 1930-32, 1942, orange, terracotta or yellow hand truck with dump bin, rare in red.	30	50	75
163 FREIGHT ACCESSORY SET: 1930-42.	175	250	350

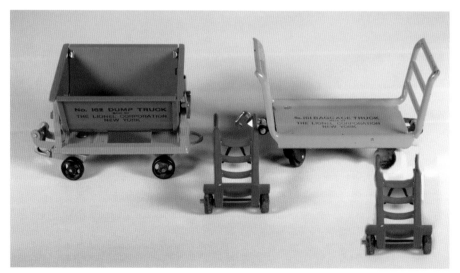

163 FREIGHT ACCESSORY SET

	C5	C7	C8

164 LOG LOADER: 1940-42, 1946-50, aluminum or **gray**-painted supporting structures.

	C5	C7	C8
	150-**200**	225-**275**	350-**400**

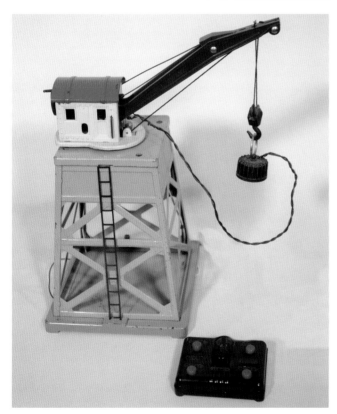

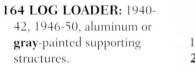

165 MAGNETIC CRANE: 1940-42, aluminum or **gray**-painted supporting structure.

	C5	C7	C8
	200-**300**	275-**375**	375-**475**

166 WHISTLE CONTROLLER: 1938-39.

	C5	C7	C8
	5	7	10

	C5	C7	C8

167 WHISTLE AND DIRECTION CONTROLLER: 1939-42.

	C5	C7	C8
167 WHISTLE AND DIRECTION CONTROLLER: 1939-42.	4	8	15
167X WHISTLE AND DIRECTION CONTROLLER: 1940-42.	10	20	30
168 MAGIC ELECTROL CONTROLLER: 1940-42, styled like 167 whistle control or 1019 controller.	10	20	30
169 DIRECTION CONTROLLER: 1940-42.	10	20	30

	C5	C7	C8
170 DC REDUCER: 1914-38.	10	20	30
171 DC TO AC INVERTER: 1936-42.	4	8	15
172 DC TO AC INVERTER: 1936-42.	4	8	15

| | **C5** | **C7** | **C8** | | **C5** | **C7** | **C8** |

184 BUNGALOW: 1923-42.   40   90   150   **185 BUNGALOW:** 1923-24.   50   100   175

186 ILLUMINATED BUNGALOW SET: 1923-32.   400   1,000   1,800

	C5	**C7**	**C8**

	C5	**C7**	**C8**

186 LOG LOADER
OUTFIT: 1940-41.

	500	800	1,200

187 BUNGALOW SET:
1931-32.

	400	1,000	1,800

191 VILLA: 1923-32.

	150	275	400

188 COAL ELEVATOR
OUTFIT: 1938-41.

	500	800	1,200

192 ILLUMINATED
VILLA SET: 1923-32.

	1,500	2,500	4,000

193 AUTOMATIC
ACCESSORY SET: 1927-
29.

	250	500	800

194 AUTOMATIC
ACCESSORY SET: 1927-
29.

	200	400	700

195 ILLUMINATED
TERRACE: 1927-30.

	400	800	1,600

196 ACCESSORY SET:
1927.

	250	500	800

189 VILLA: 1923-32.

	150	250	375

200 TURNTABLE: 1928-33,
pea green or **black** base.

	75-**200**	125-**350**	200-**550**

	C5	**C7**	**C8**

210R RIGHT HAND MANUAL TURNOUT: 1926-42, pea green or black base.

	C5	**C7**	**C8**
210R RIGHT HAND MANUAL TURNOUT: 1926-42, pea green or black base.	10	15	20

205 MERCHANDISE CONTAINERS: 1930-38. — 125 / 225 / 350

206 ARTIFICIAL COAL: 1938-42. — 5 / 10 / 15

207 SACK OF COAL: 1938-42. — 5 / 10 / 15

208 TOOL SET: 1928-42, miniature section gang tools in metal toolbox. — 50 / 150 / 275

209 BARRELS: 1930-42, Standard gauge turned wooden representations of wooden or steel drums. — 150 / 225 / 300

0209 BARRELS: 1934-42, 0 gauge turned wooden representations of wooden or steel drums. — 100 / 175 / 250

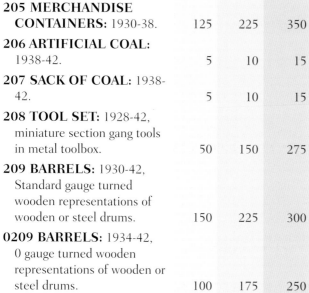

210 PAIR OF MANUAL TURNOUTS: 1926-42, Standard gauge. — 20 / 30 / 40

210L LEFT HAND MANUAL TURNOUT: 1926-42, pea green or black base. — 10 / 15 / 20

	C5	**C7**	**C8**
217 LIGHTING SET: 1914-23.	20	35	50
220 PAIR OF MANUAL TURNOUTS: 1926.	20	40	70
222 PAIR OF REMOTE CONTROL TURNOUTS: 1926-31.	40	60	100
222L LEFT HAND REMOTE CONTROL TURNOUT: 1926-31.	20	30	50
222R RIGHT HAND REMOTE CONTROL TURNOUT: 1926-31.	20	30	50
223 PAIR OF REMOTE CONTROL TURNOUTS: 1932-42, pea green or black bases.	60	90	125
223L LEFT HAND REMOTE CONTROL TURNOUT: 1932-42, pea green or black base.	30	45	60
223R RIGHT HAND REMOTE CONTROL TURNOUT: 1932-42, pea green or black base.	30	45	60
225 REMOTE CONTROL TURNOUT SET: 1929-32.	125	250	400
270 BRIDGE: 1931-42, light red, maroon, vermilion.	25	35	50

	C5	C7	C8
270 LIGHTING SET: 1915-23, for DC current.	20	35	50
271 LIGHTING SET: 1915-23, for AC current.	20	35	50
271 BRIDGES: 1931-40, except 1934.	150	250	400
272 BRIDGES: 1931-40, except 1934.	250	450	750

	C5	C7	C8
280 BRIDGE: 1931-42, gray, red, pea or 45N green.	50	80	125
281 BRIDGES: 1931-40, except 1934.	150	250	400
282 BRIDGES: 1931-40, except 1934.	250	450	750

	C5	C7	C8
300 HELL GATE BRIDGE: 1928-34, green or **aluminum-colored** superstructure.	800-1,000	1,100-1,500	1,400-2,100
308 RAILROAD SIGN SET: 1940-42, 1945-49, green base with artificial grass, rectangular base painted white, or round white bases.	35	50	75
310 TRACK: 1901-05.	75	125	200

	C5	C7	C8
313 BASCULE BRIDGE: 1940-42, 1946-49, silver or **gray**, superstructure of the bridge was painted silver.	300-**400**	525-**625**	675-**775**

	C5	C7	C8
314 PLATE GIRDER BRIDGE (Type I): 1940-1941 silver, 1942 gray.	25	35	50

	C5	C7	C8
315 ILLUMINATED TRESTLE BRIDGE: 1940-42, 1946-47, silver or **gray**.	75-**100**	100-**125**	125-**150**

	C5	**C7**	**C8**

	C5	**C7**	**C8**

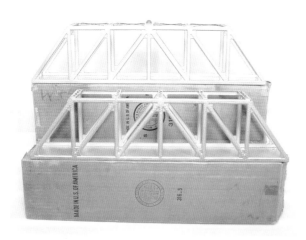

316 TRESTLE BRIDGE:
1941, 1942 and 1949,
aluminum or **gray**.

	25-**30**	40-**50**	55-**70**

435 POWER STATION:
1926-38, **terracotta walls,
gray base**, mustard walls,
gray base; ivory walls, gray
base; terracotta walls, gray
base; cream walls, gray base,
or cream walls, 45N green
base.

	125-**300**	250-**600**	400-**1,000**

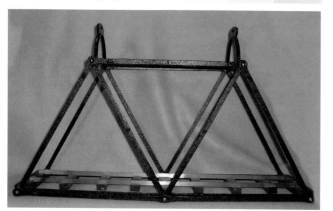

**340 SUSPENSION
BRIDGE:** 1902-05.

Too rarely, if ever, traded
to establish market
pricing.

436 POWER STATION:
1926-37, terracotta walls,
light green windows, gray
base; terracotta walls,
orange windows, gray
base; cream walls, orange
windows, gray base; cream
walls, white windows,
45N green base. Add
300 percent premium for
"EDISON SERVICE"
sign rather than "POWER
STATION".

	150	275	425

380 ELEVATED PILLARS:
1904-05.

	450	850	1,200

	C5	C7	C8

437 SWITCH SIGNAL TOWER: 1926-37, terracotta lower walls, mustard upper walls, pea green roof; terracotta lower walls, cream upper walls, peacock roof; burnt orange lower walls, mustard upper walls, pea green roof; burnt orange lower walls, light mustard upper walls, pea green roof or **yellow lower and upper walls, orange roof**.

	C5	C7	C8
	200-	350-	550-
	1,200	**1,800**	**2,500**

438 SIGNAL TOWER:
1927-39, pea green or **aluminum-painted** supports.

	C5	C7	C8
	200-	325-	500-
	300	**475**	**700**

	C5	C7	C8

439 PANEL BOARD: 1928-42, black or **white** simulated marble backgrounds mounted on red or maroon supports

	C5	C7	C8
	75-	125-	175-
	100	**150**	**200**

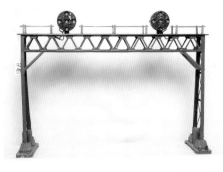

440 SIGNAL BRIDGE/0440 SIGNAL BRIDGE: 1932-35, supported by die-cast terracotta or red bases.

	C5	C7	C8
	175-	250-	350-
	200	**325**	**450**

440C PANEL BOARD:
1932-42, light, glossy or flat red, includes switches to control 440 signal bridge in addition to knife switches.

	C5	C7	C8
	75	125	175

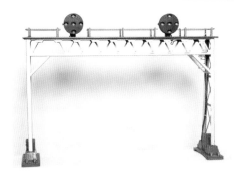

440N SIGNAL BRIDGE:
1936-42, red die-cast bases with silver or **gray** structure.

	C5	C7	C8
	175-	225-	275-
	250	**450**	**650**

	C5	**C7**	**C8**

441 WEIGHING STATION: 1932-36, Standard gauge. — 500 / 1,000 / 1,500

442 LANDSCAPED DINER: 1938-42, ivory or cream bodies with pink or red foundations and steps. — 150 / 250 / 375

444 ROUNDHOUSE: 1932-35, terracotta walls and a pea green roof with two green skylights and maroon windows. — 1,200 / 2,000 / 3,000

444-18 CLIP: 1932-35, used to join 444 sections together. — Too rarely traded to establish market pricing.

455 Electric Range: 1930, 1932-34, green and cream porcelain range. — 400 / 800 / 1,500

500 PINE BUSHES: 1927-28. — Too rarely traded to establish market pricing.

501 SMALL PINE TREES: 1927-28. — Too rarely traded to establish market pricing.

	C5	**C7**	**C8**

502 MEDIUM PINE TREES: 1927-28. — Too rarely traded to establish market pricing.

503 LARGE PINE TREES: 1927-28. — Too rarely traded to establish market pricing.

504 ROSE BUSHES: 1927-28. — Too rarely traded to establish market pricing.

505 OAK TREES: 1927-28. — Too rarely traded to establish market pricing.

506 PLATFORM: 1924-28. — Too rarely traded to establish market pricing.

507 PLATFORM: 1924-28. — Too rarely traded to establish market pricing.

508 SKY: 1924-28. — Too rarely traded to establish market pricing.

509 COMPOSITION BOARD MOUNTAINS: 1924-28. — Too rarely traded to establish market pricing.

510 CANNA BUSHES: 1927-28. — Too rarely traded to establish market pricing.

550 MINIATURE RAILROAD FIGURES: 1932-36, original box significant portion of values listed. — 225 / 375 / 550

551 ENGINEER: 1932-36, medium or dark blue clothing. — 20 / 30 / 40

552 CONDUCTOR: 1932-36. — 20 / 30 / 40

553 PORTER: 1932-36, came with a removable yellow step box. — 20 / 30 / 40

554 MALE PASSENGER: 1932-36, brown or mojave clothing. — 20 / 30 / 40

	C5	C7	C8
555 FEMALE PASSENGER: 1932-36, variety of different colored clothing	20	30	40
556 RED CAP: 1932-36, dark blue clothing and a red cap.	20	30	40
711 PAIR OF REMOTE CONTROL TURNOUTS: 1935-42.	75	125	200
711L LEFT HAND REMOTE CONTROL TURNOUT: 1935-42.	40	60	100
711R RIGHT HAND REMOTE CONTROL TURNOUT: 1935-42.	40	60	100
720 90-DEGREE CROSSING: 1935-42.	25	35	45
721 PAIR OF MANUAL TURNOUTS: 1935-42.	50	75	125
721L LEFT HAND MANUAL TURNOUT: 1935-42.	25	40	60
721R RIGHT HAND MANUAL TURNOUT: 1935-42.	25	40	60
730 90-DEGREE CROSSING: 1935-42.	30	45	60
731 PAIR OF REMOTE CONTROL TURNOUTS: 1935-42.	75	125	200
731L LEFT HAND REMOTE CONTROL TURNOUT: 1935-42.	40	60	100
731R RIGHT HAND REMOTE CONTROL TURNOUT: 1935-42.	40	60	100
760 072 TRACK: 1954-58.	50	75	120
761 CURVED TRACK: 1934-42, 072.	1	2	3
762 STRAIGHT TRACK: 1934-42, 072.	1	2	3
762S STRAIGHT TRACK: 1934-42, 072 short straight.	1	2	3
771 CURVED TRACK: 1935-42 "T-rail."	5	10	15

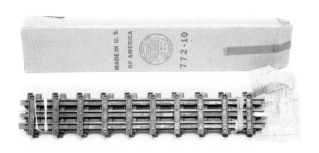

	C5	C7	C8
772 STRAIGHT TRACK: 1935-42 "T-rail."	10	15	20
772S STRAIGHT TRACK: 1935-42 "T-rail."	20	30	40
773 FISH PLATE SET: 1935-42 "T-rail."	25	50	75
812T TOOL SET: 1930-41.	50	100	150

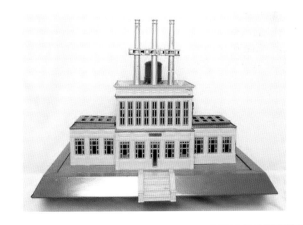

	C5	C7	C8
840 INDUSTRIAL POWER STATION: 1928-40, cream walls, orange roof or white walls with red roof.	1,000-**1,500**	1,700-**2,500**	2,500-**3,500**

	C5	C7	C8
910 GROVE OF TREES: 1932-42.	100	250	500

C5   C7   C8

C5   C7   C8

911 COUNTRY ESTATE:
1932-42, variety of color combinations. 200 500 1,000

912 SUBURBAN HOME:
1932-42, variety of color combinations. 200 500 1000

913 LANDSCAPED
BUNGALOW: 1932-42. 150 300 550

914 PARK LANDSCAPE:
1932-36, cream-colored plywood base and urn. 150 350 650

915 TUNNEL: 1932-35, 60
or **65** inches long. 100- 200- 300-
 150 **300** **650**

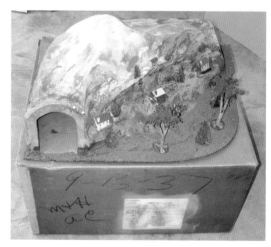

916 TUNNEL: 1932-42,
29-1/4 or **37** inches long. 100- 200- 300-
 150 **300** **550**

917 SCENIC HILLSIDE:
1932-36. 150 200 250

918 SCENIC HILLSIDE:
1932-36. 150 200 250

919 ARTIFICIAL GRASS:
1932-42. 7 7 25

	C5	C7	C8

920 SCENIC PARK: 1932-33.

	C5	C7	C8
920 SCENIC PARK: 1932-33.	1,000	2,000	3,000

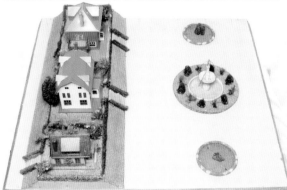

921 SCENIC PARK: 1932-33.

	C5	C7	C8
921 SCENIC PARK: 1932-33.	2,000	3,200	4,500

	C5	C7	C8

	C5	C7	C8
921C PARK CENTER SECTION: 1932-33.	750	1,500	2,250
922 LAMP TERRACE: 1932-36, with green, mojave, pea green or **copper**-colored lamp post.	100-**200**	150-**350**	200-**550**

	C5	C7	C8
923 TUNNEL: 1933-42.	100	200	400
924 TUNNEL: 1935-42.			
924 TUNNEL (Type I): 1935.	200	350	550
924 TUNNEL (Type II): 1936.	100	200	400
925 LUBRICANT: 1935-42.	1	4	10

	C5	C7	C8
927 ORNAMENTAL FLAG PLOT: 1937-42, cream base.	100	200	400
1012 WINNER STATION: 1931-33, cream walls, orange roof, two or three binding posts. Transformer mounted internally.	40	55	75

	C5	**C7**	**C8**
1012K WINNER STATION: 1932-33, same as 1012, but sans transformer.	40	55	75
1013 CURVED TRACK: 1933-42.	.25	.50	1.00
1017 WINNER STATION: 1932-33.	40	55	75
1018 STRAIGHT TRACK: 1933-42.	.25	.50	1.00
1019 REMOTE CONTROL TRACK SET: 1938-42, 1946-50.	5	8	10
1021 90-DEGREE CROSSING: 1933-42, 1945-54.	2	4	8

	C5	**C7**	**C8**
1022 TUNNEL: 1935-42.	20	40	75
1023 TUNNEL: 1934-42.	20	40	75
1024 PAIR OF MANUAL TURNOUTS: 1935-42, 1946-52.	10	15	25
1024L LEFT HAND MANUAL TURNOUT: 1934-42.	5	8	10
1024R RIGHT HAND MANUAL TURNOUT: 1934-42.	5	8	10

	C5	**C7**	**C8**
1025 ILLUMINATED BUMPER: 1940-42, 1946-47.	10	15	20

	C5	**C7**	**C8**
1027 LIONEL JUNIOR TRANSFORMER STATION: 1933-34, yellow.	40	60	85
1028 LIONEL JUNIOR TRANSFORMER STATION: 1935.	40	60	85
1029 LIONEL JUNIOR TRANSFORMER STATION: 1936.	40	60	85
1038 TRANSFORMER: 30 watt.	5	10	20
1039 TRANSFORMER: 1937-40, 35 watt.	5	10	20
1040 TRANSFORMER: 1937-39, 60 watt.	20	35	50

	C5	**C7**	**C8**
1041 TRANSFORMER: 1939-42, 60 watt.	20	35	50

	C5	**C7**	**C8**

	C5	**C7**	**C8**

1045 OPERATING WATCHMAN: 1938-42, 1946-50, with blue, dark blue, black or brown figure.

	C5	C7	C8
	20	35	50

1100 HAND CAR: 1934-37, Mickey and Minnie Mouse, red, **orange**, green or maroon base.

	C5	C7	C8
	350-**500**	600-**900**	1,100-**1,600**

1103 HAND CAR: 1935-37, Peter Rabbit Chick Mobile, metal flanged wheels or **rubber wheels**.

	C5	C7	C8
	300-**400**	600-**675**	900-**1,250**

1105 HAND CAR: 1935-36, Santa with Mickey Mouse peering from sack. Red or **green** base.

	C5	C7	C8
	500-**700**	1,000-**1,500**	2,000-**2,500**

1106 HAND CAR: Santa handcars were made without Mickey as well.

Too rarely traded to establish pricing.

1107 RAIL CAR: 1936-37 Donald Duck and Pluto, white or orange doghouse.

	C5	C7	C8
	400-**700**	600-**1,000**	900-**1,500**

1121 REMOTE CONTROL TURNOUTS: 1937-42, 1946-51.

	C5	C7	C8
	20	35	45

1550 PAIR OF MANUAL TURNOUTS: 1933-37.

	C5	C7	C8
	1	2	5

	C5	C7	C8
1555 90-DEGREE CROSSING: 1933-37.	1	2	5
1560 LIONEL JUNIOR STATION: 1933-37.	15	25	35
1569 LIONEL JUNIOR ACCESSORY SET: 1933-37, included four telegraph poles, one each semaphore, warning signal, clock and crossing gate, mounted on red or black bases. Box critical to value.	100	200	400
1571 TELEGRAPH POLE: 1933-37.	5	10	15
1572 SEMAPHORE: 1933-37, gray or pea green post mounted on black or red bases.	5	10	15
1575 CROSSING GATE: 1933-37, pea green or gray post.	5	10	15
A MINIATURE MOTOR: 1904.	50	75	100

	C5	C7	C8
A TRANSFORMER: 1921-37, 40 or 60 watts.	5	10	15
B NEW DEPARTURE MOTOR: 1906-16.	75	110	150

	C5	C7	C8
B TRANSFORMER: 1916-38, 50 or 75 watts.	5	10	25

	C5	C7	C8
C CURVED TRACK: 1906-42, Standard gauge.	1.00	1.50	2.50
CC CURVED TRACK: 1915-22, Standard gauge terminal track.	1.00	1.50	2.50
C NEW DEPARTURE MOTOR: 1906-16.	100	130	175
C TRANSFORMER: 1922-31, 75 watts.	5	10	25
D NEW DEPARTURE MOTOR: 1906-16.	100	130	175
E NEW DEPARTURE MOTOR: 1906-16.	100	130	175
F NEW DEPARTURE MOTOR: 1906-16.	100	130	175
F TRANSFORMER: 1931-37, 40 Watts.	5	10	25
G FAN MOTOR: 1909-14.	100	130	175
H TRANSFORMER: 1938-39, 75 Watts.	5	10	25
K SEWING MACHINE MOTOR: 1904-06.	100	130	175

	C5	C7	C8
K TRANSFORMER: 1913-38, 150 or 200 watts.	20	40	60
L SEWING MACHINE MOTOR: 1905.	75	100	125
L TRANSFORMER: 1913-38, 50 or 75 watts.	10	15	20
M PEERLESS MOTOR: 1915-20.	50	75	100
MS STRAIGHT TRACK: 1933-38, two-rail 027-type track.	.50	1.00	2.00
MWC CURVED TRACK: 1933-38, two-rail 027-type track.	.50	1.00	2.00
N TRANSFORMER: 1941-42, 50 watts.	5	10	15

	C5	C7	C8
OC CURVED TRACK: 1915-61, 0 gauge.	.25	.50	1.00
OCC CURVED TRACK: 1915-22, 0 gauge terminal track.	.25	.50	1.00
OCS CURVED TRACK: 1933-42, 0 gauge insulated.	.25	.50	1.00
OS STRAIGHT TRACK: 1915-61, 0 gauge	.50	1.00	2.00
OSC STRAIGHT TRACK: 1915-22, 0 gauge terminal.	.50	1.00	2.00
OSS STRAIGHT TRACK: 1933-42, 0 gauge insulated.	.50	1.00	2.00
OTC LOCKON: 1923-36.	.25	.50	1.00
Q TRANSFORMER: 1914-42, 50 or 75 watts.	10	20	40

	C5	C7	C8
R PEERLESS MOTOR: 1915-20.	75	100	125
R TRANSFORMER: 1939-42, 1946, 100 or 110 watts.	50	75	100
RCS REMOTE CONTROL TRACK: 1938-42, 1946-48, 0 gauge.	5	10	15
S STRAIGHT TRACK: 1906-42, Standard gauge.	1.00	2.00	3.00
S TRANSFORMER: 1914-17, 1938-42, 1947, 50 or 80 watts.	20	35	60
SC STRAIGHT TRACK: 1915-22, Standard gauge terminal.	1.00	2.00	3.00
SCS CURVED TRACK: 1933-42, Standard gauge insulated.	1.00	2.00	3.00
SMC CURVED TRACK: 1935-36, two-rail, 027-style track to activate the Mickey Mouse stoker.	1.00	2.00	3.00

	C5	C7	C8
SS STRAIGHT TRACK: 1933-42 insulated Standard gauge.	1.00	2.00	3.00
STC LOCKON: 1923-36, Standard gauge.	.25	.50	1.00
T TRANSFORMER (Type I): 1914-22, 75, 100, 110, or 150 watts.	10	15	25
U TRANSFORMER: 1932-33, 50 watts.	10	15	25

	C5	C7	C8
UTC LOCKON: 1936-42.	.25	.50	1.00

	C5	C7	C8
V TRANSFORMER: 1938-1942, 1946-47, 150 watts.	100	125	150
W CURVED TRACK: 1934-42, half section Standard gauge.	1.00	2.00	3.00
W TRANSFORMER: 1933-42, 75 watts.	10	15	25
WX TRANSFORMER: 1933-42, 75 watts, 25 cycle.	10	15	25
Y PEERLESS MOTOR: 1915-20.	50	75	100
Z TRANSFORMER: 1938-42, 1945-47, 250 watts.	100	125	150

| | C5 | C7 | C8 | | C5 | C7 | C8 |

POSTWAR LOCOMOTIVES AND ROLLING STOCK

41 UNITED STATES ARMY SWITCHER: 1955-57, **painted**, or *unpainted* black body.

	C5	C7	C8
	125-**200**	160-**300**	200-**400**

42 PICATINNY ARSENAL SWITCHER: 1957, unpainted olive drab body.

| 200 | 300 | 400 |

44 U.S. ARMY MOBILE MISSILE LAUNCHER: 1959-62, painted blue body.

| 150 | 225 | 350 |

45 U.S. MARINES MOBILE MISSILE LAUNCHER: 1960-62, painted olive drab.

| 175 | 275 | 425 |

50 LIONEL GANG CAR: 1954-64, **gray (1954)** or *blue* bumpers, **two-piece (1954)** or *one-piece* horn

| 40-**375** | 60-**500** | 75-**675** |

51 NAVY YARD NEW YORK SWITCHER: 1956-57, unpainted blue plastic body.

| 125 | 175 | 250 |

52 FIRE CAR: 1958-61, red-painted black plastic body.

| 125 | 200 | 300 |

53 RIO GRANDE SWITCHER: 1957-60, **"a" in Rio Grande printed normally**, or *"a" in Rio Grande reversed* (prototypically correct).

| 225-**425** | 325-**600** | 450-**900** |

54 BALLAST TAMPER: 1958-61, 1966-69, unpainted yellow plastic body.

| 150 | 225 | 325 |

55 TIE-JECTOR: 1957-61, early units had a **solid wall behind engineer**, a *vent behind the engineer* was added later.

| 150 | 225 | 325 |

56 M St L SWITCHER: 1958, body painted red, cab sides painted white.

| 300 | 550 | 800 |

	C5	C7	C8

57 AEC SWITCHER: 1959-60, unpainted white body, cab sides painted red.

| | 450 | 700 | 1,200 |

58 GREAT NORTHERN SWITCHER/ SNOWPLOW: 1959-1961, unpainted green plastic, with white cab sides equipped with a rotary snow blower.

| | 300 | 500 | 800 |

59 U.S. AIR FORCE MINUTEMAN SWITCHER: 1961-63, unpainted white body.

| | 300 | 500 | 750 |

60 LIONELVILLE RAPID TRANSIT TROLLEY: 1955-58, Yellow body, red roof; **black lettering, no vents, metal motorman silhouettes** or black lettering, no vents, no motorman silhouettes, or *blue lettering, no vents, no motormen,* or blue lettering, no motormen, with vents.

| | *100-* **200** | *175-* **300** | *250-* **400** |

65 HANDCAR: 1962-66, molded light or *dark* yellow plastic body, final version has **improved body** molding.

| | *175-* **225** | *325-* **450** | *500-* **650** |

68 EXECUTIVE INSPECTION CAR: 1958-61, gray plastic, painted red and cream.

| | 175 | 300 | 425 |

	C5	C7	C8

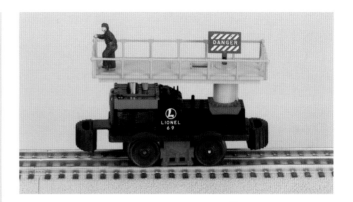

69 MAINTENANCE CAR: 1960-62, dark gray brushplate, black body, both unpainted.

| | 225 | 350 | 500 |

202 UNION PACIFIC ALCO A: 1957, painted orange.

| | 75 | 100 | 150 |

204 SANTA FE ALCO A-A: 1957, powered and dummy painted blue and yellow. Dummy has operating headlight.

| | 100 | 175 | 275 |

205 MISSOURI PACIFIC ALCO A-A: 1957-58, solid blue-painted, made **with** or *without* factory installed steel nose supports that are painted to match the unit.

| | *75-* **100** | *150-* **175** | *250-* **275** |

208 SANTA FE ALCO A-A: 1958-59, painted blue and yellow, no headlight in dummy.

| | 75 | 150 | 250 |

209 NEW HAVEN ALCO A-A: 1958 only, black, white and orange paint on molded black plastic body.

| | 400 | 600 | 1000 |

210 TEXAS SPECIAL ALCO A-A: 1958 only, painted red and white body.

| | 75 | 150 | 250 |

	C5	**C7**	**C8**		**C5**	**C7**	**C8**

211 TEXAS SPECIAL ALCO A-A

211 TEXAS SPECIAL ALCO A-A: 1962-63, 1965-66, cosmetically almost identical to the 210.

	75	150	250

212 SANTA FE ALCO A-A: 1964-66, painted red and silver. Some stamped "BLT / BY LIONEL". Others were stamped "BLT 8-57 / BY LIONEL", but no difference in value or scarcity.

	100	175	275

212 UNITED STATES MARINE CORPS ALCO A: 1958-59, painted *dark* or medium blue

	100-**150**	175-**225**	250-**325**

212(T) UNITED STATES MARINE CORPS ALCO A dummy: 1958, painted medium blue body.

	450	675	1100

213 MINNEAPOLIS & ST. LOUIS ALCO A-A: 1964, painted red.

	125	225	325

215 SANTA FE ALCO: 1965-66, painted red and silver. Sold as *A-A* with 212T or **A-B** with 218C.

	100-**110**	150-**175**	250-**275**

216 BURLINGTON ALCO A: 1958, painted silver and red.

	200	350	450

216 MINNEAPOLIS & ST. LOUIS ALCO A: 1965, painted red body, came as either *single* A unit, or with 213T as **A-A** combination.

	100-**175**	150-**225**	200-**350**

217 B & M ALCO A-B: 1959, unpainted blue plastic bodies with the roof and A-unit nose painted black.

	100	165	250

218 SANTA FE ALCO: 1959-63, painted silver and red, came either as *A-A* or in 1961 as A-B combinations. From time to time A-A units were produced which had **solid yellow nose decals** that lacked the red areas inside the perimeter.

	100-**125**	150-**175**	225-**275**

	C5	C7	C8

218C SANTA FE ALCO B UNIT: 1961-63, painted silver. — 50 / 75 / 115

219 MISSOURI PACIFIC ALCO A-A: 1959 only, uncataloged, blue-painted pair. — 100 / 175 / 290

220 SANTA FE ALCO: 1960-61, painted silver and red, sold as an *A only*, or with a dummy as an **A-A** combination. — 75-**150** / 125-**225** / 175-**300**

221 2-6-4 STEAM: 1946-47, painted either **gray** or *black*, with either **silver** or black wheels, and furnished with either 221T or **221W** tender. — 50-**100** / 75-**150** / 125-**200**

221 RIO GRANDE ALCO A: 1963-64, unpainted yellow body. — 50 / 70 / 90

221 SANTA FE ALCO A: 1964, uncataloged, unpainted olive drab body, no E-unit, wired for forward-only travel. — 250 / 500 / 750

221 UNITED STATES MARINE CORPS ALCO A: 1964, uncataloged, unpainted olive drab body. — 225 / 375 / 550

222 RIO GRANDE ALCO A: 1962, painted yellow, wired to run forward only. — 50 / 75 / 100

223 SANTA FE ALCO A-B: 1963, Painted silver and red. — 125 / 200 / 325

224 2-6-2 STEAM: 1945-46, with 2466W or 2466WX tender, with or **without** drawbar, **black** or silver railings, **squared** or rounded cab floor. — 60-**75** / 100-**125** / 150-**200**

224 UNITED STATES NAVY ALCO A-B: 1960 only, painted blue. — 150 / 225 / 350

	C5	C7	C8

225 CHESAPEAKE & OHIO ALCO A: 1960 only, painted dark blue. — 75 / 125 / 175

226 B & M ALCO A-B: 1960 only, B unit unpainted blue plastic, A unit also blue either *unpainted* or **painted**. — 100-**150** / 175-**225** / 275-**325**

227 CANADIAN NATIONAL ALCO A: 1960 only, molded gray body painted green. — 100 / 150 / 200

228 CANADIAN NATIONAL ALCO A: 1960 only, uncataloged, body painted green. — 100 / 150 / 200

229 MINNEAPOLIS & ST. LOUIS ALCO: 1961-62. Sold as single *A* or in **A-B** combination. — 75-**125** / 100-**175** / 150-**275**

	C5	**C7**	**C8**

230 CHESAPEAKE & OHIO ALCO A: 1961 only, painted dark blue. — 75 / 125 / 175

231 ROCK ISLAND ALCO A: 1961-63 painted black with white heat-stamped lettering and a white roofline stripe. *With* or **without** broad red stripe on sides. — 75-**225** / 125-**375** / 175-**500**

232 NEW HAVEN ALCO A: 1962, painted overall orange with two narrow black stripes. — 75 / 125 / 175

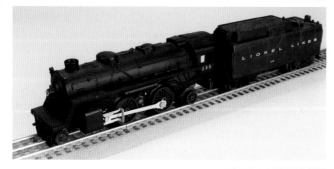

233 2-4-2 STEAM: 1961-62, with 233W tender. — 50 / 75 / 125

235 2-4-2 STEAM: 1961, supplied with either the 1050T or 1130T tender. — 150 / 250 / 350

	C5	**C7**	**C8**

236 2-4-2 STEAM: 1961-62, supplied with either the 1050T or 1130T tender. — 20 / 35 / 50

237 2-4-2 STEAM: 1963-66, paired variously with a number of different tenders, including the 1061T and 1062T slope-back models, the 242T and 1060T small streamlined, or **234W** square whistle tender. Thick or thin running boards. — 30-**60** / 50-**100** / 85-**175**

238 2-4-2 STEAM: 1963-64, furnished with the 234W whistle tender. Thick or thin running boards. — 100 / 150 / 250

	C5	C7	C8

239 2-4-2 STEAM: 1965-66, cab number either **heat** or rubber-stamped in white, and came with either **234W** or 242T tender.

	C5	C7	C8
	30-**80**	45-**125**	70-**175**

240 2-4-2 STEAM: 1964, uncataloged, came with 242T tender.

	C5	C7	C8
	150	225	375

241 2-4-2 STEAM: 1965-66, uncataloged, with 234W tender. White running board applied by **painting** or rubber-stamping.

	C5	C7	C8
	90-**100**	150-**175**	240-**275**

242 2-4-2 STEAM: 1962-66, came with 242T, 1060T, 1061T or 1062T tender.

	C5	C7	C8
	10	20	40

243 2-4-2 STEAM: 1960 only, came with the 243W tender.

	C5	C7	C8
	70	100	200

244 2-4-2 STEAM: 1960-61, came with either 244T or 1130T tender.

	C5	C7	C8
	25	35	50

245 2-4-2 STEAM: 1959, uncataloged, came with 1130T tender.

	C5	C7	C8
	40	70	90

246 2-4-2 STEAM: 1959-61, came with either the 1130T or the 244T tender.

	C5	C7	C8
	20	30	40

247 2-4-2 STEAM: 1959 only, came with 247T tender, which had a blue stripe to match the locomotive.

	C5	C7	C8
	45	65	90

	C5	C7	C8
248 2-4-2 STEAM: 1958, uncataloged, came with 1130T.	60	70	85
249 2-4-2 STEAM: 1958 only, came with 250T tender which had matching red stripe.	30	45	60
250 2-4-2 STEAM: 1957 only, came with 250T tender which had matching red stripe.	30	40	50
251 2-4-2 STEAM: 1966 only, came with 1062T tender.	150	200	350

	C5	C7	C8
400 BALTIMORE AND OHIO RDC-1: 1956-58.	150	225	300
404 BALTIMORE AND OHIO RDC-4: 1957-58.	200	300	400
520 LIONEL LINES 1-B-0 ELECTRIC: 1956-57, unpainted red plastic body with **black** or *copper*-colored plastic pantograph mounted on top.	75-**100**	120-**150**	175-**200**

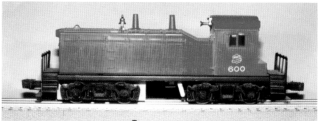

	C5	C7	C8
600 M K T NW-2: 1955 unpainted red plastic body mounted on **gray frame with yellow platform railings and blued steel steps**, or on gray or black or *blued steel* frame with blued steel railings and steps.	115-**375**	160-**550**	225-**800**
601 SEABOARD NW-2: 1956, painted black and red.	115	150	225
602 SEABOARD NW-2: 1957-58 painted black and red.	125	175	250
610 ERIE NW-2: 1955-only body painted black with yellow heat-stamped number. **Yellow**, black or *blued steel* frame.	100-**425**	150-**650**	225-**1,100**
611 JERSEY CENTRAL NW-2: 1957-58, blue and orange body, blue can be unpainted light or dark shade, or **painted**.	150-**400**	225-**600**	350-**900**
613 UNION PACIFIC NW-2: 1958 only, yellow and gray.	250	400	600
614 ALASKA RAILROAD NW-2: 1959-60, "BUILT BY / LIONEL" either in *molded color*, or **outlined in yellow**.	150-**325**	225-**475**	300-**750**

250 2-4-2 STEAM

	C5	C7	C8

616 SANTA FE NW-2:
1961-62, painted black
with white safety stripes.
Bodies came with *open but
unused E-unit and bell slots*,
or plugged E-unit slot and
open bell slot, or with **both
E-unit and bell slots
plugged**.

| | *125-* | *175-* | *250-* |
| | **200** | **325** | **450** |

617 SANTA FE NW-2:
1963, painted black with
white safety stripes. Came
with black ornamental bell,
silver ornamental horn,
head and marker light
lenses, and radio antenna.
Early units had **separately
installed frame steps**,
steps on late units integral
with frame.

| | 150 | 250 | 375 |

**621 JERSEY CENTRAL
NW-2:** 1956-57, unpainted
blue plastic body.

| | 100 | 150 | 200 |

622 A.T. & S.F. NW-2:
1949-50, black, die-cast
frame. **With** or *without* "622"
stamped on the nose of the
locomotive.

| | *150-* | *200-* | *350-* |
| | **200** | **325** | **500** |

623 A.T. & S.F. NW-2:
1952-54, black, die-cast
frame. Hood-side handrail
retained by **10** or *three*
stations.

| | *100-* | *150-* | *225-* |
| | **125** | **175** | **250** |

	C5	C7	C8

**624 CHESAPEAKE &
OHIO NW-2:** 1952-54,
medium or **light** blue,
die-cast frame. Hood-side
handrail retained by **10** or
three stations.

| | *150-* | *225-* | *375-* |
| | **300** | **450** | **700** |

**625 LEHIGH VALLEY
CENTER CAB:** 1957-58,
unpainted red body.

| | 125 | 175 | 225 |

**626 BALTIMORE AND
OHIO CENTER CAB:**
1957 only, unpainted blue
body.

| | 250 | 400 | 625 |

**627 LEHIGH VALLEY
CENTER CAB:** 1956-57,
unpainted red plastic body.

| | 75 | 115 | 150 |

**628 NORTHERN PACIFIC
CENTER CAB:** 1956-57,
unpainted black body.

| | 100 | 150 | 225 |

**629 BURLINGTON
CENTER CAB:** 1956,
silver painted body.

| | 250 | 450 | 800 |

	C5	C7	C8

633 SANTA FE NW-2: 1962, painted blue body with yellow safety stripes. — 125 / 200 / 300

634 SANTA FE NW-2: 1963, 1965-66, painted blue body, **yellow safety stripes** in 1963 only, *no stripes* 65-66. — 75-125 / 125-175 / 200-250

635 UNION PACIFIC NW-2: 1965 only, painted yellow body. — 75 / 125 / 200

637 2-6-4 STEAM: 1959-61, came with 2046W or 736W tenders. Number *rubber* or **heat**-stamped. — 75-120 / 125-175 / 200-300

638-2361 STOKELY-VAN CAMP'S BOXCAR: 1962-64, uncataloged. — 25 / 40 / 60

645 UNION PACIFIC NW-2: 1969, unpainted yellow plastic body. — 75 / 125 / 200

646 4-6-4 STEAM: 1954-58, came with 2046W tenders, silver or white cab lettering. — 175 / 250 / 350

665 4-6-4 STEAM: 1954-56, 1966. Furnished with 6026W, 2046W or 736W tender. Rubber- or heat-stamped numbers on loco. — 165 / 250 / 300

671 6-8-6 STEAM: 1946-49, 1946 locos have bulb-type smoke units, heater units used thereafter. "6200" stamped in **white** on some boiler fronts, *decaled* on most, came with 671W or **2671W** tenders, some of the later having **backup lights**. — 135-325 / 175-475 / 275-600

671R 6-8-6 STEAM: 1946-49, "Electronic Control" **bulb** or *heater*-type smoke units used. — 225-250 / 325-350 / 425-475

671 RR 6-8-6 STEAM: 1952 only, came with 2046W-50 tender. Cabs **may** or may not have the "RR" suffix stamped on them. — 185-225 / 275-350 / 350-450

675 2-6-2 STEAM: 1947-49, **white "675"** stamped on boiler front, or *red keystone decal* applied. Came with 2466WX or 6466WX tender. — 95-125 / 145-175 / 225-250

675 2-6-4 STEAM: 1952 only, with 2046W tender. — 95 / 145 / 225

681 6-8-6 STEAM: 1950-51, 1953. Came with **2671W** or 2046W-50 tender, number stamped in *silver* or white. — 165-175 / 250-275 / 350-375

682 6-8-6 STEAM: 1954-55, came with a 2046W-50 tender. — 275 / 425 / 600

685 4-6-4 STEAM: 1953 only, came with 6026W tender. **Rubber-** or *heat-*stamped numbers on loco. — 200-250 / 300-350 / 400-500

726 2-8-4 STEAM: 1946-49, 1946 locos have **bulb-type smoke units**, *heater* units used thereafter. Came with 2426W tender. — 225-300 / 350-475 / 475-600

	C5	C7	C8

726RR 2-8-4 STEAM: 1952 only, came with 2046W tender. Cabs **may** or may not have the "RR" suffix stamped on them. — 225-**300** 375-**425** 475-**600**

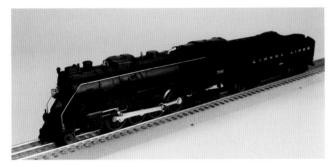

736 2-8-4 STEAM: 1950-51, 1953-68, came with **2671WX**, 2046W or 736W tender. — 200-**300** 300-**425** 400-**575**

746 4-8-4 STEAM: 1957-60, came with **long-striped** tender stamped 746W, or short-striped 746W without number stamping. — 650-**700** 850-**900** 1,200-**1,500**

773 4-6-4 STEAM: 1950 with **2426W tender**, 1964-66, 736W or 773W tender 64-66. — 600-**950** 850-**1,200** 1,100-**1,800**

1001 2-4-2 STEAM: 1948 only, **die-cast** or *plastic*, plastic with *white* or silver numbers, all with 1001T tender. — 25-**225** 40-**325** 60-**450**

1002 Lionel Gondola: 1948-52, *black*, blue, **red, silver, yellow**. — 7-**225** 10-**375** 15-**500**

	C5	C7	C8

X1004 BABY RUTH BOXCAR: 1948-52, outline or solid lettering. — 6 10 14

1005 SUNOCO TANK CAR: 1948-50, gray tank with *medium* or dark blue lettering. — 5 7 12

1007 LIONEL LINES CABOOSE: 1948-52, *red* or **tuscan** body. — 2-**75** 4-**200** 6-**300**

1050 0-4-0 STEAM: 1959 only, came with a 1050T slope-back tender. — 150 200 350

1055 TEXAS SPECIAL ALCO A: 1959-60, painted red with white lettering. — 40 60 90

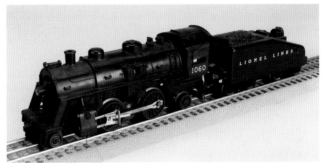

1060 2-4-2 STEAM: 1960-62, came with 1050T or 1060T tender. **Long** or *short* rainshield over loco headlight. — 10 25 50

	C5	**C7**	**C8**

1061 0-4-0 or 2-4-2 STEAM: 1963-64, 1969 used 1061T, 1062T, 1060T or 242T tenders. Numbers white *heat-stamped*, omitted or applied to **paper label**.

	10-150	25-225	45-300

1062 0-4-0 or 2-4-2 STEAM: 1963-64, used 1061T, 1062T, 1060T or 242T tenders. Streamlined tender sometimes lettered **Southern Pacific**.

	10-95	20-125	35-175

1065 UNION PACIFIC ALCO A: 1961 only, body painted yellow.

	45	65	100

1066 UNION PACIFIC ALCO A: 1964, uncataloged unpainted yellow body.

	45	65	100

1101 2-4-2 STEAM: 1948- only, with 1001T tender.

	15	35	55

1110 2-4-2 STEAM: 1949, 1951-52, with 1001T tender. **Baldwin disc** or spoked drive wheels.

	10-25	20-40	35-60

1120 2-4-2 STEAM: 1950 only, with 1001T tender.

	15	30	50

1130 2-4-2 STEAM: 1953-54, **die-cast** or *plastic*, plastic with white or *silver* numbers, with 6066T or 1130T tender.

	10-225	25-350	40-450

1615 0-4-0 STEAM: 1955-57, with 1615T tender.

	125	175	275

1625 0-4-0 STEAM: 1958 only, with 1625T tender.

	175	275	400

1654 2-4-2 STEAM: 1946-47, with 1654T or **1654W** tender.

	30-35	50-60	70-95

1655 2-4-2 STEAM: 1948-49, with 6654W tender.

	40	70	95

1656 0-4-0 STEAM: 1948-49, with 6403B tender with **separate Bakelite coal pile** or *integral die-cast coal pile*.

	200-225	300-350	425-475

1665 0-4-0 STEAM: 1946 only, with *heat-* or **rubber-** stamped 2403B tender.

	200-250	325-375	450-500

1666 2-6-2 STEAM: 1946-47, black or *silver* handrails, *moveable* or **rigid** bell.

	75-100	100-150	175-250

	C5	C7	C8		C5	C7	C8

1862 4-4-0 STEAM: 1959-62, with 1862T tender. — 125 / 200 / 300

1865 WESTERN & ATLANTIC COACH: 1959-62, body painted yellow with brown roof. — 20 / 30 / 40

1866 WESTERN & ATLANTIC MAIL-BAGGAGE: 1959-62, body painted yellow with brown roof. — 20 / 30 / 40

1872 4-4-0 STEAM: 1959-62, with 1872T tender. — 150 / 250 / 350

1875 WESTERN & ATLANTIC COACH: 1959-62, body painted yellow with brown roof. — 125 / 200 / 275

1876 WESTERN & ATLANTIC MAIL-BAGGAGE: 1959-62, body painted yellow with brown roof. — 40 / 65 / 90

1877 FLATCAR: 1959-62, unpainted brown plastic, came with a load of two white, two tan and brown, and two black horses made by Bachmann Bros. (hence the "BB" logo on the horses' bellies), and a 10-section maroon fence. — 35 / 75 / 110

1875W WESTERN & ATLANTIC COACH WITH WHISTLE: 1959-62, body painted yellow with brown roof. — 60 / 100 / 140

1872 4-4-0 STEAM

	C5	C7	C8

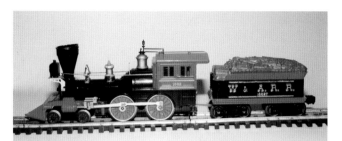

1882 4-4-0 STEAM: 1960-only, came with 1882T tender.

	C5	C7	C8
	425	550	800

1885 WESTERN & ATLANTIC COACH: 1960, painted blue with brown roof.

	C5	C7	C8
	175	250	350

1887 FLATCAR: 1960-only, unpainted brown plastic, came with a load of two white, two tan and brown, and two black horses made by Bachmann Bros. (hence the "BB" logo on the horses bellies), and a 10-section fence.

	C5	C7	C8
	140	200	275

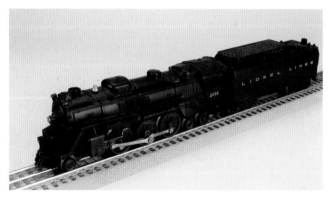

2016 2-6-4 STEAM: 1955-56, with 6026W tender. Number *heat*- or **rubber**-stamped in white.

	C5	C7	C8
	75-150	100-250	175-350

	C5	C7	C8

2018 2-6-4 STEAM: 1956-59, came with **6026W**, *6026T* or *1130T* tenders.

	C5	C7	C8
	50-65	65-100	100-150

2020 6-8-6 STEAM: 1946-49, 1946 locos have **bulb**-type smoke units, *heater* units used thereafter. "6200" stamped in **white** on some boiler fronts, *decaled* on most, came with 2020W or 6020W tender.

	C5	C7	C8
	150-175	200-250	275-350

2023 UNION PACIFIC ALCO A-A: 1950-51, came in **yellow with gray roof and nose**, yellow with gray roof, and *silver with gray roof*.

	C5	C7	C8
	175-2,000	300-2,800	450-3,800

2024 CHESAPEAKE & OHIO ALCO A: 1969 only, unpainted dark blue body.

	C5	C7	C8
	40	60	90

2025 2-6-2 STEAM: 1947-49, **white "2025"** stamped on boiler front, or *red keystone decal* applied. Came with 2466WX or 6466WX tender.

	C5	C7	C8
	70-125	100-175	175-250

2025 2-6-4 STEAM: 1952 only, with 6466W tender.

	C5	C7	C8
	85	125	200

	C5	C7	C8

2026 2-6-2 STEAM: 1948-49, **Baldwin disc** or *spoke* wheels, with 6466WX tender. — **50-75** | *75-***100** | *100-***150**

2026 2-6-4 STEAM: 1951-53, with 6066T, 6466T or **6466W** tender, loco numbers rubber-stamped in *silver* or heat-stamped in **white**. — **40-90** | *60-***125** | *100-***185**

2028 PENNSYLVANIA GP-7: 1955, **gold** or yellow rubber-stamped lettering, *gold* or **tan** frame. — *225-***350** | *350-***600** | *500-***900**

2029 2-6-4 STEAM: 1964-69, came with *1060T, 234T* or 234W "Lionel Lines" or **234W "Pennsylvania"** tender, the later carries a $200 premium above listed prices. — **35-55** | **50-75** | *80-***125**

2031 ROCK ISLAND ALCO A-A: 1952-54, painted black with broad red stripe. — 250 | 375 | 550

2032 ERIE ALCO A-A: 1952-54, painted black with narrow yellow striping. — 150 | 225 | 350

	C5	C7	C8

2033 UNION PACIFIC ALCO A-A: 1952-54 painted silver with silver roof. — 175 | 275 | 450

2034 2-4-2 STEAM: 1952 only, came with a 6066T tender. — 15 | 35 | 60

2035 2-6-4 STEAM: 1950-51 came with the 6466W tender. — 85 | 125 | 200

2036 2-6-4 STEAM: 1950 only, with 6466W tender. — 100 | 150 | 225

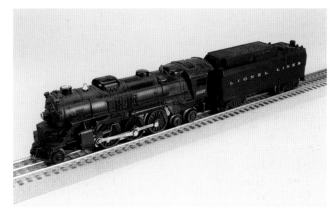

2037 2-6-4 STEAM: 1953-55, 1957-63, came with 6026W, 233W or 234W whistle tender, or non-whistling 6066T, 6026T or 1130T tender. Reduce the values listed one third for non-whistle tender. — 75 | 120 | 175

2037-500 2-6-4 STEAM: 1957-58, pink, with 1130T-500 pink tender. — 500 | 700 | 950

2041 ROCK ISLAND ALCO A-A: 1969, unpainted black plastic bodies with wide red stripe. — 75 | 115 | 150

	C5	**C7**	**C8**

2046 4-6-4 STEAM: 1950-51, 1953, came with 2046W tender. Silver numbers with **die-cast trailing truck**, or white numbers with plastic and sheet-metal trailing truck.

140 200 275

2055 4-6-4 STEAM: 1953-55, came with 6026W or 2046W tender.

140 200 275

2056 4-6-4 STEAM: 1952 only, came with 2046W tender.

175 250 350

2065 4-6-4 STEAM: 1954-56, came with 6026W or 2046W tender.

175 250 325

2240 WABASH F-3 A-B: 1956 only, molded in medium blue painted blue with the roof and upper body painted gray, the white band was silk-screened on. The final segment of the B-unit's white stripe, near "Built by Lionel" is 1/2-inch long.

500 750 1,150

	C5	**C7**	**C8**

2242 NEW HAVEN F-3 A-B: 1958-59, heat-stamped white "NH" on the nose door.

750 1,250 2,000

2243 SANTA FE F-3 A-B: 1955-57 **high-profile** or flush molded cab door ladder.

300- 450- 675-
350 500 750

2243C SANTA FE F-3 B UNIT: 1955-57, not originally sold separately, but often sold individually on the collector market.

150 225 300

2245 THE TEXAS SPECIAL F-3 A-B: 1954-55, painted glossy red with white silk-screened lower panels. The red lettering on the sides of the units was actually the red paint which had been masked off. Horizontal motors in 1954, vertical in 1955, late 1955 B-units have **closed porthole** openings.

400- 550- 800-
750 1,000 1,400

2257 LIONEL-SP CABOOSE: 1947, *red no stack, red-orange no stack,* red-orange with matching stack, **tuscan with matching stack,** *heat or* rubber-stamped markings.

3-300 5-500 10-775

	C5	**C7**	**C8**

2321 LACKAWANNA FM:
1954-56, **maroon** or *gray* roof.

	375-	500-	750-
	550	**800**	**1,200**

2322 VIRGINIAN FM:
1965-66, *unpainted blue* plastic with painted-on yellow trim, or both blue and yellow **painted** on.

	400-	600-	800-
	500	**750**	**960**

2328 BURLINGTON GP-7:
1955-56, painted silver body, red frame.

	300	450	750

2329 VIRGINIAN EL-C RECTIFIER: 1958-59, blue-painted body with yellow frame.

	500	800	1,200

2330 PENNSYLVANIA GG1: 1950, painted green.

	800	1,400	2,200

	C5	**C7**	**C8**

2331 VIRGINIAN FM:
1955-58 **molded gray body painted yellow and blue**, or molded gray body painted black and yellow, or *molded blue* body with yellow painted on.

	600-	800-	1,100-
	1,000	**1,350**	**2,000**

2332 PENNSYLVANIA GG1: 1947-49 *green*, or VERY dark, almost **black** green.

	300-	450-	750-
	600	**1,000**	**2,000**

2333 SANTA FE F-3 A-A:
1948-49, **clear, unpainted body**, or *silver and red painted body*.

	300-	600-	1,200-
	3,000	**5,000**	**9,000**

2334 NEW YORK CENTRAL F-3 A-A: 1948-49, **rubber-stamped** or *heat-stamped* lettering.

	300-	600-	1,200-
	350	**650**	**1,250**

2337 WABASH GP-7: 1958, unpainted blue plastic body.

	250	350	525

	C5	C7	C8

2338 THE MILWAUKEE ROAD GP-7: 1955-56, translucent orange plastic body with **orange stripe on cab**, or translucent orange plastic body with no cab stripe, or *opaque* orange plastic bodies with *no cab stripe*.

	175-**1,000**	275-**1,500**	400-**2,200**

2339 WABASH GP-7: 1957, unpainted blue plastic body.

	200	300	450

2340 PENNSYLVANIA GG1: 1955, painted *green* or Tuscan **red**.

	800-**1,000**	1,250-**1,500**	2,100-**2,500**

	C5	C7	C8

2341 JERSEY CENTRAL FM: 1956 only, molded blue plastic body, with **gloss** or *matte* orange paint applied.

	1,250-**1,500**	2,000-**2,350**	2,800-**3,500**

2343 SANTA FE F-3 A-A: 1950-52, painted red and silver.

	300	500	1,200

2343C SANTA FE F-3 B-UNIT: 1950-55, screen-type (50-51) or *molded louver* roof vents.

	150	250	450

2344 NEW YORK CENTRAL F-3 A-A: 1950-52.

	350	600	1,100

2344C NEW YORK CENTRAL F-3 B-UNIT: 1950-55. Screen-type (50-51) or *molded louver* roof vents.

	175	300	450

2345 WESTERN PACIFIC F-3 A-A: 1952 painted silver and orange.

	1,250	2,100	3,000

2343 SANTA FE F-3 A-A

2344 NEW YORK CENTRAL F-3 A-A

	C5	**C7**	**C8**

2346 BOSTON AND MAINE GP-9: 1965-66, black plastic body painted blue. — 200 | 300 | 425

2347 CHESAPEAKE & OHIO GP-7: 1965 only, body painted blue with yellow heat-stamped markings. — 1,500 | 2,500 | 3,500

2348 MINNEAPOLIS & ST LOUIS GP-9: 1958-59, painted red, and a white stripe painted on the middle of each side, the cab roof was painted blue, and red and white lettering was heat-stamped on. — 250 | 350 | 500

	C5	**C7**	**C8**

2349 NORTHERN PACIFIC GP-9: 1959-60, painted black brilliant gold-painted ends and side stripes. — 300 | 450 | 600

2350 NEW HAVEN EP-5: 1956-58, **orange "N", a black "H", painted nose**; or orange "N", a black "H", decal nose; or white "N", orange "H", painted nose; or *white "N", orange "H", decal nose*. — 300-**1,000** | 400-**1,600** | 550-**2,400**

2351 MILWAUKEE ROAD EP-5: 1957-58, yellow-painted body with a maroon-painted stripe in the middle and a black-painted upper quarter and roof, heat-stamped yellow lettering. — 350 | 500 | 750

2352 PENNSYLVANIA EP-5: 1957-58, Tuscan-painted body. — 350 | 500 | 750

2353 SANTA FE F-3 A-A: 1953-55, painted silver and red. — 350 | 650 | 1,100

2354 NEW YORK CENTRAL F-3 A-A: 1953-55. — 300 | 550 | 950

C5   C7   C8   **C5   C7   C8**

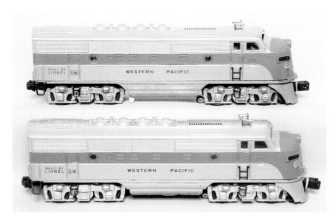

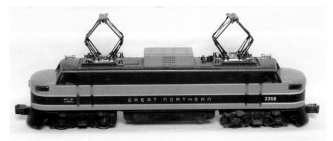

2355 WESTERN PACIFIC
F-3 A-A: 1953, silver and
orange paint.   1,100   1,800   2,800

2358 GREAT NORTHERN
EP-5: 1959-60 "Great
Northern" heat-stamped on
sides in yellow, end markings,
number and "BLT BY
LIONEL" were a large decal.   700   1,100   1,800

2359 BOSTON AND
MAINE GP-9: 1961-62,
black plastic body painted
blue, cab painted black,
white heat-stamped lettering.   200   300   450

2360 PENNSYLVANIA
GG1: 1956-58, green with
five stripes, **Tuscan with
five stripes**, or Tuscan with
single applied by rubber-
stamping, *painting or decal*.   750-   1,100-   1,750-
                                 900   1,500   2,500

2356 SOUTHERN F-3 A-
A: 1954-56, green-painted
body had its lower side
panels and nose painted gray
with rubber-stamped yellow
stripes and lettering.   800   1,250   2,000

2363 ILLINOIS CENTRAL
F-3 A-B: 1955-56,
unpainted or *painted* orange
stripe.   400   800   1,500

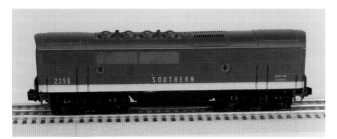

2356C SOUTHERN F-3 B-
UNIT: 1954-56 decorated to
match the 2356 A-A units.   275   400   550

2357 LIONEL-SP
CABOOSE: 1947-48,
Tuscan body and stack, or red
body no stack, or **red body
and stack**.   18-   25-   30-
                         250   450   750

2365 CHESAPEAKE AND
OHIO GP-7: 1962-63,
painted blue with yellow
heat-stamped markings.   200   325   475

	C5	C7	C8		C5	C7	C8

2378 MILWAUKEE ROAD F-3 A-B

2367 WABASH F-3 A-B: 1955 only, molded in royal blue plastic, A unit painted, B-unit unpainted. The final segment of white stripe on B unit, near the "Built by Lionel" marking is 1/8-inch long. **Rubber-stamped** or *heat-stamped* B-unit lettering.

	C5	C7	C8
	725-	*1,150-*	*1,700-*
	1,200	**1,900**	**3,000**

2368 BALTIMORE AND OHIO F-3 A-B: 1956 only, *unpainted* blue plastic or **blue-painted** gray plastic body.

	1,600-	*2,400-*	*3,400-*
	2,000	**2,800**	**4,000**

2373 CANADIAN PACIFIC F-3 A-A: 1957, painted gray and brown with yellow heat-stamped stripes and lettering.

1,200	1,800	2,800

2378 MILWAUKEE ROAD F-3 A-B: 1956-only, unpainted gray bodies, painted-on red stripe and yellow heat-stamped delineating stripes. Each unit **with** or without a thin yellow roofline stripe, matched combinations are preferred.

1,500	2,400	3,300

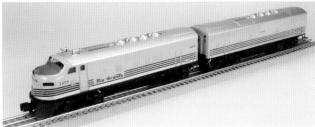

2379 RIO GRANDE F-3 A-B: 1957-58, painted yellow, black horizontal stripes and side lettering were heat-stamped.

1,100	1,600	2,300

2383 SANTA FE F-3 A-A: 1958-66, *silver and red,* or silver and orange-red.

300	450	700

2400 MAPLEWOOD PULLMAN: 1948-49, painted green with yellow stripes and window outlines, dark gray roof.

90	140	200

2401 HILLSIDE OBSERVATION: 1948-49, matches 2400.

85	125	175

2402 CHATHAM PULLMAN: 1948-49, matches 2400.

90	140	200

2404 SANTA FE VISTA DOME: 1964-65, no lights or silhouetted window strips.

35	70	100

2405 SANTA FE PULLMAN: 1964-65, matches 2404.

35	70	100

2406 SANTA FE OBSERVATION: 1964-65, matches 2404.

30	60	90

	C5	**C7**	**C8**

2408 SANTA FE VISTA DOME: 1966 only, has lights and silhouetted window strips. | 40 | 70 | 100

2409 SANTA FE PULLMAN: 1966 only, matches 2408. | 40 | 70 | 100

2410 SANTA FE OBSERVATION: 1966 only, matches 2408. | 35 | 60 | 90

2411 FLATCAR: 1946-48, loaded with **steel pipe** with groove inside or three 7-inch long 3/8-inch diameter *wooden dowels.* | 20-**75** | 30-**100** | 42-**140**

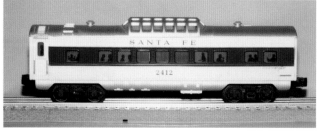

2412 SANTA FE VISTA DOME: 1959-63, blue stripe, illuminated, with silhouetted window strips. | 30 | 60 | 90

2414 SANTA FE PULLMAN: 1959-63, matches 2412. | 30 | 60 | 90

2416 SANTA FE OBSERVATION: 1959-63, matches 2412. | 25 | 55 | 80

	C5	**C7**	**C8**

2419 D. L. & W WRECKING CAR: 1946-47. | 25 | 35 | 50

2420 D. L. & W WRECKING CAR: 1946-47, dark gray cab on **light** or dark gray die-cast frame. *Heat-stamped serif* or rubber-stamped sans-serif lettering. | 60-**150** | 100-**200** | 150-**300**

2421 MAPLEWOOD PULLMAN: 1950-51 **gray** roof, 1952-53 silver roof. | 50-**60** | 75-**90** | 100-**125**

2422 CHATHAM PULLMAN: 1950-53, matches 2421. | 50-60 | 75-90 | 100-125

	C5	**C7**	**C8**

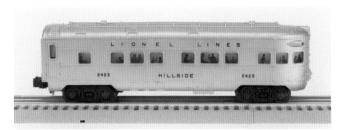

2423 HILLSIDE OBSERVATION: 1950-53, matches 2421

	C5	C7	C8
	50-**60**	70-**80**	90-**100**

2429 LIVINGSTON PULLMAN: 1952-53, matches 2421.

	*90-***100**	*125-***150**	*180-***225**

2430 PULLMAN: 1946-47, sheet-metal with blue body with silver roof.

	20	50	80

2431 OBSERVATION: 1946-47, matches 2430.

	20	50	80

2432 CLIFTON VISTA DOME: 1954-58, silver, illuminated, with silhouetted window strips and red lettering.

	25	50	75

2434 NEWARK PULLMAN: 1954-58, matches 2432.

	25	50	75

2435 ELIZABETH PULLMAN: 1954-58, matches 2432.

	40	75	125

2436 SUMMIT OBSERVATION: 1954-56, matches 2432.

	35	60	100

2436 MOOSEHEART OBSERVATION: 1957-58, matches 2432.

	35	60	100

2440 PULLMAN: 1946-47, two-tone green sheet-metal silver rubber-stamped white heat-stamped lettering.

	25	50	75

2441 OBSERVATION: 1946-47, two-tone green sheet-metal silver rubber-stamped white heat-stamped lettering.

	25	50	75

2442 PULLMAN: 1946-48, brown sheet-metal, silver rubber-stamped or white heat-stamped lettering.

	25	50	75

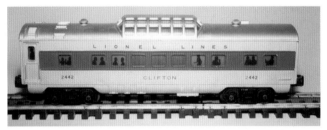

2442 CLIFTON VISTA DOME: 1956 red stripe illuminated with silhouetted window strips.

	75	125	175

2443 OBSERVATION: 1946-48, brown sheet-metal, silver rubber-stamped or *white heat-stamped* lettering.

	25	45-55	70-90

2444 NEWARK PULLMAN: 1956 matches 2442.

	75	125	175

2445 ELIZABETH PULLMAN: 1956 matches 2442.

	100	175	225

2446 SUMMIT PULLMAN: 1956 matches 2442.

	75	125	175

	C5	C7	C8
2452 PENNSYLVANIA GONDOLA: 1945-47.	12	20	40
2452X PENNSYLVANIA GONDOLA: 1946-47.	12	20	40
X2454 BABY RUTH BOXCAR: 1946-47.	15	25	35
X2454 PENNSYLVANIA: 1946 only, **orange** or *brown* doors.	80-**125**	150-**175**	225-**250**
2456 LEHIGH VALLEY HOPPER: 1948 only, black painted body.	15	25	35
2457 PENNSYLVANIA CABOOSE: 1945-47, "477618" on side, **brown** or *red* body, **red** or *black* window frames. Has illumination and glazed windows.	20-**60**	30-**100**	40-**150**
X2458 PENNSYLVANIA BOXCAR: 1946-48, brown 9 1/4" double-door automobile car.	20	45	65

	C5	C7	C8
2460 BUCYRUS ERIE CRANE: 1946-50, dark or light **gray**, or *black* cab.	60-**125**	80-**200**	100-**275**
2461 TRANSFORMER CAR: 1947-48, **red** or *black* transformer load.	40-**60**	75-**100**	100-**150**

	C5	C7	C8
2465 SUNOCO TANKER: 1946-48, "SUNOCO" logo decal **centered** or *offset*	5-**100**	8-**150**	12-**250**
2472 PENNSYLVANIA CABOOSE: 1946-47, numbered "477618" on sides, red, no illumination or window glazing.	15	25	35

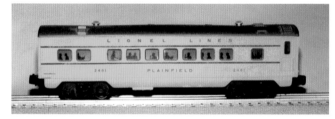

	C5	C7	C8
2481 PLAINFIELD PULLMAN: 1950, yellow, red markings, gray roof.	150	225	375
2482 WESTFIELD PULLMAN: 1950, matches 2481.	150	225	375
2483 LIVINGSTON OBSERVATION: 1950, matches 2481.	125	200	325

	C5	C7	C8
2521 OBSERVATION / PRESIDENT McKINLEY: 1962-66, extruded aluminum.	75	110	150

	C5	**C7**	**C8**

2522 VISTA DOME / PRESIDENT HARRISON: 1962-66, matches 2521. — 75 / 110 / 150

2523 PULLMAN / PRESIDENT GARFIELD: 1962-66, matches 2521. — 75 / 110 / 150

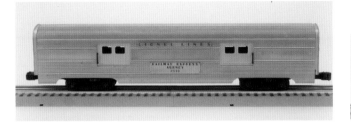

2530 LIONEL LINES / RAILWAY EXPRESS AGENCY: 1954-60, extruded aluminum baggage car with **large** or *small* doors. — 75-**250** / 125-**400** / 175-**550**

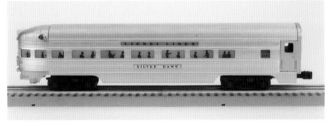

2531 LIONEL LINES / SILVER DAWN OBSERVATION: 1952-60, extruded aluminum. *With* or **without** fluted channels above and below the windows. — 60-**125** / 75-**160** / 100-**200**

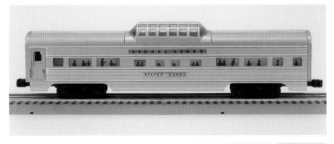

2532 LIONEL LINES / SILVER RANGE DOME: 1952-60, matches 2531. — 60-**125** / 100-**160** / 125-**200**

	C5	**C7**	**C8**

2533 LIONEL LINES / SILVER CLOUD PULLMAN: 1952-60, matches 2531. — 60-**125** / 100-**160** / 125-**200**

2534 LIONEL LINES / SILVER BLUFF PULLMAN: 1952-60, matches 2531. — 60-**125** / 110-**200** / 150-**275**

2541 PENNSYLVANIA / ALEXANDER HAMILTON OBSERVATION: 1955-56, extruded aluminum *Congressional.* — 125 / 200 / 275

2542 PENNSYLVANIA / BETSY ROSS DOME: 1955-56, matches 2541. — 125 / 200 / 275

2543 PENNSYLVANIA / WILLIAM PENN PULLMAN: 1955-56, matches 2541. — 125 / 200 / 275

2544 PENNSYLVANIA / MOLLY PITCHER PULLMAN: 1955-56, matches 2541. — 125 / 200 / 275

2550 BALTIMORE AND OHIO RDC-4: 1957-58. — 350 / 550 / 700

	C5	C7	C8
2551 CANADIAN PACIFIC / BANFF PARK OBSERVATION: 1957 extruded aluminum.	150	225	325
2552 CANADIAN PACIFIC / SKYLINE 500 DOME: 1957, matches 2551.	150	250	325
2553 CANADIAN PACIFIC / BLAIR MANOR PULLMAN: 1957, matches 2551.	225	350	500
2554 CANADIAN PACIFIC / CRAIG MANOR: PULLMAN: 1957, matches 2551.	225	350	500

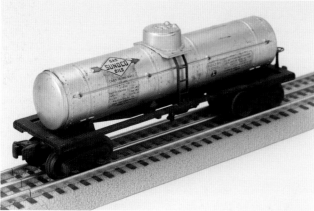

	C5	C7	C8
2555 SUNOCO TANKER: 1946-48, with or without "GAS" and "OILS" in SUNOCO logo, "2555" on **side** or bottom of the car.	25-**35**	40-**45**	55-**60**
2559 BALTIMORE AND OHIO RDC-9: 1957-58, non-powered.	200	300	400
2560 LIONEL LINES CRANE: 1946-47, similar to prewar 2660 crane, green, brown or black two-piece boom.	45	65	110
2561 SANTA FE / VISTA VALLEY PULLMAN: 1959-61, extruded aluminum.	175	225	325
2562 SANTA FE / REGAL PASS DOME: 1959-61, matches 2561.	200	250	375

	C5	C7	C8
2563 SANTA FE / INDIAN FALLS PULLMAN: 1959-61, matches 2561.	200	250	375

	C5	C7	C8
2625 IRVINGTON PULLMAN: 1946-50, *plain* or **silhouetted** windows (1950 only).	125-**150**	225-**275**	350-**400**
2625 MADISON PULLMAN: 1947, plain windows.	175	300	425
2625 MANHATTAN PULLMAN: 1947, plain windows.	175	300	425
2627 MADISON PULLMAN: 1948-50, *plain* or **silhouetted** windows (1950 only).	125-**150**	250-**300**	325-**400**

	C5	C7	C8
2628 MANHATTAN PULLMAN: 1948-50, *plain* or **silhouetted** windows (1950 only).	125-**150**	250-**300**	325-**400**
2755 SUNOCO TANKER: 1945 only, silver.	70	100	185
X2758 PENNSYLVANIA BOXCAR: 1945-46, brown 9-1/4-inch double-door automobile car.	25	50	75

	C5	C7	C8

	C5	C7	C8

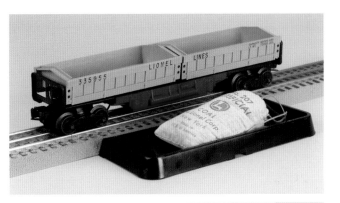

2855 SUNOCO TANKER: 1946-47, **black** or *gray*, with or without "GAS" and "OILS" in SUNOCO logo.

100- **145** | *175-* **225** | *225-* **350**

3309 TURBO MISSILE LAUNCHING CAR: 1962-64, *light* or **cherry** red, non-operating couplers.

20- **45** | 35-**70** | *55-* **100**

3330 FLATCAR WITH OPERATING SUBMARINE KIT: 1960-62, submarines lettered 3830, those lettered 3330 are forgeries.

100 | 150 | 200

3349 TURBO MISSILE FIRING CAR: 1962-65, unpainted red plastic, two operating couplers.

30 | 50 | 65

3349-100 TURBO MISSILE LAUNCHING CAR: 1963-64, *red* or **olive drab**, one operating coupler.

20- **200** | *35-* **350** | *55-* **500**

3356 SANTA FE HORSE CAR WITH CORRAL: 1956-60, 1964-66, bar-end *metal* or AAR-**plastic** trucks. Reduce value by 50 percent if corral is missing.

100- **125** | *150-* **175** | *180-* **250**

3357 HYDRAULIC PLATFORM MAINTENANCE CAR: 1962-64, with overhead "bridge," trip and police and hobo figures.

35 | 65 | 100

3359 LIONEL LINES DUMP CAR: 1955-58.

40 | 60 | 80

3360 BURRO CRANE: 1956-57, with actuator, yellow, **painted** or *unpainted*.

175- **425** | *275-* **650** | *400-* **850**

3361 LOG DUMP CAR: 1955-59, serif or sans-serif lettering, "336155" either to right or left of "LIONEL LINES."

30 | 42 | 55

3362 HELIUM TANK UNLOADING CAR: 1961-63, unpainted dark green plastic, white rubber-stamped "LIONEL LINES 3362", 3 "helium tanks" AAR trucks with operating couplers.

15 | 20 | 45

	C5	C7	C8

3362/3364 OPERATING UNLOADING CAR: 1969, unpainted dark green plastic, no markings, 2 "helium tanks," non-operating couplers.

| | 15 | 35 | 75 |

3364 OPERATING LOG UNLOADING CAR: 1965-66, 1968, Identical to the 3362, and rubber-stamped "3362", came 3-5/8 x 6-inch wooden dowels stained brown.

| | 15 | 30 | 70 |

3366 CIRCUS CAR: 1959-61 unpainted white body and doors, red-painted roofwalk. Reduce value 50 percent if matching corral and 9 white horses are missing.

| | 150 | 250 | 350 |

3370 WELLS FARGO SHERIFF AND OUTLAW: 1961-64. Action simulates gunfight.

| | 25 | 50 | 75 |

3376 BRONX ZOO: 1960-66, 1969, giraffe "ducks" to avoid obstacle. Includes telltale and operating plate assembly. *White* or **yellow** (1969) lettering on blue body.

| | 40-**175** | 65-**300** | 90-**450** |

3376-160 BRONX ZOO: Green body with yellow lettering.

| | 85 | 110 | 150 |

	C5	C7	C8

3386 BRONX ZOO: 1960 only, blue with white markings, arch-bar trucks and non-operating couplers.

| | 60 | 80 | 115 |

3409 OPERATING HELICOPTER LAUNCHING CAR: 1960-62, came with an operating single rotor helicopter with a gray body heat-stamped "NAVY".

| | 100 | 150 | 225 |

3410 HELICOPTER LAUNCHING CAR: 1961-63, and carried a *gray-bodied* single rotor helicopter with heat-stamped "NAVY" with separate pale yellow tail rotor or solid yellow helicopter with integral tail.

| | 65 | 100 | 150 |

3413 MERCURY CAPSULE LAUNCHING CAR: 1962-64, unpainted red plastic chassis with gray plastic superstructure. Came with parachute-equipped rocket.

| | 100 | 160 | 225 |

3413-150 MERCURY CAPSULE LAUNCHING CAR: 1963, equipped with one operating and one non-operating coupler.

| | 100 | 160 | 225 |

3376 BRONX ZOO

	C5	**C7**	**C8**

	C5	**C7**	**C8**

3419 OPERATING HELICOPTER LAUNCHING CAR: 1959-65, its body was made of blue plastic, which ranged from medium blue to a dark, almost purple shade. In 1959 the launch spindle was 2 inches in diameter, in subsequent years a 1-3/8-inch spindle was used. Black or plated operating mechanism, single or two blade gray "Navy" helicopter, or all-**yellow helicopter**.

60-80 | 90-120 | 150-180

3424 WABASH BOXCAR WITH BRAKEMAN: 1956-58, with two contactor/pole-support assemblies and two telltale poles. The brakeman figures came in two colors; blue and white, and the car bodies came molded in both medium and dark blue, but there is no difference in value associated with either variation.

50 | 75 | 125

3428 UNITED STATES MAIL OPERATING BOXCAR: 1959-60, red, white and blue boxcar. Rubber figure of a blue or gray mailman ejects rubber "bag" of mail.

50 | 85 | 125

3429 U.S.M.C. OPERATING HELICOPTER LAUNCHING CAR: 1960, painted olive drab and white heat-stamped "BUILT BY/ LIONEL U. S. M. C. 3429". Came with single rotor operating helicopter with a gray body heat-stamped "USMC" on the tail boom.

350 | 425 | 650

3434 OPERATING POULTRY DISPATCH: 1959-60, 1964-66, bar-end metal trucks early, AAR plastic trucks 64-66.

65-75 | 100-110 | 150-175

3435 TRAVELING AQUARIUM: 1959-62, gold circle around "L" logo and gold "TANK No. 1" and "TANK No. 2" markings; or gold markings without "TANK No. 1" and "TANK No. 2" or circle, or *yellow* markings.

125-650 | 200-1,100 | 275-1,650

3444 ERIE OPERATING GONDOLA: 1957-1959.

50 | 75 | 110

3451 OPERATING LUMBER CAR: 1946-48, **rubber-stamped** and *heat-stamped* lettering.

25-30 | 35-40 | 50-60

	C5	**C7**	**C8**

3454 AUTOMATIC MERCHANDISE BOXCAR: 1946-47, painted silver, *blue* or **red** lettering.

	C5	**C7**	**C8**
3454	80-**600**	110-**1,000**	160-**1,600**

3456 N & W HOPPER: 1950-55, operating doors.

3456	25	45	65

3459 LIONEL LINES DUMP CAR: 1946-48, **aluminum**, green or *black* colored dump bin.

3459	30-**150**	50-**225**	80-**375**

3460 FLATCAR WITH TRAILERS: 1955-1957, unpainted green plastic trailers with removable roofs, die-cast landing gear, and metal side signs reading "LIONEL TRAINS".

3460	40	70	100

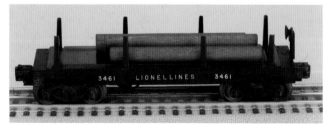

3461 OPERATING LUMBER CAR: 1949-55, *black* or **green** frame.

3461	25-**30**	35-**45**	50-**50**

3462 AUTOMATIC REFRIGERATED MILK CAR: 1947-48, **gloss cream**, matte cream or matte cream or *white* painted body. If platform and milk cans are absent, the values should be reduced by 50 percent.

3462	30-75	45-**125**	60-**200**

X3464 A.T. & S.F. BOXCAR: 1949-52, 9 1/4-inches long, *orange* or **tan** body.

X3464	12-**275**	20-**400**	30-**650**

X3464 NYC BOXCAR: 1949-52, 9 1/4-inches long, tan.

X3464	12	20	30

3469 LIONEL LINES: 1949-55, black.

3469	30	40	60

3470 AERIAL TARGET LAUNCHING CAR: 1962-64, dark blue flat car.

3470	50	75	100

3470-100 AERIAL TARGET LAUNCHING CAR: 1963, powder blue.

3470-100	200	325	450

	C5	**C7**	**C8**

3472 AUTOMATIC REFRIGERATED MILK CAR: 1949-53, painted cream or unpainted white with aluminum doors, or *unpainted white with plastic doors*. If platform and milk cans are absent, the values should be reduced by 50 percent. — 30, 45, 60

3474 WESTERN PACIFIC BOXCAR: 1952-53, silver 9-1/4-inches long. — 35, 55, 80

3482 AUTOMATIC REFRIGERATED MILK CAR: 1954-55, 9-1/4-inches long unpainted white milk car. Right of door stamped **RT3472** or *RT3482*. If platform and milk cans are absent, the values should be reduced by 50 percent. — 40-75, 60-100, 85-150

3484 PENNSYLVANIA OPERATING BOXCAR: 1953, 10 5/8-inches long. — 30, 50, 80

3484-25 A T & S F OPERATING BOXCAR: 1954, 1956 10-5/8-inches long. Orange body with **black** or *white* lettering. — 50-700, 80-900, 125-1,400

3494-1 PACEMAKER OPERATING BOXCAR: 1955, 10-5/8-inches long. — 75, 110, 165

3494-150 MISSOURI PACIFIC LINES OPERATING BOXCAR: 1956, 10 5/8-inches long. — 60, 100, 160

3494-275 STATE OF MAINE OPERATING BOXCAR: 1956-58, 10 5/8-inches long. With or **without** "3494275" stamped to the left of the door. — 60-100, 80-175, 125-250

3494-550 MONON OPERATING BOXCAR: 1957-58, 10 5/8-inches long. — 200, 325, 500

3494-625 SOO LINE OPERATING BOXCAR: 1957-58 10 5/8-inches long. — 200, 325, 525

3509 SATELLITE LAUNCHING CAR: 1961, unpainted dark green, gray and yellow. — 40, 65, 100

3510 SATELLITE LAUNCHING CAR: 1962, bright red, no number on car. — 100, 150, 225

3512 OPERATING FIREMAN AND LADDER CAR: 1959-61, *black* or **silver** extension ladder. — 75-100, 125-160, 180-225

3519 OPERATING SATELLITE LAUNCHING CAR: 1961-64, dark green unpainted plastic. — 35, 55, 80

3520 LIONEL LINES SEARCHLIGHT CAR: 1952-53, **serif** or *sans-serif* lettering. — 35-75, 55-125, 75-180

	C5	**C7**	**C8**

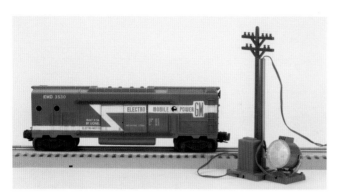

3530 ELECTRO MOBILE POWER GENERATOR CAR: 1956-58 through 1958, white stripe stops at ladder, or extends through the molded-in ladder on the right-hand end of the car. 60 100 150

3535 OPERATING SECURITY CAR WITH ROTATING SEARCHLIGHT: 1960-61. 75 115 175

3540 OPERATING RADAR CAR: 1959-62. 100 175 250

3545 OPERATING TV MONITOR CAR: 1961-62. 125 200 275

3559 COAL DUMP: 1946-48, black or brown Bakelite mechanism housing. 20 35 50

3562-1 A.T. & S. F. OPERATING BARREL CAR: 1954 *black* with black or yellow trough, or **gray with red lettering**. 110-800 175-1,200 250-1,700

3562-25 A.T. & S. F. OPERATING BARREL CAR: 1954 only. Gray painted body marked 356225 on car side, with **red** or *blue* heat-stamped markings 40-250 65-400 85-625

3562-50 A.T. & S. F. OPERATING BARREL CAR: 1955-56, marked 356250 on car side, yellow **painted** or *unpainted* body. 45-60 70-95 85-150

3562-75 A.T. & S. F. OPERATING BARREL CAR: Orange unpainted body marked 356275. 60 90 150

3619 HELICOPTER RECONNAISSANCE CAR: 1962-64, spring-loaded mechanism launches a red HO gauge helicopter through the roof of this boxcar. *Light* or **dark** yellow unpainted plastic. 60-100 100-175 150-250

3620 LIONEL LINES: 1954-56, *gray* or **orange** searchlight housing. 30-100 40-140 60-200

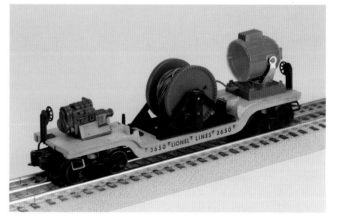

3650 LIONEL LINES: 1956-59 came with *light gray*, dark gray, or **olive gray** frame. 40-125 60-175 80-250

	C5	**C7**	**C8**

3656 LIONEL LINES OPERATING CATTLE

CAR: 1949-55. Reduce value 50 percent if matching corral and cattle are missing. Heat-stamped **black lettering**, adhesive "Armour" logo, heat-stamped white lettering, adhesive "Armour" logo, heat-stamped white lettering, *no "Armour"* logo.

	C5	**C7**	**C8**
	50-**150**	75-**225**	110-**300**

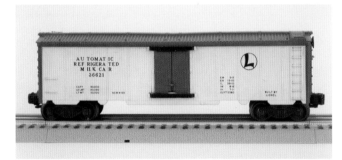

3662 AUTOMATIC REFRIGERATED MILK

CAR: 1955-60 and 1964-66. If platform and milk cans are absent, the values should be reduced by 50 percent. **Painted** or *unpainted* white.

	C5	**C7**	**C8**
	45-**50**	70-**75**	100-**115**

3665 MINUTEMAN: 1961-64, unpainted white body with red and white rocket with blue rubber nose cone **light** or *dark* (almost purple) blue roof.

	C5	**C7**	**C8**
	60-**150**	90-**200**	125-**325**

3666 MINUTEMAN: Unpainted white body housing large olive drab cannon with four wooden artillery shells.

	C5	**C7**	**C8**
	350	550	800

3672 CORN PRODUCTS CO.-BOSCO: 1959-60. If

platform and milk cans are absent, the values should be reduced by 50 percent.

	C5	**C7**	**C8**
	225	350	500

	C5	**C7**	**C8**

3820 U.S.M.C. OPERATING SUBMARINE CAR: 1960-

62, painted olive drab body carrying factory-assembled gray "U.S. NAVY 3830" submarine. Be aware that in addition to reproduction 3830 submarines, forgeries stamped "U.S.M.C. 3820" also exist.

	C5	**C7**	**C8**
	150	225	350

3830 SUBMARINE CAR:

1960-63, unpainted blue carrying submarine lettered "U.S. NAVY 3830".

	C5	**C7**	**C8**
	90	115	150

3854 AUTOMATIC MERCHANDISE CAR:

1946-47, with six plastic "crates" (actually cubes) engraved "BABY RUTH".

	C5	**C7**	**C8**
	375	600	850

3927 LIONEL LINES TRACK CLEANING

CAR: 1956-60.

	C5	**C7**	**C8**
	40	65	90

4357 LIONEL-SP CABOOSE: 1948-49,

Tuscan-painted plastic body.

	C5	**C7**	**C8**
	85	150	250

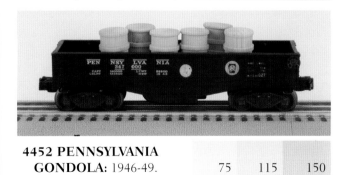

4452 PENNSYLVANIA GONDOLA: 1946-49.

	C5	**C7**	**C8**
	75	115	150

	C5	**C7**	**C8**

X4454 BABY RUTH BOXCAR: 1946-49.

	C5	C7	C8
X4454 BABY RUTH BOXCAR: 1946-49.	100	175	300
4457 PENNSYLVANIA CABOOSE: 1946-47, steel-bodied caboose painted red.	75	150	250

	C5	C7	C8
5459 LIONEL LINES DUMP CAR: 1946-49.	100	175	275
6002 NEW YORK CENTRAL GONDOLA: 1950 only. It was not supplied with a load.	12	20	30
X6004 BABY RUTH BOXCAR: 1950 only, unpainted orange.	5	7	10
6007 LIONEL LINES CABOOSE: 1950 only, unpainted red plastic.	5	10	15
6012 LIONEL GONDOLA: 1951-56, unpainted black plastic body.	5	8	15
6014 AIREX BOXCAR: 1959 only.	35	50	75
X6014 BABY RUTH BOXCAR: 1951-56, These cars had metal trucks. **Red** or *white* body.	4-7	8-**12**	*10*-**16**
6014 BOSCO BOXCAR: 1958 AAR-type trucks, unpainted red, **white** or orange body.	6-**30**	9-**50**	*12*-**75**
6014 CHUN KING BOXCAR: 1956.	100	150	250

	C5	C7	C8
6014 FRISCO BOXCAR: 1957, 1963-69, red, white or **orange** body.	4-**40**	6-**60**	10-**80**
6014 WIX FILTERS BOXCAR: 1959 only.	100	150	250

	C5	C7	C8
6015 SUNOCO TANKER: 1954-55, painted or unpainted yellow tank.	5-65	8-100	10-150
6017 LIONEL LINES CABOOSE: 1951-62, red body, tuscan, semi-gloss tuscan, gloss tuscan, maroon, tile red, *brown*.	2-75	4-125	6-200
6017 LIONEL CABOOSE: 1956 only, often mistaken for the common 6017 Lionel Lines.	35	60	90
6017-50 UNITED STATES MARINE CORPS CABOOSE: 1958 only, dark blue.	35	60	90
6017 LIONEL LINES CABOOSE: 1958 only, painted light gray.	15	30	45
6017 BOSTON AND MAINE CABOOSE: 1959, 1962 and 1965-66. Light, medium or **dark** blue.	20-**275**	35-**425**	60-**650**
6017 A.T.&S.F. CABOOSE: 1959-60, painted light gray	20	30	45
6017-200 UNITED STATES NAVY CABOOSE: 1960 only.	50	75	110
6017-235 A. T. & S. F. CABOOSE: 1962 only, painted red.	30	50	75
6024 RCA WHIRLPOOL BOXCAR: 1957 only.	35	60	80
6024 SHREDDED WHEAT BOXCAR: 1957 only.	12	20	30

	C5	**C7**	**C8**

	C5	**C7**	**C8**

6025 GULF TANK CAR:
1956-58, black, gray or
orange tank.

| | 5-16 | 10-**25** | 15-**40** |

**6027 ALASKA RAILROAD
CABOOSE:** 1949 only,
painted dark blue, heat-
stamped in yellow.

| | 40 | 65 | 95 |

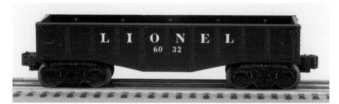

6032 LIONEL GONDOLA:
1952-54, unpainted black
plastic.

| | 5 | 8 | 15 |

**X6034 BABY RUTH
BOXCAR:** 1953-54,
unpainted orange.

| | 7 | 10 | 14 |

**6035 SUNOCO TANK
CAR:** 1952-53, unpainted
gray body.

| | 3 | 8 | 15 |

**6037 LIONEL LINES
CABOOSE:** 1952-54,
unpainted *Tuscan* or **red**
bodies.

| | 3-**25** | 5-**40** | 7-**65** |

6042 LIONEL GONDOLA:
1959-64 equipped with
archbar or AAR trucks,
with or without operating
couplers. Black or blue.

| | 5 | 8 | 12 |

6044 AIREX BOXCAR:
1959-61, *medium*, teal or
very dark (approaching
purple) blue

| | 10-175 | 18-275 | 25-400 |

**6044-1X McCALL'S-
NESTLE'S BOXCAR:**
Produced in the early 1960s,
unpainted blue body was
decorated by pasting a
miniature McCall's-Nestle's
billboard on each side.

| | 700 | 1,000 | 1,500 |

**6045 LIONEL LINES
TANK CAR:** 1959-64,
unpainted gray, beige or
orange tank.

| | 15-**20** | 30-**50** | 45-**75** |

**6045 CITIES SERVICE
TANK CAR:** 1960-61,
green.

| | 20 | 50 | 75 |

**6047 LIONEL LINES
CABOOSE:** 1959-62,
unpainted medium *red* or
coral-pink

| | 3-**20** | 5-**40** | *10*-**65** |

	C5	C7	C8
6050 LIBBY'S TOMATO JUICE BOXCAR: 1963, unpainted white body with red and blue lettering and a red, blue and green tomato juice logo.	20	35	60
6050 LIONEL SAVINGS BANK BOXCAR: 1961, "BUILT BY LIONEL" **spelled** out or *abbreviated* as "BLT".	*20-50*	30-**75**	45-**100**
6050 SWIFT BOXCAR: 1962-63, unpainted red with white heat-stamped lettering.	12	20	30
6057 LIONEL LINES CABOOSE: 1959-62, 1969, **painted** or *unpainted* red, or coral-pink body.	6-**35**	10-**60**	*15-90*
6057-50 LIONEL LINES CABOOSE: 1962, unpainted orange.	15	25	40

	C5	C7	C8
6059-50 M & St L: 1963-64, unpainted red body with white heat-stamped markings.	12	18	25
6062 NEW YORK CENTRAL GONDOLA: 1959-1962, 1969, Black, with or without metal underframe.	15-25	20-40	28-60
6067 CABOOSE: 1961-62, unlettered, red, yellow or brown plastic.	2-20	4-35	7-50
6076 A T S F HOPPER: unpainted gray, black heat-stamped lettering.	15	30	40
6076 LEHIGH VALLEY HOPPER: Black, red or gray unpainted, or painted pale yellow body.	10-400	14-800	18-1100
6110 2-4-2 STEAM: 1950 only, with a 6001T tender.	25	40	55

6058 CHESAPEAKE AND OHIO CABOOSE: 1961, painted dark yellow.

	C5	C7	C8
	20	35	60

6111/6121 FLATCAR: 1955-58, assorted colors.

	C5	C7	C8
	10	15	20

6059 M & St L CABOOSE: 1961-69, **painted** or *unpainted* red or unpainted maroon.

	C5	C7	C8
	4-15	8-**20**	*12-30*

6112 LIONEL GONDOLA: 1956-58, *Black*, blue or **white** body.

	C5	C7	C8
	5-**15**	8-**30**	*12-50*

| | C5 | C7 | C8 | | C5 | C7 | C8 |

6119 D.L. & W. WORK CABOOSE: 1955-56, unpainted red open tool compartment and unpainted red plastic cab.

| | 12 | 25 | 40 |

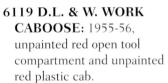
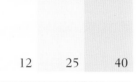

6119-25 D.L. & W. WORK CABOOSE: 1956 only, overall orange work caboose.

| | 20 | 35 | 55 |

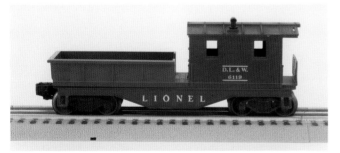

6119-50 D.L. & W. WORK CABOOSE: 1956 only, all-brown 6119.

| | 25 | 45 | 75 |

6119-75 D.L. & W. WORK CABOOSE: 1957 **serif** or *sans-serif* frame lettering.

| | 12-125 | 25-225 | 45-350 |

6119-100 D.L. & W.WORK CABOOSE: 1957-66 unpainted gray tool compartment and an *unpainted* or **painted** red cab.

| | 8-60 | 15-100 | 25-150 |

6119-125 RESCUE CABOOSE: 1964 only, cab and tool compartment unpainted olive drab plastic.

| | 100 | 175 | 250 |

6120 UNDECORATED CABOOSE: Unpainted yellow tool compartment and cab.

| | 20 | 30 | 40 |

6130 A. T. S. F. CABOOSE: 1961-65, 1969, red tool compartment and a red cab.

| | 16 | 25 | 40 |

6142 LIONEL GONDOLA: 1963-66, 1969, black, green, blue or **olive drab** body.

| | 5-75 | 8-110 | 12-165 |

6151 FLATCAR WITH RANGE PATROL TRUCK: 1958 only.

| | 65 | 110 | 160 |

	C5	C7	C8

6162 NEW YORK CENTRAL GONDOLA: 1959-68, blue, teal or **red** body.

	C5	C7	C8
	10-**85**	12-**125**	15-**200**

6162-60 ALASKA RAILROAD GONDOLA: 1959.

40	55	80

6167 LIONEL LINES CABOOSE: 1963-64. *Unpainted* or **painted** red.

4-**60**	7-**100**	10-**175**

6167 UNDECORATED CABOOSE: Unpainted olive drab.

200	375	550

6167-25 UNDECORATED CABOOSE: 1963-64. Red.

5	7	10

6167-50 UNDECORATED CABOOSE: Unpainted yellow body.

12	20	35

6167-85 UNION PACIFIC CABOOSE: 1963-66, 1969, unpainted yellow body black heat-stamped markings.

10	16	25

6167-100 LIONEL LINES CABOOSE: 1963-64, unpainted red body.

5	10	14

6167-125 UNDECORATED CABOOSE: 1963-64, unpainted red body.

5	7	10

	C5	C7	C8

6167-150 LIONEL LINES CABOOSE: 1963-64, unpainted red body.

5	10	14

6167-1967 T. T. 0. S. HOPPER: (Toy Train Operating Society): 1967, unpainted olive with metallic gold heat-stamped lettering.

50	65	100

6175 ROCKET FLATCAR: 1958-61, white plastic rocket load heat-stamped "BUILT BY / LIONEL" and "U S NAVY" in blue. Unpainted red or black plastic.

40	60	85

6176 LEHIGH VALLEY HOPPER: 1964-66, 1969, bright yellow, dark yellow, gray or black.

10	15	20

6219 C&O WORK CABOOSE: 1960, tool compartment and cab painted dark blue.

30	50	75

6220 A.T. & S.F. NW-2: 1949-50, black, die-cast frame. **With** or *without* "6220" stamped on the nose.

150-**200**	200-**325**	350-**500**

	C5	C7	C8

6250 SEABOARD NW-2:
1954-55 "SEABOARD"
lettering applied with decal,
rubber-stamped or *wide-spaced rubber-stamping*
(about 2 13/16 to 2 23/32
inches long).

175-
500
275-
675
375-
950

6257 LIONEL-SP CABOOSE: 1948-52
painted red, red-orange, tile
red or painted dark tile red,
as was **smokejack**.

2-**200** 5-**400** 8-**650**

6257X LIONEL-SP CABOOSE: 1948-only.

15 25 35

6257 LIONEL CABOOSE:
1953-55, red body, tile red,
or dark red.

5 8 10

6257-100 LIONEL LINES CABOOSE: 1963-64,
unpainted red body, with die-cast smokejack.

15 25 40

6262 WHEEL CAR:
1956-57, unpainted **red** or
unpainted *black* body.

50-
400
75-
1,000
100-
1,500

6264 LUMBER CAR: 1957-
58, unpainted red body came
with 12 timbers.

30 50 75

6311 FLATCAR WITH PIPES: 1955 only,
unpainted brown, with three
silver-gray plastic pipes.

20 40 65

	C5	C7	C8

6315 GULF TANK CAR:
1956-58, with flat burnt-orange, glossy burnt-orange,
true orange bands, bands
painted on the ends.

25-60
55-125
80-175

6315 LIONEL LINES TANK CAR: 1963-66, all
orange tank. **Painted** or
unpainted orange tank.

*10-***75**
*20-***125**
*40-***225**

6315 GULF: 1968-69,
unpainted orange tank.

20 35 75

6342 NYC CULVERT GONDOLA: 1956-58,
1966-69.

15 25 40

6343 BARREL RAMP CAR: 1961-62.

25 40 65

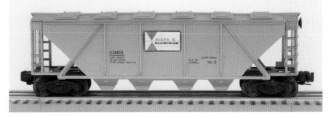

6346 ALCOA COVERED HOPPER: 1956, painted
silver, multi-colored ALCOA
marking was adhesive-backed paper label; heat-stamped *blue*, black or **red**
heat-stamped lettering.

30-
500
50-
800
75-
1,200

6352 PACIFIC FRUIT EXPRESS BOXCAR:
1955-57, unpainted orange
body with black heat-stamped lettering; **three** or
four lines of data rubber-stamped on ice compartment
door.

75-**90**
100-
150
150-
225

	C5	C7	C8

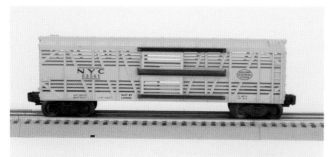

	C5	C7	C8

6356 NYC STOCK CAR: 1954-55, painted yellow; **rubber** or *heat*-stamped markings. — 25-**50** / 35-**75** / 50-**100**

6357 LIONEL-SP CABOOSE: 1948-53. — 15 / 22 / 35

6376 CIRCUS STOCK CAR: 1956-57, unpainted white plastic, with red trim and markings. — 60 / 100 / 150

6401 FLATCAR: 1965, unpainted gray body. — 2 / 5 / 10

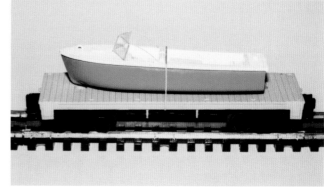

6357 LIONEL CABOOSE: 1953-61, Tuscan or maroon, with *black* or **maroon** die-cast smokejack. — 15-**275** / 22-**425** / 35-**600**

6357-50 A.T.&S.F. CABOOSE: 1960 only, painted red with white heat-stamped markings. — 600 / 1,000 / 1,600

6361 TIMBER TRANSPORT CAR: 1960-61, 1964-66, and 1968-69, unpainted *dark* or **light** green body. — 40-**75** / 70-**125** / 100-**175**

6362 RAILWAY TRUCK CAR: 1955-57, *shiny* or **pale** orange. — 30-**125** / 45-**175** / 70-**250**

6402 FLATCAR: 1962, 1964-66, 1969, gray or brown with two empty LIONEL *cable reels* or 6801-75 **boat** with blue hull. — 8-**50** / 13-**65** / 20-**95**

6404 FLAT CAR WITH AUTOMOBILE: Black plastic body heat-stamped "6404" and "BUILT BY LIONEL" in white. With **yellow, red,** *kelly green or brown* auto with gray bumpers. — 40-**150** / 60-**200** / 85-**260**

6405 FLATCAR WITH VAN: 1961, heat-stamped "6405" furnished with a yellow plastic van with single rear wheels. — 20 / 35 / 60

	C5	**C7**	**C8**

6406 FLATCAR WITH AUTO: 1961, gray or maroon plastic, unlettered flatcar carrying a single yellow automobile with gray bumpers. — 50, 75, 100

6407 FLATCAR WITH MISSILE: 1963, with a large missile with removable Mercury capsule produced by Sterling Plastics. The Sterling Plastics name ALWAYS was molded into the base of the capsules. — 300, 500, 700

6408 FLATCAR WITH PIPES: 1963, unpainted red plastic flatcar with five gray plastic pipes held on with a rubber band. — 15, 25, 35

6409-25 FLATCAR WITH PIPES: 1963, unpainted red plastic flatcar with three gray plastic pipes held on with a rubber band. — 15, 25, 35

6411 FLATCAR: 1948-50, medium-gray flat car with three 7-inch long wooden 3/8-inch dowels. — 20, 30, 40

6413 MERCURY CAPSULE CARRYING CAR: 1962-63; *unpainted blue*, painted blue or **unpainted blue-green** body. — *100-***300**, *150-***400**, *210-***600**

6414 EVANS AUTO LOADER: 1955-66, unpainted red body, black sheet metal superstructure. With four 4 5/16-inch long plastic automobiles. Metal trucks and one each red, white, yellow and green automobiles. — 75, 110, 165

AAR-type trucks with one each red, white, yellow and green automobiles. — 70, 100, 150

"6414" to the left of "LIONEL", four red autos with gray bumpers. — 100, 150, 200

"6414" to the left of "LIONEL", four yellow autos with gray bumpers. — 200, 300, 500

"6414" to the left of "LIONEL", four kelly green autos with gray bumpers. — 750, 1,000, 1,500

"6414" to the left of "LIONEL", four brown autos with gray bumpers. — 750, 1,000, 1,500

Decaled "6414 AUTO LOADER" legend, four light red automobiles with gray bumpers. — 200, 400, 650

6414-85 EVANS AUTO LOADER: 1964, two yellow and two red automobiles adaptations from Lionel's slot cars with molded-in tires. — 450, 600, 850

6415 SUNOCO TANK CAR: 1953-55, 1964-66 and 1969. — 10, 20, 35

	C5	C7	C8

6416 BOAT LOADER:
1961-63, with four boats with white-painted hulls, blue-painted cabin and brown-painted interior. — 125 / 175 / 250

6417 PENNSYLVANIA CABOOSE: 1953-57, *with* or **without** "NEW YORK ZONE". — *20-***200** / *30-***300** / *45-***425**

6417-25 LIONEL LINES CABOOSE: 1954 only. — 20 / 30 / 55

6417-50 LEHIGH VALLEY CABOOSE: 1954 only, painted *gray* or **Tuscan**. — *75-***600** / *125-***1,000** / *175-***1,500**

6418 MACHINERY CAR:
1955-57, 16-wheel car with two unnumbered black plastic girders with "LIONEL" in raised white letters. — 75 / 100 / 125

With two unnumbered orange plastic girders with "LIONEL" in raised white lettering. — 90 / 115 / 150

Orange girders with "LIONEL" in raised black lettering. — 75 / 100 / 125

Orange girders without the raised "LIONEL" having accent color. — 75 / 100 / 125

Unnumbered orange plastic girders painted light gray. — 90 / 115 / 150

Girders pinkish red-oxide primer color with raised "U.S. STEEL" lettering outlined in black. — 90 / 115 / 150

Girders black with raised "U.S. STEEL" lettering outlined in white. — 75 / 100 / 125

	C5	C7	C8

6419 D. L. & W. CABOOSE: 1948-50, 1952-55, gray work caboose with die-cast frame. — 25 / 35 / 50

6419-25 D. L. & W. CABOOSE: 1954-55, gray work caboose with die-cast frame and one coupler. — 25 / 35 / 50

6419-50 D. L. & W. CABOOSE: 1956-57, gray work caboose, short die-cast smokejack, bar-end trucks and two magnetic couplers. — 25 / 40 / 60

6419-75 D. L. & W. CABOOSE: 1956, gray work caboose identical to the 6419-50, but with one coupler. — 25 / 40 / 60

6419-100 N & W CABOOSE: 1957-58, gray work caboose. — 100 / 150 / 250

6420 D. L. & W. CABOOSE: 1948-50, dark gray work caboose with operating searchlight. — 60 / 100 / 150

6424 TWIN AUTO CAR:
1956-59, unpainted black plastic, with automobiles with chrome bumpers. — 30 / 50 / 75

	C5	C7	C8

6425 GULF TANK CAR: 1956-58, Triple dome. — 15 | 30 | 50

6427 LIONEL LINES CABOOSE: 1954-60, Tuscan numbered "64273". — 20 | 30 | 45

6427-60 VIRGINIAN CABOOSE: 1958, painted dark blue with yellow heat-stamped lettering. — 125 | 250 | 450

6427-500 PENNSYLVANIA CABOOSE: 1957-58, painted sky blue and was decorated with white heat-stamped lettering, including the number "576427". — 200 | 350 | 525

6428 UNITED STATES MAIL BOXCAR: 1960-61, 1965-66, red, white and blue. — 20 | 35 | 50

6429 D. L. & W. CABOOSE: 1963 only, gray work caboose. — 150 | 275 | 450

6430 COOPER-JARRETT VAN CAR: 1956-58, unpainted red flatcar with vans. — 45 | 70 | 100

6431 PIGGY-BACK CAR WITH TRAILER TRUCKS AND TRACTOR: 1966, packaged with two trailers and a road tractor. Car heat-stamped 6430, the 6431 number appearing exclusively on the end of the original box. — 175 | 250 | 375

6434 POULTRY DISPATCH STOCK CAR: 1958-59, painted red, illuminated. — 45 | 70 | 100

6436 LEHIGH VALLEY HOPPER: 1955-56, 1966, open-top hopper;
Black, marked "646361", without spreader bar. — 50 | 65 | 90
Black, marked "646361" with spreader bar. — 20 | 35 | 50
Maroon, marked "643625" without spreader bar. — 50 | 75 | 100
Maroon, marked "643625" with spreader bar. — 20 | 35 | 50

6436 LEHIGH VALLEY HOPPER (Type V): 1963-68, red, cataloged as 6436-110. Stamped **with** or *without* "NEW 3-55" on sides. — 20-35 | 30-50 | 50-85

6436 LEHIGH VALLEY HOPPER: 1957-58, lilac painted, with maroon heat-stamped lettering numbered "643657", part of "Girl's Set." — 150 | 250 | 375

6436-1969 T C A HOPPER (Train Collectors Association): 1969. — 75 | 90 | 125

6437 PENNSYLVANIA CABOOSE: 1961-68. — 17 | 25 | 40

	C5	C7	C8

6440 PULLMAN: 1948-49, brown sheet metal. — 25 — 40 — 70

6440 FLATCAR WITH PIGGY-BACK VANS: 1961-63, red flatcar with unpainted gray plastic trailers with only single rear wheels and no decoration. — 60 — 100 — 140

6441 OBSERVATION: 1948-49, brown sheet metal. — 25 — 35 — 60

6442 PULLMAN: 1949, brown sheet metal. — 30 — 60 — 90

6443 OBSERVATION: 1949, brown sheet metal. — 30 — 60 — 90

6445 FORT KNOX GOLD RESERVE: 1961-63. — 80 — 125 — 175

6446 N & W COVERED HOPPER: 1954-55, gray or black-painted body and cover, without spreader-brace holes, marked "546446". — 30 — 45 — 60

6446 (-25) N & W: 1955-57, 1963, gray or black-painted body and cover marked "644625". — 25 — 40 — 60

	C5	C7	C8

6446 LEHIGH VALLEY HOPPER (6446-60) 1963 body painted red, roof and hatches unpainted red. — 110 — 175 — 275

6447 PENNSYLVANIA CABOOSE: 1963 only. — 200 — 325 — 500

6448 TARGET RANGE BOXCAR: 1961-64, red roof and ends and white side panels, or white roof and ends and red side panels. — 18 — 25 — 40

6452 PENNSYLVANIA GONDOLA: 1948-49, numbered "6462" or "6452" on side and rubber-stamped "6452" on bottom of the frame. — 12 — 16 — 25

X6454 A.T.&S.F. BOXCAR: 1948, painted orange with black markings. — 25 — 40 — 60

X6454 BABY RUTH BOXCAR: 1948, painted light orange. — 125 — 250 — 375

X6454 ERIE BOXCAR: 1949-52, brown with white markings. — 30 — 45 — 70

X6454 N Y C BOXCAR: 1948 only, *tan,* brown or **orange** body. — 20-75 — **30-125** — **45-200**

	C5	**C7**	**C8**

X6454 PENNSYLVANIA BOXCAR: 1949-52, brown. — 30 | 45 | 70

X6454 SOUTHERN PACIFIC BOXCAR: 1949-52, brown. — 30 | 45 | 70

6456 LEHIGH VALLEY: 1948-55, painted black, maroon, gray, or glossy **red**. — 8-75 | 10-110 | 15-175

6457 LIONEL CABOOSE: 1949-52. — 15 | 25 | 35

6460 BUCYRUS ERIE CRANE: 1952-54; *black* or **red**. — 40 | 75 | 95

6461 TRANSFORMER CAR: 1949-50, gray die-cast flatcar with black transformer load. — 50 | 75 | 100

	C5	**C7**	**C8**

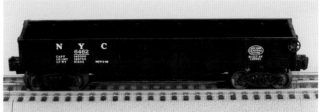

6462 NEW YORK CENTRAL GONDOLA: 1949-56, black, red or **green**. — 10-15 | 13-22 | 16-32

6462-500 NEW YORK CENTRAL GONDOLA: 1957-58, pink. — 150 | 200 | 300

6463 ROCKET FUEL TANK CAR: 1962-63, painted snow-white with bright red rubber-stamped lettering. — 15 | 25 | 60

6464-1 WESTERN PACIFIC BOXCAR: 1953-54, painted silver, blue or red heat-stamped markings. — 55-975 | 85-1,600 | 110-2,400

6464-25 GREAT NORTHERN BOXCAR: 1953-54, painted orange with white heat-stamped lettering. — 60 | 75 | 100

	C5	**C7**	**C8**

6464-50 MINNEAPOLIS & ST LOUIS: 1953-56, four full columns of rivets to the right of the door.

	50	70	100

6464-75 ROCK ISLAND: 1953-54, 1969, green-painted body.

	60	80	100

6464-100 WESTERN PACIFIC: 1954-55, silver (see 6464-250 for orange).

	100	130	190

6464-125 PACEMAKER BOXCAR: 1954-56, red and gray decorated with white.

	75	110	150

	C5	**C7**	**C8**

6464-150 MISSOURI PACIFIC BOXCAR: 1954-55, 1957, circular Missouri Pacific Lines herald stamped in the panel immediately to the **left of the door**, or in the *fourth panel* from the left end of the car.

	75-**850**	125-**1,250**	160-**1,900**

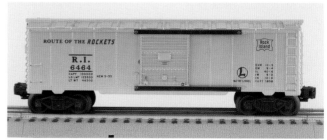

6464-175 ROCK ISLAND: 1954-55, painted silver; markings in *blue*, or **black**.

	75-**750**	110-**1,000**	175-**1,600**

6464-200 PENNSYLVANIA BOXCAR: 1954-55, 1969, Tuscan-painted doors and body.

	75	110	150

6464-225 SOUTHERN PACIFIC BOXCAR: 1954-56.

	75	110	150

	C5	C7	C8

6464-250 WESTERN PACIFIC BOXCAR: 1954, 1966, orange stamped **6464-100** or *6464-250*

	C5	C7	C8
	130-**600**	200-**850**	275-**1,200**

6464-275 STATE OF MAINE BOXCAR: 1955, 1957-59, solid **red door** or *striped door*.

	C5	C7	C8
	60-**100**	90-**165**	125-**250**

6464-300 RUTLAND BOXCAR: 1955-56, Rutland herald has a **solid dark green** or *yellow* background.

	C5	C7	C8
	75-**2,000**	125-**2,700**	175-**3,500**

	C5	C7	C8

6464-325 BALTIMORE & OHIO SENTINEL BOXCAR: 1956 only, painted silver and aqua.

	C5	C7	C8
	400	625	875

6464-350 M-K-T (Missouri-Kansas-Texas) BOXCAR: 1956 only.

	C5	C7	C8
	200	300	400

6464-375 CENTRAL OF GEORGIA BOXCAR: 1956-57, 1966.

	C5	C7	C8
	75	110	150

	C5	**C7**	**C8**

	C5	**C7**	**C8**

6464-400 BALTIMORE & OHIO BOXCAR: 1956-57, 1969, marked **"BLT 5-54 BY LIONEL"** on one side and **"BLT 2-56 BY LIONEL"** on the other or *matching built dates.*

C5	C7	C8
70-**500**	100-**850**	150-**1,200**

6464-425 NEW HAVEN BOXCAR: 1956-58.

C5	C7	C8
40	60	80

6464-450 GREAT NORTHERN BOXCAR: 1956-57, 1966.

C5	C7	C8
75	125	175

6464-475 BOSTON AND MAINE BOXCAR: 1957-60, 1965-68.

C5	C7	C8
35	50	65

6464-500 TIMKEN BOXCAR: 1957-59, 1969.

C5	C7	C8
75	125	175

6464-510 PACEMAKER BOXCAR: 1957-58, pastel blue.

C5	C7	C8
500	675	950

6464-515 M-K-T BOXCAR: 1957-58, pastel yellow.

C5	C7	C8
500	675	950

| | **C5** | **C7** | **C8** | | **C5** | **C7** | **C8** |

**6464-525 MINNEAPOLIS
& ST. LOUIS:** BOXCAR:
1957-58, 1964-66.   35   60   100

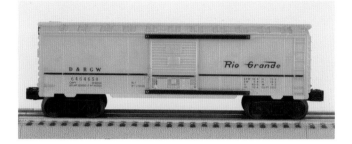

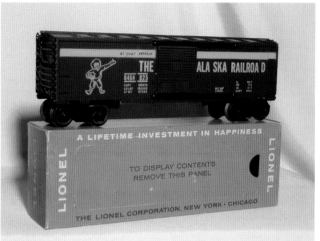

**6464-650 RIO GRANDE
BOXCAR:** 1957-58, 1966.   75   125   175

**6464-825 ALASKA
RAILROAD BOXCAR:**
1959-60, blue.   175   275   375

**6464-700 SANTA FE
BOXCAR:** 1961, 1966.   80   125   185

**6464-900 NEW YORK
CENTRAL BOXCAR:**
1960-66, jade green.   60   110   150

**6464-1965 TRAIN
COLLECTORS
ASSOCIATION
BOXCAR:** 1965,
uncataloged commemorative
for the 1965 TCA convention
in Pittsburgh, painted blue
body.   80   200   250

**6464-725 NEW HAVEN
BOXCAR:** 1962-66, 1968-
69, *orange* or **black** body.   *45-* **200**   *60-* **275**   *100-* **375**

	C5	C7	C8

6465 SUNOCO TANK CAR: 1948-56, two-dome painted silver, technical data ends with the word *"TANK"* or **"6465"**.

	C5	C7	C8
	5-10	*10-15*	*15-25*

6465 GULF/LIONEL LINES TANK CAR: 1958, *gray* or **black** tank.

	C5	C7	C8
	15-40	*18-55*	25-85

6465 LIONEL LINES TANK CAR: 1959, 1963-66, **black** or *orange* tank.

	C5	C7	C8
	4-15	8-40	12-55

	C5	C7	C8

6465 CITIES SERVICE TANK CAR: 1960-62, painted green.

	C5	C7	C8
	15	25	35

6467 MISCELLANEOUS FLATCAR: 1956 only, molded red plastic body white heat-stamped "LIONEL 6467". Unpainted black plastic bulkhead, four spring-steel 2411-4 posts, no load furnished.

	C5	C7	C8
	30	45	70

6468 BALTIMORE & OHIO BOXCAR: 1953-55, painted *blue*, or **Tuscan**.

	C5	C7	C8
	40- **250**	*65-* **350**	*100-* **475**

6468-25 NEW HAVEN BOXCAR: 1956-58, orange body, black doors; "N" of NH logo *black* or **white**.

	C5	C7	C8
	50- **150**	*75-* **225**	*110-* **325**

	C5	**C7**	**C8**

6469 LIQUIFIED GAS CAR: 1963 only, unpainted red plastic with orange tint, heat-stamped "Lionel" in white, black molded plastic bulkheads glued in place. The load was a cardboard tube wrapped in glossy white paper. On it, printed in black, was the car number "6469" and an Erie herald. Sheet-metal caps were painted white and crimped on each end of the tube.   **40** **90** **140**

6470 EXPLOSIVES BOXCAR: 1959-60.   **30** **50** **70**

6472 REFRIGERATOR: 1950-53.   **25** **35** **50**

6473 HORSE TRANSPORT CAR: 1962-66, 1969.   **25** **35** **50**

6475 PICKLES: 1960-62, vat car.   **25** **45** **65**

6475 LIBBY'S CRUSHED PINEAPPLE: 1963-64, vats covered in adhesive silver paper with Libby's logos.   **30** **40** **60**

6476 LEHIGH VALLEY HOPPER: 1957-69, red, gray or black body.   **10** **16** **22**

6476-1 TOY TRAIN OPERATING SOCIETY HOPPER: 1969 only, uncataloged.   **40** **65** **110**

6476 LEHIGH VALLEY: 1959-63, *red*, **coral pink**, or black body.   **8-15** *10-30* *15*-**50**

6476-135 LEHIGH VALLEY: 1964-66, 1968, listed in various catalogs was a yellow 6476 hopper. Be advised, however, that no yellow hopper cars were produced with the numbered "6476" stamped on them. Rather, the 6476 number denoted two operating couplers. The cars themselves used various black Lehigh Valley heat stamps, with various numbers and built and new dates.   SEE OTHER LISTINGS

6477 MISCELLANEOUS CAR WITH PIPES: 1957-58, red plastic body, black plastic bulkheads, four spring-steel 2411-4 posts, load of five silver-gray plastic pipes.   **30** **60** **80**

6480 EXPLOSIVES BOXCAR: 1961 only, red.   **30** **50** **70**

	C5	C7	C8

6482 REFRIGERATOR: 1957 only, white. — 40 — 55 — 85

6500 BEECHCRAFT BONANZA TRANSPORT CAR: 1962, unnumbered, unpainted black flatcar with red and white airplane. Four rivets bind each wing together. Red or **white** upper wings and fuselage. — 425-**550** — 550-**700** — 750-**950**

6501 FLATCAR WITH MOTORBOAT: 1962-63, boat propelled by pellets of baking soda. — 90 — 125 — 175

6502 STEEL GIRDER TRANSPORT CAR: 1962-63, with a single unpainted orange girder with "LIONEL" in raised lettering retained by a 6418-9 elastic band. Unpainted *black* or **red** plastic body. — 20-**50** — 35-**80** — 60-**125**

6502-50 STEEL GIRDER TRANSPORT CAR: Circa 1963, unlettered, unpainted blue plastic car with single unpainted orange "LIONEL" girder retained by a 6418-9 elastic band. — 25 — 40 — 60

6511 PIPE CAR: 1953-56, furnished with five standard silver-gray plastic pipes and a small envelope containing 13 2411-4 spring steel posts. — 20 — 45 — 65

6512 CHERRY PICKER CAR: 1962-63. — 75 — 100 — 150

6517 LIONEL LINES CABOOSE: 1955-59, **with** or *without* underscoring beneath "BLT 12-55" and "LIONEL". — 40-**45** — 60-**75** — 80-**100**

6517-75 ERIE CABOOSE: 1966 only, bay window caboose. — 250 — 400 — 525

6517/1966 TCA CABOOSE: 1966, uncataloged commemorative caboose. — 75 — 125 — 200

6518 TRANSFORMER CAR: 1956-58, upper transformer panel heat-stamped in white "6518", lower panel heat stamped "LIONEL TRANSFORMER CAR". — 75 — 115 — 155

6519 ALLIS-CHALMERS HEAT EXCHANGER CAR: 1958-61, molded medium, dark or milky orange plastic. — 55-100 — 85-140 — 125-200

6520 LIONEL LINES: 1949-51, simulated generator hid an off-on switch that could be actuated with a remote control uncoupling track. Beware of reproduction generators.

	C5	C7	C8
Tan generator.	425	700	1,000
Green generator.	225	350	475
Orange generator	35	50	75
Maroon generator.	50	75	100

6530 FIREFIGHTING INSTRUCTION CAR: 1960-62, unpainted red plastic body and unpainted white plastic opening doors. — 65 — 100 — 150

	C5	C7	C8

6536 M & St. L HOPPER: (Minneapolis & St. Louis): 1958-59, 1963, this large open-topped hopper. — 35 / 55 / 85

6544 MISSILE FIRING CAR: 1960-64, came with two small envelopes, each containing four 44-40 rockets. Control panel heat-stamped in *white* or **black**. — 100-**225** / 140-**375** / 225-**550**

6555 SUNOCO TANK CAR: 1949-50, tank painted silver. — 20 / 40 / 65

6556 M-K-T STOCK CAR: 1958 only, red. — 150 / 250 / 450

6557 LIONEL SMOKING CABOOSE: 1958-59. — 150 / 250 / 400

6560 BUCYRUS ERIE CRANE: 1955-64, 1966-69. **Gray** or *red* cab. — 30-**60** / 45-**80** / 60-**110**

656025 BUCYRUS ERIE: 1956, red cab, frame heat-stamped 656025. — 65 / 105 / 140

6561 CABLE REEL CAR: 1953-56, unpainted gray or orange reels wound with solid aluminum wire. — 45 / 65 / 90

6562 NEW YORK CENTRAL GONDOLA: 1956-58, gray, red or black gondola, usually included a load of four red canisters with "Lionel Air Activated Container" lettering. — 28 / 45 / 60

6572 RAILWAY EXPRESS AGENCY REFRIGERATOR: 1958-59, 1963, **dark** or *light* green. — 65-**80** / 95-**125** / 125-**175**

	C5	C7	C8

6630 MISSILE LAUNCHING CAR: 1961, unpainted black plastic body with pivoting blue plastic launcher base. — 75 / 110 / 165

6636 ALASKA RAILROAD HOPPER: 1959-60, black. — 35 / 55 / 85

6640 U.S.M.C. MISSILE LAUNCHING CAR: 1960, body painted olive drab and was heat-stamped "U.S.M.C. 6640" in white. Unpainted olive drab plastic launcher base with a black plastic launch rail. — 150 / 225 / 325

6646 LIONEL LINES STOCK CAR: 1957 only, orange. — 25 / 35 / 55

6650 MISSILE LAUNCHING CAR: 1959-63, unpainted red plastic body heat-stamped "6650 LIONEL". Pivoting unpainted blue plastic launcher base with a black plastic launch rail. — 35 / 50 / 75

6651 U.S. MARINE CORPS CANNON FIRING CAR: 1964-65. — 125 / 225 / 300

6656 LIONEL LINES STOCK CAR: 1950-53, yellow, **with** or *without* adhesive-backed "Armour" emblem applied to their doors. — 18-**50** / 25-**75** / 35-**100**

6657 RIO GRANDE CABOOSE: 1957-58, silver and yellow. — 75 / 125 / 200

6660 BOOM CAR: 1958, equipped with a pair of outriggers. — 50 / 75 / 115

	C5	C7	C8

6670 DERRICK CAR: 1959-60 No outriggers. — 40 · 60 · 90

6672 SANTA FE REFRIGERATOR: 1954-56, *two* or **three** lines of data to the right of the door. — *45-***150** · *75-***250** · *100-***425**

6736 DETROIT & MACKINAC HOPPER: 1960-62, red. — 25 · 45 · 65

6800 AIRPLANE CAR: 1957-60, unpainted red flatcar, undecorated yellow and black plastic aircraft with identifying markings molded into the underside of the fuselage. These markings read: "NO. 6800-60 AIRPLANE THE LIONEL CORPORATION NEW YORK, N.Y. MADE IN U.S. OF AMERICA". Either black upper surfaces and yellow propeller or yellow upper surfaces with black propeller. Only three rivets to bind the wing halves. — 150 · 200 · 300

6801 BOAT CAR: 1957-60, unpainted red flatcar with boat in unpainted gray plastic cradle. Metal or plastic trucks, white-hulled boat with brown deck that had no Lionel markings. — 70 · 100 · 150

6801-50 BOAT CAR: AAR-type trucks, yellow boat hull marked "NO. 6801-60 BOAT MADE IN U.S. OF AMERICA" and "THE LIONEL CORPORATION NEW YORK, N.Y." — 70 · 100 · 150

6801-75 BOAT CAR: AAR-type trucks, blue boat hull marked "NO. 6801-60 BOAT MADE IN U.S. OF AMERICA" and "THE LIONEL CORPORATION NEW YORK, N.Y." — 70 · 100 · 150

6802 FLATCAR WITH GIRDERS: 1958-59, red flatcar with two black "U.S. STEEL" girders. Car stamped "6802 LIONEL". — 20 · 25 · 35

6803 FLATCAR WITH MILITARY UNITS: 1958-59, with USMC tank and a truck with swiveling loudspeakers. — 125 · 200 · 300

6804 FLATCAR WITH MILITARY UNITS: 1958-59, with USMC antiaircraft and loudspeaker trucks. — 125 · 200 · 300

6805 RADIOACTIVE WASTE CAR: 1958-59, with two illuminated radioactive waste containers painted gray. — 75 · 125 · 175

6806 FLATCAR WITH MILITARY UNITS: 1958-59, with USMC medical and radar trucks. — 100 · 175 · 275

6807 FLATCAR WITH DUCK: 1958-59, with amphibious 2-1/2 ton 6x6 truck. — 75 · 100 · 150

6808 FLATCAR WITH MILITARY LOAD: 1958-59, with searchlight truck and M19 Gun Motor Carriage. — 200 · 275 · 400

6809 FLATCAR WITH MILITARY UNITS: 1958-59, with medical van and antiaircraft trucks. — 125 · 200 · 300

6810 FLATCAR WITH COOPER-JARRETT VAN: 1958, with one white Cooper-Jarrett trailer. — 35 · 50 · 70

	C5	C7	C8

6812 TRACK MAINTENANCE CAR: 1959-61, body unpainted red plastic heat-stamped "6812" to the left of "LIONEL" in white serif letters.

| | 50 | 80 | 125 |

6814 RESCUE UNIT: 1959-61, gray frame with white tool compartment insert, two molded plastic stretchers, oxygen tank and a blue rubber figure.

| | 50 | 100 | 165 |

6816 FLATCAR WITH ALLIS-CHALMERS CRAWLER TRACTOR: 1959-60, red or **black** flatcar, if dozer has black hood lettering, increase values shown $150-300.

| | 300-**1,000** | 475-**1,650** | 650-**2,700** |

6817 FLATCAR WITH ALLIS-CHALMERS SCRAPER: 1959-60, red or **black** flatcar. If scraper has black hood lettering, increase values shown $150-300.

| | 350-**1,250** | 450-**2,300** | 600-**3,600** |

6818 FLATCAR WITH TRANSFORMER: 1958, red car with black transformer heat-stamped "6818" on the upper panel.

| | 35 | 50 | 70 |

6819 FLATCAR WITH HELICOPTER: 1959-61, with non-operating helicopter with opaque yellow tail rotor, and gray fuselage unmarked or heat-stamped "NAVY".

| | 50 | 75 | 110 |

6820 AERIAL MISSILE TRANSPORT CAR: 1960-61, helicopter equipped with two huge, non-firing missiles.

| | 150 | 250 | 400 |

	C5	C7	C8

6821 FLATCAR WITH CRATES: 1959-60, cargo was modification of the crate load created for the 3444 animated gondola.

| | 20 | 30 | 40 |

6822 NIGHT CREW SEARCHLIGHT: 1961-69, black or gray superstructure.

| | 5 | 40 | 60 |

6823 FLATCAR WITH I.R.B.M. MISSILES: 1959-60, carried two matching 6650-type missiles in 6801-64 boat cradles.

| | 40 | 60 | 80 |

6824 U.S.M.C. CABOOSE: 1960, cab, tool compartment, tool compartment insert and frame all painted olive drab. All markings in white. With blue rubber figure with painted hands and face, a white plastic air tank and two white plastic stretchers.

| | 125 | 200 | 300 |

6824-50 FIRST AID CABOOSE: 1964, black frame, no crewman, tool compartment insert, stretchers or oxygen tank.

| | 50 | 100 | 150 |

6825 FLATCAR WITH ARCH TRESTLE BRIDGE: 1959-62, with black HO-sized bridge.

| | 30 | 50 | 75 |

	C5	**C7**	**C8**

6826 FLATCAR WITH CHRISTMAS TREES: 1959-60, four spring-steel 2411-4 posts keep the foliage load in place.

| | 100 | 150 | 215 |

6827 P & H POWER SHOVEL CAR: 1960-63, black flatcar was heat-stamped "6827" to the left of "LIONEL" in white. Its cargo was a well-detailed and elaborate kit of a P & H power shovel, which was packaged, along with the booklet "P & H: The Story of a Trademark" in a special yellow and black P & H box.

| | 125 | 175 | 250 |

6828 P & H MOBILE CONSTRUCTION CRANE CAR: 1960-63, 1966. Load was a kit of a crane produced by the Harnischfeger Corporation.. This kit, in its own yellow and black P & H box, was packaged along with the flatcar inside a Lionel box. Flatcar was unpainted *black* and **red** plastic.

| | *150-*
500 | *225-*
650 | *300-*
1,000 |

	C5	**C7**	**C8**

6830 SUBMARINE CAR: 1960-61, with a non-operating Lionel submarine was produced. With 6830 black heat-stamped number on sub.

| | 100 | 140 | 200 |

6844 MISSILE CARRYING CAR: 1959-60, rack held six white 44-40 missiles.

Unpainted *black* or **red** plastic frames.

| | *45-*
600 | *70-*
750 | *110-*
1,200 |

UNNUMBERED FLATCAR: Gray unpainted 1877-style flatcar with no markings, no truss rods, and AAR-type trucks. Carried either a moss-green tank, or moss-green Jeep and cannon, made by Payton Plastics.

There is not sufficient information to determine market value, however, an authentic load is key to its scarcity.

UNMARKED HOPPER: 1963-69, short hopper, yellow, red, black, *gray*, or **olive**.

| | *15*-**50** | *18*-**75** | *25-*
110 |

LIONEL POSTWAR ACCESSORIES, TRACK AND TRANSFORMERS

One of the key elements in Lionel's success, both prewar and postwar, was its numerous operating accessories. Joshua Cowen felt it was important to provide a means for children and adults to interact with the trains, as well as providing a semi-realistic setting to operate them in.

Initially the postwar accessories were carryovers of their prewar counterparts. The 45 Gateman, 115 Station, 313 Bascule Bridge, 97 and 164 coal and lumber loaders were all introduced before World War II. Soon, however, new designs poured from the Lionel shops. The 132 station, 397 coal loader and 364 lumber loader, all less expensive to produce than their prewar designed counterparts, pushed the earlier models from the catalog.

More than any other component, the development of the vibrator motor allowed Lionel to create a bewildering array of animated yet inexpensive accessories including operating forklift platforms, animated news stands, culvert loaders and unloaders.

Not all accessories provided action. Bridges crossed gorges, street lamps illuminated the miniature villages of Lionelville and Plasticville, the latter dotted with buildings sold by Lionel, but made by Bachmann.

Today Lionel's accessories retain their appeal to operators and collectors alike. Children, young or old, still delight in watching day to day tasks being performed in miniature by these accessories.

Despite their appeal, compared to trains and starter sets in particular, all accessories are relatively scarce. Even the most common of accessories, like the 145 gateman, is more difficult to locate than a common train car, such as the 6462 gondola.

Also cataloged as accessories by Lionel were various easily lost loads and a few fragile repair parts. Virtually every part of every item was available through Authorized Lionel Service Stations, but the parts cataloged as accessories were available to any Lionel retail outlet. Whereas repair parts typically came in blue and manila envelopes that were hand-labeled as to contents, the "accessory" parts came in conventional retail packaging. It is this retail packaging that warrants the values listed for such items, the items themselves as a rule are easily located. Representative examples of these accessory items are included in the following listings as well. During the 1960s, certain small- to medium-sized accessory items were packaged on blister cards for retail sales. Today, these items in unopened condition are highly sought after collectibles, and bring a substantial premium over the prices listed here. For more information about these, as well as more detailed information about the many variations of accessories, consult *The Standard Catalog of Lionel Trains, 1945-1969.*

	C5	C7	C8
011-11 INSULATING PINS: 1946-60, one dozen insulating pins for 0 gauge track. The collector value of this item is in the packaging.	1	2	3
011-43 INSULATING PINS: 1961, one dozen 0 gauge insulating pins.	1	2	3
020 90 DEGREE CROSSOVER: 1915-61, excluding 1943-45, 0 gauge.	5	7	10
020X 45 DEGREE CROSSING: 1915-59, excluding 1943-45.	6	9	14
022 REMOTE CONTROL SWITCHES: 1945-66 pair of 0 gauge turnouts.	60	75	90
022LH REMOTE CONTROL SWITCH: 1950-61, left-hand 0 gauge turnout with controller.	35	45	55
022RH REMOTE CONTROL SWITCH: 1950-61, right-hand 0 gauge turnout with controller.	35	45	55
022A REMOTE CONTROL SWITCH: 1947, unusual version of a pair of 0 gauge switches built in 1947. Due to materials shortages, these switches were built without fixed voltage capabilities or bottom plates.	100	150	275
022-500 0 GAUGE ADAPTER SET: 1957-61, allowed the use of 0 gauge switches with Super 0 track. Much of the value is in the packaging.	2	3	4

	C5	C7	C8
025 BUMPER: 1946-47, illuminated black-painted die-cast bumper attached to a piece of 0 Gauge track.	15	20	30
26 BUMPER: 1948, **gray**, 1949-50, red.	10-**30**	15-**40**	25-**50**

	C5	C7	C8
30 WATER TOWER: 1947-50, it had a dark gray die-cast base and a solenoid-lowered plastic spout.	80	125	200
31 CURVED TRACK: 1957-66, Super 0.	1	2	4

	C5	C7	C8

31-15 GROUND RAIL PIN: 1957-66, one dozen pins for outer rails of Super 0 track. — 1 / 2 / 3

31-45 POWER BLADE CONNECTOR: 1961-64, envelope contains 12 copper connectors. — 1 / 2 / 3

32 STRAIGHT TRACK: 1957-66, Super 0. — 2 / 4 / 6

32-10 INSULATING PIN: 1957-60, one dozen insulating pins for use in the outer rails of Super 0 track. — 1 / 2 / 3

32-20 POWER BLADE INSULATOR: 1957-60, this package contained one dozen insulating connectors for use on the center power blade of Super 0 track. — 1 / 2 / 3

32-45 POWER BLADE INSULATOR: 1961-66, this package contained one dozen insulating connectors for use on the center power blade of Super 0 track. — 1 / 2 / 3

32-55 INSULATING PIN: 1961-66, one dozen insulating pins for use in the outer rails of Super 0 track. — 1 / 2 / 3

33 HALF CURVED TRACK: 1957-66, half section of Super 0 curved track. — 1 / 2 / 3

34 HALF STRAIGHT TRACK: 1957-66, half section of Super 0 straight track. — 1 / 2 / 3

	C5	C7	C8

35 BOULEVARD LAMP: 1945-49. — 20 / 35 / 55

36 OPERATING CAR REMOTE CONTROL SET: 1957-66, track set includes two control blades, a 90 controller and the needed hook up wire. This allowed operating cars powered through sliding shoes to be operated on Super 0 track. — 8 / 12 / 18

37 UNCOUPLING TRACK SET: 1957-66, 1 1/2-inch long Super 0 track section containing an electromagnet. Packaged with a 90 controller and hook up wire. — 10 / 15 / 20

	C5	**C7**	**C8**

38 WATER TOWER: 1946-47, with internal pump. Supplied with a turned metal finial to plug the roof top fill hole, a small funnel and a packet of tablets to use to color the water. Black supporting structure and either brown or dark gray-painted roof or brown supporting structure, and red roof.

250-275	325-375	450-500

38 ACCESSORY ADAPTER TRACKS: 1957-61, pair of special Super 0 tracks with only four crossties was need to allow the attachment of track trips or installation on accessory bases.

8	12	15

40 HOOK UP WIRE: 1950-51, 1953-63, orange or gray reels, wrapped with 50 feet of 18-gauge single conductor wire insulated in either yellow, maroon, blue or white plastic. The earlier production was wrapped in Lionel imprinted cellophane.

5	20	40

40-25 CABLE REEL: 1955-57, orange reel holding 15 inches of the same black four-conductor wire as used on Lionel remote control track sections. It came packaged in a preprinted manila envelope, and it is that envelope that actually has the values listed here.

75	150	300

	C5	**C7**	**C8**

40-50 CABLE REEL: 1960-61, this orange reel holding 15 inches of the same black three-conductor wire as used on Lionel switch controls. It came packaged in a preprinted manila envelope, and it is that envelope that actually has the values listed here.

75	150	300

042 MANUAL SWITCHES: 1946-59, pair manually operated 0 gauge turnouts.

40	50	60

43 POWER TRACK: 1959-66, special Super 0 1 1/2-inch track section with built-in fahnstock clips.

5	7	10

44-80 MISSILES: 1959-60, set of four replacement missiles.

10	20	30

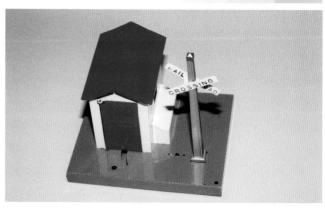

45 GATEMAN: 1946-49.

40	50	60

	C5	C7	C8
45N GATEMAN: 1945.	50	65	80
48 INSULATED STRAIGHT TRACK: 1957-66, Super 0.	5	7	10
49 INSULATED CURVED TRACK: 1957-66, Super 0.	5	7	10
56 LAMP POST: 1946-49.	30	45	60
58 LAMP POST: 1946-50, ivory-colored.	35	50	65
61 GROUND LOCK ON: 1957-66, Super 0.	1	2	3
62 POWER LOCK ON: 1957-66, Super 0.	1	2	3

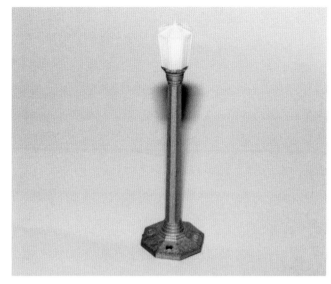

	C5	C7	C8
71 LAMP POST: 1949-59.	15	20	30
75 GOOSE NECK LAMPS: 1961-63, pair of 6 1/2-inch tall black plastic lamps.	15	25	40

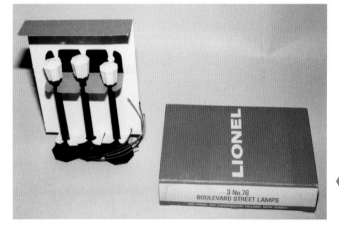

	C5	C7	C8
76 BOULEVARD STREET LAMPS: 1956-69, green plastic.	15	25	40
88 CONTROLLER: 1946-50.	1	2	10
89 FLAGPOLE: 1956-58, stitched-edged flag.	30	50	75
No stitched edge.	25	40	60
90 CONTROLLER: 1955-66, with shiny metal clip retaining a piece of cardstock.	3	8	14
No metal clip.	1	2	10

	C5	C7	C8
64 HIGHWAY LAMP POST: 1945-49.	45	60	75
70 LAMP POST: 1949-50, has a die-cast tilting head.	25	40	60

	C5	C7	C8
"No. 90 CONTROL" molded into the case.	1	2	10
91 CIRCUIT BREAKER: 1957-60.	20	25	30
92 CIRCUIT BREAKER CONTROLLER: Packaged in a manila envelope.	5	10	15
Packed in a traditional box.	5	10	15
Carded blister pack.	-	90	150

	C5	C7	C8
97 COAL ELEVATOR:	100	175	225
108 TRESTLE SET: 1959, packaged in overstamped 1044 transformer box. Only 12 trestle piers provided (two each lettered A-F).	30	45	85

109 TRESTLE SET: 1961, set of 12 piers.

No value established.

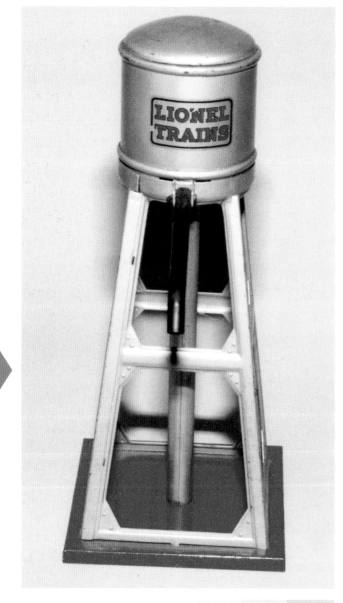

	C5	C7	C8
110 TRESTLE SET: 1955-69.	18	22	35

	C5	C7	C8
93 WATER TOWER: 1946-49, painted silver.	25	40	65
96C CONTROLLER: 1945-54.	1	2	5
111 TRESTLE SET: 1956-69, set of 10 "A" piers.	15	25	35

	C5	**C7**	**C8**
112 SUPER 0 SWITCHES: 1957 only, pair.	55	90	100
112R SUPER 0 SWITCHES: 1958-66, pair.	65	100	125
112-125 SUPER 0 SWITCH: 1957-61, left-hand remote control with 022C controller.	40	60	80
112-150 SUPER 0 SWITCH: 1957-61, right-hand remote control with 022C controller.	40	60	80
112LH SUPER 0 SWITCH: 1962-66, left hand remote control turnout with a 022C controller.	40	60	80
112RH SUPER 0 SWITCH: 1962-66, right hand remote control turnout with a 022C controller.	40	60	80

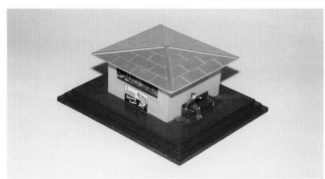

	C5	**C7**	**C8**
114 NEWS STAND WITH HORN: 1957-59.	75	115	150

	C5	**C7**	**C8**
115 LIONEL CITY STATION: 1946-49.	250	350	500

	C5	**C7**	**C8**
118 NEWSSTAND WITH WHISTLE: 1957-58.	60	100	125
119 LANDSCAPED TUNNEL: 1957-58, 14 inches long, 10 inches wide, 8 inches high vacu-formed plastic tunnel.	Too infrequently offered in Lionel packaging to establish value.		
120 90 DEGREE CROSSING: 1957-66, 90 degree Super 0 crossing.	5	10	15
121 LANDSCAPED TUNNEL: 1959-66, styrofoam tunnel. The Lionel packaging is essential to its value as a Lionel collectable.	Too infrequently offered in Lionel packaging to establish value.		

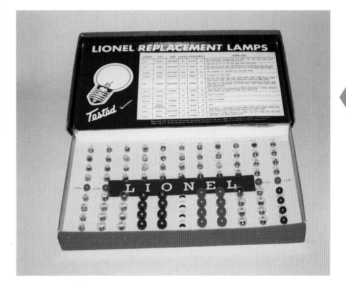

	C5	**C7**	**C8**
123 LAMP ASSORTMENT: 1953-59.	150	250	400

	C5	C7	C8

123-60 LAMP ASSORTMENT: 1960-63.

	C5	C7	C8
	200	300	500

125 WHISTLE SHACK: 1950-55.

	C5	C7	C8
	25	45	60

128 ANIMATED NEWSSTAND: 1957-60.

	C5	C7	C8
	125	175	225

130 60 DEGREE CROSSING: 1957-66, Super 0 60 degree crossing.

	C5	C7	C8
	10	14	18

	C5	C7	C8

131 CURVED TUNNEL: 1957-66, styrofoam tunnel. Lionel packaging is essential to its value as a Lionel collectible.

Too infrequently offered in Lionel packaging to establish value.

132 ILLUMINATED STATION WITH AUTOMATIC TRAIN CONTROL: 1949-55, brick red chimney.

	C5	C7	C8
	75	110	150

133 ILLUMINATED PASSENGER STATION: 1957, 1961-62, 1966, green chimney.

	C5	C7	C8
	50	75	100

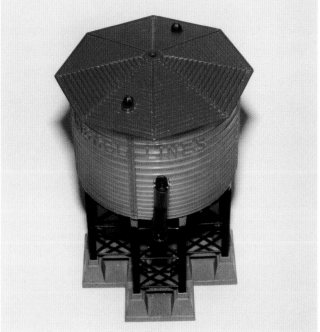

138 WATER TANK: 1953-57, unpainted gray plastic roof.

	C5	C7	C8
	100	150	175

	C5	C7	C8

140 AUTOMATIC BANJO SIGNAL: 1954-66, packed in a box.

	C5	C7	C8
140 AUTOMATIC BANJO SIGNAL: 1954-66, packed in a box.	30	40	55
142 MANUAL SWITCHES: 1957-66, pair Super 0 manual turnouts.	30	40	55
142-125 SUPER 0 SWITCH: 1957-61, single left-hand Super 0 manual.	20	30	40
142-150 SUPER 0 SWITCH: 1957-61, single right-hand Super 0 manual.	20	30	40
142LH SUPER 0 SWITCH: 1962, separate sale left hand Super 0 manual turnout.	20	30	40
142RH SUPER 0 SWITCH: 1962, separate sale right hand Super 0 manual turnout.	20	30	40

145 AUTOMATIC GATEMAN: 1950-66.

	C5	C7	C8
145 AUTOMATIC GATEMAN: 1950-66.	30	40	55

	C5	C7	C8
145C CONTACTOR: 1950-60, SPST pressure-activated normally open momentary contact switch. Collectible value is in the box.	1	2	10
147 WHISTLE CONTROLLER: 1961-66, contained a D cell battery.	2	4	10
148 DWARF SIGNAL: 1957-60, furnished with 148C switch.	50	65	100

150 TELEGRAPH POLE SET: 1947-50, set of six brown plastic poles with metal base clips.

	C5	C7	C8
150 TELEGRAPH POLE SET: 1947-50, set of six brown plastic poles with metal base clips.	40	60	75

151 SEMAPHORE: 1947-69.

	C5	C7	C8
151 SEMAPHORE: 1947-69.	20	28	40

	C5	**C7**	**C8**

	C5	**C7**	**C8**

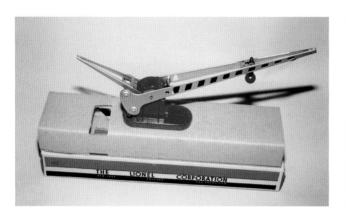

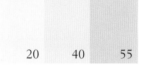

152 AUTOMATIC CROSSING GATE: 1945-49, main and pedestrian gates painted silver.

	C5	C7	C8
	20	40	55

154 AUTOMATIC HIGHWAY SIGNAL: 1956-69.

	C5	C7	C8
	30	40	50

153 AUTOMATIC BLOCK SIGNAL AND CONTROL: 1945-59.

	C5	C7	C8
	30	40	50

153C CONTACTOR: single pole, double throw pressure-activated momentary contact switch. Collectible value is in box.

	C5	C7	C8
	1	2	10

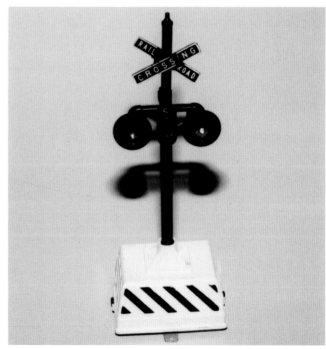

155 BELL RINGING SIGNAL: 1955-57, no "feet."

	C5	C7	C8
	45	60	75

	C5	**C7**	**C8**

156 ILLUMINATED STATION PLATFORM:

1946-51, two sections of black plastic picket fence between roof supports, and provided with a separate fence section to connect two or more platforms together. Four lithographed tin miniature billboards hung from the fences.

	C5	**C7**	**C8**
156 Illuminated Station Platform	60	85	125

157 ILLUMINATED STATION PLATFORM:

1952-59, four lithographed tin miniature billboards hung from fences.

	C5	**C7**	**C8**
157 Illuminated Station Platform	30	45	60
161 MAIL PICKUP SET: 1961-1963.	65	100	140
163 SINGLE TARGET BLOCK SIGNAL: 1961-69, packaged in box.	30	40	55

	C5	**C7**	**C8**

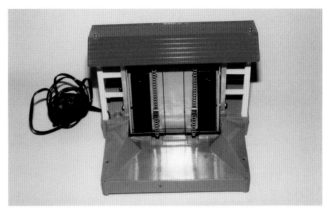

164 LOG LOADER:

1946-50, power terminals protruded through the top of the base, adjacent to the loading bin.

	C5	**C7**	**C8**
164 Log Loader	150	225	350
167 WHISTLE CONTROLLER: 1946-57.	4	8	15

175 ROCKET LAUNCHER:

1958-60.

	C5	**C7**	**C8**
175 Rocket Launcher	125	250	400

175-50 EXTRA ROCKET:

1959-60. Replacement rockets for the 175 launcher and 6175 flatcar. Prices shown are for original six-pack box.

	C5	**C7**	**C8**
175-50 Extra Rocket	150	225	400

	C5	C7	C8

182 TRIPLE ACTION MAGNET CRANE: 1946-49, a nicely detailed electro-magnet, which lifted the 182-22 scrap steel supplied with the crane, was marked "Cutler Hammer". Note: The cab of the 182 ALWAYS had a smokestack, and the smokestack was NEVER molded as part of the cab.

| | 150 | 250 | 325 |

192 OPERATING CONTROL TOWER: 1959-60.

| | 150 | 200 | 275 |

193 INDUSTRIAL WATER TOWER: 1953-55, with flashing red warning light.

| | 85 | 115 | 160 |

195 FLOODLIGHT TOWER: 1957-69.

| | 45 | 60 | 75 |

	C5	C7	C8

195-75 EIGHT BULB FLOODLIGHT EXTENSION: 1957-60, this was a standard eight-bulb array from a 195 floodlight tower, plus two extension posts. This could be used to increase the light output from a 195.

| | 20 | 35 | 60 |

196 SMOKE PELLETS: 1946-47, contained 100 smoke pellets made of ammonium nitrate for use in bulb-type smoke units only.

| | 40 | 75 | 125 |

197 ROTATING RADAR ANTENNA: 1957-59, **orange** or gray platform structure.

| | 80-**100** | 100-**125** | 150-**190** |

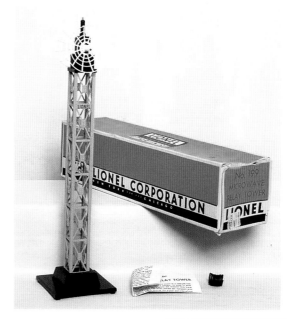

199 MICROWAVE RELAY TOWER: 1958-59.

| | 40 | 75 | 120 |

	C5	C7	C8		C5	C7	C8

206 ARTIFICIAL COAL:
1946-59, half-pound cloth
bags lettered with red "No.
206" "ARTIFICIAL COAL"
and Lionel markings filled
with ground Bakelite "coal."

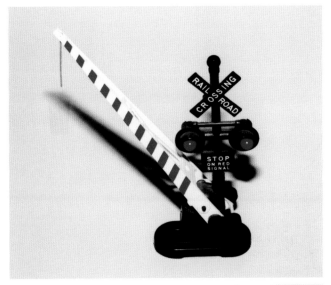

**262 HIGHWAY CROSSING
GATE:** 1962-69, packaged
in box.

Item	C5	C7	C8
206 ARTIFICIAL COAL	5	10	15
214 PLATE GIRDER BRIDGE: 1953-69, metal base, plastic sides.	15	20	30
252 CROSSING GATE: 1950-63.	25	30	40
253 AUTOMATIC BLOCK SIGNAL: 1956-59.	20	30	45

256 FREIGHT STATION:
1950-53, dark or **light green**
roof.

**257 FREIGHT STATION
WITH DIESEL HORN:**
1956-57, the correct base
has "257" molded into it.
Dark or **light green** roof.

260 BUMPER: 1951-69,
red-painted die-cast metal or
unpainted black plastic.

Item	C5	C7	C8
256 FREIGHT STATION	40-75	60-**125**	75-**175**
257 FREIGHT STATION	60-75	75-**125**	100-**175**
260 BUMPER	15-30	20-**40**	25-**50**

Item	C5	C7	C8
262 HIGHWAY CROSSING GATE	50	75	100

**264 OPERATING FORK
LIFT:** 1957-60.

282 GANTRY CRANE:
1954-55, electromagnet
has blackened sheet metal
housing, crane cab screwed
in place.

282R GANTRY CRANE:
1956-57, electromagnet
housing bright metal, crane
cab was snapped in place.

Item	C5	C7	C8
264 OPERATING FORK LIFT	250	325	400
282 GANTRY CRANE	140	190	250
282R GANTRY CRANE	140	190	250

	C5	C7	C8

299 CODE TRANSMITTER SET: 1961-63, packaged with a 299-25 telegraph key.

	C5	C7	C8
299 Code Transmitter Set	100	125	175
308 Railroad Sign Set	35	50	75

308 RAILROAD SIGN SET: 1945-49, included five different die-cast sign posts.

309 YARD SIGN SET: 1950-59, nine plastic signs with die-cast metal bases.

310 BILLBOARD: 1950-68, five unpainted green plastic billboard frames furnished with perforated diecut sheets of cardboard billboards.

	C5	C7	C8
309 Yard Sign Set	20	30	45
310 Billboard	5	10	40

313 BASCULE BRIDGE: 1946-49, L-shaped gearbox. Supplied with a black steel alignment frame.

313-82 FIBER PINS: 1946-60, one dozen 027 insulating pins.

313-121 FIBER PINS: 1961, one dozen 027 insulating pins.

314 PLATE GIRDER BRIDGE: 1945-50, gray rounded-end die-cast girder sides rubber-stamped "LIONEL" in black.

315 ILLUMINATED TRESTLE BRIDGE: 1946-47, with red light mounted mid-span.

	C5	C7	C8
313 Bascule Bridge	300	525	675
313-82 Fiber Pins	1	2	3
313-121 Fiber Pins	1	2	3
314 Plate Girder Bridge	25	35	50
315 Illuminated Trestle Bridge	75	100	125

	C5	**C7**	**C8**

316 TRESTLE BRIDGE:
1949. 25   40   55

317 TRESTLE BRIDGE:
1950-56.   25   35   50

321 TRESTLE BRIDGE:
1958-64, sheet metal base
with unpainted gray plastic
sides and top. It was shipped
unassembled and the buyer
was to assemble it.   20   35   50

**332 ARCH UNDER
BRIDGE:** 1959-66, gray
plastic sides with black-
painted metal deck. It was
shipped unassembled and
the buyer was to assemble it.   30   45   60

**334 DISPATCHING
BOARD:** 1957-60.   175   250   310

342 CULVERT LOADER:
1956-58, came with 6342.   200   275   350

	C5	**C7**	**C8**

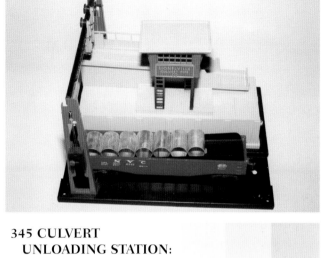

**345 CULVERT
UNLOADING STATION:**
1957-59, came with 6342.   250   350   425

**346 OPERATING
CULVERT UNLOADER:**
1965-66, manual version of
the 345.   100   150   250

**347 CANNON FIRING
RANGE SET:** 1964.   200   600   1000

**348 OPERATING
CULVERT UNLOADER:**
1966-69, manual version of
the 345. Came with 6342.   125   175   250

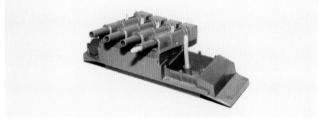

	C5	C7	C8

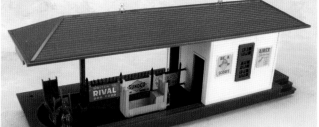

350 ENGINE TRANSFER TABLE: 1957-60.   150   325   450

350-50 TRANSFER TABLE EXTENSION: 1957-60.   125   175   225

352 ICE DEPOT: 1955-57, came with 6352 ice car.   175   250   325

353 TRACK SIDE CONTROL SIGNAL: 1960-61.   20   30   45

	C5	C7	C8

356 OPERATING FREIGHT STATION: 1952-57, dark green roof. With one each dark green and orange baggage carts. Early production came with a colorful lithographed tin insert for one of the baggage carts, add $75 to values listed for this item. With dark green and orange baggage carts or one tomato red baggage cart and one light green baggage cart.   60-125   95-160   140-220

362 BARREL LOADER: 1952-57, commonly with blue rubber man, if white rubber man add $25 to listed values.   70   100   150

362-78 BARRELS: 1952-57, box of six brown-stained small wooden barrels.   5   10   20

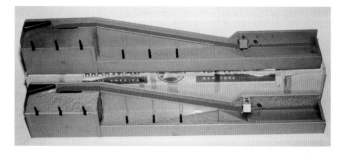

364 LUMBER LOADER: 1948-57, **dark crackle gray** finish or light gray hammer tone finish.   90-**100**   125-**150**   175-**200**

364C ON-OFF SWITCH: 1959-64.   2   8   16

	C5	**C7**	**C8**
365 DISPATCHING STATION: 1958-59.	80	115	140
375 TURNTABLE: 1962-64.	125	175	225
390C SWITCH: 1960-64.	5	10	20

394 ROTARY BEACON: 1949-53. Unpainted aluminum, or painted red or **dark green**.	**C5** 20-**50**	**C7** 30-**75**	**C8** 45-**100**

395 FLOODLIGHT TOWER: 1949-56, unpainted aluminum, or painted red, silver, green or **yellow**.	25-**100**	40-**140**	60-**200**

	C5	**C7**	**C8**

397 COAL LOADER: 1948-57, **yellow** or blue GM motor housing.	125-**250**	175-**350**	225-**450**

410 BILLBOARD BLINKER: 1956-58.	30	50	70
413 COUNTDOWN CONTROL PANEL: 1962 only.	45	75	100
415 DIESEL FUELING STATION: 1955-67.	100	145	200

	C5	**C7**	**C8**

419 HELIPORT: 1962-only, included yellow helicopter.

	175	425	600

443 MISSILE LAUNCHING PLATFORM WITH EXPLODING AMMUNITION DUMP: 1960-62.

	25	40	80

445 OPERATING SWITCH TOWER: 1952-57.

	40	75	100

	C5	**C7**	**C8**

448 MISSILE FIRING RANGE SET: 1961-63, with 6448 Target Range Car with red sides and white lettering, roof and ends. Accessory packaged with lichen "bushes."

	90	175	250

450 SIGNAL BRIDGE: 1952-58, included two signal heads.

	50	65	80

450L SIGNAL BRIDGE HEAD: 1952-58, blackened die-cast twin lamp socket. Much of the value is in the small Traditional box it was packed in.

	40	60	100

452 GANTRY SIGNAL BRIDGE: 1961-63.

	75	110	150

	C5	**C7**	**C8**

455 OPERATING OIL DERRICK: 1950-54, furnished with four turned solid aluminum oil drums and a separate sign reading "SUNOCO OIL DERRICK No. 455". 175 225 275

456 COAL RAMP: 1950-55, supplied with a special 456-100 controller, a 3456 operating hopper car, 456-83 maroon plastic receiving bin, two 456-85 coal pin mounting posts, a 456-84 coal bin door and a bag of 206 coal. **Dark gray, braided steel wire handrails** or dark or light gray with handrails made of fishing line. 150-**200** 225-**275** 300-**350**

	C5	**C7**	**C8**

460 PIGGY BACK TRANSPORTATION SET: 1955-57, came with 3460 flatcar and trailers. With two green plastic "LIONEL TRAINS" trailers with "FRUEHAUF" and "DURAVAN" signs on the front. 100 150 175

460P PIGGY BACK PLATFORM: Platform only without trailers or flatcar. The box must be present in order for this to have any real value. 300 500 700

461 PLATFORM WITH TRUCK AND TRAILER: 1966, lacks depressions molded into the top to receive trailer wheels. Came with a white single axle Lionel-made trailer and a red die-cast tractor made by Midge. 100 150 200

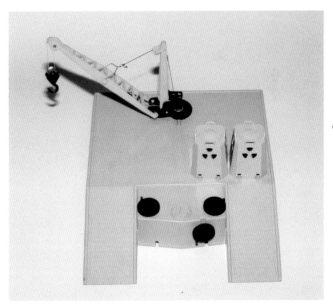

462 DERRICK PLATFORM SET: 1961-62, with two 6805-type containers without illumination but with wire bales attached to handles. 200 275 350

	C5	C7	C8

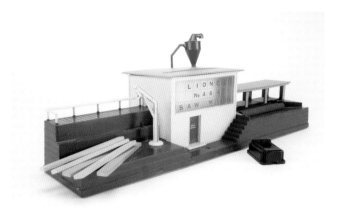

464 LUMBER MILL: 1956-60.

	C5	C7	C8
464 LUMBER MILL	125	175	225

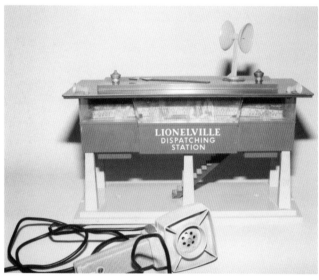

465 SOUND DISPATCHING STATION: 1956-57, came with a gray plastic microphone equipped with two red buttons.

470 MISSILE LAUNCHING PLATFORM WITH EXPLODING TARGET CAR: 1959-62, came with exploding 6470 target car.

494 ROTARY BEACON: 1954-66.

	C5	C7	C8
465 SOUND DISPATCHING STATION	100	140	175
470 MISSILE LAUNCHING PLATFORM	100	150	210
494 ROTARY BEACON	30	40	50

	C5	C7	C8

497 COALING STATION: 1953-58.

671-75 SPECIAL SMOKE BULB:

703-10 SPECIAL SMOKE BULB:

760 072 TRACK: 1950, 1954-58, box of 16 sections of 072 track.

	C5	C7	C8
497 COALING STATION	125	160	230
671-75 SPECIAL SMOKE BULB	10	20	30
703-10 SPECIAL SMOKE BULB	15	30	45
760 072 TRACK	50	75	120

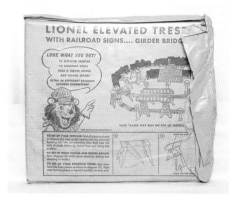

902 ELEVATED TRESTLE SET: 1959-60, came packaged in a paper sack printed with the label "902 ELEVATED TRESTLE SET".

908 RAILROAD TERMINAL: circa 1964.

909 SMOKE FLUID: 1957-68.

	C5	C7	C8
902 ELEVATED TRESTLE SET	-	100	250
908 RAILROAD TERMINAL	Too rarely traded to establish value.		
909 SMOKE FLUID	5	20	45

	C5	C7	C8

910 U. S. NAVY SUBMARINE BASE: 1961, made entirely of cardboard.

Too rarely traded to establish value.

919 ARTIFICIAL GRASS: 1946-64, half-pound bag of green-dyed sawdust.

	C5	C7	C8
919	7	7	25

928 MAINTENANCE AND LUBRICANT KIT: 1960-63.

	C5	C7	C8
928	20	40	70

920 SCENIC DISPLAY SET: 1957-58.

	C5	C7	C8
920	40	100	150

920-2 TUNNEL PORTALS: 1958-59, set of two "HILLSIDE" gray plastic tunnel portals.

920-2	20	35	50

920-3 GREEN GRASS: 1957-58, the clear plastic bag of green-dyed sawdust "grass."

920-3	2	10	30

920-4 YELLOW GRASS: 1957-58, the clear plastic bag of yellow-dyed sawdust "grass."

920-4	2	10	30

920-5 ARTIFICIAL ROCK: 1957-58, expanded vermiculite.

920-5	5	30	50

920-8 LICHEN: 1958

920-8	5	25	50

927 LUBRICATING AND MAINTENANCE KIT: 1950-59.

927	10	30	60

943 EXPLODING AMMUNITION DUMP: 1959-61.

	C5	C7	C8
943	30	60	90

950 U.S. RAILROAD MAP: 1958-66, packed in a tube.

950	60	90	150

951 FARM SET: 1958.

951	125	175	400

952 FIGURE SET: 1958.

952	125	175	400

	C5	**C7**	**C8**
953 FIGURE SET: 1959-62.	125	175	400
954 SWIMMING POOL AND PLAYGROUND SET: 1959.	125	175	400
955 HIGHWAY SET: 1958.	125	175	400
956 STOCKYARD SET: 1959.	125	175	400
957 FARM BUILDING AND ANIMAL SET: 1958.	125	175	400
958 VEHICLE SET: 1958.	150	250	475
959 BARN SET: 1958.	150	250	475
960 BARNYARD SET: 1959-61.	125	175	400
961 SCHOOL SET: 1959.	125	175	400
962 TURNPIKE SET: 1958.	175	275	500
963 FRONTIER SET: 1959-60.	150	250	475
963-100 FRONTIER SET: 1960.	300	450	700
964 FACTORY SITE SET: 1959.	150	250	475
965 FARM SET: 1959.	125	175	400
966 FIRE HOUSE SET: 1958.	125	175	400
967 POST OFFICE SET: 1958.	125	175	400

	C5	**C7**	**C8**
968 TV TRANSMITTER SET: 1958.	150	250	475
969 CONSTRUCTION SET: 1960.	150	250	475
970 TICKET BOOTH: 1958–60, 46 inches tall, 22 inches wide, 11 inches deep cardboard ticket booth.	-	125	175

	C5	**C7**	**C8**
971 LICHEN: 1960-64.	75	175	300

	C5	**C7**	**C8**
972 LANDSCAPE TREE ASSORTMENT: 1961-64.	150	300	500
973 COMPLETE LANDSCAPING SET: 1960-64.	300	1000	1500

	C5	C7	C8

974 SCENERY SET: 1962-63.

	C5	C7	C8
974 SCENERY SET: 1962-63.	700	2500	4000
980 RANCH SET: 1960.	125	200	400

	C5	C7	C8
981 FREIGHT YARD SET: 1960.	125	200	400
982 SUBURBAN SPLIT LEVEL SET: 1960.	125	200	400
983 FARM SET: 1960-61.	125	200	400
984 RAILROAD SET: 1961-62.	125	200	400
985 FREIGHT AREA SET: 1961.	125	200	400
986 FARM SET: 1962.	125	200	400
987 TOWN SET: 1962.	400	700	1000
988 RAILROAD STRUCTURE SET: 1962.	150	275	450
1008 UNCOUPLING UNIT: 1957-62.	1	2	5
1008-50 UNCOUPLING TRACK SECTION: 1957-62	1	2	5
1009 MANUMATIC UNCOUPLER: xxxx	1	2	5
1010 TRANSFORMER: 1961-66, 35-watt.	10	20	25
1011 TRANSFORMER: 1948-52 25-watt.	10	15	20
1011X TRANSFORMER: 1948-52 25-watt, 125-volt, 25-cycle.	10	15	20

	C5	C7	C8
1012 TRANSFORMER: 1950-54, 35-watt.	20	30	40
1014 TRANSFORMER: 1955, 40-watt.	15	25	40
1015 TRANSFORMER: 1955-60, 45-watt.	25	35	45
1016 TRANSFORMER: 1959-60, 35-watt, 110-volt primary transformer had a speed control and circuit breaker, but no fixed voltage taps or whistle control. It was available 1959-60.	10	20	30
1019 REMOTE CONTROL TRACK SET: 1946-50, 027 uncoupling track.	5	8	10
1020 90 DEGREE CROSSING: 1955-69, 027 90 degree crossing.	2	4	7
1021 90 DEGREE CROSSING: 1945-54, 027 90 degree crossing.	2	4	8
1022 MANUAL SWITCHES: 1953-69, pair of 027 turnouts.	15	20	30
1022LH MANUAL SWITCH: 1953-69, manual 027 left hand turnout.	8	10	16
1022RH MANUAL SWITCH: 1953-69, manual 027 right hand turnout.	8	10	16
1023 45 DEGREE CROSSING: 1956-69, 027 crossing.	3	6	10
1024 MANUAL SWITCHES: 1946-52, pair of metal-based 027 manual turnouts.	10	20	25
1025 ILLUMINATED BUMPER: 1946-47, die-cast black illuminated bumper, attached to a section of 027 straight track.	10	15	20
1025 TRANSFORMER: 1961-66, 1969 45-watt.	25	35	45
1026 TRANSFORMER: 1961-64 25-watt.	10	15	20

	C5	**C7**	**C8**
1032 TRANSFORMER: 1948, 75-watt.	20	35	60
1032M TRANSFORMER: 1948, 75-watt 125-volt, 50-cycle.	30	45	70

	C5	**C7**	**C8**
1033 TRANSFORMER: 1948-56.	40	60	90

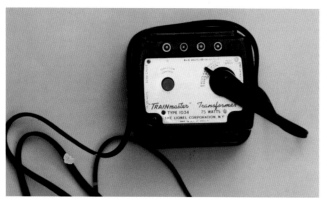

	C5	**C7**	**C8**
1034 TRANSFORMER: 1948-54, 75-watt.	20	35	60
1035 TRANSFORMER: 1947, 60-watt.	5	10	15
1037 TRANSFORMER: 1946-47, 40-watt.	10	15	25
1041 TRANSFORMER: 1945-46, 60-watt.	20	35	50
1042 TRANSFORMER: 1947-48, 75-watt.	25	40	60

	C5	**C7**	**C8**
1043 TRANSFORMER: 1953-58, 50-watt.	20	35	50

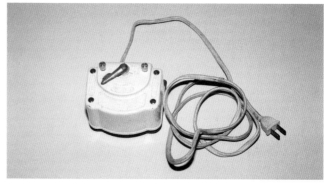

	C5	**C7**	**C8**
1043-500 TRANSFORMER: Ivory-colored case, white cord and gold-colored handle, 60 watts.	75	125	175
1043M TRANSFORMER: 1953-58, 50-watt 125-volt, 25-cycle.	40	55	75
1044 TRANSFORMER: 1957-69, 90-watt.	40	65	90
1044M TRANSFORMER: 1957-69, 90-watt, 125-volt, 25-cycle.	40	65	90
1045 OPERATING WATCHMAN: 1946-50.	20	35	50

	C5	C7	C8

1047 OPERATING SWITCHMAN: 1959-61. 90 125 170

1053 TRANSFORMER: 1956-60, 60-watt. 20 35 45

1063 TRANSFORMER: 1960-64, 75-watt. 25 40 60

1063-100 TRANSFORMER: 1961-75-watt. 30 45 65

1073 TRANSFORMER: 1961-66, 60-watt. 20 30 50

1121 REMOTE CONTROL SWITCHES: 1946-51, pair of 027 turnouts. 20 35 45

1122 REMOTE CONTROL SWITCHES: 1952-53, pair of 027 turnouts. 17 30 35

1122E REMOTE CONTROL SWITCHES: 1953-69, pair of 027 turnouts. 20 35 45

1122LH SWITCH: 1955-69, single left-hand 027 turnout. 12 18 25

1122RH SWITCH: 1955-69, single right-hand 027 turnout. 12 18 25

1122-234 FIBER PINS: 1958-60, one dozen 027 insulating pins. 1 2 3

1122-500 0-27 GAUGE ADAPTER: 1957-66, conversion pins to use 027 switches with Super 0 track. 1 2 3

1144 TRANSFORMER: 1961-66 75-watt. 10 20 40

	C5	C7	C8

1232 TRANSFORMER: 1948, 75-watt, 220-volt primary. 50 100 150

1241 TRANSFORMER: 1947-48, 60-watt, 220-volt primary. 50 100 150

1244 TRANSFORMER: 1957-66, 90-watt, 220-volt primary. 50 100 150

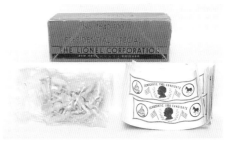

1640-100 PRESIDENTIAL SPECIAL: 1960, bag of plastic people and paper signs for passenger cars indicating Secret Service, Press Corps and both political parties. 100 225 400

3330-100 OPERATING SUBMARINE KIT: 1960-61, packaged in cardboard box with elaborate artwork. 100 200 300

6009 UNCOUPLING SECTION: 1953-55, 027. 3 6 10

6019 REMOTE CONTROL TRACK: 1948-66, 027. 4 6 10

6029 UNCOUPLING TRACK SET: 1955-63, 027. 3 5 7

6149 REMOTE CONTROL UNCOUPLING TRACK: 1964-69, 027. 1 5 7

6418 BRIDGE: See 214.

6800-60 AIRPLANE: 1957-58, individually boxed for separate sale. 150 350 450

A TRANSFORMER: 1947-48, 90-watt. 20 40 50

A220 TRANSFORMER: 1947-48, 90-watt 220-volt. 50 70 100

	C5	C7	C8
AX TRANSFORMER: 1947-48 90-watt, 110-volt, 25-hertz primary.	20	40	50

CTC LOCKON: 1947-69.	-	-	1.00
ECU-1 ELECTRONIC CONTROL UNIT: 1946-49.	40	75	100
KW TRANSFORMER: 1950-65, 190-watts.	100	150	200
LTC LOCKON: 1950-69 illuminated.	2	5	12
LW TRANSFORMER: 1955-56, 125-watts.	75	100	125
OC CURVED TRACK: 1945-61, 0 gauge curve track.	-	.50	1.00

	C5	C7	C8
OC-18 STEEL PINS: 1946-60, one dozen steel pins for 0 gauge track. The collectible is the envelope, not the pins.	-	-	1.00
OC-51 STEEL PINS: This small envelope, available only in 1961, contained one dozen steel pins for 0 gauge track. The collectible is the envelope, not the pins.	-	-	1.00
OS STRAIGHT TRACK: 1945-61, 0 gauge straight track.	.50	1.00	2.00
OTC LOCKON:	1	2	4
Q TRANSFORMER: 1946, 75-watts	20	40	60
R TRANSFORMER: 1946,100-watts, 1947, 110 watts.	50	75	100
RCS REMOTE CONTROL TRACK: 1946-48, 0 Gauge.	5	10	15
R220 TRANSFORMER: 1948, this transformer was the same as an R, but was adapted for the European market by the use of a 220-volt primary coil rather than the standard 110-volt U.S.-type coil.	50	100	150
RW TRANSFORMER: 1948-54, 110-watts.	50	75	100
S TRANSFORMER: 1947, 80-watts.	20	35	60
SW TRANSFORMER: 1961-66, 130-watts.	60	90	125

	C5	C7	C8
SP SMOKE PELLETS: 1948-69, bottle of 50 pills.	10	20	30

	C5	**C7**	**C8**

TOC CURVED TRACK:
1962-69 0 gauge curved track. — .50 1.00

TOC-51 STEEL PINS:
1962-69, one dozen steel pins for 0 gauge track. The collectable is the envelope, not the pins. — — 1.00

TOS STRAIGHT TRACK:
1962-69, 0 gauge straight track. .50 1.00 2.00

TW TRANSFORMER:
1953-60, 175-watts. 75 125 150

T020 90 DEGREE CROSSOVER: 1962-69, 90 degree 0 gauge crossing. 5 7 10

T022-500 0 GAUGE ADAPTER SET: 1962-66, allows the use of 0 gauge switches with Super 0 track. Much of the value is in the packaging. 2 3 4

UCS REMOTE CONTROL TRACK: 1949-69, 0 gauge. 8 14 18

	C5	**C7**	**C8**

UTC LOCKON: 1945-46, fits Standard gauge track as well as 0-27, and 0 gauge track. 1 2 4

V TRANSFORMER: 1946-47, four-throttle 150-watts. 100 125 150

VW TRANSFORMER:
1948-49, four-throttle 150-watts. 120 140 175

Z TRANSFORMER: 1945-47 four-throttle 250-watts. 100 125 150

ZW TRANSFORMER:
1948-49; 250-watts, 1950-66; **275-watts**. 100-**150** 150-**225** 250-**300**

HO GAUGE

	C5	C7	C8
0039 TRACK CLEANING CAR: 1961	70	100	200
0050 GANG CAR: 1959	60	100	200
0055 LOCOMOTIVE: 1961, M&StL switcher	50	100	200
0056 LOCOMOTIVE: 1959, A.E.C. Switcher	75	150	300
0057 LOCOMOTIVE: 1959, U.P. Switcher	50	100	200-
0058 LOCOMOTIVE: 1960, R.I. Switcher	40	80	150
0059 LOCOMOTIVE: 1960, U.S. Air Force Switcher	50	100	200
0068 INSPECTION CAR: 1961	50	100	200
0100 POWER PACK: 1961	15	20	40
0101 POWER PACK: 1961	15	20	40
0103 POWER PACK: 1959	15	20	40
0103-800 POWER PACK: 1961	15	20	40
0104 POWER PACK: 1961	15	20	40
0110 TRESTLE SET: 1958	15	20	40
0111 TRESTLE SET: 1959	15	20	40
0114 ENGINE HOUSE: 1958, w/horn	75	100	200
0115 KIT: 1961, engine house	52	70	150

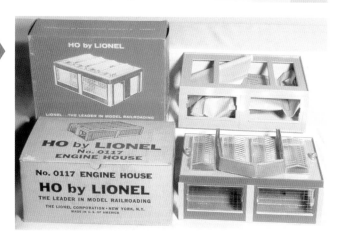

	C5	C7	C8
0117 ENGINE HOUSE: 1959	68	90	175
0118 ENGINE HOUSE: 1958, with whistle	75	100	200
0119 TUNNEL: 1959	10	15	30
0140 BANJO SIGNAL: 1962	33	45	75

	C5	C7	C8
0145 GATEMAN: 1959, automatic	45	60	100
0150 RECTIFIER: 1958	3	4	10
0181 CAB CONTROL: 1958	13	25	50
0197 RADAR ANTENNA: 1958	30	40	75
0214 GIRDER BRIDGE: 1958	5	15	25
0222 DECK BRIDGE: 1961	15	20	35
0224 GIRDER BRIDGE: 1961	10	15	30
0226 TRUSS BRIDGE: 1961	10	15	30
0245-200 CONTACTOR: 1960	5	7	15
0252 CROSSING GATE: 1959	30	40	75
0300 LUMBER CAR: 1960, operating	15	25	50
0301 DUMP CAR: 1960, operating	20	40	75
0301-16 CARGO BIN: 1960	5	7	15
0319 HELICOPTER CAR: 1960, operating	25	50	100
0337 GIRAFFE CAR: 1961, operating	25	50	100
0349 TURBO MISSILE FIRING CAR:	50	100	200

	C5	C7	C8
0357 COP AND HOBO CAR: 1962	20	40	75

	C5	C7	C8

0365 MISSILE LAUNCHING CAR: 1962 — 30 / 50 / 100

0366 MILK CAR: 1961, operating — 30 / 60 / 110

0370 SHERIFF AND OUTLAW CAR: 1962 — 20 / 40 / 75

0410 SUBURBAN RANCH HOUSE: 1959 — 15 / 20 / 45

0411 FIGURE SET: 1959 — 15 / 20 / 45

0412 FARM SET: 1959 — 15 / 20 / 45

0413 RAILROAD STRUCTURE SET: 1959 — 15 / 20 / 45

0414 VILLAGE SET: 1959 — 15 / 20 / 45

0425 FIGURE SET: 1962 — 10 / 15 / 30

0430 TREE ASSORTMENT: 1959 — 10 / 14 / 25

0431 LANDSCAPE SET: 1959 — 15 / 20 / 40

0432 TREE ASSORTMENT: 1961 — 10 / 15 / 30

0470 MISSILE LAUNCHING PLATFORM: 1960 — 40 / 65 / 125

0480 MISSILE FIRING RANGE SET: 1961 — 10 / 15 / 30

0500 LOCOMOTIVE: 1957, C&NW FM C-liner powered A unit — 50 / 100 / 150

0501 LOCOMOTIVE: 1957, T&P FM C-Liner powered A UNIT — 75 / 120 / 200

0502 LOCOMOTIVE: 1957, Wabash FM C-Liner powered A unit — 30 / 65 / 125

0503 LOCOMOTIVE: 1957, WP FM C-Liner powered A unit — 30 / 65 / 125

0504 LOCOMOTIVE: 1957, SP FM C-Liner powered A unit — 75 / 120 / 200

	C5	C7	C8

0505 LOCOMOTIVE: 1957, IC FM C-Liner powered A unit — 25 / 50 / 100

0510 LOCOMOTIVE: 1957, C&NW FM C-Liner dummy A unit — 50 / 100 / 150

0511 LOCOMOTIVE: 1957, T&P FM C-Liner Dummy A Unit — 30 / 65 / 125

0512 LOCOMOTIVE: 1957, Wabash FM C-Liner dummy A unit — 25 / 50 / 100

0513 LOCOMOTIVE: 1957, WP FM C-Liner Dummy A unit — 25 / 50 / 100

0514 LOCOMOTIVE: 1957, SP FM C-Liner Dummy A unit — 50 / 100 / 150

0515 LOCOMOTIVE: 1957, IC FM C-Liner Dummy A unit — 25 / 50 / 100

0520 LOCOMOTIVE: 1957, C&NW FM C-Liner Dummy B unit — 50 / 100 / 150

0521 LOCOMOTIVE: 1957, T&P FM C-Liner Dummy B unit — 30 / 65 / 125

0522 LOCOMOTIVE: 1957, Wabash FM C-Liner Dummy B unit — 25 / 50 / 100

0523 LOCOMOTIVE: 1957, WP FM C-Liner Dummy B unit — 25 / 50 / 100

0524 LOCOMOTIVE: 1957, SP FM C-Liner Dummy B unit — 50 / 100 / 150

0525 LOCOMOTIVE: 1957, IC FM C-Liner Dummy B unit — 25 / 50 / 100

	C5	C7	C8
0530 LOCOMOTIVE: 1958, DRGW, Diesel F-3 powered A	30	60	125
0531 LOCOMOTIVE: 1958, C.M. ST. P&P, Diesel F-3 powered A	30	65	125
0532 LOCOMOTIVE: 1958, Diesel F-3 powered A, B&O	30	65	125
0533 LOCOMOTIVE: 1958, New Haven, Diesel F-3 powered A,	30	65	125
0535 LOCOMOTIVE: 1962, Santa Fe, Diesel ALCO, AB	30	65	125
0536 LOCOMOTIVE: 1963, Santa Fe, Diesel ALCO	30	65	125
0537 LOCOMOTIVE: 1966, Diesel ALCO, AB Santa Fe	30	65	125
0540 LOCOMOTIVE: 1958, DRGW, Diesel F-3, Dummy B	25	50	100
0541 LOCOMOTIVE: 1958, CMST P&P, Diesel F-3, dummy B	25	50	100
0550 LOCOMOTIVE: 1958, DRGW, Diesel F-3, dummy A	25	50	100
0555 LOCOMOTIVE: 1963, Santa Fe, Diesel F-3 powered A	30	65	125
0561 ROTARY SNOWPLOW: 1959, MSTL	60	100	200

0564 LOCOMOTIVE: 1960, C&O, Diesel ALCO, powered A

	C5	C7	C8
0564 LOCOMOTIVE: 1960, C&O, Diesel ALCO, powered A	30	65	125

	C5	C7	C8
0565 LOCOMOTIVE: 1959, Santa Fe, Diesel ALCO, powered A	30	65	125
0566 LOCOMOTIVE: 1959, Texas Special, Diesel ALCO, powered A	30	65	125
0567 LOCOMOTIVE: 1959, Alaska, Diesel ALCO, powered A	30	65	125
0568 LOCOMOTIVE: 1962, Union Pacific, Diesel ALCO, powered A	30	65	125
0569 LOCOMOTIVE: 1963, Union Pacific, Diesel ALCO, powered A	30	65	125
0570-1 NAVY YARD SWITCHER:	60	100	200

	C5	C7	C8
0571 LOCOMOTIVE: 1963, PRR, Diesel ALCO, powered A	30	65	125
0576 LOCOMOTIVE: 1959, Texas Special, Diesel F-3, dummy B	30	65	125

	C5	C7	C8

0577 LOCOMOTIVE: 1959, Alaska, Diesel F-3, dummy B — 30 / 65 / 125

0581 LOCOMOTIVE: 1960, PRR, Rectifier — 30 / 65 / 125

0586 LOCOMOTIVE: 1959, Texas Special, Diesel F-3, dummy A — 25 / 50 / 100

0587 LOCOMOTIVE: 1959, Alaska, Diesel F-3, dummy A — 25 / 50 / 100

0591 LOCOMOTIVE: 1959, New Haven, Rectifier — 30 / 65 / 125

0592 LOCOMOTIVE: 1966, Santa Fe, Diesel GP9 — 30 / 65 / 125

0593 LOCOMOTIVE: 1963, Northern Pacific, Diesel GP9 — 30 / 65 / 125

0594 LOCOMOTIVE: 1963, Santa Fe, Diesel GP9 — 30 / 65 / 125

0595 LOCOMOTIVE: 1959, Santa Fe, Diesel F-3, dummy A — 25 / 50 / 100

0596 LOCOMOTIVE: 1959, NYC, diesel GP9 — 30 / 65 / 125

0597 LOCOMOTIVE: 1961, Northern Pacific, Diesel GP9 — 30 / 65 / 125

0598 LOCOMOTIVE: 1961, NYC, diesel GP7 — 30 / 65 / 125

0602 0-6-0 STEAM LOCOMOTIVE: 1960 — 25 / 50 / 100

	C5	C7	C8

0605 0-4-0 TANK-TYPE STEAM LOCOMOTIVE: 1959 — 30 / 65 / 125

0625 4-6-2 STEAM LOCOMOTIVE: 1959 — 45 / 90 / 175

0626 4-6-2 STEAM LOCOMOTIVE: 1963 — 35 / 65 / 125

0635 4-6-2 STEAM LOCOMOTIVE: With Smoke, 1963 — 30 / 65 / 125

0636 4-6-2 STEAM LOCOMOTIVE: 1963 — 30 / 65 / 125

0637 4-6-2 STEAM LOCOMOTIVE: 1963 — 30 / 65 / 125

0642 2-4-2 STEAM LOCOMOTIVE: 1961 — 30 / 65 / 125

0643 2-4-2 STEAM LOCOMOTIVE: 1963 — 30 / 65 / 125

0645 4-6-2 STEAM LOCOMOTIVE: With Smoke, 1962 — 30 / 65 / 125

0646 4-6-2 STEAM LOCOMOTIVE: With Smoke, 1963 — 30 / 65 / 125

0647 4-6-2 STEAM LOCOMOTIVE: With Smoke, 1966 — 30 / 65 / 125

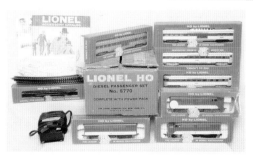

0704 BAGGAGE CAR: 1959, Texas Special — 30 / 60 / 125

	C5	C7	C8
0705 PULLMAN: 1959, Texas Special	30	60	125
0706 VISTA DOME: 1959, Texas Special	30	60	125
0707 OBSERVATION CAR: 1959, Texas Special	30	60	125
0708 BAGGAGE CAR: 1960, Pennsylvania	10	20	40
0709 VISTA DOME: 1960, Pennsylvania	13	25	50
0710 OBSERVATION CAR: 1960, Pennsylvania	10	20	40
0711 BAGGAGE CAR: 1960, Pennsylvania	10	20	40
0712 BAGGAGE CAR: 1961, Santa Fe	25	45	100
0713 PULLMAN: 1961, Santa Fe	25	45	100
0714 VISTA DOME: 1961, Santa Fe	13	25	50
0715 OBSERVATION CAR: 1961, Santa Fe	10	20	40
0723 PULLMAN: 1963, Pennsylvania	10	20	40
0725 OBSERVATION CAR: 1963, Pennsylvania	10	20	40
0733 PULLMAN: 1964, Santa Fe	10	20	40
0735 OBSERVATION CAR: 1964, Santa Fe	10	20	40
0800 FLATCAR: 1958, with airplane	30	60	125
0801 FLATCAR: 1958, with boat	15	30	60

	C5	C7	C8
0805 AEC CAR: 1959, with light	20	40	75
0806 FLATCAR: 1959, with helicopter	25	50	100

	C5	C7	C8
0807 FLATCAR: 1959, with bulldozer	25	45	90

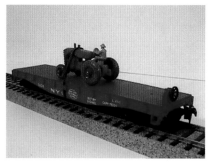

	C5	C7	C8
0808 FLATCAR: With tractor, 1959-60, red NYC	25	45	90
0809 HELIUM TRANSPORT CAR: 1961	20	35	75
0810 GENERATOR TRANSPORT CAR: 1961	15	25	50
0811-25 FLAT: 1958, with stakes	10	20	40
0813 MERCURY CAPSULE CAR: 1962	15	30	60

	C5	C7	C8
0814 AUTO TRANSPORT CAR: NYC	25	50	100
0814 AUTO TRANSPORT CAR: SP	25	50	100
0815 TANK CAR: 1958	20	35	75

	C5	C7	C8
0815-75 TANK CAR: Lionel Lines, orange, 1963 stamped 0815200	10	25	50
0815-50 TANK CAR: 1964	10	25	50

	C5	C7	C8
0815-85 TANK CAR: 1964	10	25	50
0815-110 SUNOCO TANK CAR: Black	65	150	350
0816-50 ROCK FUEL TANK CAR: 1962	13	25	50
0816 ROCKET FUEL TANK CAR: 1962	13	25	50
0817 CABOOSE: 1958	12	25	50
0817-250K CABOOSE: 1959, Texas Special	10	20	40
0817-300 CABOOSE: 1959, Southern Pacific	10	20	40
0817-275 CABOOSE: 1959, New Haven	10	20	40
0817-200 CABOOSE: 1959, AEC	10	20	40
0817-225 CABOOSE: 1959, Alaska	10	20	40
0817-150 CABOOSE: 1960, Santa Fe	10	20	40
0817-350 CABOOSE: 1960, Rock Island	10	20	40
0819-1 WORK CABOOSE: 1958, P.R.R.	13	25	50
0819-100 WORK CABOOSE: 1958, B&M	13	25	50
0819-200 WORK CABOOSE: 1959, B&M	13	25	50
0819-225 WORK CABOOSE: 1960, Santa Fe	13	25	50
0819-250 WORK CABOOSE: 1960, NP	13	25	50
0819-275 WORK CABOOSE: 1960, C&O	13	25	50
0819-285 WORK CABOOSE: 1963, C&O	13	25	50
0821 PIPE CAR: 1960	13	25	50
0821-100 PIPE CAR: 1963	15	30	65
0821-50 PIPE CAR: 1964	13	25	50
822 CABOOSE: O GA., 1915	40	75	150
0823 TWIN MISSILE CAR: 1960	35	70	150
0824 FLATCAR: 1958, with two cars	20	45	100
0827 CABOOSE: 1961, Lionel	10	20	40

	C5	C7	C8
0827-50 CABOOSE: 1963, AEC	10	20	40
0827-75 CABOOSE: 1963, Lionel	10	20	40
0830 FLATCAR: 1958, W/TWO VANS	20	40	75
0834 POULTRY CAR: 1959	20	40	80

	C5	C7	C8
08361 HOPPER: 1959-63, Alaska, red	10	20	40
0836-100 HOPPER: 1964, Lionel	10	20	40
0836-60 HOPPER: 1966, Alaska	10	20	40
0837 CABOOSE: 1961, M&STL	8	15	30
0837-100 CABOOSE: 1963, M&STL	10	20	40
0838 CABOOSE: 1961, Lackawanna	10	20	40
0840 CABOOSE: 1961, NYC	10	20	40
0841 CABOOSE: 1961	10	20	40
0841-50 CABOOSE: 1962, Union Pacific	10	20	40
0841-175 CABOOSE: 1962, Santa Fe	10	20	40
0842 CULVERT PIPE CAR: 1960	12	25	50
0845 GOLD BULLION CAR: 1962	40	75	150
0847-100 EXPLODING TARGET CAR: 1960	30	60	125
0847 EXPLODING TARGET CAR: 1960	10	20	40
0850-100 MISSILE LAUNCHING CAR	20	40	75
0850 MISSILE LAUNCHING CAR: 1960	20	35	75
0860 DERRICK: 1958	15	30	65
0861 TIMBER TRANSPORT CAR: 1960	10	20	40

	C5	C7	C8
0861-100 TIMBER TRANSPORT CAR: 1961	13	25	50
0862 GONDOLA: 1958	5	10	30

	C5	C7	C8
0862-200 GONDOLA: 1958	60	100	200
0863 RAIL TRUCK CAR: 1960	13	25	50
0864-175 BOXCAR: 1958, Timken	10	20	40
0864-225 BOXCAR: 1958, Central of Georgia	30	60	125
0864-25 BOXCAR: 1958, NYC	10	20	40
0864-200 BOXCAR: 1958, Monon	10	20	40
0864-250 BOXCAR: 1958, Wabash	10	20	40
0864-125 BOXCAR: 1958, Rutland	10	20	40
0864-50 BOXCAR: 1958, State of Maine	10	20	40
0864-1 BOXCAR: 1958, Seaboard	10	20	40
0864-100 BOXCAR: 1958, New Haven	10	20	40
0864-150 BOXCAR: 1958, M&STL	10	20	40
0864-900 BOXCAR: 1959, NYC	10	20	40
0864-300 BOXCAR: 1959, Alaska	10	20	40
0864-325 BOXCAR: 1959, D.S.S.A.	10	20	40
0864-350 BOXCAR: 1959, State of Maine	15	30	60
0864-400 BOXCAR: 1960, B&M	10	20	40
0864-700 BOXCAR: 1961, Santa Fe	10	20	40

	C5	C7	C8
0864-275 BOXCAR: 1962, State of Maine	10	20	40
0864-935 BOXCAR: 1963, NYC	10	20	40
0864-925 BOXCAR: 1964, NYC	10	20	40
0865 GONDOLA: 1958, with canisters	15	30	65
0865-225 GONDOLA: 1960, with scrap iron	13	25	50
0865-250 GONDOLA: 1960, with crates	13	25	50
0865-300 GONDOLA: 1963, with crates	13	25	50
0865-350 GONDOLA: 1963, NYC	10	20	40
0865-375 GONDOLA: 1963, NYC	10	20	40
0865-400 GONDOLA: 1963, NYC with crates	10	20	40
0865-435 GONDOLA: 1964	10	20	40
0866-1 CATTLE CAR: 1958, M.K.T.	10	20	40
0866-25 CATTLE CAR: 1958, Santa Fe	10	20	40
0866-200 CIRCUS CAR: 1959	15	32	65
0870 MAINTENANCE CAR: 1959, with generator	15	30	60
0872-50 REEFER: 1958, El Capitan	10	20	40
0872-25 REEFER: 1958, Illinois Central	10	20	40
0872-1 REEFER: 1958, Fruit Growers	10	20	40
0872-200 REEFER: 1959, Railway Express	10	20	40

	C5	C7	C8
0873 RODEO CAR: 1962	10	20	40

	C5	C7	C8
0874 BOXCAR: 1964, NYC	25	50	100
0874-60 BOXCAR: 1964, B&M	10	20	40
0874-25 BOXCAR: 1965, NYC	10	20	40
0875 FLATCAR: 1959, with missile	20	35	75
0877 MISCELLANEOUS CAR: 1958	10	20	40
0879 DERRICK: 1958	13	25	50
0880 MAINTENANCE CAR: 1959, with light	30	60	125
0900 OPERATING PLATFORM: 1960	20	35	75
902-5 ROCKS: 1958	—	3	5
0903 TRACK: 1958, straight, 3"	—	—	1
0905 TRACK: 1958, straight, 1-1/2"	—	—	1
0906 TRACK: 1968, straight, 6"	—	—	1
0909 TRACK: 1958, straight, 9"	—	—	1
0922 REMOTE CONTROL SWITCH: 1958, right	2	3	5
0923 REMOTE CONTROL SWITCH: 1958, left	2	3	5
0925-10 INSULATING CLIP: 1960	—	—	1
0925 TERMINAL TRACK: 1958, straight	—	1	2
0929 UPCOUPLING TRACK: 1958, 9"	1	3	5

	C5	C7	C8
0930 30 DEGREES CROSSING: 1960	1	3	5
0939 UNCOUPLER: 1958	1	3	5
0942 MANUAL SWITCH: 1958, right	1	3	5
0943 MANUAL SWITCH: 1958, left	1	3	5
0950 RE-RAILER: 1958	1	3	5
0960 BUMPER TRACK: 1960	—	1	2
0961 BUMPER TRACK: 1961, illuminated	—	1	2
0975 TERMINAL TRACK: 1958, curved	1	1	2
0983 CURVED TRACK: 1958, curved, 3", 18" radius	—	—	1
0984 CURVED TRACK: 1958, 4-1/2", 18" radius	—	—	1
0985 CURVED TRACK: 1958, 9", 15" radius	—	—	1
0986 TRACK: 1958, curved, 4-1/2", 15" radius	—	—	1
0989 TRACK: 1958, curved, 9", 18" radius	—	—	1
0990 90 DEGREES CROSSING: 1958	5	7	10
5402 RAILROAD AND ROADWAY CROSSING: 1963	1	2	5

MARX

Toy trains bearing the maker's mark of Marx dominated the shelves of dime stores and other economy retailers for much of the 20th century. Initially, Marx's toys were actually produced by others, and only sold by Marx. The first trains were produced by the Girard Model Works. They were sold by Marx as "The Joy Line." Joy Line trains were sold through 1936.

Marx bought the Girard plant in 1935, and trains continued to be produced there through 1975, three years after the company was bought by Quaker Oats.

JOY LINE

Marx sold Joy Line trains from 1927 through 1936.

STEAM

	C6	C8
(101) STEAM, 0-4-0, 1930-31, black, cast-iron, electric with headlight.	155	210
(102) STEAM, 1930-31, black, cast iron, mechanical, screw or **slip-on key**.	50-65	75-100
(103) STEAM, 1933-35, red, mechanical.	45	80
(104) STEAM, 1933-35, black, mechanical, sparkler, dummy or battery-operated headlight.	40	80
(105) STEAM, 1932-35, Red body, black frame, mechanical, dummy or battery-operated headlight.	40	80

	C6	C8
(106) STEAM, 1932-35, black body, red frame, electric.	50	100

	C6	**C8**

		C6	C8
107) BUNNY LOCOMOTIVE, 1935-36, pink and blue, mechanical		800	1,200
350 STEAM, 0-4-0, 1927-30, yellow, black, red, blue, mechanical.		300	425

ROLLING STOCK

	C6	C8
351 TENDER, 1927-35, yellow and blue, black, or red, long or short body, **"351 Koal Kar"** or no number.	25-75	45-125
352 GONDOLA, 1927-36, "Venice Gondola," blue, or red or orange floor toy.	40	80
(352) GONDOLA, 1935-36, "Bunny Express," frame lavender, or light blue or green.	150	250
353 TANK, 1927-34 "Everful Tank Car," gold body, red or black ends, blue or black frame.	50	75
354 SIDE DUMP, 1927-34, "Contractor Dump Car," yellow body, blue or black ends, blue or black frame.	50	80
355 BOXCAR, 1927-34, "Hobo Rest," red body, blue or black frame, blue, yellow, black or orange roof.	40	80
(356) CABOOSE, 1926-34, "Eagle Eye Caboose," red body, blue or black frame, yellow, black or orange roof. **Illuminated** or non-illuminated.	40-80	75-115

	C6	C8
357 COACH, 1931-34, "The Joy Line Coach," green body, blue or black frame, red, orange or **yellow** roof.	50-75	65-100

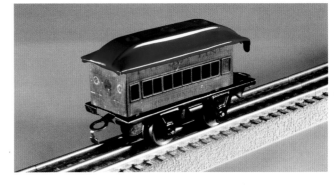

	C6	C8
458 OBSERVATION, 1931-34, "The Joy Line," green lithography, red or orange roof, **with** or without illuminated "Joy Line" drumhead.	40-150	50-200

C6   C8   C6   C8

ARTICULATED STREAMLINERS

M10000 POWER CARS

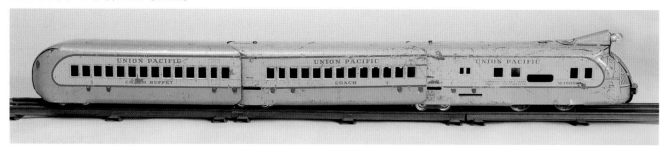

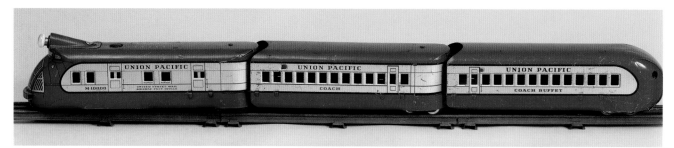

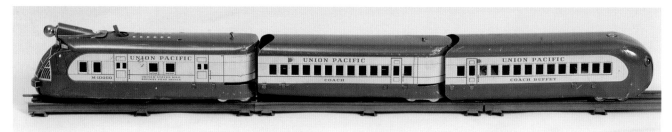

Three variations of the M100000

M10000 Union Pacific power car, electric, 1934-37, many variations.   30   80

M10000 Union Pacific power car, mechanical, 1934-37, many variations.   30   80

PASSENGER CARS FOR M10000 SETS

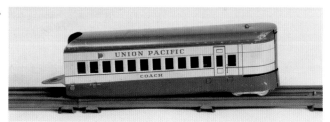

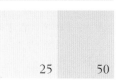

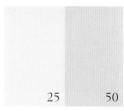

(657) UNION PACIFIC "COACH," 1934-37, two- or four-wheel. Many variations matching M10000 power car.   25   50

(658) UNION PACIFIC "COACH BUFFET," observation, 1934-37, with or without illumination. Many variations matching M10000 power car.   25   50

	C6	C8		C6	C8

M10005 POWER CARS

**(732) MECHANICAL OR
ECECTRIC,** 1936-40, cream
with green and orange trim.

40   60

(732GMD) ELECTRIC, 1948,
white with green and orange
trim, pin or tab coupler.

30   60

**(791) MECHANICAL OR
ELECTRIC,** 1940, 1948-52,
silver w/ red and blue trim.

20   40

735) MECHANICAL, 1946-50,
yellow and brown with or without
reverse.

40   80

(735D) DUMMY, 1951-53,
yellow and brown with orange
trim, tab coupler on front.

30   70

PASSENGER CARS FOR M10005 SETS

(657G) UNION PACIFIC,
1936-40, Cream w/ green roof,
orange trim, **"RPO, REA/
RPO,"** or Coach lettered either
Los Angeles, Omaha or Denver.

15-30   30-60

(658G) UNION PACIFIC,
1936-40, "Squaw Bonnet,"
observation, matches (657G).

20   30

(757) UNION PACIFIC, 1937-
40, yellow, brown roof, orange
trim, RPO, REA/RPO, **Diner**
or Coach lettered Los Angeles,
Omaha or Denver.

20-200   40-400

(757A) UNION PACIFIC,
1948-50, white with green roof,
or **silver, red and blue,** RPO,
REA/RPO, or Observation,
or Coach lettered either Los
Angeles, Omaha or Denver.

15-40   30-80

(758) UNION PACIFIC, 1937-
40, "Squaw Bonnet" observation,
matches (757).

25   35

(758A) UNION PACIFIC, 1945-
50, "Squaw Bonnet," observation,
white, green, and orange, or
silver, red, and blue.

20   30

	C6	C8

PASSENGER CARS FOR MERCURY SETS

(657) NEW YORK CENTRAL, 1938-40, gray body and roof (various shades), "US Mail-Bag," "Toledo" "Coach," **"Cleveland" "Coach,"** "Chicago". — C6 40-60, C8 80-**125**

(657CQ) NEW YORK CENTRAL, 1939-47, brass body and roof, black trim, illuminated, or non-illuminated), "US Mail-Bag," "Toledo," "Coach," "Cleveland," "Coach," "Chicago," "Coach." — C6 50, C8 100

(657RA) NEW YORK CENTRAL, 1937-40, 1948, "Coach," red body and roof, white trim. "Toledo," "Cleveland" or "Chicago". — C6 40, C8 100

(658) NEW YORK CENTRAL, 1940, observation, gray, "Detroit." — C6 45, C8 90

(658CQ) NEW YORK CENTRAL, 1939-41, observation, brass, "Detroit." — C6 60, C8 100

(658RA) NEW YORK CENTRAL, 1937-40, observation, red, "Detroit" red. — C6 50, C8 100

DIESEL LOCOMOTIVES

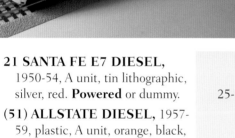

21 SANTA FE E7 DIESEL, 1950-54, A unit, tin lithographic, silver, red. **Powered** or dummy. — C6 25-**30**, C8 50-**60**

(51) ALLSTATE DIESEL, 1957-59, plastic, A unit, orange, black, powered or dummy. — C6 110, C8 150

(51) ALLSTATE DIESEL, 1957-59, plastic, B unit, orange, black. — C6 100, C8 160

(52) UNION PACIFIC E7 DIESEL, 1960, plastic, A unit, powered orange. — C6 125, C8 175

(52) UNION PACIFIC E7 DIESEL, 1960, plastic, B unit, powered orange. — C6 150, C8 200

	C6	C8

54 KCS DIESEL, 1956-60, tin lithographed, A unit powered or dummy, red, black, yellow.

(55) KCS DIESEL, 1957-60, B unit, four- or eight-wheel.

62 B&O DIESEL, 1953-54, 1958, 1967 tin, A unit, silver, blue, powered or dummy.

	C6	C8
54 KCS DIESEL	80	125
(55) KCS DIESEL	50	100
62 B&O DIESEL	40	80

81 MONON DIESEL, 1955-56, 1958-59, tin, A unit, powered or dummy, two- or four-wheel, gray, red, "81F."

(82) MONON DIESEL, 1958-59, B unit, four- or eight-wheel.

99 ROCK ISLAND DIESEL, 1958-74, plastic, A unit, powered or dummy, black, red.

(99X) ROCK ISLAND DIESEL, 1958-61, B unit.

112 LV DIESEL, 1974-76, switcher, red.

588 NEW YORK CENTRAL DIESEL, 1958-62, switcher, black, maroon, **gray**.

	C6	C8
81 MONON DIESEL	50	80
(82) MONON DIESEL	40	75
99 ROCK ISLAND DIESEL	50	80
(99X) ROCK ISLAND DIESEL	40	75
112 LV DIESEL	20	40
588 NEW YORK CENTRAL DIESEL	25-50	50-75

	C6	C8

702 WESTERN PACIFIC DIESEL, 1972-74, switcher, green with gold, yellow or **cream** trim.

799 ROCK ISLAND DIESEL, 1959-65, switcher, black and red.

799 WESTERN PACIFIC DIESEL, switcher, 1959-65, green and yellow.

(800) MISSOURI PACIFIC DIESEL, switcher, 1975-76, blue.

(801 ILLINOIS CENTRAL GULF DIESEL, switcher, 1974-75, with or without reverse mechanism, orange and white "Split Rail" scheme.

901 WESTERN PACIFIC DIESEL, E-7A, 1956-60 plastic, powered or dummy, green and yellow or **gray and yellow**.

	C6	C8
702 WESTERN PACIFIC DIESEL	30-60	50-80
799 ROCK ISLAND DIESEL	30	45
799 WESTERN PACIFIC DIESEL	60	80
(800) MISSOURI PACIFIC DIESEL	50	90
(801 ILLINOIS CENTRAL GULF DIESEL	30	60
901 WESTERN PACIFIC DIESEL	50-90	75-125

(902) WESTERN PACIFIC DIESEL, E-7B unit, 1957-58, green and yellow or **gray and yellow**.

	C6	C8
(902) WESTERN PACIFIC DIESEL	60-100	85-135

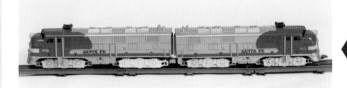

1095 SANTA FE DIESEL, plastic, E-7A unit, 1952, gray, red, yellow, powered or dummy.

(1096) SANTA FE DIESEL, E-7B unit, catalog No. 1095B, 1955-71.

	C6	C8
1095 SANTA FE DIESEL	40	75
(1096) SANTA FE DIESEL	25	40

C6   C8   C6   C8

1798 CAPE CANAVERAL EXPRESS DIESEL, switcher, 1959-64, red, white and blue. 85 110

(1998) ALLSTATE DIESEL, 1959, blue, eight-wheel. 130 220

(2002) HANDCAR 30 45

1998 AT&SF SWITCHER, 1955-62, eight-wheel, maroon or **black**. 40-80 85-125

1998 ROCK ISLAND DIESEL SWITCHER, 1962, gray and red, eight-wheel, powered or dummy, black or **silver trucks**. ..... 80-**100** 115-**140**

2002 NEW HAVEN DIESEL, plastic, E-7A unit, 1960-74, black, white, orange "McGinnis scheme," powered or dummy.

Powered 50 75

Dummy 60 74

(2003) NEW HAVEN DIESEL, E-7B unit, 1960-74, black, white, orange "McGinnis scheme." 50 75

1998 UNION PACIFIC DIESEL, 1955-62, eight-wheel, powered or dummy. 80-100 115-140

	C6	C8

4000 SEABOARD DIESEL, 1955-62, tin, A unit, green, yellow, electric, mechanical or dummy. — 50 — 75

(4001) SEABOARD DIESEL, 1962, B unit, four-wheel. — 175 — 225

6000 SOUTHERN PACIFIC DIESEL, 1952-54, tin, A unit, power or dummy, orange, silver or **white** stripe. — 25-**35** — 40-**60**

2124 B&M DIESEL, RDC, 1958-59, silver gray. — 200 — 275

4000 NEW YORK CENTRAL DIESEL, 1953-55, 1959-69, 1971-74, plastic, black and white, powered or dummy, many variations. — 85 — 150

4000 PENN CENTRAL DIESEL, 1971-73, plastic, E-7A unit, powered or dummy, turquoise green, **with** or without white stripe and painted grilles. — 175-**275** — 225-**400**

STEAM LOCOMOTIVES

1 STEAM, 1959-60, Wm. Crooks locomotive, plastic, 4-4-0 with smoke, 1973, 0-4-0 no smoke, plastic. — 75 — 100

(198) STEAM, 0-4-0, 1962, plastic, Marlines, **red** or black. — 40-**80** — 60-**115**

333 STEAM, 4-6-2, 1949-53, die-cast, black, with or without smoke. — 60 — 100

391 STEAM, 2-4-2 1938, 1942, 0-4-0 1939-41, all black or **black with red trim.** — 40-**60** — 75-**100**

396 STEAM, 0-4-0 or 2-4-2, 1941-42, sheet metal, black or **copper.** — 40-**50** — 60-**75**

397 STEAM, 2-4-2, 1941, **copper** or black boiler. — 60-**70** — 85-**100**

C6   **C8**   **C6**   **C8**

400 STEAM, 0-4-0, 1953-54, locomotive, plastic, black or **olive drab**.   15-**50**   20-**75**

500 STEAM, 0-4-0 or 2-4-2, 1938-42, Army, olive drab.   75   100

(591) STEAM, 0-4-0, 1953-60, electric, black.   10   20

(593) STEAM, 0-4-0, 1953-60, electric.   10   20

(595) STEAM, 0-4-0, 1959-60, electric.   10   20

(597) STEAM, 0-4-0, 1934-52, Commodore Vanderbilt, *black*, red, gray, **olive drab**.   25-**150**   50-**250**

(635) STEAM, 0-4-0, 1938-41, Mercury, *black*, red, gray.   35-60   60-110

490 STEAM, 0-4-0, 1962-75, black or gray.   20   25

666 STEAM, 2-4-2, 1955, die-cast, black or **olive drab**.   25-**60**   35-**85**

(833) STEAM, 0-4-0, 1947-52, black.   15   20

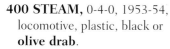

(494/495) STEAM, 0-4-0 or 2-4-2, 1939-41, 1946-52, Marlines, numbered "3000," many variations, the most valuable of which included a red cab and boiler.   25-**80**   50-**120**

897 STEAM, 0-4-0, 1939, lithographed black or **olive drab**.   60-**125**   85-**200**

898 STEAM, 0-4-0, 1946-52, black.   15   20

	C6	**C8**
994 STEAM, 0-4-0, **with** or without number on cab.	25-40	50-80
(995) STEAM, 0-4-0, same as 994, black or **red**.	25-150	50-250

999 STEAM, 2-4-2, 1941-42, 1947, black, die-cast, **open**, closed or embossed pilot.	25-75	50-125

	C6	**C8**
1666 STEAM, 2-4-2, plastic, with or without smoke, black or **gray**.	20-50	25-75

1829 STEAM, 4-6-4, black, **with** or without smoke.	40-50	70-100
3000 STEAM, 0-4-0 or 2-4-2, 1939-41, 1946-52, many variations, all equal value except **red** boiler with light blue, silver and black running board apron.	55-75	100-150
3000 See (494/495)		

MECHANICAL STEAM LOCOMOTIVES

(1) STEAM, 0-4-0, 1962, Wm. Crooks, black.	50	100
(198) STEAM, 0-4-0, 1962, Marlines, plastic, black or **red**.	30-60	50-100
(232) STEAM, 0-4-0, 1934-48, Commodore Vanderbilt, black, red, green, gray, or **silver**.	40-225	50-300
(233) See (635)		
400 STEAM, 0-4-0, 1952-56, 1958, 1965-76, black, many variations, all equal value except **with rubber bulb smoke puffer**.	15-30	20-60
(401) STEAM, 0-4-0, 1962, Marlines, black.	8	12
(591) STEAM, 0-4-0, 1950-58, black.	10	20
(635) STEAM, 0-4-0, 1938-40, Mercury, black, gray, red or **blue**.	50-100	75-175
666 STEAM, 0-4-0, mechanical, uses same body as does electric 999.	500	1,000
734 STEAM, 0-4-0, 1950-52, Mickey Mouse locomotive.	175	225

(735) STEAM, 0-4-0, 1950-52, black.	15	30
(833) STEAM, 0-4-0, 1947-52, black.	15	25
897 STEAM, 0-4-0, 1940, tin lithographed, black and white or **olive drab**.	60-175	100-250.
898 STEAM, 0-4-0, 1940, 1946-48, black.	20	40
994 STEAM, 0-4-0, black.	20	40
3000 STEAM, 0-4-0, Canadian Pacific, maroon or **blue and white** sideboards.	125-150	175-200
(198A) MARLINES TENDER, used with 198 Steam, black or **blue** plastic.	25-40	40-60
(451) CANADIAN PACIFIC TENDER, 1937-41, 6", four-wheel frame. Silver, red, **maroon** or lettered Pennsylvania.	20	50
(461) CP TENDER, 1935-39, 6", eight-wheel frame, automatic couplers. Silver, maroon or **light blue**.	30-50	60-75

	C6	C8		C6	C8

TENDERS

500 (851 M) ARMY SUPPLY TRAIN TENDER, 1935-40, 6", four-wheel, olive drab or lime-olive body. — 50 — 75

(551) NEW YORK CENTRAL, 1934-36, Commodore Vanderbilt wagon top tender, four-wheel, black, **silver**, blue, red, gray, copper. — 10-150 — 15-250

(941) TENDER, 1949-52, four-wheel frame, lithographed tin, **red** or black NKP or red, green yellow "Mickey Mouse." — 10-100 — 15-225

(951) TENDER, 1939-42, 1951-58, four- or eight-wheel, New York Central or **NKP.** — 15-100 — 20-160

952 OLIVE DRAB TENDER, "Army Supply Train," 1940, four-wheel. — 150 — 175

(961) EIGHT-WHEEL SLOPE BACK TENDER, 1962-64, 1967-68, 1972, 1974, black, plastic or **gray**, assorted road names. — 15-25 — 20-30

(971) NEW YORK CENTRAL TENDER, 1938-48, two-wheel, articulated, pin couplers. Brass, gray and red. — 50 — 75

(1951) TENDER, black plastic, 1952-74, four- or eight-wheel, assorted road names, including **Canadian Pacific**. — 10-50 — 15-75

(2451) CP TENDER, 1937-38, 1941, 6", eight-wheel frame, hook couplers, **light blue** or maroon, yellow or gold lettering. — 40-50 — 60-75

(2551) NEW YORK CENTRAL, 1938-40, Commodore Vanderbilt, eight-wheel frame and rivets. — 15 — 30

2731 SANTA FE TENDER, 1953, 1955, 1959-60, black plastic used with 1829. — 25 — 40

(3551) TENDER, Union Pacific, New York Central or **"1st Div. S.P. & P.R.R.",** 1955-57, 1959, 6", four-wheel frame, formed metal. — 15-50 — 20-75

(3651) WILLIAM CROOKS TENDER, 1959-62, 1973 black plastic, "Tales of Wells Fargo", or "1st Div. St. P. & P.R.R." — 20 — 40

(3661) See (198A)

(3991) NEW YORK CENTRAL, 1949-54, die-cast, black. — 40 — 70

EARLY SIX-INCH CARS

201 OBSERVATION, 1934-35 cherry red, Joy Line couplers. — 50 — 65

245 PULLMAN, 1934-36, "Bogota," cherry red. — 20 — 40

246 COACH, 1934-36, "Montclair," cherry red. — 20 — 40

547 BAGGAGE, New York Central, 1934-35, cherry red, Joy Line couplers. — 45 — 65

	C6	C8
(550) CRANE, 1934-35, New York Central, orange cab, red boom, red or black crane cab base, Joy Line couplers.	20	40
(551) WAGON TOP TENDER, 1934-36, New York Central Commodore Vanderbilt four-wheel, black, **silver**, blue, red, gray, copper.	10-**150**	15-**250**
552 GONDOLA, CRI&P, 1934-36, cherry red.	20	30
553 TANK CAR, Santa Fe, 1934-36, bright yellow.	15	30
(559) DOUBLE FLOODLIGHT CAR with two nickel or black lights.	75	150

	C6	C8
694 CABOOSE, New York Central, 1934-36, cherry red.	15	30
817 See 91453		
1678 HOPPER, Northern Pacific, 1934-35, olive bronze, Joy Line couplers.	20	35
1935 MAIL CAR, New York Central, 1934-36, dark green, Joy Line couplers.	45	90
91453 REFRIGERATOR CAR, C&S, 1934-35, yellow, Joy Line couplers.	30	50

SIX-INCH FOUR-WHEEL CARS

The "six-inch" four-wheel cars, (actually 6-3/4" long) were sold from 1934 into 1942. After a break due to World War II, the car returned in 1946 and remained in the line through 1972. Plastic couplers were introduced on part of the line about 1953.

BAGGAGE, EXPRESS, MAIL CARS

	C6	C8
547 BAGGAGE/MAIL CAR, New York Central, 1936-37, red body, yellow, silver or **black lettering**.	35-**45**	60-**85**
1935 "U.S. MAIL CAR," New York Central, 1936-37, green or red body.	40	90

	C6	C8
5011-5026 BAGGAGE/MAIL CAR, New York Central, 1957, blue and gray body.	35	60

| | C6 | C8 | | C6 | C8 |

BOXCARS

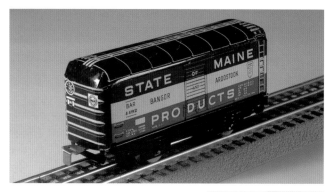

4485-4500 BAR, "State of Maine Products," 1960, 1962, blue, white and red, solid doors. 50 75

37960-37975 PRR, "Merchandise Service", 1954, gray and red, solid doors, also produced without number on side in 1965. 15 30

46010 SSW, "Cotton Belt Route", 1940, cobalt blue, orange, yellow, brown, crimson red, candy apple red. 30-65 75-125

51998 C&NW, "400 Streamliners", 1939-40, cobalt blue, orange, yellow, brown, crimson red, candy apple red. 30-65 75-125

90171 B&LE, 1940, 1948, 1953, 1955, cobalt blue, **orange, yellow,** brown, crimson red, candy apple red, caramel, salmon red. 30-**55** 75-**115**

174580-174595 NEW YORK CENTRAL, Pacemaker, red and gray body, white and black detail, sliding doors. 75 125

384299 B&O, 1940, 1954-55, 1957, cobalt blue, **orange, yellow,** brown, crimson red, candy apple red. 30-**65** 75-**125**

	C6	**C8**

CABOOSES

556 NEW YORK CENTRAL,
red, **with** or without illumination.

	C6	C8
556 NEW YORK CENTRAL, red, **with** or without illumination.	15-50	20-125
694 NEW YORK CENTRAL, dark red, many variations.	20	30
956 SAL, green and yellow.	50	75

	C6	C8
3824 UP, yellow and brown body, orange, **brown** or black frame.	15-25	20-40
5563 KCS, red, yellow and black.	75	125
20102 NEW YORK CENTRAL, red and gray, **with** or without illumination.	5-90	10-175

	C6	C8
31055 MONON, red and gray.	75	125

FLATCARS AND MISCELLANEOUS WORK CARS

Note: If loads listed are missing, value of car should be reduced 75 percent or more.

	C6	C8
(550) CRANE, 1934-35, New York Central, orange cab, red or black crane cab base.	20	40
(559) DOUBLE FLOODLIGHT, no lettering or lithography, black or **red** frame, brass, black or **red deck**, black or **nickel lights**.	20-50	40-90

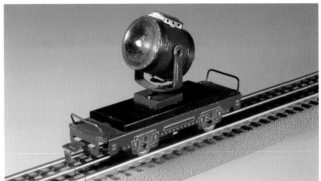

	C6	C8
(561) SEARCHLIGHT, with single large brass, red-painted metal or red plastic light.	25	65
(562) FLATCAR, black, with dump or stake truckload.	125	175
(563) LUMBER CAR, with load of four pieces of square lumber.	40	60
(566) CABLE CAR, black, with wooden cable reel wound with rope.	50	75
(572A) AIRPLANE CAR, black car with various colors of airplanes as load, red most common.	125-150	200-275
(574) BARREL CAR, black, with seven wooden barrels.	50	75
(663) POLE CAR, black, with 15 dowel load.	40	50
Unnumbered RAIL TRANSPORT CARS (sold as a pair), black, with rail load.	175	225
Unnumbered WHEEL CAR, with wheel load.	100	125

| | **C6** | **C8** | | **C6** | **C8** |

GONDOLAS

548 CRI&P "Guernsey Milk," 1939-40, turquoise, cream, wood milk cans held by cardboard insert. — 75 / 125

552 CRI&P, 1937-38, 1940, red, green or blue. — 15 / 25

552G CRI&P, "Groceries and Sundries," yellow, brown, with box load. — 50 / 100

28500 LV high-sided, green and silver, 1953, 1960. — 10 / 20

86000 DLW high-sided, iridescent blue, red, 1956. — 30 / 50

91257 Seaboard RR, 1957, red, brown, **dark blue**. — 15-**50** / 20-**85**

554 NP "General Coal Co.," 1935-40, 1946, 1950, blue with red interior, or red with yellow interior. — 15 / 25

241708 B&O, 1953, yellow exterior, with **black**, gray or red interior. — 5-**20** / 15-**50**

738701 PRR, 1940, 1952, 1954 high-sided, red. — 20 / 35

	C6	C8		C6	C8

HOPPERS

1678 NORTHERN PACIFIC, "General Coal Co.," 1936, olive-bronze, red interior. — 30 — 40

86000 DLW, "Lackawanna," 1953, blue. — 20 — 25

738701 PRR hopper, "Pennsylvania", 1940 tuscan with tuscan or **black** interior. — 15-20 — 25-**35**

MILITARY CARS

(552M) (298/6) GONDOLA, "Ordnance Dept." olive **with** or without **bullet load.** — 60-**100** — 110-**200**

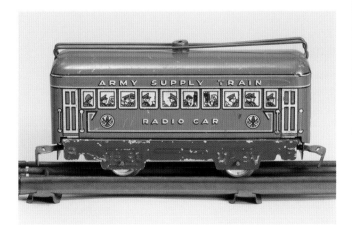

(557M) COACH, "Army Supply Train", "Radio Car", olive lithographed body, **with** or without antennas. — 50-**75** — 75-**100**

(558M) OBSERVATION, "Army Supply Train," "Official Car," olive lithography, with or without illumination, nickel or brass platform rail. — 50 — 100

(561M) SEARCHLIGHT CAR, olive drab; 1939, red, black or olive handle; mirror lens and **dummy searchlight,** 1941. — 35-**100** — 65-**125**

(572) FIELD GUN CAR, 1940, olive drab. — 70 — 100

(572A) FLATCAR, with olive or red airplane, 1940. — 150 — 250

(572D) FLATCAR, olive dump or cargo truck. — 150 — 225

	C6	**C8**

(572G) SIEGE GUN CAR, 1940, cannon has 5/8" bore, olive drab.

	C6	C8
(572G) SIEGE GUN CAR	125	150
(572M) FLATCAR	60	80

(572M) FLATCAR, olive, 1940, 1957, various metal or plastic truck loads.

(572AA) ANTI-AIRCRAFT GUN CAR, 1940, cannon has 5/16" bore, olive drab.

	C6	C8
(572AA) ANTI-AIRCRAFT GUN CAR	100	125

(572MG) MACHINE GUN CAR, 1940, olive drab.

(572ST) FLATCAR, with tank, 1940, various tanks used, including tumbling and sparkling; painted and lithographed.

	C6	C8
(572MG) MACHINE GUN CAR	100	125
(572ST) FLATCAR	125-225	250-425

PASSENGER CARS

	C6	**C8**
201 "OBSERVATION," 1934-36, cherry red.	50	75

	C6	C8
245 PULLMAN, 1934-36, cherry red, "Bogota."	25	40
246 PULLMAN, 1934-36, cherry red, "Montclair."	30	50
246 COACH, Canadian Pacific, 1938-40, wine-maroon body, "Montreal."	125	250
247 COACH, Canadian Pacific, 1938-40, wine-maroon body, "Toronto."	125	250
248 COACH, Canadian Pacific, 1938-40, wine-maroon body, "Quebec."	125	250
249 COACH, Canadian Pacific, 1938-40, wine-maroon body, "Ottawa."	125	250
250 COACH, Canadian Pacific, 1938-40, wine-maroon body, "Winnipeg."	125	250
251 COACH, Canadian Pacific, 1938-40, wine-maroon body, "Vancouver."	125	250
252 COACH, Canadian Pacific, 1938-40, wine-maroon body, "Calgary."	125	250
253 COACH, Canadian Pacific, 1938-40, wine-maroon body, "Hamilton."	125	250

	C6	C8

2071 COACH, New York Central, silver. | 40 | 75

2072 OBSERVATION, New York Central, matches 2071. | 70 | 100

Unnumbered "Montclair," commonly with red body, sometimes with **blue and white** or green and yellow lithographed body. Silver, red, blue or black frame, with or without illumination. | 20-**75** | 40-**125**

Unnumbered "Bogota," commonly with red body, sometimes with **blue and white** or green and yellow lithographed body. Silver, red, blue or black frame, with or without illumination. | 20-**75** | 40-**125**

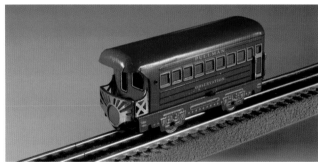

Unnumbered "Observation," commonly with red body, sometimes with **blue and white** or green and yellow lithographed body. Silver, red, blue or black frame, with or without illuminated interior and drumhead. | 20-**75** | 40-**125**

REFRIGERATOR CARS

555 "Colorado & Southern Refrigerator," 1937-42, 1953-54, cream body, blue or **red roof**, red, black or **silver frame**, sliding doors or **man in door**. | 20-**175** | 40-**275**

10961-10976 FGEX, 1940-49, 1954-56, yellow car with sliding doors and gray roof. | 150 | 275

91453 "Colorado & Southern Refrigerator," 1936-38, yellow with sliding doors. | 25 | 40

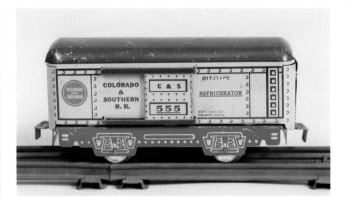

C6   C8   C6   C8

SIDE DUMP CARS

TANK CARS

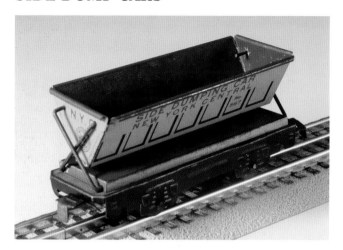

567 NEW YORK CENTRAL
"Side Dumping Car," yellow with
brass, brown or copper deck.   20   40

STOCK CARS

553 TANK CAR, Santa Fe, 1934-
36, bright yellow or silver, flat or
domed ends.   15   30

59 STOCK CAR, Union Pacific,
slotted or solid lithographed
tuscan car sides.   20-40   35-60

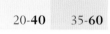

553 TANK CAR, UTLX, silver,
black or tin dome and ends.   20   30

C6 C8

C6 C8

| 19847 TANK CAR, SDRX, black or **green**. | 20-**30** | 30-**80** |

SIX-INCH EIGHT-WHEEL CARS

Offered from 1936 into 1942, these cars used the same bodies as their four-wheel counterparts, but were equipped with swiveling four-wheel trucks.

BAGGAGE, EXPRESS, MAIL CARS

547 BAGGAGE/MAIL CAR, New York Central, 1936-37, red body, yellow lettering.	70	100
1935 "U.S. Mail Car," New York Central, 1936-37, red body.	60	90

BOXCARS

46010 SSW, "Cotton Belt Route," 1940, cobalt blue, **orange, yellow**, brown, crimson red.	30-**65**	75-**125**
51998 C&NW, "400 Streamliners," 1939-40, cobalt blue, **orange, yellow**, brown, crimson red.	30-**65**	75-**125**
90171 B&LE, 1940, cobalt blue, **orange, yellow**, brown, crimson red, caramel, salmon red.	30-**55**	75-**115**
384299 B&O, 1940, cobalt blue, **orange, yellow**, brown, crimson red.	30-**65**	75-**125**

CABOOSES

556 NEW YORK CENTRAL, red, with black or **red frame**.	15-**25**	25-**50**

FLATCARS AND MISCELLANEOUS WORK CARS

Note: If loads listed are missing, value of car should be reduced 75 percent or more.

(2550) CRANE, New York Central, orange cab, red or black crane cab base.	30	65
(2561) SEARCHLIGHT, with illuminated or dummy lamp.	60-75	100-125

	C6	C8
(2562) FLATCAR, black or **red**; with dump or stake truckload.	125-175	175-**225**
(2563) LUMBER CAR, black or **red**; with load of four pieces of square lumber.	40-80	60-175
(2566) CABLE CAR, black, with wooden cable reel wound with rope.	50	75
(2574) BARREL CAR, black, with seven wooden barrels.	50	75
(2663) POLE CAR, black or **red**, with 15 dowel load.	30-80	60-**175**

GONDOLAS

	C6	C8
548 CRI&P "Guernsey Milk", 1939-40, turquoise, cream, wood milk cans held by cardboard insert.	100	150

	C6	C8
552 CRI&P, 1937-38, 1940, green with black or red frame.	15-25	25-45

	C6	C8
552G CRI&P, "Groceries and Sundries", yellow, brown, with box load.	75	150

	C6	C8
554 NP "General Coal Co.," 1936-40, red with yellow interior.	15	35
738701 PRR, 1940, high-sided, red.	20	35

MILITARY CARS

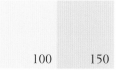

	C6	C8
(2552M) GONDOLA, "Ordnance Dept." olive, **with** or without **bullet load**.	60-**100**	110-**200**
(2561MD) SEARCHLIGHT CAR, olive drab; 1939, dummy searchlight.	100	150
(2572) FIELD GUN CAR, 1940, olive drab.	125	175
(2572G) SIEGE GUN CAR, 1940, cannon has 5/8" bore, olive drab.	125	175
(2572MG) MACHINE GUN CAR, 1940, olive drab.	175	250
(2572ST) FLATCAR with tank, 1940, painted olive or lithographed red and yellow tank.	300	400

	C6	C8

PASSENGER CARS

246 COACH, Canadian Pacific, 1938-40, wine-maroon body, "Montreal." — 125 / 250

247 COACH, Canadian Pacific, 1938-40, wine-maroon body, "Toronto." — 125 / 250

248 COACH, Canadian Pacific, 1938-40, wine-maroon body, "Quebec." — 125 / 250

249 COACH, Canadian Pacific, 1938-40, wine-maroon body, "Ottawa." — 125 / 250

250 COACH, Canadian Pacific, 1938-40, wine-maroon body, "Winnipeg." — 125 / 250

251 COACH, Canadian Pacific, 1938-40, wine-maroon body, "Vancouver." — 125 / 250

252 COACH, Canadian Pacific, 1938-40, wine-maroon body, "Calgary." — 125 / 250

253 COACH, Canadian Pacific, 1938-40, wine-maroon body, "Hamilton." — 125 / 250

Unnumbered "Bogota," black or **red frame**. — 30-**50** / 50-**70**

Unnumbered "Montclair," black or **red frame**. — 30-**50** / 50-**70**

Unnumbered "Observation," black or **red frame**. — 30-**50** / 50-**70**

REFRIGERATOR CARS

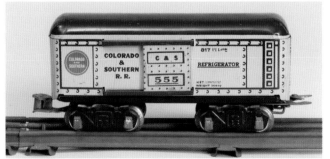

555 COLORADO & SOUTHERN REFRIGERATOR, 1937-42, cream body, blue or red roof, red or black frame. — 30 / 60

SIDE DUMP CARS

567 NEW YORK CENTRAL "Side Dumping Car," yellow with brass, brown or copper deck. — 20 / 40

STOCK CARS

59 STOCK CAR, Union Pacific, **slotted** or solid lithographed tuscan car sides. — 20-**40** / 35-**60**

TANK CARS

553 SANTA FE, silver, flat or dome-shaped ends, black or **red frame**. — 20-**25** / 35-**45**

C6   C8   C6   C8

MARX SEVEN-INCH CARS

Marx produced the cars in this series for 10 years, beginning in 1949.

BOXCARS

1476 "MICKEY MOUSE TRAIN," 1950-57, yellow.   90   165

4484 BAR, "State of Maine," 1956-57.   20   30

37950-37959 PRR, "Merchandise Service," 1950-55, red and gray.   15   25

CABOOSES

C-504-C-518 B&O, 1955-57, blue, gray, and black, four or eight wheels.   45   65

956 NICKEL PLATE ROAD, 1950-58, red and gray.   15   25
969-980 KCS, 1956-57, yellow, red, and black.   125   175

1235 SP, 1952-55, red, maroon, and silver.   15   20
1951 AT&SF, 1951-53, red and black.   15   20

3855 MONON, 1956-57, red, gray and white.   30   75

	C6	C8

**20110-20124 NEW YORK
CENTRAL,** 1954-58,
"Pacemaker."

	20	30

**691521 "MICKEY MOUSE
TRAIN METEOR,"** 1950-51.

	70	110

GONDOLAS

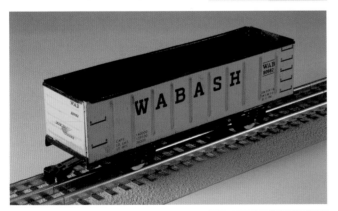

36000 C&O, 1956-57, brown.

	20	35

80982 WABASH, 1950-53,
yellow.

	15	20

**Unnumbered "MICKEY
MOUSE TRAIN,"** 1950-51,
blue and yellow.

	75	115

	C6	C8

PASSENGER CARS (1860 PERIOD)

1 COMBINE, St. Paul & Pacific,
1959-60, 1962, yellow with black
roof, four- or eight-wheel.

	40	75

3 COACH, St. Paul & Pacific,
1959-60, 1962, yellow with black
roof, four- or eight-wheel.

	40	75

C6   C8   C6   C8

MARX PLASTIC FREIGHT CARS

These were produced from 1952 through 1975. Some of the same tooling is in use today by new owners.

BOXCARS

2858 "USAX ORDNANCE," olive drab. — 225 | 400

3280 SANTA FE, four-wheel, orange or white. — 15 | 20

5595 "FARM MASTER BRAND," 1959, automatic boxcar, cream or white. — 25 | 40

13975 AT&SF, four- or eight-wheel, brown, red or **yellow**. — 15-25 | 20-60

18918 GREAT NORTHERN, brown. — 50 | 90

20053 SEABOARD, 1957, 1959, four-door boxcar, tuscan or **red**. — 60-115 | 85-165

34178 GREAT NORTHERN, 1961, 1975, lime or **dark green**. — 15-25 | 20-40

43461 PACIFIC FRUIT EXPRESS, 1955, white. — 15 | 20

54099 MISSOURI PACIFIC, 1956-57, 1960, 1974, **orange, green or yellow**, or red automatic. — 25-125 | 40-200

77003 BOSTON AND MAINE, 1952, 1955, 1957, blue. — 20 | 30

147815 ROCK ISLAND, 1952-59, red or **tuscan**. — 20-45 | 45-70

	C6	C8
161755 NEW YORK CENTRAL, 1952, yellow, four-wheel.	15	20
174479 NEW YORK CENTRAL, "Pacemaker," green, four-wheel.	30	50

	C6	C8
176893 NEW YORK CENTRAL, 1973-74, dark green.	30	50
186028 UNION PACIFIC, 1955, dark red.	30	60
249319 MARLINES OPERATING BOXCAR, operating, 1955, 1959, red or white.	30	50
259199 CANADIAN PACIFIC, tuscan.	100	125
467110 B&O.	15	20
Unnumbered MARLINES, 1952, red or blue.	30	60

CABOOSES

	C6	C8
45 SP-STYLE CABOOSE, 1973, dark brown.	35	45
234 "US ARMY," 1957, olive drab.	30	50
C350 MONON, maroon or red, four- or eight-wheel.	25	35
X467 "ROCKET COMPUTING CENTRE" CABOOSE, red, four-wheel.	40	55
504 B&O, 1953, blue, four-wheel.	190	250
564 "ALLSTATE," 1959.	5	20
586 ROCK ISLAND, work caboose, brown.	20	30

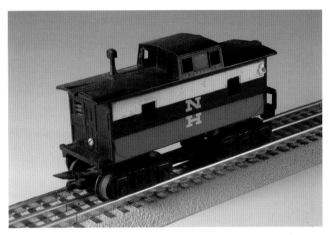

	C6	C8
635 NEW HAVEN, maroon, brown or black, white and orange **"McGinnis scheme,"** four- or eight-wheel.	15-**25**	20-**40**
643 WESTERN PACIFIC, SP-style caboose, green, four-wheel.	20	30

	C6	C8
643 WESTERN PACIFIC, bay window caboose, 1973, green.	65	115
969 KCS, red, four- or eight-wheel.	50	75
1015 ICG WORK CABOOSE, 1974, black, orange, white.	35	50
MP1231 "MISSOURI PACIFIC SYSTEM," 1974, white, four-wheel.	30	50
1500 RIO GRANDE, 1974, orange.	65	90
1963 USAX, 1963, work caboose	100	150
(1972) SANTA FE, 1974, brown or red.	10	15

	C6	C8

1977 AT&SF, 1973-75, red, maroon or **red, silver and yellow,** four- or eight-wheel.

	C6	C8
1977 AT&SF	10-15	15-25
1988 B&LE, 1974, orange.	25	50
2130 USA WORK CABOOSE, olive drab.	125	225

	C6	C8
2225 SANTA FE, 1958-66, bay window, maroon.	50	75
(2225) "ALLSTATE", 1953-59, bay window, orange or turquoise blue.	80	125
2366 CANADIAN PACIFIC, maroon.	75	100
3824 UNION PACIFIC, 1956, 1962, bay window, maroon.	60	85
3900 UNION PACIFIC, 1974-75, orange, brown, yellow, or orange and black, four- or eight-wheel.	10-30	15-50

	C6	C8
4427 SANTA FE, 1952-59, red.	15	25

	C6	C8
4546 NEW YORK CENTRAL CABOOSE, dark red, large-type, 74.	20	30

	C6	C8
(4556) SOUTHERN PACIFIC, 1953-75, red or brown.	10	15
(4564) NEW YORK CENTRAL, red or brown.	15	20
4586 UNION PACIFIC, 1957-58, work caboose, red, with or **without searchlight**.	25-30	35-50
(4587) SANTA FE, 1962, work caboose w/ light, maroon.	30	50
(4588) "ALLSTATE", 1955, work caboose w/ light, tuscan.	30	60
(4589) NEW YORK CENTRAL, 1957, track-cleaning work caboose.	75	125
(4590) AT&SF, 1955-62, **red,** brown, or brown and red.	15-20	20-30
5586 WESTERN PACIFIC, 1957, work caboose, dark red.	20	30
17858 ROCK ISLAND, 1958-59, SP-style caboose, tuscan, four- or eight-wheel.	15	25
17858 ROCK ISLAND, bay window, maroon.	35	70

	C6	C8

18326 NEW YORK CENTRAL, 1956-74, **black, white and green**, or numerous other colors, four- or eight-wheel. 15-**30** 20-**50**

18326 PENN CENTRAL. 15 25

95050 LEHIGH VALLEY, 1974, red, four-wheel. 7 12

Unnumbered MARLINES, 1952, 1974, red, four-wheel. 25 50

Unnumbered W.T. GRANT, 1972, light orange, similar to 4556. 20 30

CRANES

5590 NEW YORK CENTRAL, black plastic cab, die-cast base, with or without searchlight. 40-75 50-115

IC-1020X35 ILLINOIS CENTRAL, brown and orange. 25 45

	C6	C8

Unnumbered NEW YORK CENTRAL, gray and black, or black. 15 25

DUMP CARS

967(A) NEW YORK CENTRAL, 1957-58, blue or **black**, four-wheel. 100-**125** 175-**225**

Unnumbered ERIE, eight-wheel log dump w/ five-log load, maroon or blue mechanically operated, or maroon electrically operated. 20 35

FLATCARS

Note: If loads listed are missing, value of car should be reduced 75 percent or more.

24 ILLINOIS CENTRAL, with searchlight, 1974, black. 25 40

56(A) BROWN, 1973, with yellow fence and wood load. 25 35

586 ERIE, maroon. 5 10

586 USA, olive drab, various silver military loads. 50 90

1024 ILLINOIS CENTRAL GULF, 1974, black, yellow rails. 25 50

1796 ROCKET LAUNCHER, 1959-60, white or blue and gray, four- or eight-wheel. 100 175

2246 USA, 1957, olive drab, with two silver plastic military loads, six different individual possible cargo items. 75 125

	C6	**C8**
2824 "US ARMY," 1957, depressed center car, olive drab, missiles and launcher.	100	200
4528A ERIE, 1956, maroon or **orange** with red, **gray or green** tractors.	40-**150**	75-**275**
4566 CWEX, 1955, blue depressed center car (various shades) with gray or **yellow** cable reels.	50-**100**	75-**250**

	C6	**C8**
4571 WECX, 1955-65, red depressed center car with gray searchlight and generator.	25	50
4581 BKX, red, with two lights and a generator.	50	75

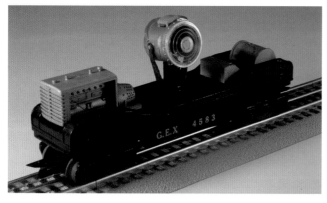

	C6	**C8**
4583 GEX, 1955, black.	50	100
5545 CB&Q, 1957, red or maroon, commonly with black girder marked.	35	60
5545 CB&Q, also came with two each of a variety of trailers, including Allstate, **Walgreens**, Burlington, Western Auto or New York Central.	125-**200**	175-**275**

	C6	**C8**
(5561) WECX, 1956-57, red, depressed, with gray searchlight.	40	65

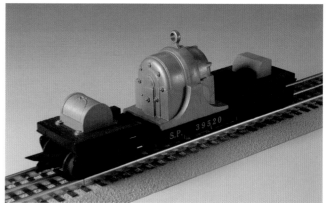

	C6	**C8**
39520 SP, 1958, depressed center, black or maroon with generator.	40	75
44535 SAL, gray, with eight-piece pipe load.	35	60

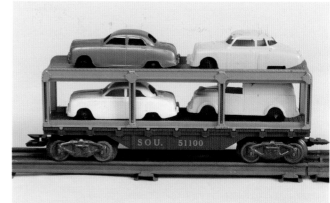

	C6	**C8**
51100 SOUTHERN, 1955-73, auto loader, red, or maroon or **blue base** with gray or yellow rack and four cars.	25-**30**	55-**65**
74563 ACL, 1961, red, with red rails and a four-piece lumber load.	60	90
Unnumbered ERIE, four- or eight-wheel, with lumber, cable reel, two autos, two tractors, Atomic Light Generator, a generator or variety of trailers, of which **Walgreens** and **Western Auto** are the most valuable.	20-**125**	25-**200**

	C6	C8

GONDOLAS

Note: If loads listed are missing, value of car should be reduced 75 percent or more.

1799 USAX, 1959, **red, eight-** wheel or blue, four-wheel, with missile load. — 65-**80** / 110-**125**

2236 USA, 1957, olive drab, with missile load. — 50 / 80

2824 MISSILE LAUNCHER, 1961-62, yellow. — 50 / 75

5532 "ALLSTATE," 1959-62, light or dark blue, eight- or **four-wheel**. — 15-**35** / 20-**65**

20309 L&N, 1959, 1961, brown or yellow. — 60 / 125

51170 ERIE, black, blue, **orange** or gray. — 15-**80** / 20-**150**

131000 SCL, 1973, yellow or blue, eight-wheel. — 15 / 20

39234 CANADIAN PACIFIC, 1957, 1960-62, brown, black, tuscan, removable ends. — 50 / 70

347100 PRR, 1952-73, four- or eight-wheel. — 10 / 20

715100 NEW YORK CENTRAL, 1970-74, four- or eight-wheel. — 15 / 20

Unnumbered MARINES, 1952, yellow, four-wheel. — 20 / 30

	C6	C8

HOPPERS

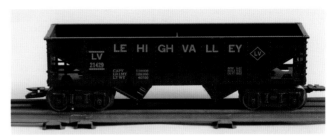

21429 LEHIGH VALLEY, 1965-76, many variations. — 20 / 30

21913 LEHIGH VALLEY, 1965-74, many variations — 10 / 20

28236 VIRGINIAN, 1955, 1974, **red** or brown. — 15-**75** / 30-**150**

TANK CARS

246 "CHEMICAL ROCKET FUEL," cream or white. — 15 / 25

284 UTLX, 1954, 1964, three-dome. — 15 / 25

2532 "CITIES SERVICE," 1966-70, green, four-or eight-wheel. — 10 / 15

(5543) FLAT w/ two tanks, 1955-74, Cities Service, Allstate or **Gulf**. — 25-**125** / 50-**225**

	C6	C8
(5553) ALLSTATE, Exxon or "**Milk,**" three-dome, 1960-74.	25-**225**	50-**300**
(9553) "ALLSTATE," "Allstate Rocket Fuel" or **Gulf,** 1959-74, single dome, four- or eight-wheel.	15-**35**	25-**60**
X-246 "CHEMICAL ROCKET FUEL," four-wheel.	15	20

MARX ACCESSORIES

Marx marked no numbers on the accessories they produced, requiring reference to catalogs for proper identifications. For that reason, they are listed here in alphabetical order.

	C6	C8
(3832) AIRPORT, plastic.	30	50
(3741) ARMY BARRACKS, plastic.	30	50
(3861) BARN, plastic barn and silo.	15	25
(3862) BARN.	15	25
(1456) BARREL LOADER, automatic.	50	75
(6102) BATTERY BOX, black.	15	20
(0446) BEACON, rotating.	20	30
(0226) BILLBOARD, plastic, **yellow lighted** or green non-illuminated, two-piece set.	10-**20**	20-**35**

	C6	C8
(404) BLOCK SIGNAL, two lights, 6-1/2 inches tall.	5	10
(404) BLOCK SIGNAL, three lights, 6-1/2 inches tall.	5	10
(405) BLOCK SIGNAL, with rheostat and three lights.	15	20
(434) BLOCK SIGNAL, 1952, single target 8 inches tall.	**12**	**20**
(434) BLOCK SIGNAL, three lights, black, 6-1/2 inches tall.	12	20
(454) BLOCK SIGNAL, 1952, two lights, black, 7 inches.	5	10

	C6	C8
(464) BLOCK SIGNAL, plastic, 1957, double target type, gray or black.	1	15
(1402) BLOCK SIGNAL, two lights, black, 6-1/2 inches tall.	5	10
(1404) BLOCK SIGNAL, position type, metal, five lights, 9 inches tall.	75	100
(1404) BLOCK SIGNAL, position type, plastic.	30	40
(1405) BLOCK SIGNAL, three lights, with control.	60	80
Unnumbered BLOCK SIGNAL, green.	10	15
(1303) BRIDGE, black, "Erie".	8	15
(1304) BRIDGE, girder, metal.	10	15
(1305) BRIDGE.	15	30
(1310) BRIDGE, girder, metal.	15	35
(1320) BRIDGE, 18-inch through-truss.	10	25
(1324) BRIDGE, similar to 1320 with beacon added.	30	50
(1350) BRIDGE, silver, 24-inches long.	10	20
(1380) BRIDGE, silver, 24-inches, with beacon added.	30	50
(6110) BUILDINGS, cardboard, set of eight.	30	50
(505) BUMPER, non-illuminated, red or black metal, or gray or white plastic.	5	10

	C6	C8

(605) BUMPER, illuminated, metal or plastic, black. — 5 — 10

(304) CATTLE CORRAL, metal, black or silver. — 20 — 30

(3856) CHICKEN COOP, lithographed. — 25 — 35

(3851) CHURCH, plastic. — 20 — 25

(3852) CHURCH, 1952, identical to 3851. — 20 — 25

(409) CIRCUIT BREAKER, 25 watts. — 5 — 10

(415) CIRCUIT BREAKER, 50 watts. — 5 — 10

(419) CIRCUIT BREAKER, 30 watts. — 5 — 10

(420) CIRCUIT BREAKER, black. — 10 — 15

(420A) CIRCUIT BREAKER, black. — 5 — 10

(425) CIRCUIT BREAKER. — 5 — 10

(424) CONTROL TOWER, metal. — 25 — 45

(6101) CONTROLLER. — 3 — 5

(1601) COUPLER ADAPTER. — 5 — 10

(409) CROSSING FLASHER, red or black. — 12 — 18

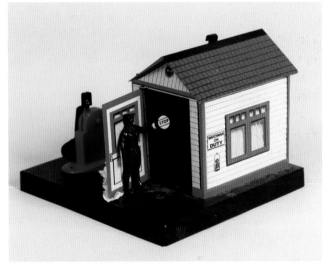

(414) CROSSING BELL, 7-1/2 inches tall. — 15 — 20

(417) CROSSING SIGN, red and chrome. — 12 — 18

(317) CROSSING GATE, manual, black or red, 8 inches. — 8 — 12

(064) CROSSING GATE, plastic. — 3 — 5

(428) CROSSING GATE, automatic, 7-inch, gray or black plastic. — 5 — 10

	C6	C8

(0217) CROSSING GATE, gray plastic. — 3 — 5

(1438) CROSSING GATE, 1952, with double arms. — 12 — 20

(321) CROSSING SET, four pieces. — 12 — 25

(430) CROSSING SET, three pieces. — 10 — 20

(1420) CROSSING SHANTY, 1957, with gate and attendant. — 25 — 50

(1439) CROSSING SHANTY, with gate and attendant. — 25 — 50

(1440) CROSSING SHANTY, illuminated, with gate and attendant. — 40 — 65

(314) CROSSING SIGN, "Caution", "High Speed Trains." — 5 — 10

(067) CROSSING SIGNAL, plastic. — 2 — 5

(069) CROSSING SIGNAL, plastic. — 2 — 5

(418) CROSSING SIGNAL, 1952, with bell. — 10 — 15

(421) CROSSING SIGNAL, plastic, with flashing lights. — 10 — 15

(423) CROSSING SIGNAL, 1952, black and chrome, with flashing lights. — 10 — 15

| | C6 | C8 |

(438) CROSSING SIGNAL, with automatic gate, 1952, black or red. — 10 — 15

(1426) CROSSING SIGNAL, banjo-type, plastic, with flashing light. — 10 — 15

(0218) CROSSING WATCHMAN SHED, 1956, red. — 10 — 15

(412) DERRICK, black and red, or orange. — 25 — 40

(422) DERRICK, black and red lithographed. — 30 — 50

(0442) DERRICK, gray and red plastic. — 10 — 15

(1450) DIESEL, fuel station. — 50 — 75

(3771) DINER, plastic. — 22 — 35

(1614) DUMP UNIT. — 75 — 100

(1615) DUMP UNIT, identical to 1614. — 75 — 100

(403) DWARF SIGNAL. — 25 — 40

(3812) FACTORY. — 25 — 35

(316) FENCE, black or silver (value per section). — 5 — 7

(6111) FENCE AND RAMP. — 10 — 15

(782) FIGURE SET, plastic. — 7 — 12

(6114) FIGURE SET, farm animals, lithographed, eight-piece set. — 30 — 60

Unnumbered FIGURE SET, soldiers and tents. — 30 — 50

| | C6 | C8 |

(3781) FIREHOUSE, plastic. — 10 — 25

(0416) FLOODLIGHT TOWER, 1952-53, four lights, plastic, 13-1/2 inches tall. — 15 — 25

(0436) FLOODLIGHT TOWER, 1952-53, gray and black, plastic, 13-1/4 inches tall. — 10 — 15

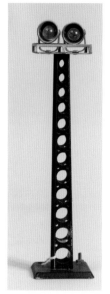

(416) FLOODLIGHT TOWER, twin lights, black, **green**, red or silver. — 10-15 — 20-**35**

(416A) FLOODLIGHT TOWER, twin lights, 11-1/2 inches tall. — 15 — 25

(5420) FREIGHT STATION, 1952, lithographed metal. — 75 — 100

(5424) FREIGHT STATION, same as 5420, with accessories, 1953-54. — 100 — 125

(1460) GANTRY CRANE, 1955-57. — 65 — 100

(2959) GIRARD WHISTLING STATION, red and gray. — 25 — 45

(2960) GIRARD WHISTLING STATION, red and gray. — 25 — 45

(2970) GIRARD WHISTLING STATION, illuminated. — 30 — 50

(1600) GLENDALE FREIGHT STATION. — 50 — 75

	C6	C8

(1900) GLENDALE STATION, with warning signal. — 50 / 75

(2900) GLENDALE STATION, with lamp and signals. — 75 / 100

(3880) GLENDALE STATION, plastic. — 15 / 25

(4116) GLENDALE STATION, kit, lithographed. — 50 / 75

(4412) GLENDALE STATION, lithographed metal. — 50 / 75

(4416) GLENDALE STATION, with light and accessories. — 50 / 75

(4418) GLENDALE STATION, talking station. — 75 / 100

(066) GRADE CROSSING, brown plastic stamped "RR." — 1 / 3

(6103) GRADE CROSSING, brown, stamped "RR Crossing." — 2 / 5

(2940) GRAND CENTRAL TERMINAL, lithographed, buff-yellow. — 75 / 100

(Unnumbered) GRAND CENTRAL TERMINAL, blue, yellow or tan, red. — 45 / 60

(068) HIGH-TENSION POLES, brown plastic, set of six. — 10 / 15

(3802) HOUSE, colonial. — 10 / 20

(500) KEY, for mechanical locomotives. — 2 / 8

(062) LAMP POST, plastic, 6 inches tall. — 1 / 2

(072) LAMP POST, plastic, 6 inches tall. — 1 / 2

(073) LAMP POST, set of three, 6-1/2 inches tall. — 10 / 15

(074) LAMP POST, plastic, 6-1/4 inches tall. — 3 / 5

(078) LAMP POST, plastic, 6-1/2 inches tall. — 3 / 5

(308) LAMP, street, metal body, 7 inch tall, battery operated, assorted colors. — 10 / 25

(408) LAMP, street lamp, black or red. — 10 / 15

(419) LAMP, street lamp, 7 1/2-inch tall, black or red. — 10 / 15

(426) LAMP, street, gray, plastic, 7-1/2 inch tall. — 5 / 10

(429) LAMP, street, 1952. — 10 / 15

(1392) LIFT BRIDGE, silver, Illinois Central herald. — 45 / 80

(B-25) LIGHT, extension. — 10 / 15

(X-5) LIGHT BULB KIT, five replacement 12-volt bulbs. — 10 / 20

(X-10) LUBRICANT, tube. — 2 / 5

Unnumbered NEWSSTAND. — 5 / 10

(2979) OAK PARK STATION, yellow and green. — 40 / 70

(2980) OAK PARK STATION, yellow and green. — 40 / 70

(2990) OAK PARK STATION, with light. — 60 / 90

(3721) POLICE STATION. — 10 / 20

Unnumbered POWER HOUSE, with transformer inside. — 60 / 125

(0161) POWER POLE, set of 12 plastic. — 5 / 10

(3871) RANCH HOUSE, plastic. — 10 / 15

(3872) RANCH HOUSE, identical to 3871. — 10 / 15

(3792) RANCH SET, plastic. — 15 / 25

(421) RHEOSTAT. — 5 / 10

(6112) ROCKET ACCESSORIES SET, Cape Canaveral. — 50 / 75

	C6	C8
(390C) RAILROAD ACCESSORY SET, consists of a 390 tunnel and two 313 telltales.	18	25
(399) RAILROAD ACCESSORY SET, consists of a 390 tunnel, two 313 telltales and one 1310 girder bridge.	30	45
(6106) SCALE, plastic.	5	10
(3822) SCHOOL, plastic.	10	25
(436) SEARCHLIGHT TOWER, black.	15	25
(310) SEARCHLIGHT, battery-operated, green.	17	30

	C6	C8
(410) SEARCHLIGHT, square pedestal, 5-1/4 inches tall.	15	25
(063) SEMAPHORE, plastic, 6 inches tall.	10	15
(311) SEMAPHORE, manual, red or black, 9-1/2 inches tall.	10	15
(312) SEMAPHORE, manual, green base, 9-1/2 inches tall.	10	15
(439) SEMAPHORE, black, illuminated, 9-1/4 inches tall.	10	15
(0211) SEMAPHORE, plastic, manual.	2	5
(3891) SERVICE STATION, plastic.	10	20
(3892) SERVICE STATION, plastic, identical to 3891.	10	20
(6108) SHOVEL.	10	20

	C6	C8
(1624) SIGN, "Uncouple Here".	1	2
(Unnumbered) SIGN, "40".	2	5
(Unnumbered) SIGN, "Notice, No Trespassing, RR Property".	2	5
(Unnumbered) SIGN, "Reduce Speed".	2	5
(Unnumbered) SIGN, "W".	2	5
(Unnumbered) SIGN, "Curve."	2	5
(348) SIGN SET, 1953-55, five-piece, right-of-way.	15	20
(1136) SIGN SET, seven signs.	10	20
(1180) SIGN SET, 12 signs.	15	25
(1182) SIGN SET, 12 signs.	15	25
(1281) SIGN SET, 12 signs.	15	25
(1282) SIGN SET, 12 right-of-way signs.	15	25
(1434) SIGNAL, overhead bridge, silver.	30	50
(0221) SIGNAL SET, automatic.	8	15
(430) SIGNAL SET, 29 pieces, plastic.	15	25
(406) SINGLE BULL'S-EYE CROSSING SIGNAL.	10	15
(333F) SMOKE REFILL, green glass bottle.	2	5
(0405) SPOTLIGHT, black and red, plastic.	5	10
(2899) STATION, whistling lithographed.	25	40
(3881) STATION, with accessories and figures.	10	20
(3882) STATION, identical to 3881.	10	20
(3381) STATION AND ACCESSORY SET, plastic.	10	20
(6104) STATION PLATFORM, plastic, six people.	10	15
(6109A) SUITCASE, tan lithographed.	50	75
(3841) SUPERMARKET, plastic.	15	20
(3842) SUPERMARKET, plastic identical to 3841.	15	20
(413A) SWITCHMAN TOWER, metal.	20	30

	C6	C8		C6	C8
(2920) SWITCHMAN TOWER, plastic.	25	35	(061) TELEPHONE POLE SET, 12 brown plastic poles.	5	10
(2939) SWITCHMAN TOWER, plastic, illuminated.	25	35	(313) TELLTALE, paper or rubber tales.	10	15
(2940) SWITCHMAN TOWER, 1952-58, with two moving men.	35	50	TRACK, curved or straight.	.10	.25
			(464/C) TRACK CONNECTION PACKAGE, four pieces.	1	3

TRANSFORMERS   Prices typically are .25 per watt of rated power output.

	C6	C8		C6	C8
(299) TRESTLE SET, eight pieces.	15	25	(392) TUNNEL, 1950, lithographed.	5	10
(612) TRESTLE, black.	2	5	Various numbers TURNOUT, manual or remote, with controller if applicable.	5	10
(615) TRESTLE, black.	2	5	Various numbers UNCOUPLERS.	1	2
(1414) TRESTLE, graduated, and bridge set.	10	15	(1830) UNION STATION, blue and red.	40	60
(6113) TRESTLE AND BRIDGE SET, with plastic tunnel.	10	15	(1430) UNION STATION, blue and yellow.	35	55
(1412) TRESTLE SET, 24-piece plastic.	7	12	(0165) WATER TOWER, gray plastic.	10	15
(4376) TRESTLE SET, 14-piece plastic.	5	10	(065) WATER TOWER, plastic, with spout, black, gray and red or **green and yellow**.	15-25	20-40
(6105) BAGGAGE TRUCK, four-wheel, plastic.	5	10	(465) WATER TOWER, bubbling, gray, 14-1/2 inches tall.	35	50
6107) BAGGAGE TRUCK, two-wheel, plastic.	10	15	(1379) WATER TOWER, identical to 0165.	8	12
(6109) TRUNK, steamer, lithographed.	30	50	(700) WHISTLE, two-tone.	5	10
(309) TUNNEL, red, green, yellow.	30	50	(701) WHISTLE, two-tone.	5	10
(390) TUNNEL, 1939-53, metal or fiber.	5	10			

PLASTICVILLE

Although they are not trains, for toy train enthusiasts of the 1950s and '60s, Plasticville USA pieces were as much a part of their railroads as were products of Lionel and American Flyer. Plasticville USA is a product of Philadelphia's Bachmann Brothers. The product line began in 1947 with the introduction of a fence for use with Christmas gardens. This fence quickly came to the attention of toy train enthusiasts, and within a year a plastic village was being created.

By 1950, the name "Plasticville USA" began appearing on the boxes. Notable for their ease of assembly without the use of adhesive, this series of structures and accessories was created to an ambiguous scale in order for them to be used in conjunction with both 0 and S gauge trains. Later the product line was expanded to include HO items as well. Other companies, most notably Marx and Skyline, produced similar series of buildings, but these have not achieved the collectible status of Plasticville. However, the distinction is easily blurred, as Bachmann bought the former Skyline tooling in 1953, and the tooling of the rival Littletown line of plastic structures in 1956.

Many of these kits were produced for a number of years, in numerous color combinations and with various catalog numbers. The serious student of Plasticville can assemble quite a large and colorful collection.

Just as with all toy trains, collectors most desire vintage Plasticville items in their original packaging. Least desirable are kits that have been glued together or have broken pieces. Beware, for just as in the case of trains, the commonly missing or damaged parts have been skillfully reproduced. Particularly sought after by collectors are kits whose components are made of marbleized brown-black or gray-black plastic.

Because unlike most trains the catalog number of Plasticville items does not appear on the item itself, the following listings are arranged in alphabetic order to ease reference. Be aware that for a C8 rating these items must still be sealed in their cellophane wrappings (such wrappings, however, were not introduced until 1959), or in their plastic bags with header cards attached, with the parts still on their sprues.

Current production of Plasticville is made in China, ironic for a product line once promoted as "Plasticville U.S.A." Unless otherwise noted, all items listed are 0/S gauge.

	C5	C7	C8

CS-5 5 & 10, tan walls, red roof | 10 | 40 | 50 |

AD-4 AIRPORT ADMIN BUILDING, white walls, blue roof and trim. | 20 | 125 | 200 |

AP-1 AIRPORT HANGAR, white walls with blue roof and red doors or **yellow roof and gray doors.** | 10-20 | 40-**80** | 60-**125** |
1503 APARTMENT ADD-A-FLOOR, tan walls, maroon trim. | 10 | 15 | 30 |

	C5	C7	C8
1907 APARTMENT HOUSE, tan walls, maroon trim, white or **tan roof**.	15	35	45
1963 APARTMENT HOUSE, red walls, tan roof and trim.	10	15	20
1975 AUTUMN TREES, assorted colors, 1961.	50	200	350

BK-1 BANK, 1955, gray walls, green roof, red lights, red lettering.	15	30	60
1801 BANK, 1956, gray walls, green roof, red lights, red lettering.	15	30	60
1960 BANK, 1987, gray walls, green roof, white lights, gray lettering.	10	20	30
FR-5 BARBECUE, gray, 1950.	1	2	3
1004 BARBECUE, gray, 1957.	1	2	3

BN-1 BARN, white walls, red roof, chrome trim, or white walls, green roof, or red walls and green roof. 1950-55. | 10 | 15 | 25 |

	C5	C7	C8
1601 BARN, white walls, red roof, chrome trim, or white walls, green roof, or red walls and green roof. 1956-63.	10	15	25
1704 BARN, white walls, red roof, chrome trim, or white walls, green roof, or red walls and green roof. 1964-70.	10	30	60
1811 BARN, white walls, red roof, chrome trim, or white walls, green roof, or red walls and green roof. 1971.	10	15	25
1851 BARN, white walls, red roof, chrome trim, or white walls, green roof, or red walls and green roof.	10	15	25
1987 BARN, white walls, red roof, chrome trim, or white walls, green roof, or red walls and green roof. 1987.	10	15	25
5601 BARN, white walls, red roof, chrome trim, or white walls, green roof, or red walls and green roof, polybagged with header. 1963.	10	150	200
2602 BARN, HO	1	3	5
BY-4 BARNYARD ANIMAL SET, 1952.	15	25	40
1606 BARNYARD ANIMAL SET, 1957.	15	25	40
BB-9 BILLBOARD, white or green, 1950.	1	2	3
1028 BILLBOARD, white or green, 1957.	1	2	3
CBR BIRD BATH, red, yellow or blue bird, 1950.	2	5	10
1305 BLOCK SIGNAL, black, set of two.	15	30	60
SL-1 BOULEVARD LIGHT, 1950.	.50	1.00	2.00
1026 BOULEVARD LIGHT, 1957.	.50	1.00	2.00
1938 BOULEVARD AND STREET LIGHT, 1981, set of 12 each.	4	6	8

	C5	C7	C8
BL-2 BRIDGE AND POND, various shades of green, 1950.	10	15	20
2417 BRIDGE AND POND, HO.	10	30	50
1629 BUNGALOW, white sides, gray or **green roof**, 1962.	20-40	60-125	100-175
1810 BUNGALOW, white sides, gray or **green roof**, 1967.	20-40	60-125	100-175
5629 BUNGALOW, in poly bay with header card, 1963.	20	200	300

	C5	C7	C8
HP-8 CAPE COD HOUSE, 1950.	10	100	200
HP-9 CAPE COD HOUSE, white, salmon, blue or yellow walls, assorted roof colors, 1951.	10	25	35

	C5	**C7**	**C8**
1400 CAPE COD HOUSE, white, salmon, blue or yellow walls, assorted roof colors, 1956.	10	25	35
1502 CAPE COD HOUSE, white, salmon, blue or yellow walls, assorted roof colors, 1957.	10	25	35
1630 CAPE COD HOUSE, white, salmon, blue or yellow walls, assorted roof colors, 1963.	10	25	35
2300 CAPE COD HOUSE, HO.	3	5	10
C-18 CATHEDRAL, 1955, white walls, gray roof.	20	45	65
1623 CATTLE LOADING PEN, 1958.	20	75	125
2611 CATTLE LOADING PEN.			
CC-9 CHURCH, white walls, gray roof, 1953.	10	20	30

	C5	**C7**	**C8**
1600 CHURCH, white walls, gray roof, 1953.	10	20	30
1818 CHURCH, white walls, gray roof, 1953.	10	20	30
5600 CHURCH, polybagged with header card, 1963.	10	125	175
PF-4 CITIZENS WITH PAINT, 1953.	10	20	40
1605 CITIZENS WITH PAINT.	10	20	40

	C5	**C7**	**C8**
1619 CITIZENS WITH PAINT.	10	20	40
1915 CITIZENS WITH PAINT, 1971.	10	20	40
1955 CITIZENS WITH PAINT, 1981.	10	20	40
1975 COALING STATION.	10	20	35
1976 COALING STATION, 1964	10	40	75
1957 COALING STATION.	5	10	20
2808 COALING STATION, HO.	1	3	5
1803 COLONIAL CHURCH, 1957, red walls, gray roof.	15	30	45
1910 COLONIAL CHURCH, 1957, red walls, gray roof.	15	30	45
HO-71 COLONIAL HOUSE, HO.	3	5	10
2401 COLONIAL HOUSE, white and green, HO.	3	5	10
1703 COLONIAL MANSION, white walls, red, green, blue or **gray roof,** 1957.	20-**50**	40-150	60-**225**
1850 COLONIAL MANSION, white walls, red, green, blue or **gray roof,** 1971.	20-**50**	40-150	60-**225**
1626 CORNER STORE, 1960- white walls and gray roof or gray walls with white roof.	15	30	50
CC-8 COUNTRY CHURCH, 1950, white walls, brown or gray roof.	10	15	25
1805 COVERED BRIDGE, rust sides, tan roadway, 1960.	15	30	50
1920 COVERED BRIDGE, rust sides, gray roadway, 1975,	15	30	50
2802 COVERED BRIDGE, HO	5	15	30
WG-2 CROSSING GATE, 1950, white arm with black or **red base.**	-	.50-**2**	1-**5**

	C5	C7	C8
1029 CROSSING GATE, white arm with black or **red base.**	-	.50-**2**	1-**5**
1937 CROSSING GATE, white arm with black, 1981,	-	.50-2	1-5
1304 CROSSING SIGNAL, white, set of two	5	20	40
1622 DAIRY BARN, red or **tuscan** walls, gray roof, 1957.	10-**15**	20-**25**	30-**35**
1932 DAIRY BARN, red walls white roof, 1980.	5	10	15
DE-7 DINER KIT, chrome or gray walls, red or yellow roof, 1952-57.	10-**15**	30-**60**	50-**75**
1500 DINER KIT, 1958-59.	20	40	65
1853 DRUG STORE, tan front, white sides and rear.	20	70	100
2406 DRUG AND HARDWARE STORE, HO.	10	30	50
CT-6 EVERGREEN TREE, white, green, **red or translucent colors,** 1950.	.50-**5**	1-**10**	2-**20**
1906 FACTORY, gray or brown roof, green or gray doors, 1957.	25	60	90
1988 FACTORY, gray or brown roof, green or gray doors, Scenic Classics.	20	40	60
2801 FACTORY, HO.	3	5	10
1617 FARM BUILDINGS AND ANIMALS, white walls and red trim or red walls and white trim, 1956.	15	30	75
2612 FARM BUILDINGS AND ANIMALS, HO.	5	10	20
1981 FARM BUILDINGS AND EQUIPMENT, 1980.	30	60	100
1302 FARM IMPLEMENTS, assorted colors produced.	25	60	125

	C5	C7	C8
FH-4 FIRE HOUSE, white walls, red roof, 1950-56, white or gray siren. Gray siren warrants a 300 percent premium.	15	20	30
1607 FIRE HOUSE, white walls, red roof, 1957, white siren.	15	20	30
1921 FIRE HOUSE, white walls, red roof, 1976, white siren.	15	20	30
FP-5 FLAG POLE, white, 48-star US flag, 1953.	2	4	6
1027 FLAG POLE, white, 48-star US flag, 1957.	2	4	6
FB-8 FLOCK OF BIRDS, red, blue, yellow, 1950.	.25 ea	.50 ea	1.00 ea
PB-5 FOOTBRIDGE, brown, 1950.	1	3	5
2412 FREIGHT STATION, HO.	5	10	15
2610 FREIGHT STATION, HO.	2	5	8
FB-1 FROSTY BAR, salmon walls, white roof, white walls, salmon roof, yellow walls, white roof, white walls, yellow roof. A chrome counter warrants a slight premium. 1954.	10	20	40

	C5	C7	C8

1401 FROSTY BAR, salmon walls, white roof, white walls, salmon roof, yellow walls, white roof, white walls, yellow roof. A chrome counter warrants a slight premium. 1956,

	C5	C7	C8
1956,	10	20	40

2400 FROSTY BAR, HO.

| | 5 | 10 | 15 |

GO-2 GAS STATION, small, white walls, red roof, light or dark inserts, red lettering, 1950, includes T-shaped island, gas pumps, and oil rack.

| | 10 | 20 | 35 |

1962 GAS STATION, small, white walls, red roof, white lettering, 1987, single island, not T-shaped.

| | 5 | 10 | 15 |

GO-3 GAS STATION, large, white walls, red roof, 1955, includes two islands with pumps and oil racks.

| | 10 | 20 | 40 |

	C5	C7	C8
1800 GAS STATION, large, white walls, red roof, 1956, includes two islands with pumps and oil racks.	10	20	40
1909 GAS STATION, large, white walls, red roof, 1967, no Plasticville logo, includes two islands with pumps and oil racks.	10	30	60
5800 GAS STATION, large, white walls, red roof, 1963, polybagged with header card, includes two islands with pumps and oil racks.	10	125	200
2608 GAS STATION, HO, white and red.	5	10	15
2807 GAS STATION, HO.	1	3	5
1804 GREENHOUSE, white sides and gray base, or gray sides and white base, 1957.	25	60	125
5804 GREENHOUSE, white sides and gray base, or gray sides and white base, polybagged with header, 1963.	25	125	175
2609 GREENHOUSE, HO.	5	10	15

	C5	C7	C8
1627 HOBO SHACKS, two buildings with brown sides and gray roof or gray sides and brown roof.	50	125	250
5627 HOBO SHACKS, two buildings with brown sides and gray roof or gray sides and brown roof. Polybagged with header card.	50	225	350

	C5	C7	C8
HS-6 HOSPITAL, no furniture or floor, 1953, red lettering on building, blue roof.	15	30	45
HS-6 HOSPITAL, with cardboard floor and 22 pieces of furniture, 1954-56, red lettering on building, blue roof	40	70	95
1902 HOSPITAL, w/ furniture,1957-74, red lettering on building, blue roof.	20	40	65
1919 HOSPITAL, w/ furniture, black lettering on building, blue roof, 1975-86.	20	40	65
1961 HOSPITAL, no furniture or floor, gray roof, 1987, white lettering on building.	7	12	15
HF-2 HOUSE FENCE AND GATE.	2	5	10
1624 HOUSE under Construction, 1959.	30	75	100
2803 HOUSE under Construction.	3	5	10
2616 HOUSE TRAILER, HO.	5	10	20
1776 INDEPENDENCE HALL, 1956, red sides, gray roof.	40	50	75
2921 INDEPENDENCE HALL, 1975, tuscan walls, dark gray roof.	30	40	65
1620 LOADING PLATFORM, brown with gray roof, or gray with brown roof, with three carts. 1957.	5	15	25
1707 LOADING PLATFORM, brown with gray roof, or gray with brown roof with three carts. 1964.	5	150	200
1809 LOADING PLATFORM, brown with gray roof, or gray with brown roof with three carts. 1967.	5	15	25
1817 LOADING PLATFORM, brown with gray roof, or gray with brown roof with three carts. 1971.	5	15	25

	C5	C7	C8
5620 LOADING PLATFORM, brown with gray roof, or gray with brown roof with three carts. 1963.	5	150	200
1952 LOADING PLATFORM and Watchman Shanty.	5	15	20
LC-2 LOG CABIN, brown, with or without **rifle,** 1951.	10-**100**	20-**200**	40-**300**
MT-2 MAPLE TREE, green, 1950.	1 ea	2 ea	3 ea
2905 MEN'S STORE, HO.	1	3	5
1504 MOBILE HOME, white walls, blue roof, or blue walls and white roof, 1961.	20	40	80

	C5	C7	C8
1621 MOTEL, white walls, salmon roof, or salmon walls, white roof.	6	10	15
1913 MOTEL, white walls, salmon roof, or salmon walls, white roof.	6	10	15
2607 MOVIE THEATER, HO.	5	10	15

	C5	C7	C8
MH-2 NEW ENGLAND RANCH HOUSE, tan or white walls, brown, gray or charcoal roof, brown, red, green, blue, buff or yellow windows.	10	20	35

	C5	C7	C8
1701 NEW ENGLAND RANCH HOUSE, tan or white walls, brown, gray or charcoal roof, brown, red, green, blue, buff or yellow windows, 1956.	10	20	35
1808 NEW ENGLAND RANCH HOUSE, tan or white walls, brown, gray or charcoal roof, brown, red, green, blue, buff or yellow windows, 1966.	10	20	35
1912 NEW ENGLAND RANCH HOUSE, tan or white walls, brown, gray or charcoal roof, brown, red, green, blue, buff or yellow windows, 1971.	10	20	35
5701 NEW ENGLAND RANCH HOUSE, polybagged with header card, 1963.	10	150	200
SA-9 OUTHOUSE, red, white, beige, brown or **olive,** 1950.	2-4	3-9	6-12
2907 NEW CAR SHOWROOM, HO.	2	5	10
1918 PARK ASSORTMENT, 1975	20	35	55
DH-2 PHARMACY/ HARDWARE, black font, tan sides and rear, 1953.	5	15	25
1611 PHARMACY/ HARDWARE, black font, tan sides and rear, 1963-.	5	15	25
CT-5 PICKET FENCE.	.25 ea	.50 ea	1.00 ea
FG-12 PICKET FENCE.	.25 ea	.50 ea	1.00 ea
1002 PICKET FENCE.	.25 ea	.50 ea	1.00 ea
1101 PICKET FENCE, small, carded, 1959.	-	15	25
CG-10 PICKET FENCE GATE, white.	.50	1.00	2.00
1031 PICKET FENCE GATE, white.	.50	1.00	2.00
1404 PINE TREE ASSORTMENT, 1957.	5	20	40

	C5	C7	C8
PH-1 PLASTICVILLE HALL, 1955, tan sides, red roof.	30	40	65
1905 PLASTICVILLE HALL, 1956, red or tan sides, gray or red roof.	40	50	75
1406 PLAYGROUND EQUIPMENT, 1957.	15	25	40

	C5	C7	C8
PD-3 POLICE DEPARTMENT, gray or **sandstone walls,** green roof, 1951.	10-20	30-60	40-90
1614 POLICE DEPARTMENT, gray walls, green roof, 1957.	10	60	90
2408 POLICE DEPARTMENT, HO-scale.	2	5	10
1409 POPLAR TREE.	10	20	40
PO-1 POST OFFICE, gray front wall, tan rear and side walls, gray or **red roof,** 1953-57.	10-30	40-150	40-300
1602 POST OFFICE, gray front wall, tan rear and side walls, gray or **red roof,** 1958-.	10-30	40-150	40-300
2407 POST OFFICE, HO.	2	5	10
1405 RAILROAD AND STREET SIGNS.	10	15	30
1625 RAILROAD WORK CAR, 1960, brown with gray roof, gray with brown roof, maroon with gray roof, gray with maroon roof.	20	30	45

	C5	C7	C8
1917 RAILROAD WORK CAR, 1974, brown with gray roof, gray with brown roof, maroon with gray roof, gray with maroon roof.	20	30	45
2701 RAILROAD WORK CAR, HO.	3	7	10

	C5	C7	C8
RH-1 RANCH HOUSE, many color combination variations, aqua and dark blue with gray roofs and white windows warrant substantial premium, 1951.	5	15	25
1603 RANCH HOUSE, many color combination variations, aqua and dark blue with gray roofs and white windows warrant substantial premium, 1956.	5	15	25
1705 RANCH HOUSE, many color combination variations, aqua and dark blue with gray roofs and white windows warrant substantial premium, 1964.	5	15	25
1812 RANCH HOUSE, many color combination variations, aqua and dark blue with gray roofs and white windows warrant substantial premium, 1967.	5	15	25
1852 RANCH HOUSE, many color combination variations, aqua and dark blue with gray roofs and white windows warrant substantial premium, 1971.	5	15	25

	C5	C7	C8
1934 RANCH HOUSE, many color combination variations, aqua and dark blue with gray roofs and white windows warrant substantial premium, 1980.	5	15	25
5603 RANCH HOUSE, polybagged with header card, 1963.	5	150	200
2301 RANCH HOUSE, HO.	2	4	8
2618 RANCH HOUSE, HO.	3	5	10
1806 ROADSIDE STAND, white walls, green or gray roof, molded sign, 1962.	15	35	60
1923 ROADSIDE STAND, white walls, green or gray roof, decal sign, 1977.	10	25	40
5806 ROADSIDE STAND,, white walls, green or gray roof, decal sign, polybagged with header card. 1963.	10	125	175
RF-1 RUSTIC FENCE, 1950.	.25 ea	.50 ea	1.00 ea
1007 RUSTIC FENCE.	.25 ea	.50 ea	1.00 ea
RG-3 RUSTIC GATE, 1950.	.25 ea	.50 ea	1.00 ea
1034 RUSTIC GATE.	.25 ea	.50 ea	1.00 ea

	C5	C7	C8
SC-4 SCHOOL, 1951-56, red walls, light or dark gray, or **white roof.**	10-**25**	20-**40**	30-**60**
1608 SCHOOL, 1957-, red walls, light or dark gray, or white roof.	10-25	20-40	30-60
1914 SCHOOL, 1971 red walls, light or dark gray, or **white roof.**	10-**25**	20-**40**	30-**60**

	C5	C7	C8
2814 SCHOOL, HO.	2	5	10
1982 SCHOOL, with playground equipment, scenic classics, 1980.	25	40	60
BS-6 SHRUB, green, brown, or buff, 1950.	.25 ea	.50 ea	1.00 ea
1628 SHADE TREES, 1961.	15	40	100
SG-3 SIGNAL BRIDGE, black, 1954.	10	20	30
1403 SIGNAL BRIDGE, black, 1956.	5	10	15
1632 SIGNAL BRIDGE, black, 1967.	10	20	30
1815 SIGNAL BRIDGE, black, 1971.	10	20	30
5403 SIGNAL BRIDGE, black, polybagged with header card, 1963.	10	160	200
2620 SIGNAL BRIDGE, HO.	3	5	10
1951 SIGNAL BRIDGE and Switch Tower, 1963.	5	10	20
TP-5 SIGNS and Telephone Poles, 1950.	5	10	15
1000 SIGNS and Telephone Poles, 1957.	5	10	15
1630 SIGNS and Telephone Poles, 1971.	5	10	15
1931 SIGNS and Telephone Poles, 1981.	5	10	15
1908 SPLIT LEVEL HOUSE, gray walls, pink, tan or turquoise windows, 1959.	15	25	35
1953 SPLIT LEVEL HOUSE, gray walls, pink, tan or turquoise windows, 1980.	15	25	35
TR-6 SPRUCE TREE, green or white.	.50 ea	1.00 ea	2.00 ea
1001 SPRUCE TREE, green or white.	.50 ea	1.00 ea	2.00 ea
LM-3 STATION PLATFORM, Brown and gray, 1950.	5	10	20
1200 STATION PLATFORM, Brown and gray, 1956.	5	10	20

	C5	C7	C8
LP-9 STREET LIGHTS, green or black, 1950, carded.	1	2	4
1025 STREET LIGHTS, green or black, 1957, carded.	1	2	4
1938 STREET AND BOULEVARD LIGHTS, green or black, 1981, box of 12 each.	4	6	8
SS-5 STREET NAME SIGNS, green, 1950.	.25	.50	1.00
ST-1 STREET ACCESSORIES UNIT, 15 pieces, 1952.	22	33	45
1609 STREET ACCESSORIES UNIT, 15 pieces, 1963.	22	33	45

	C5	C7	C8
12A STREET SIGNS, boxed set of 12.	10	20	30
RS-7 SUBURBAN STATION, white walls, green or gray roof, brown or gray platform. 1950.	5	15	25

	C5	C7	C8
RS-8 SUBURBAN STATION, white walls, green or gray roof, brown or gray platform. 1951.	5	15	25
1616 SUBURBAN STATION, white walls, green or gray roof, brown or gray platform. 1956.	5	15	25

	C5	C7	C8
1706 SUBURBAN STATION, white walls, green or gray roof, brown or gray platform. 1964.	5	15	25
1813 SUBURBAN STATION, white walls, green or gray roof, brown or gray platform. 1967.	5	15	25
1911 SUBURBAN STATION, white walls, green or gray roof, brown or gray platform. 1971.	5	15	25
1954 SUBURBAN STATION, white walls, green or gray roof, brown or gray platform. 1980.	5	15	25
5616 SUBURBAN STATION, white walls, green or gray roof, brown or gray platform, polybagged with header card. 1963.	5	150	200
2605 SUBURBAN STATION, HO.	5	25	50
2806 SUBURBAN STATION, HO.	3	5	10
SM-7 SUPERMARKET, large, green front, tan sides and rear, brown or **red roof**, 1953-57.	10	25-**35**	40-**65**
1613 SUPERMARKET, large, green front, tan sides and rear, brown or **red roof**, 1958-.	10	25-**35**	40-**65**

	C5	C7	C8
SW-2 SWITCH TOWER, 1954, brown sides, gray roof, or gray sides, brown roof.	5	15	25
1402 SWITCH TOWER, brown sides, gray roof, or gray sides, brown roof.	5	15	25
1631 SWITCH TOWER, brown sides, gray roof, or gray sides, brown roof.	5	15	25
1814 SWITCH TOWER, brown sides, gray roof, or gray sides, brown roof.	5	15	25
5402 SWITCH TOWER, brown sides, gray roof, or gray sides, brown roof, poly bagged with header card, 1963.	5	75	125
1951 SWITCH TOWER, and Signal Bridge, 1989.	5	15	25
HO-72 SWITCH TOWER, HO.	1	3	5
2619 SWITCH TOWER, HO.	1	3	5
1090 TELEPHONE BOOTH, blue and white, or white and blue.	7	12	20
5000 TELEPHONE POLES, polybagged with header card.	-	140	200
2950 TOWN HALL, tuscan walls, dark gray roof.	50	60	85
CC-7 TOY CHURCH, 1950.	10	15	25
2904 TOY AND HOBBY SHOP, HO.	2	5	10
BR-2 TRESTLE BRIDGE, black, 1955.	10	25	50

	C5	C7	C8
SM-6 SUPERMARKET, small, white walls, red roof, light or dark window inserts, 1950-.	5	15	30

	C5	C7	C8
1604 TRESTLE BRIDGE, black, 1956.	10	25	50
2810 TRESTLE BRIDGE, HO.	1	3	5
1900 TURNPIKE INTERCHANGE, blue walls, white roof, 1956.	35	75	150
1618 TV STATION, white walls, red roof, or red walls, white roof.	20	40	65
1964 TV STATION, white walls, red roof, or red walls, white roof, lettering in molded color only.	10	15	25
2613 TV STATION, gray walls, white roof, HO.	5	10	15
LH-4 TWO STORY COLONIAL HOUSE, tan, white, red or yellow walls, red, green or gray roof, 1954.	10	15	25
1700 TWO STORY COLONIAL HOUSE, tan, white, red or yellow walls, red, green or gray roof, 1956.	10	15	25
1807 TWO STORY COLONIAL HOUSE, tan, white, red or yellow walls, red, green or gray roof, 1966.	10	15	25
1922 TWO STORY COLONIAL HOUSE, tan, white, red or yellow walls, red, green or gray roof, 1977.	10	15	25
1936 TWO STORY COLONIAL HOUSE, tan, white, red or yellow walls, red, green or gray roof, 1981.	10	15	25
5700 TWO STORY COLONIAL HOUSE, polybagged with header card, 1963.	10	150	200
1901 UNION STATION, white walls, green roof, gray platform, plastic clock.	15	30	45
1958 UNION STATION, white walls, green roof, gray platform, clock was a decal.	10	15	25

	C5	C7	C8
1407 WATCHMAN SHANTY, brown with gray roof and trim, or gray with brown roof and trim.	5	15	25
1633 WATCHMAN SHANTY, brown with gray roof and trim, or gray with brown roof and trim.	5	15	25
1816 WATCHMAN SHANTY, brown with gray roof and trim, or gray with brown roof and trim.	5	15	25
5407 WATCHMAN SHANTY, brown with gray roof and trim, or gray with brown roof and trim, polybagged with header.	5	150	175
1952 WATCHMAN SHANTY and Loading Platform.	5	15	20
1615 WATER TANK, brown tank, gray roof, or gray tank with brown roof, 1957.	10	20	30
1916 WATER TANK, brown tank, gray roof, or gray tank with brown roof, 1974.	10	15	25
1935 WATER TANK, brown tank, gray roof, or gray tank with brown roof, 1980.	10	15	25
2600 WATER TANK, HO.	5	10	20
2812 WATER TANK, HO.	1	3	5
WW-3 WISHING WELL, 1950.	3	8	10
1033 WISHING WELL, 1957.	3	8	10
1408 WINDMILL, gray, 1958.	15	45	60
2412 WINDMILL, gray, HO.	5	10	15
YW-4 YARD PUMP, brown, 1950.	1	2	3
1005 YARD PUMP, brown, 1957.	1	2	3

UNIQUE

The Unique Art Manufacturing Company was a toy manufacturer based in Newark, N.J. The company's strength was attractively lithographed mechanical toys, which it had produced from 1916. These toys came in a variety of forms, including cars and typewriters. Particularly popular were sophisticated dancing musical windup toys, which are today quite sought after. Under the direction of Samuel I. Berger, windup trains were added to the product line in 1949, and electric trains soon after. The company's established distribution channels, the booming train market and the local availability of tooling–no doubt at a bargain price from the 15-year defunct Dorfan firm–led to the decision to enter this market. The Dorfan tooling was not used as it was, but rather was modified to create cars that minimized the labor required to assemble them.

However, another lithographed toy manufacturer took Unique's incursion into train manufacturing very seriously. Louis Marx and Company responded to Unique's entry by developing a line of cars to compete directly with the newcomer. Faced with this stiff competition, plus a materials shortage due to rationing during the Korean War, Unique withdrew from the toy train market in 1951. During its brief production history, Unique produced a few items that are today coveted by collectors, including its Circus Set and its 105 animated caboose.

	C5	C7	C8
CONTROL TOWER, lithographed tin, two-story building containing power supply, cream w/green roof, some have reverse button, 3" x 2" x 4".	15	30	60
HIGH SIDE GONDOLA, tin, orange w/red inside, without punched out sides, black lettering reads "Unique Lines," 7-1/2" long.	30	45	60
HOBO BOXCAR, lithographed tin, clockwork, rolls along floor w/dog biting hobo.	500	750	1,000
100 BOXCAR, tin, silver w/red lettering reads "Unique Lines" and "3509," 7-1/2" long.	40	60	80
101 HOPPER CAR, tin, orange w/red inside, black lettering reads "Unique Lines," 7-1/2" long.	25	38	50

	C5	C7	C8
102 PASSENGER CAR, 9" long tin, blue body w/silver roof, white and black lettering reads "Pullman" and "City of Joplin".	100	150	200
102 PASSENGER CAR, tin, blue body w/silver roof, white and black lettering reads "Pullman" and "Garden City," 9" long.	100	150	200
105 CABOOSE, tin, red w/ yellow lettering reads "Unique Lines," 7-1/2" long.	30	45	60
105 CABOOSE, tin, red w/ yellow w/swing-out, lettering read "Unique Lines" and "Benny the Brakeman" on the rear platform, 7-1/2" long.	40	65	100
107 CATTLE CAR, tin, red w/yellow roof, marked "Unique Lines," 7-1/2" long.	50	75	100

	C5	C7	C8
109 CIRCUS CAR, tin, mostly red w/open roof, marked "Jewel T Circus," elephant in center panel, 7-1/2" long, hard to find.	100	150	200
109 CIRCUS CAR, tin, mostly red w/yellow roof, marked "Jewel T Circus," lion in center panel, 7-1/2" long.	50	75	100
109 CIRCUS CAR, tin, mostly red w/open roof, marked "Jewel T Circus," lion in center panel, 7-1/2" long, desirable.	100	150	200
109 CIRCUS CAR, tin, mostly red w/yellow roof, marked "Jewel T Circus," elephant in center panel, 7-1/2" long.	50	75	100
515 HILLBILLY EXPRESS, lithographed tin, clockwork, runs back and forth along inclined track.	100	150	200
702 FINNEGAN THE BAGGAGE MAN, lithographed tin, clockwork, package has cut-out cardboard luggage.	50	75	100

	C5	C7	C8
742 ENGINE, tin, clockwork, multicolored and gray w/ tender, marked "Unique Lines," 7-1/2" long tender, 10" long engine.	40	60	90

	C5	C7	C8
1950 ENGINE, tin, electric w/reverse and headlight, multicolored and blue, w/tender, marked "Unique Lines," 7-1/2" long tender, 10" long engine.	30	45	80
1950 ENGINE, tin, multicolored and blue, w/tender, marked "Unique Lines," 7-1/2" long tender, 10" long loco.	30	45	80

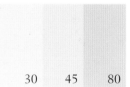

	C5	C7	C8
2000 ENGINE, tin, diesel, powered A and dummy A, multicolored and maroon, marked "Rock Island," 14" long.	30	45	80

Many of the photos in this volume were provided by Stout Auctions, one of the nation's premier toy train auctioneers. Located in both Williamsport, Indiana and West Middlesex, Pennsylvania, Stout specializes in liquidating collections of premium quality trains, including the previous owner of Lionel and other high profile individuals. Stout currently has many record auction items including one of the most important toy trains ever sold- the brass Lionel 700E scale Hudson that sat in Joshua Lionel Cowen's office. Consigned items are offered for both on-site and internet bidding. For more information call 765-764-6901, or visit www.stoutauctions.com

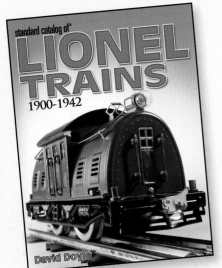
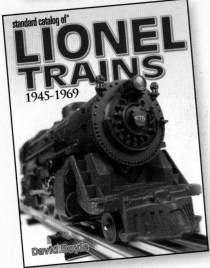
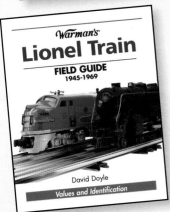